Changing Paths

Changing Paths

INTERNATIONAL DEVELOPMENT AND
THE NEW POLITICS OF INCLUSION

Edited by Peter P. Houtzager and Mick Moore

UNIVERSITY OF MICHIGAN PRESS
Ann Arbor

2006   2005   2004   2003   4   3   2   1

A CIP catalog record for this book is available from the British Library.

Library of Congress Cataloging-in-Publication Data

Changing paths : international development and the new politics of
    inclusion / edited by Peter P. Houtzager and Mick Moore.
       p.   cm.
    Includes bibliographical references (p.   ) and index.
    ISBN 0-472-11322-4 (cloth : alk. paper)
       1. Economic development—Political aspects.   2. Poverty—
    Government policy.   3. Distributive justice.   I. Houtzager, Peter P.
    II. Moore, Mick.
    HD87 .C418   2003
    320'.6—dc21   2002156535

Contents

Tables

Chapter 8

Chapter 9

Acknowledgments

Encounters between scholars and policymakers do not always have happy outcomes. This book is the product of an encounter that—for a series of reasons related to personalities, professional positions, and historical timing (notably, the end of a long period of ascent of neoliberal ideas)—was unusually fruitful. The book began to take shape during two meetings in 1999 that assembled scholars from Brazil, Bangladesh, India, Nigeria, the United Kingdom, and the United States, and policymakers from the UK Department for International Development and World Bank. The intellectual backdrop to our discussions in the splendid surroundings of Eynsham Hall and Castle Donnington in the UK was a shared concern about the depoliticization of debates on international development policy and an awareness of a growing interest in empowerment of the poor, pro-poor policy-making, and good governance. Our immediate concern was the politics of poverty reduction and the longer term distributional and political consequences of different bundles of pro-poor public policies.

The policy actors with whom we had contact prior to the meetings complained that much public policy in low- and middle-income countries failed to bear the expected fruit because of political dynamics. Yet these dynamics were invisible in policy analysis and pronouncements and in many recent academic analyses. A number of scholar-colleagues made similar observations and commented that scholars in the international development debate have played an important role in legitimizing and reproducing the technification of development discourse. We hope that the chapters assembled here are an antidote.

All the authors assembled here have earned special appreciation for their patience with the persnickety editors. Particular thanks are due to the one author who finally did complain about the successive rounds of revisions, but nonetheless met all the deadlines and proved a model and stimulating collaborator. Carol Spencer cheerfully bore the burden of seeing the manuscript to the publisher and then to the press. We are very grateful to Ron Herring for providing the valuable and much needed support that ensured the manuscript found its way into the hands of such a competent publisher. For providing valuable discussion that helped shape the direction the volume ultimately took, and for feedback on the specific essays assembled here, we want to thank the participants of the two workshops. In addition to the contributors, they include Michael Anderson, Catherine Boone, Teddy Brett, Kathryn Clarke, Monica Dasgupta, Garth Glentworth, Merilee Grindle, Naomi Hossain, Ravi Kanbur, Jennifer Leavy, David Lehman, Fernando Limongi, Kimberly Niles, Dele Olowu, James Putzel, Rehman Sobhan, Richard Thomas, Ashutosh Varshney, Roger Wilson, David Wood, and Geof Wood. Finally, individual ideas only materialize into collective products when the requisite material conditions are present. For ensuring these conditions, as well as for playing a central role in instigating this endeavor, we thank our gracious colleague Roger Wilson, Chief Governance Advisor to the UK Department for International Development.

1 *Introduction*

FROM POLYCENTRISM TO THE POLITY

Peter P. Houtzager

T he new politics of inclusion is the progeny of disquiet. Two decades of marketizing reform have succeeded in disassembling developmental states—their bases of legitimacy, the political coalitions that sustained them, and of course many of their concrete manifestations (from parastatal companies to interventionist economic policies and universal social programs).[1] They have also fostered greater economic integration across national boundaries. The disquiet, in what is now a postdevelopment state period, grows out of the failure of marketizing reforms to significantly reduce absolute poverty (a quarter of the world's population exists on less than one dollar a day) and out of historically unprecedented levels of inequality between and within countries.[2] Antiglobalization protests and a new wave of international terrorism targeting the symbols of global capitalism are widely interpreted (not always accurately) as manifestations of the exclusionary nature of current marketizing development models. As a result, an array of national and international actors has recently become preoccupied with the inclusion of the poor in the gains from economic growth and the capacity of poor social groups to have their voices heard in national policy debates.[3] The shift in concern from "getting prices right" to pro-poor growth and empowerment of the poor is helping to create new opportunities for differentially situated poor groups to challenge their economic and political exclusion.

This volume explores the forms the new politics of inclusion can take in the postdevelopmental state period. In doing so, it casts a critical eye on the two dominant intellectual trends in international development—neoliberal and poststructuralist—that have converged on a set of beliefs that, if pursued in practice, may undermine the current opportunity to expand inclusion. These intellectual trends are rooted in the belief that the uncoordinated and decentralized actions of civil society, market, and state actors are likely to create a mutually reinforcing movement that can produce all good things for all people—democracies in which citizens enjoy actual legal equality and rights, higher standards of living, greater socioeconomic equality, and (lately) "empowerment of the poor." A key feature of this radical polycentric zeitgeist is an indiscriminate hostility toward large *political* organizations, be they state entities, political parties, or groups organized across many localities such as labor movements and professional associations. At a time of unprecedented concentration of capital and power in the hands of a few private individuals and corporate conglomerates, the prescriptions for more equitable, affluent, and democratic societies all emphasize decentralization of action, association, and governance.

The construction and interpretation of a new politics of inclusion, this volume argues, must concern itself centrally with how societal and state actors democratically negotiate large-scale collective solutions across the public-private divide. There is little evidence for the belief that the uncoordinated action of a multiplicity of local actors in either civil society or the market alone can either solve problems such as market and state failure or challenge authoritarian political elites on a scale sufficient to lift large numbers of people out of poverty and political subordination.[4] One of the principal obstacles to greater inclusion is the dearth of reform-oriented political actors and coalitions that can aggregate and negotiate competing interests both within society and between society and agents of the state. Constructing reform-oriented coalitions requires refocusing our attention from the decentralized and autarkic engagements of civil society and market actors toward the political arena and the institutions of representative and deliberative democracy.

What analytic lens should we use to refocus? This chapter suggests a "polity approach" that draws on the insights of Skocpol (1992) and Tilly (1978, 1997) and different lineages of comparative institutionalism, including that proposed by Evans (1995, 1996).[5] The polity approach is also built on, and attempts to provide a broad theoretical core to, a sprawling body of work that shares many assumptions of historical institutionalism in sociology and comparative politics. Such work has focused to varying degrees on the agency of political leaders, institutional dynamics, and forms of state-society synergy.[6]

The polity approach focuses on how societal and state actors are constituted, how they develop a differential capacity to act and form alliances, and how they cooperate and compete across the public-private divide to produce purposeful change. The capacity and nature of both state and societal actors are understood as the outcome of a two-way exchange that is shaped in substantial ways by the institutional terrain in which it takes place. The ability of political actors to produce a politics of inclusion is in large measure contingent on their ability to engineer *fit* with political institutions that grant some actors greater leverage in the policy process than others. The capacity to engineer fit, however, is severely constrained by a variety of factors, including institutional ones.

The volume's essays address three types of questions that the polity frame brings to fore. First, what reform-oriented collective actors, particularly from within subordinated social sectors, and broad political coalitions can be constructed to transcend the fragmentation and localism of much current organizing and activism? Second, and conversely, what forms of distributive and redistributive policies can gather sufficient support to be politically sustainable and can enhance the ability of subordinated groups to organize and acquire voice? And, third, how do particular features of the polity—national and subnational regime types, decentralization of state institutions, and various dimensions of governance—affect the ability of the poor to acquire voice and a greater share of material wealth? These questions are, in varying ways, tackled in a comparative manner. The essays compare either a small number of countries over time, a large number of countries at a particular point in time, or different regions within a single country across several periods.

The essays also make an important conceptual move. They draw on the growing literature on path dependence in economic history and comparative historical sociology to suggest that change can usefully be thought of as occurring in an incremental, bounded way *within* particular paths or as episodic large-scale shifts *between* paths. By explicitly addressing different patterns of change, the essays bring to the fore the varying degrees of agency actors enjoy at different points in time and the ways in which the causal importance of events (or policy interventions) is tied to their timing—that is, where they fall in a causal sequence or path. Similar events or actions that occur at different points in time, or in different contexts, can have markedly dissimilar consequences.

To make our task manageable, we have framed our analyses within a number of analytic boundaries. One of the most important is to limit our focus to political dynamics within territorially based, national political communities in which states have at least a minimum capacity to maintain physical borders, though not necessarily to maintain order within them. Our choice may mystify those who argue the birth of global civil society, the rise of global social movements and overlapping centers and levels of authority, or the withering of the territorially defined nation-state under these and other pressures of globalization and localization. Clearly, the constraints imposed by international capital mobility, the dictates of competition within international markets, and U.S. international hegemony have played a central role in undermining developmental states and social democratic models and in ushering in a period of marketized economic models and neoliberal states. The argument for an internationalized perspective is well made by Held et al. (1999, 50), who note that

> although governments and states remain, of course, powerful actors, they now share the global arena with an array of other agencies and organizations. The state is confronted by an enormous number of intergovernmental organizations (IGOs), international agencies and regimes which operate across different spatial reaches, and by quasi-supranational institutions, like the European Union. Nonstate actors or transnational bodies, such as multinational corporations, transnational pressure groups, transnational professional associations, social movements and so on, also participate intensively in global politics.

This volume's concern, however, is the politics of inclusion, and three questions need to be answered to set the appropriate analytic boundaries. Where does authority reside in the policy areas of central concern to us? For the social groups with which we are concerned, what are the boundaries of the political community? And what are the institutional arrangements that appear to shape public policies, collective actors, and reform-oriented coalitions? On these criteria, political dynamics within the nation-state clearly deserve special attention, although a variety of international factors will impinge on them and should be taken into account. The territorially defined nation-state today remains the only actor able to extract the vast resources from society that make possible significant distributive and redistributive policies and the only actor capable of providing public goods on a significant scale. It is also the organizational form of authority with which most people have contact in their daily lives and that provides the most readily available route for poor social groups to influence the conditions of their own lives. More generally, the state is also the only actor with a legitimate monopoly over violence, with the potential to make war in the international arena and maintain order domestically. No supranational institution approximates the capacity of even weak nation-states in these areas.

RADICAL POLYCENTRISM

The principal positions in the debate on the politics of inclusion—neoliberal and poststructuralist—embody forms of radical polycentrism. The hegemonic view in international development is, broadly speaking, neoliberal, and places its faith in a market regulated by a minimalist (night watchman) state[7] and in a political democracy in which civil society limits (rather than builds) public authority.[8] The recently constructed international governance agenda reflects this set of beliefs. This agenda, or at least progressive versions that are moved by concerns with growing inequality and persistent poverty, brings together decentralization (administrative, fiscal, and policy-making), the strengthening of civil society, and popular participation as a prescription for pro-poor growth and greater voice of the poor.[9] For the World Bank (2000, 15), and several other international development actors, poverty itself now includes "voicelessness and powerlessness" alongside material deprivation or ill-being. There is particular optimism about the role civil society has to play. The Development Assistance Committee (DAC) of the Organization for Economic Cooperation and Development (OECD), which coordinates bilateral aid donors, argues that "active civil societies are central to the evolution of participatory and transparent systems of government, which are essential for economic development."[10] And in a concise statement of the dominant thinking, the United Nations Development Program (UNDP) (2000, 11–12) argues that poverty reduction requires "shifting decision-making power closer to poor communities by devolving authority to local government, . . . opening up local government to popular participation and building partnerships with civil society organizations."

These new elements (decentralization, civil society, and participation), however, are built on a suspicion of the state, and large political organizations in general, and leave the late-twentieth-century agenda of market-driven growth, deregulation, privatization, and trade liberalization firmly in place. Nor has the emergence of the new institutional economics (NIE) fundamentally challenged the market-based model. Its recognition of the degree to which markets depend on state institutions and actions has, however, considerably expanded views of where state regulation is required to ensure that the invisible hand does not lose its touch.[11]

The counterhegemonic view of the poststructuralists has been concerned with the new politics of inclusion since at least the early 1980s, but it also is radically polycentric. Rather than follow neoliberals back to the nineteenth century for its postdevelopmental state prescriptions, this group of scholars, policymakers, and activists has abandoned the modernist project of the old Left and, along with it, belief in the virtues of the state, the party, and working class movements as agents of transformation. Instead they propose a radical democratic politics and an "alternative to development" that, in Escobar's (1995, 215) words, emphasizes "a critical stance . . . [toward] established scientific knowledge; an interest in local autonomy, culture and knowledge; and the defense of localized, pluralistic grassroots movements."[12] Adopting a "decentered" view of power and politics, poststructuralists have deserted formal institutions to focus on the democratization of social relations—that is, on challenging authoritarianism in the life world. This challenge comes through the decentralized grassroots struggles of a wide assortment of actors such as new social movements across multiple social arenas. Contestation over

identities, knowledge creation, and discursive practices figure prominently. The old Left's dream of seizing state power through a vanguard
party and/or guerrilla movement and directing transformation from
above is rejected.[13] Civil society is held to be the carrier of all public and
private good—a force against state and market and a space where
authoritarian social relations are challenged, individual empowerment is
possible, and identities are under constant negotiation.

These two variants of radical polycentrism suffer from various faults,
but three are particularly troubling in their implications for the new politics of inclusion. First, there is a disconnection between prescriptions
that emphasize fragmented localized action and the forces that shape
most peoples' lives. *Forbes* informs us that the world's 322 wealthiest
individuals had a combined net worth of $1.1 trillion in 2000, which is
greater than the entire gross national product (GNP) of China ($0.9 tril-
lion, population 1.25 billion) and almost triple that of India ($0.44 tril-
lion, population 1 billion). Furthermore, only six countries in the world
produce greater GNPs than those 300-odd individuals: France, Germany,
Italy, Japan, the United Kingdom, and the United States. According to
Fortune, General Motors (ranked at the top of the Fortune 500) had
annual revenues in 2000 that were three times greater than Mexico's tax
revenue and thirteen times that of Egypt.[14] If a basic tenet of political
economy holds true—that the concentration of economic power enables,
and sometimes necessitates, the concentration of political power (see
chap. 3, this volume)—then suggestions such as those made by UNDP
(2000, 12) that "the foundation of poverty reduction is *self-organization
of the poor at the community level*" seem at best hopelessly naive.

Second, the hegemonic (neoliberal) variant of radical polycentrism
contains strong echoes of the 1950s and 1960s debates on what were then
called modernizing countries, which were founded on the belief that economic development, political order, and democracy went hand in hand
and were mutually reinforcing.[15] Lost is the lesson from Samuel Huntington's *Political Order in Changing Societies* (1968), which surveyed the
sharp increase in coups d'état, revolutionary revolts, and communal violence to conclude that this belief in the "unity of goodness" (1968, 5) was
ill-founded. Postwar modernization had produced political disorder, not
stable democracies, for modernization had triggered an expansion of
political participation that far outpaced the capacity of political institutions to integrate newly mobilized groups.[16] Paradoxically, *Political
Order* was published at a time when developmental states—which had
succeeded in creating legitimate order through a combination of state-led
projects of socioeconomic transformation and political exclusion—were
helping to produce nearly double-digit economic growth in countries
such as Brazil, South Korea, and Taiwan.

Huntington's thesis excited considerable controversy, not least because of the conservative implications of its focus on political order, but this early "governance agenda" had two virtues. It offered a clear understanding of the importance of political integration and the creation of legitimate political order, lest polarization in society degenerate into violent revolt, revolution, and genocide, and it focused on political institutions as central to such integration. Agreement down the political spectrum, however conceived, on the value of democratic politics and political pluralism since the late 1970s represents a fundamental, and fundamentally desirable, shift on the part of both conservative and progressive groups; support for armed struggle of the Right and the Left, and for dictatorship in its many forms, has evaporated.

Radical polycentrism (of power, identity, etc.), however, is so preoccupied with limiting the action of large political organizations that it is blind to the need for collective actors that make it possible for people to aggregate and negotiate demands, coordinate action on a sufficient scale to produce large collective solutions, obtain representation, and indeed help governments to govern. In their keen focus on civil society, hegemonic and counterhegemonic ideations have colluded to hide a critical dimension of political life, that is, political conflict and cooperation structured, limited, and integrated by national institutions, including party systems and substantial collective actors. This trend is at the heart of polycentrism and is explored in more depth in the next section.

WHY CIVIL SOCIETY IS NOT ENOUGH

"Just as retailers, bankers, and commercial employees had organized into economic interest groups," Fritzsche (1990, 76, quoted in Berman 1997, 415) observes of interwar Germany, "so also did gymnasts, folklorists, singers and churchgoers gather into clubs, rally new members, schedule meetings, and plan a full assortment of conferences and tournaments." Indeed, associational life in both Wilhelmine and Weimar Germany, particularly of the middle classes, was so vigorous that "contemporaries spoke of the *Vereinsmeierei* (roughly, "association fetishism or mania") that beset German society and joked that whenever three or more Germans gathered they were likely to draw up by-laws and found an association" (Berman 1997, 407). Confirming Weber's fear that German civic associations, unlike those of the United States, did not promote active participation of their members in the polity, during the interwar period associations were marked by a profound distrust of mass political parties and the popular mobilization they engendered. They were characterized by a "militant localism" and came to be seen as a "sanctuary" from the divisiveness and baseness of institutionalized national politics.[17] This vigorous associational life in fact further fragmented an already deeply divided society as people organized within and not across groups and associations, "hiving" members from each other (426).

Berman (1997) and a new generation of scholars argue that, with the onset of the Great Depression and the dissolution of established political parties, to which the apoliticism of civil society contributed in important ways, the explosive growth of the National Socialist German Workers' Party (NSDAP) was made possible by its ability to penetrate the dense local organizational fabric of German communities. Contrary to neo-Tocquevillians, Berman concludes (402) that "high levels of association-ism, absent strong and responsive national government and political parties, served to fragment rather than unite German society. It was weak political institutionalization rather than weak civil society" that produced the rise of Nazism.

The city of Porto Alegre, in southern Brazil, has a very different but equally revealing civil society story. The municipal government's partici-patory budgeting process has become one of the most heralded instances of direct democracy and civil society activism. Since 1989, Porto Alegre has sought popular participation, through local budget forums, in decid-ing how to allocate capital investment expenditures—investment in paved streets, sewer systems, school buildings, and so forth.[18] Participa-tion has been remarkably high. In 1996, for example, 14,267 people par-ticipated in the two principal popular assemblies in which the principal budgetary decisions are made; according to the Mayor's Office, this num-ber would grow to approximately 100,000 people, about 8 percent of the city's population, if participants in the hundreds of preparatory meetings were included.[19] Abers (1998) shows that this instance of civil society activism was in large measure a product of the initiative of a strong left-wing party with an abiding commitment to popular government. Partici-patory budgeting was a *policy* the Workers Party (PT) adopted upon assuming the mayoralty in 1989. Its municipal government worked hard to foster participation, and the effort by its community organizers to "politicize the pothole" was particularly important. Organizers "acted as external agents, visiting unmobilized neighborhoods, seeking out new leaders, helping people organize, and disseminating information about what could be gained through collective action" (532).

The policy has worked very well. On the one hand, it has enabled the PT to keep control of the mayor's office and circumvent the municipal Chamber of Deputies (the local legislative body that approves municipal budgets), where the party has consistently been in the minority.[20] On the other hand, poor neighborhoods have received better municipal services and "innumerable new neighborhood organizations have appeared in response to the policy, often in areas that were previously dominated by closed, ineffective associations that served as little more than tools of clientelist political parties" (Abers 1998, 511). In Porto Alegre, purposive state action has strengthened civil society.

The Weimar Republic and Porto Alegre experiences illustrate that the uncoordinated activity of large numbers of voluntary associations can have varied effects and the direction of causality between political dynamics and associationalism can run both ways. Academics, policymakers, and activists often misinterpret what civil society can contribute to greater inclusion. They tend to conceive civil society as isolated from both the state and political society. This blinds them to the critical role that state and political society play in the constitution of civil society itself and to the limits of what can be achieved by the uncoordinated actions of a multiplicity of local actors.

To move our discussion forward, we first need to clear some conceptual ground. Two centuries ago civil society was understood to constitute an arena of social activity that was "market-regulated, privately controlled or voluntarily organized" (Keane 1988, 1). Today the most common definition employed is considerably more narrow. It retains the idea of an arena, or sphere, of organizations and activities that are (i) entered into voluntarily and that are (ii) autonomous from the state, but the term is increasingly used to denote organizations outside of the market, or the sphere of production and exchange. The overlapping categories of primordial, coerced, and primarily economic forms of organization and their activities are excluded (Kumar 1993, 375–95). In addition, as the civic engagement debate has gained steam there has been a trend toward excluding large political organizations—political parties, labor movements, and even some interest groups.[21] All concepts that acquire a certain popular currency—democracy, culture, and of course civil society—are recruited into a variety of scholarly and political programs and hence acquire a variety of competing meanings. Here we are speaking in general terms of the core elements that make up the dominant view of civil society today.

This view is built around civil society's perceived democratic duty. Because of this duty, voluntarism and polycentrism are seen as the core virtues of civil society. Hence Putnam (1993, 89–90) observes that "civil associations contribute to the effectiveness and stability of democratic government . . . both because of their 'internal' effects on individual members and because of their 'external' effects on the wider polity. Internally, associations instill in their members habits of cooperation, solidarity, and public spiritedness. . . . Externally . . . a dense network of secondary associations . . . contribute to effective social collaboration."[22] Pluralism, the lack of central coordination, ensures the distribution of power in society and political life (hence the emphasis on autonomy and multiplicity) that is central to checking the power of state and ensuring that the interests of diverse groups are expressed. Civil society is also expected to produce democrats, as civic organizations are seen as the schools of democracy, which broaden citizens' interests and teach the requisite skills for democratic negotiation.

In both the neoliberal and poststructuralist imaginations, the distinction between civil society and the market has become important, but only poststructural analyses fully appreciate its significance. In the neoliberal view, civil society and market-based activity are mutually reinforcing and civil society can serve as a corrective to market failure. Poststructuralist views overlap significantly with that expressed by Young (1999, 145), when she writes:

> If a purpose of theorizing the functions of civil society is to describe the possibilities of free self-organization and their potential for limiting power and democratizing its exercise, however, then it is important to distinguish civil society from economy as well as state. Private firms, some of which are larger and more powerful than many states, dominate economic life in contemporary capitalist societies. Their internal organization is typically far less democratic than most governments, and persons whose lives are affected by the policies and actions of such economic institutions often lack the means to confront them. The structural consequences of market imperatives and profit-orientation as followed by these powerful economic actors, moreover, severely limit the options of individuals, groups, and sometimes states.

The current narrow reading of civil society, however, has lost the important distinction Tocqueville, Linz and Stepan (1996), Young (1999) and many others draw between civil and political associations within the larger set of organizations and practices labeled civil society. This distinction is at the heart of the current trend toward polycentrism. To neglect it provokes three types of errors. One is to deny the role of political organizations in the constitution of civil society. Tocqueville himself appears to have pointed the causal arrows from the political to the civic arena, arguing that politics spreads "the general habit and taste for association" so that "one may think of political associations as great free schools to which all citizens come to be taught the general theory of association."[23] The second is to ignore democracy's need for institutions such as parties to "aggregate and represent *differences between* democrats" (Linz and Stepan 1996, 10). Political society is the terrain where aggregation of interests and substantial coordinated action are negotiated and hence where the activities of large organizations feature prominently (such as those of political parties, labor movements, professional associations, and various kinds of non-production-based interest groups).

Finally, the current reading blinds one to the fact that political society is where collective actors and individuals "contest the legitimate right to exercise control over public power and the state apparatus" (Stepan 1988, 4). Because of the possibility of negotiated interests and large-scale coordination of action, Tocqueville and others argue that it is in political society that state accountability and responsiveness are obtained.[24]

Conceiving civil society separate from its relationship with the state is an understandable historical product of the collapse of the Communist bloc, the struggles against authoritarian rule in Latin America, and U.S. liberal hegemony in the international arena. Implicit in much of the work on civil society over the past two decades is the assumption that state and society are engaged in a zero-sum struggle. A "large" or vigorous state disrupts the bases for associational life and "crowds out" civil groups.[25] This view, however, is profoundly misleading and an analytic dead end. It mirrors the error of the early statist analyses which, in their efforts to isolate the state as a subject of inquiry, contributed to the mystification of its autonomy and transformative capacity (Migdal 1997, 211).

State actors have, in a variety of contexts, played a central role in the constitution of local associational life and collective actors.[26] This has taken place either by design or as an unintended consequence. In the former category, one can highlight, in addition to the Porto Alegre experience (Abers 1998; Baiocchi 2001; Heller 2001), the experience of Bhiwandi, a town bordering Bombay, where local police created neighborhood committees that kept communal peace even as other parts of India witnessed horrific Hindu-Muslim violence (Varshney 2001, chap. 12), state programs in Mexico that have contributed to the "scaling up" of local networks into organizations capable of pressuring subnational governments (Fox 1994, 1996), and recent work on social movements that develops the idea that states (as well as political parties and religious organizations) often support the emergence and reproduction of movements by acting as institutional hosts for them (Houtzager 2000, 2001a).[27] Among the unintended consequences, Herring (chap. 3, this volume) points out that state action and sometimes unfulfilled state promises can become nodes around which people organize to demand public action. Whitehead and Gray-Molina (chap. 2, this volume) suggest that targeted pro-poor policies create, over the long run, important opportunities for the development of political capabilities among subordinated social groups.[28]

A final conceptual point: focus on the *form* of organizational activity (i.e., civic) says little about the values and interests of the organizations and activities involved. Not only do social groups have differential abilities to organize and participate in associational life, but such activity can be a "source of political and antipolitical sentiment, democratic and antidemocratic impulses" and of both conservative and progressive values (Pasha and Blaney 1998, 422–23).[29] Discussions of civil society that focus on associational life *writ large* often lose one of the most important lessons of the past forty years of scholarship on democracy: powerful labor-controlling landlords have historically been the most significant obstacles to democratization, while organized working-class movements, when these have been allied with other (particularly middle-class) sectors, have most consistently pressed for the enlargement of citizens' rights and for democratization (Moore 1966; Rueschemeyer, Stephens, and Stephens 1992). Organized labor has of course played a central role in countering market-based exploitation, including by pressuring for universal social rights. Labor's neglect in much work on civil society is problematic, but the manner in which civil society discussions are framed itself leads one away from looking at the content of specific actors.[30]

Moving beyond conceptual problems, polycentrist expectations of what can be accomplished by the types of organizations and activities identified with civil society are also problematic. One cannot create a politics of inclusion solely, or even primarily, around civil society. The very strength of civil society, its lack of coordination and pluralism, is also its weakness. It spreads power thin and wide relative to the concentration of power of market and state actors. The ability of civic associational life, no matter how well networked, to act as an effective restraint on the state and to counter market-based inequality and exploitation by large corporate actors is severely limited. The required coordination of action for such tasks is particularly difficult because civic life itself suffers profound inequality and division—it often reproduces forms of social stratification (around gender, class, ethnicity, language group, etc.) and power relations embedded in social and economic relations. Hence Keane, a staunch proponent of both the concept of civil society and its empirical referent, observes that the state plays a crucial role in offsetting the "poor coordination, disagreement, niggardliness and open conflict engendered by plural structures of civil society" (1988, 22–23). One can make such a claim for political society as well.

Similarly, the role of civic associations in economic and social undertakings is limited by the difficulty of coordination. Young (1999, 158–59) makes a compelling argument that "civil society alone cannot do the major work of directing investment toward meeting needs and developing skills and usefully employing its members. Ensuring investment in needs, infrastructure, and education and training enough to support self-development for everyone who is able to do meaningful work requires much society-wide decision making and coordinated action."

State and political society therefore have a fundamental role in the politics of inclusion. The state has a central role to play in achieving large collective goals, facilitating coordination within civil society, countering market-based exploitation, and regulating civil society itself. Enforcing property rights and contracts, protecting individual civil and political liberties, and providing minimal public goods is not enough. Political society, as we have seen, has a central role in aggregating interests, negotiating compromise among contending groups, and balancing state power. Negotiating the boundaries of the politics of inclusion occurs in political society.

There is a growing body of work that critiques the way in which the concept of civil society has been used, but few coherent alternative perspectives have emerged that bring together an understanding of the dynamics of political society, local associational life, and various levels and sectors of the state. Developing such a perspective entails moving beyond both the idealization and essentialization of civil society that characterizes much of the writing in hegemonic and counterhegemonic work and simplistic statist notions that, as Migdal (1997) observes, have projected a myth of the state as a cohesive entity that is autonomous of social forces.[31] The rest of the chapter takes a step toward linking state and society and, for the reasons given earlier, moves away from the language of civil society, preferring instead to talk of collective actors, coalitions, and institutions. Such language highlights power dynamics and strategic interactions between political actors.

(RE)CONNECTING STATE AND SOCIETY: THE POLITY

The polity approach interprets the ways in which state and societal actors are constituted, become politically significant, and interact across the public-private divide to produce purposeful change. It is a close cousin of the framework Skocpol (1992) deploys in her interpretation of social policy in the United States, which links state capacity and public policy to the capabilities and goals of nonstate political actors.[32] Societal and state actors' capacities for action are constructed in iterative cycles (or episodes) of interaction. In the discussion that follows, it will become evident that the idea of path dependence—of change that occurs within and between institutionally defined paths—provides the causal structure of the polity approach. It provides a basis for distinguishing change in the direction of greater inclusion along two dimensions—by its speed (or time frame) and its scope. This allows us to speak of incremental change over extended periods of time that occurs within paths and of change between paths that produces dramatic breaks with past political patterns over relatively shorter time periods.[33]

The relationship between state and societal actors is at the center of the approach. Instead of assuming the autonomy and coherence of the state, as did some earlier statist approaches, the polity approach helps problematize the state. It is seen to vary in presence and relations with social groups across geographic and social space—systems of social stratification—and policy areas (O'Donnell 1993; Migdal 1994; Whitehead and Gray-Molina, this volume; Moore, this volume; Houtzager, this volume). This variability is closely linked to the highly uneven capacity for public action of all states, an idea central to the approach.

The ability of societal and state actors to produce a politics of inclusion depends on the second component of the polity approach, what Skocpol (1992, 41) calls the *fit* between these actors and "the historically changing points of access and leverage allowed by a nation's political institutions." Political institutions give some political actors and alliances greater access and leverage over public decision-making centers than others (and hence greater influence over the policy process).[34] The features of political institutions that influence which actors will enjoy fit, or will succeed in engineering it, vary considerably across national political systems, and across subnational systems of countries with large national territories or populations. There are generic dimensions, however, that appear to be particularly important.

Skocpol highlights the degrees of centralization and bureaucratization of the state and party system. The extreme decentralization of U.S. political institutions in the early 1900s—a product of federalism, the separation of powers, and the central political role of legislatures—meant, for example, that reformers were successful in changing social policy "only when they were allied with popular constituencies associated across many localities and legislative districts" (1992, 46–47). Along with early male suffrage and patronage-based parties, this structure made class-based demand making by urban labor, which was concentrated in large urban centers, extremely difficult. "Maternalist forces" were more successful during this period—they were able to forge alliances between national reformers and locally rooted women's organizations to pressure government at the local, state, and federal levels across a broad swath of U.S. territory.

We should not become victims of our own metaphors, however. One of the most important insights of the polity approach, and its third component, is that political institutions severely constrain the ability of actors to engineer fit. Political institutions have significant organizing effects on society—they influence which social groups coalesce into collective actors, how these actors organize (around what types of demands and identities), and what types of alliances they construct. The organizing effects of political institutions are in many instances constitutive of what we call "society." The conflict and cooperation that constitute "normal" political life occur within institutionally defined boundaries and produce incremental patterns of change. Skocpol (1992, 49), for example, attributes the failure of the North American working class to form a labor-based party, and develop strong class consciousness, to the particular combination of early universal male suffrage (in the 1840s) and late state bureaucratization. Similar to what takes place in many contemporary political systems outside of the OECD, nineteenth-century mass-based parties in the United States "colonized all levels of public administration, and . . . relied heavily on distribution of public jobs and publicly funded divisible benefits to appeal to locally situated constituents." Together with the inclusion of men into the polity without the need to mobilize along class lines, this undermined efforts to construct a broad class consciousness and meant that workers' organizations could not form alliances with autonomous bureaucrats in their workplace-based struggles. In contrast, women prior to the 1930s were excluded from the polity and hence from parties and political spoils. This exclusion, Skocpol suggests, facilitated the construction of a maternalist collective consciousness and nonpartisan national federations around social policies for mothers and women workers.

There are also more localized institutional effects. The particular form state presence takes in communities has important ramifications for both societal and state actors.[35] Houtzager and Kurtz (2000) suggest that collective actors representing subordinated social groups tend to crystallize around *structural linkages* that bind state and society, that is, around institutional arrangements—legal frameworks and administrative organizations—and public policies through which the state exercises its diverse productive, social, and regulatory functions.[36] Authoritarian state elites in Brazil and Chile, they argue, pursued extensive agricultural modernization projects by constructing contrasting types of linkages with rural social groups. In Brazil, an interventionist state sought to reorganize labor relations, land tenure, and social provision and to dramatically expand its presence in rural communities; in Chile, a minimalist state relied heavily on market forces to produce a pluralist and highly decentralized system of labor relations, a privatized pension system, and a new land market. These two patterns of modernization "contributed decisively to distinct political outcomes [in the postauthoritarian countrysides]—the dramatic increase in popular mobilization in Brazil . . . and the virtual collapse of a formerly potent rural union movement in Chile" (395).

Why such different outcomes? Structural linkages are manifestations of public action and as such encourage the formation of collective actors. There are three broad reasons why. First, they draw issues into the public sphere and legitimize contestation around them. This reduces the risk of repression, which becomes more costly for state and societal actors alike, and facilitates coalition building across class and other cleavages as political actors (state or societal) note the reduced risk and rightful or lawful nature of the claims being made. Second, structural linkages create new collective interests. Legislation that grants new rights to legally constituted categories of people, and public programs serving particular constituencies, creates interests that cut across previous cleavages, facilitating the formation of actors across otherwise heterogeneous social groups. In some contexts, such linkages will create new bases for alternative collective identities, particularly when state policies treat large and highly differentiated populations as a single category. This has been the case for the Rural Workers Union Movement in Brazil, which since the 1970s has constructed and reconstructed a political identity around the legal category of rural worker. The latter is an unlikely invention of the 1960s political elites that includes agricultural wage laborers, sharecroppers, and small farmers and has since become the basis for claiming a variety of social rights (Houtzager 2001a, 2001b). Part of structural linkages' organizing effects is explained by, and contingent on, the physical points of access to the state that they provide. The extent of a linkage's effect comes in part from its salience in a people's lived experience and in part from the facility they create for petitioning, protesting, and negotiating.

When actors crystallize around structural linkages, they help reproduce those linkages, becoming their natural constituencies and defenders. In this manner, an iterative cycle of state-society interactions is set in motion, creating a pattern of change within paths.

From the vantage point of state actors, structural linkages and ties to the "right" societal actors are vital to conceiving, finding support for, and implementing new types of inclusionary policies. We know from Evans (1995, 11) that states vary markedly in their internal structures and relationships with societal actors and that different combinations of these "create different capacities for state action." The nature of their ties to particular societal actors, the coherence of the civil service, the degree of centralization of authority, and the existence of a set of specialized public agencies all influence what kinds of policies state actors may adopt. Policymakers are more likely to pursue policies that can be implemented by the state agencies at their command or that require relatively low cost institutional adaptation. If state agents lack the bureaucratic capacity and linkages to societal groups required to implement particular policies, or cannot readily develop them, the policies are far less likely to be adopted (Skocpol 1992, 42).

The source of change that is internal to the polity approach, its fourth component, is the iterative nature of state-society interactions, that is, sequenced episodes of mutual adjustment through conflict and negotiation. The terrain on which current interactions unfold—which is populated by constituted actors with varying resources and capacities to engineer fit—is to a substantial degree the product of previous episodes of state-society interaction. On the one hand, public policy, once enacted, alters the terrain on which future political activity takes place. "Policies transform or expand the capacities of the state," Skocpol observes (1992, 58), and "change the administrative possibilities for official initiatives in the future." Second, they alter relations to constitute societal actors, and, third, they create or reinforce structural linkages that "affect the social identities, goals, and capabilities of groups that subsequently struggle or ally in politics." The creation of entirely new institutions, or significant institutional reform such as some of the recent decentralization initiatives, can have a major impact on the capacities of both state and societal actors and hence on their patterns of interaction. On the other hand, the constitution of societal actors and their alliance-building work alters the policy-making terrain and on occasion the constitution of the actors that are bounded by a set of particular rules and draw on a particular type of authority that collectively we call the state.

Of course, there are also multiple sources of change exogenous to the polity, such as slow processes of socioeconomic change (e.g., urbanization) or sudden geopolitical or economic crises (e.g., war or foreign exchange or debt crises). These types of change are fundamental to understanding when change *between* institutionally defined paths occurs. Such change, Krasner observes (1984, 234–35), tends to be difficult, traumatic, and crisis driven, for "institutional structures do not respond in any rapid and fluid way to alterations in the domestic or international environment . . . [large scale] institutional change is episodic and dramatic rather than continuous and incremental." Paradoxically, such moments are marked by high contingency, for political actors acquire greater agency and the array of options before them broadens beyond that of "normal" politics, raising the possibility of changing developmental paths.[37] Hence Grindle (2000, 202) concludes that in Latin America major institutional crises that threatened the stability and legitimacy of the political system, and democratic institutions in particular, have played a central role in episodes of significant institutional innovation.

Finally, the ability of groups to engineer fit with political institutions and forge proreform alliances, as Nelson suggests in this volume, is also limited by a variety of nonpolitical factors. These include the "natural" size of the group (there are more women than workers, more users of roads than of airports, etc.), the physical distribution of group members, and the nature of the social networks and community institutions that bind them together and enhance the opportunity for sharing ideas, information, and values. These "nonpolitical factors," however, are at least in part the product of political dynamics themselves. Public policies, for example, that render labor markets more "flexible"—that is, that give corporate actors greater leeway in hiring and firing employees—have important effects on the work-based networks that support working-class movements. As these networks are eroded, labor movements weaken vis-à-vis other actors and their ability to influence public policy declines, as does their attractiveness as a coalition member.

THE CHAPTERS: SEEING THE POLITY FROM BELOW, ABOVE, AND THE SIDE

The chapters explore the political processes that can, or are believed to, contribute to the emergence of a new politics of inclusion. The essays engage in dialogue with each other and do not all agree on either the direction change can take or on the scope and speed of the change that is possible today. They do all challenge important parts of the current conventional wisdom in international development. And they agree on the centrality of the polity and the new opportunities for coalition building that have emerged as the historic coalitions supporting the developmental state unravel. The chapters give a clear sense that many contemporary diagnoses of international development have read the opportunities for new distributive and redistributive policies, and new forms of political organization and participation of subordinated groups, too narrowly.

The chapters by Whitehead and Gray-Molina and by Herring open up the analytic lens by looking at long-term (cross-generational) processes of change that favor more equitable distribution of wealth and power. They explore how substantial asset redistribution—in the form of agrarian reform—has helped set in motion broadly inclusionary developmental paths in Bolivia and the Indian state of Kerala. Most of the poverty and political exclusion in the world remains rural and derives from the concentration of control over productive assets. Agrarian reform offers benefits over the long term that are more enduring and greater than many alternative antipoverty policies. The benefits, Herring argues, include restructuring "the field of power to which state functionaries respond, and therefore enables a more effective and responsive state, without which all other antipoverty options—including growth—are reduced in efficacy."

Whitehead and Gray-Molina show how high levels of participation by the rural poor in Bolivia's decentralization reform of the 1990s (Popular Participation Reform) can be explained in terms of a long path of political action by poor groups that was set in motion during the 1950s. The path's founding moment was the state-led agrarian reform of 1953, launched in the wake of the National Revolution, in which redistribution of hacienda lands was combined with "a continuous process of state-led rural mobilization" through new agrarian unions. Subsequent cycles of interaction between agrarian unions and state antipoverty initiatives led to an iterative construction and diffusion of political capabilities, that is, of the "institutional and organizational means as well as collective ideas available for effective political action." The development of capabilities varied between regions and over time, they argue, as a result of the different ways in which the institutional features of the state, the organizational resources of the poor, and the content of policies targeting the poor combined. Herring, in turn, offers a remarkable comparison of the historical experience of the U.S. South after the Civil War and the Indian state of Kerala following the 1970s. To those who argue for the political impossibility of such asset redistribution in the current context, his essay points to an array of new possible coalitional bases that are emerging and suggests that political conditions are not nearly as limiting in the current period as is assumed.

Coalition building in national contexts characterized by weak party systems and highly variable levels of state authority is particularly difficult. Houtzager compares one episode in a cycle of state-society interactions in the Philippines and Peru, respectively, during which subordinated groups attempted to escape the fragmentation and localism of much current political action and succeeded, for a period, to acquire leverage over national decision-making centers. The chapter highlights the possibilities, and some of the limits, of "NGO brokered coalitions" as partial functional equivalents of political parties. It finds that the coalitions had the most leverage when they faced a relatively coherent state (with a professional bureaucracy) whose authority was broadly accepted. It suggests that the high degree of institutional flux, particularly in state authority, which is not uncommon in Third Wave democracies (where high levels of political conflict over basic parameters of the political system continue) made sustaining the coalitions and their access to state decision-making centers particularly difficult.

In their chapters, Nelson and Kurtz examine the political feasibility of different social policy packages in a generally neoliberal context. Nelson calls into question the political sustainability of the social policy models in place since the 1980s, in which antipoverty programs, in a variety of ways, narrowly target particular segments of the poor. Echoing earlier work on social democracy such as that of Esping-Andersen (1990), she argues that the chances of sustaining pro-poor policies are higher when they are backed by broad alliances. This entails constructing universal programs or targeted policies embedded in universal programs. Kurtz's analysis of social policy in Chile and Mexico shows that even in countries that have, or are, pursuing strong marketizing reforms, political leaders have the scope to make significant policy choices. Chile in the 1990s pursued a mix of productivist policies to correct market failure and quasi-universal consumption-support policies; in contrast, Mexico has combined the former with programs that narrowly target the poor. Chile's shift toward the current mix has been incremental, but the effects are substantial.

What types of political coalitions can support the programs Nelson and Kurtz highlight? The answer, Nelson suggests, lies in the extent to which there is overlap in the interests of the poor and the lower middle strata. She suggests that the form and extent of overlapping interests are shaped by a range of factors, depending on national context: income gap and lifestyle; class position; geographic intermingling; income generation patterns; and ethnic, religious, or other group identities that cut across rather than coincide with income categories. Kurtz adds an important caveat. The boundaries of social policy in Chile and Mexico, he argues, are set by the neoliberal economic model and its accompanying ideology. The "development ideologies" that come with development models can place strict limits on state action, for ideologies frame the very definition of the problem of poverty and thus the political terrain within which solutions are debated. The policy differences observed between Chile and Mexico, he argues, can be explained by dynamics central to the polity.

One of the core premises of the debate on political inclusion is the positive relationship between democracy, the voice of subordinated social groups, and poverty reduction. This reasonable premise has two parts. One, democratic government will be responsive to pressure from below for poverty-reducing measures, and, two, under such regimes poor social groups are better able to organize and create such pressure from below. In fact, however, the relationship between democracy and the politics of inclusion appear to be far more complicated. The Moore, Harriss, and Crook chapters suggest that, at this historical moment, speaking of democracy writ large as a single, particular constellation of national institutions and dynamics is in fact unhelpful. Differences among formal democracies are so substantial that we need a much finer focus to distinguish the ways in which particular institutional arrangements and political processes associated with democracy, in given types of national contexts, can contribute to the articulation of voices of the poor and production of more equitable distribution of wealth.

Moore and his collaborators set the stage for such a shift in analytic focus. The chapter takes an entirely different approach from the previous one and enters the miasma of quantitative (national-level) governance and poverty measures. They emerge to produce a new and sharp indicator, relative income conversion efficiency (RICE), which captures "the relative efficiency of national political economies in converting national material resources into human development." Using RICE, the chapter finds that there is no statistically significant relationship between democracy and poverty reduction. In addition, it finds that the better governments score on the most widely used governance indicator, the international country risk guide (ICRG), the worse they score on RICE. This last finding, the chapter concludes, throws into doubt the assumption that good governance is essentially a linear, unidimensional variable and points to "a more 'traditional' conclusion: that there is an element of direct conflict between policies that favor (international) capital and policies that favor the poor." The ICRG measure is often used as a proxy for the general quality of governance. Unlike RICE, however, it focuses on the responsiveness of governments to the needs of international investors and lenders.

Harriss moves the analysis from democracy as a national and unitary regime to different subnational regime types in India, defined by the nature of the party system (based on the presence of leftist parties, relatively institutionalized populist parties, and others) and the balance of caste or class power. He identifies variations in the poverty reduction performance of thirteen major Indian states and explores the degree to which patterns of economic and social development can account for the different levels. He then looks at how differences in regime types influence policies, expenditure patterns, and poverty outcomes and the extent to which they break from their respective state trajectories. Within the constraints of long-run historical patterns of path dependence, regime type does have an impact on poverty reduction: regimes with well-organized, left of center parties and relatively well-institutionalized populist parties have been able to deliver pro-poor policies and reductions in poverty and have fared far better than other regimes.

The last substantive issue the volume tackles is one of the most debated in international development today. When does decentralization contribute to greater state responsiveness to the poor and better poverty reduction outcomes? Much has been bet on the potential for decentralization, which is often linked to local participation and democratization, and reforms have been undertaken by state elites under a diverse set of regimes. In their chapter, Crook and Sverrisson assess the record of such reforms in twelve countries and find that their contribution to greater political and economic inclusion are in fact rare.[38] Positive outcomes occurred when the central government had a strong commitment to promoting the interests of the poor at the local level. The disappointing results are rooted primarily in the political dynamics that decentralization reforms trigger. Such reforms seek to alter the distribution of power and resources within the state and among ruling elites and are inevitably entangled in the politics of central-local relations. Heller (2001, 133) observes that such reforms try to create a major break with the past and entail large political shifts that have occurred only under quite particular circumstances. The reform in West Bengal, for example, is the only case that produces "unambiguously" positive results for the poor and was driven by a leftist coalition elected in 1978 "in order to challenge the power of the Congress Party and the landlord classes in the countryside, and to provide a strong popular power base."

The volume's concluding chapter, by Moore, takes up some of the core ideas developed in the essays and interprets their implications for the scope and pace of change possible under a new politics of inclusion. It reinforces the central message of the volume. The developmental state was the product of a particular historical moment that has passed. What should replace it, *Changing Paths* argues, is not a radical polycentric associative sphere and unregulated markets but a polity in which societal actors and state agents compete and cooperate to produce purposeful change through a combination of representative and deliberative institutions. In such a polity, constituted actors will compete for, and reach out to, excluded groups, while such groups will coalesce into political actors and negotiation coalitions from below and across the public-private divide. These are the dynamics that will produce a politics that has as one of its principal concerns the need to enhance the material wealth and political voice of historically subordinated peoples and groups.

NOTES

This chapter has benefited from the comments of Mick Moore, Marcus Kurtz, Judith Tendler, Ruth Berins Collier, David Collier, Arnab Acharya, Kate Gooding, Zainab Latif, and Farah Nageer.

   1. The developmental state is part of a semantic field populated by the regulatory (night watchman) state associated most often with the United States, the welfare state identified with postwar Western Europe (continental), and the central-planning state of the former Communist bloc. In the vast literature on developmental states, three defining features are broadly agreed upon: (i) the state's central role and "pervasive discretion" in determining the allocation of resources and profits, (ii) its reliance on "market-conforming" methods of economic intervention, and (iii) legitimacy based on the state elite's commitment to a transformative, "developmentalist," project and on achievement of this goal (Johnson 1999, 52–53; Schneider 1999, 280). A corollary of the third feature is political exclusion; representative institutions were either nonexistent or had no real power over state behavior.

   2. If we are more generous and look at how many people live on under two dollars a day, the figure shoots up to almost half of the world's population, 2.8 billion people (World Bank 2000, 3). The gap in average income of the richest and poorest twenty countries has more than doubled in the last forty years, with the former enjoying an average income that is thirty-seven times higher than that of the latter (World Bank 2000). Between 1987 and 2000, the share of the world's population living in absolute poverty in fact fell from 28 to 24 percent, yet due to

population growth the number of people in extreme poverty remains essentially unchanged (21–24). The region that accounts for most of the relative decline, East Asia, was led by developmental states that did not embrace marketizing prescriptions (see Amsden 1989; Wade 1990; and Deyo 1987).

3. A series of conferences sponsored by the United Nations (UN) during the 1990s have, for example, produced international development targets that center on poverty reduction. The targets are the following: the reduction of the share of people living in extreme income poverty (less than one dollar a day) by half, universal primary education, elimination of gender disparity in primary and secondary education, reduction of infant mortality by two-thirds, reduction of maternal mortality by three-quarters, universal access to reproductive health services, and implementation of national strategies for sustainable development that will reverse the loss of environmental resources. These are to be met by 2015, with the exception of the elimination of gender disparity in education, which is set for 2005. The term *missing link* comes from UNDP 2000.

4. Vigorous civil society activity in the context of democratic institutions in countries such as Brazil, Mexico, and South Africa has neither been able to counter a series of "antipoor" policies nor to slow down the dismantling of social safety nets, let alone reverse the trend toward growing social inequality.

5. See also Migdal, Kohli, and Shue 1994; Migdal 1997; and Tendler 1997.

6. For an earlier effort to provide such a core based on the concepts of social capital and state-society synergy, see the essays edited by Evans (1996). Other work might include Fox 1992, 1994, 1996; and Grindle 1996, 1997, 2000.

7. The term *neoliberal economic model* is used here to denote a bundle of policies associated with the Washington Consensus, including deregulation of the domestic markets, privatization of public enterprises, liberalization of trade and investment regimes, and strict fiscal discipline. See World Bank 1998 (1); and Gore 2000 (789–90).

8. Huntington (1968, 7) pointed out the U.S. bias toward limiting public authority "When an American thinks about the problem of government-building, he directs himself not to the creation of authority and the accumulation of power but rather to the limitation of authority and the division of power. Asked to design a government, he comes up with a written constitution, bill of rights, separation of powers, checks and balances, federalism, regular elections, competitive parties—all excellent devices for limiting government. The Lockean American is so fundamentally anti-government that he identifies government with the restrictions on government."

9. There are today various competing, and sometimes overlapping, "governance agendas." Among the most prominent is the one focused on corruption and strengthening the rule of law (often read as the enforcement of private contracts and property rights).

10. Quoted in Bonvin and Martinez 1998, 7.

11. The most stimulating work in NIE remains North 1990, while Harriss, Hunter, and Lewis (1995) offer a useful collection of theoretically oriented essays on NIE in the context of development.

12. See, for example, some of the essays in Crush 1995 and Grillo and Stirrat 1997. Much of the poststructuralist work on new social movements is influenced

by Laclau and Mouffe (1985). In Latin America, the work of, for example, Alvarez, Dagnino, and Escobar (1998) has become influential. Some of the post-structuralist tenets are now shared by advocates of "alternative development," which prescribes local participation, forms of direct democracy, and participatory development practices that focus on the poor as an alternative to state-led development projects. See, for example, Fals-Borda and Rahman 1991 and the discussion in Manzo 1991, 27–30.

13. For a useful critique of this position in the Latin American context, see Roberts 1998 (67–74).

14. General Motors' revenues in 2000 were $189 billion, while Mexico's tax revenue in 1998 was $55.7 billion and Egypt's was $14.5 billion (*Fortune* 2000; World Bank 2000).

15. See, for example, Almond and Powell 1978 (252).

16. Modernization for Huntington entailed several interrelated processes, including urbanization, industrialization, increases in literacy, and the rise of mass media.

17. Koshar 1987 (3–5, quotes on 276).

18. Municipal budgets in Brazil have three components: personnel, public services, and capital investment. Local government has the most discretion in allocating in the last category.

19. The majority of participants, a 1995 survey found, belonged to popular classes: 40 percent have household incomes below three minimum wages and only elementary education, and around 60 percent have incomes of up to five times the minimum wage (Santos 1998, 485–86). Baiocchi (2001, 49) finds slightly lower rates of participation but traces a steady increase from 1991 (3,694 people) to 1998 (13,687 people).

20. Santos (1998, 467) makes the interesting point that the participatory budget has no legal standing—the mayor's office, "in strict legal terms, limits itself to submitting to the [chamber] a budget proposal that the [chamber] is free to approve, change, or defeat. In political terms, however, because the executive's proposal is sanctioned by the participatory budgeting institutions and thus by the citizens and community organizations and associations that participate in them, the executive's proposal becomes a fait accompli for the legislative body." Not surprisingly the majority in the chamber claims that the executive, through the participatory budgeting process, has usurped its role in the budgeting process.

21. Originators of this debate include Coleman (1990) and Putnam (1993). An interesting repositioning of this debate can be found in Skocpol and Fiorina 1999.

22. Quoted in Berman 1997 (405).

23. Tocqueville (1990, 119) further notes that "in their political associations the Americans, of all conditions, minds, and ages daily acquire a general taste for association and grow accustomed to the use of it. There they meet together in large numbers, they converse, they listen to one another, and they are mutually stimulated to all sorts of undertakings. They afterwards transfer to civil life the notions they have thus acquired and make them subservient to a thousand purposes." His discussion of civil society is in volume 2 of *Democracy in America,* in a section entitled "Influence of Democracy on the Feelings of the Americans,"

while the causes of democracy are discussed in volume 1 in "Principal Causes Which Tend to Maintain the Democratic Republic in the United States." Much of the latter discussion focuses on the particularities of America's religious universe, which created "habits of restraint" that are "indispensable to the maintenance of republican institutions" because they counter the extreme equality and freedom granted in law (316).

24. Kumar (1993, 381) notes that, for Tocqueville, "political society supplies 'the independent eye of society' that exercises surveillance over its public life."

25. Tocqueville was an early critic of state presence in associational life. Later critics include pluralists like Dahl (1989) and Lipset (1994) and some social capital theorists like Putnam (1993) and Coleman (1990). In Latin America, the surge of social movement activity during the late 1970s and 1980s has been linked by some scholars to the crisis of the "developmental state"; the decline of the state is seen to open up new political space where autonomous social groups can organize (Escobar and Alvarez 1992).

26. See the essays in Evans 1996 and Nugent 1993.

27. Houtzager (2001a, 3) suggests that some elite actors intentionally stimulate group formation and play the role of institutional hosts for new actors. These elite actors "draw unorganized peoples into their organizational and ideological fields, help redefine them as social groups, and sponsor their constitution as new collective political actors. While allies support existing actors in various ways, institutional hosts attempt to create *new* actors and thereby remake political cleavages and re-orient political contestation. Unlike allies, hosts intentionally contribute in critical ways to the local social networks, organizational resources, and ideological material needed to overcome the obstacles to collective action. The degree of autonomy such actors are able to negotiate from their hosts varies over time according to broader political regime dynamics."

28. See also Fox 1996; and Joshi and Moore 2000.

29. See also Howell 2000 (14); and Kasfir 1998 (5).

30. See Collier 1999 for a nuanced account of the role of organized labor in early and late episodes of democratization.

31. For national leaders, claims of the state's coherence, autonomy, and capacity serve important political needs—that is, to project state power and legitimize its exercise in terms of the collective good (hence the emphasis on autonomy).

32. Skocpol (1992, 41) summarizes her polity-centered framework as focusing on four processes: "(1) the establishment and transformation of state and party organizations through which politicians pursue policy initiatives; (2) the effects of political institutions and procedures on the identities, goals, and capacities of social groups that become involved in the politics of social policymaking; (3) the 'fit'—or lack thereof—between the goals and capacities of various politically active groups, and the historically changing points of access and leverage allowed by a nation's political institutions; and (4) the ways in which previously established social policies effect subsequent politics." Largely neglected by students of comparative politics and sociology, as well as within development studies, Skocpol's work has perhaps gone furthest in formulating a relatively coherent

framework that makes the relationship between state and societal actors the centerpiece of analysis (Katznelson 1997, 106).

33. On path dependence, see Krasner 1984; Pierson 2000a, 2000b; and Mahoney 2000.

34. See also Thelen and Steinmo 1992 (8); Krasner 1984 (225); Kitschelt 1986 (61–62); Hall 1986; March and Olson 1984; and Pierson and Skocpol 2000.

35. Tilly (1978, 1997) has long argued that the centralization of state authority provokes basic changes in how people organize to make public claims. He offers a particularly compelling example of the parliamentarization of collective action in England between the late eighteenth and early nineteenth centuries (1997). See also Tarrow 1994.

36. These include the systems of labor relations, social welfare, and land tenure. These institutional arrangements stand in contrast to *political linkages*— that is, the political regime—which encompass the formal and informal institutions involved in the aggregation of interests, leadership selection, and regulation of political conflict, such as party systems and forms of clientelism. See also Houtzager 2000, 2001a.

37. Path dependence therefore has two temporal components. The first is marked by high contingency; hence political actors have a broad array of options open to them and the room for agency is causally significant. The second, subsequent component is marked by relative determinism in that the outcome of the first component carries over and shapes subsequent events (Mahoney 2000, 507–8). Change from then on is bounded and occurs within the path established previously (even when the original conditions that gave rise to the path are no longer present). See also Pierson 2000a, 2000b; and Levi 1997.

38. The cases are of either devolved local governments or mixed forms of devolution with deconcentrated administrations.

REFERENCES

Abers, Rebecca. 1998. "From Clientelism to Cooperation: Local Government, Participatory Policy, and Civic Organization in Porto Alegre, Brazil." *Politics and Society* 26, no. 4: 511–37.

Almond, Gabriel, and G. Bingham Powell. 1978. *Comparative Politics: System, Process, and Policy.* Boston: Little, Brown.

Alvarez, Sonia, Evelina Dagnino, and Arturo Escobar. 1998. "Introduction: The Cultural and the Political in Latin American Social Movements." In Sonia Alvarez, Evelina Dagnino, and Arturo Escobar, eds. *Cultures of Politics/Politics of Cultures: Re-visioning Latin American Social Movements.* Boulder: Westview Press.

Amsden, Alice. 1989. *Asia's Next Giant: South Korea and Late Industrialization.* New York: Oxford University Press.

Baiocchi, Gianpaolo. 2001. "Participation, Activism, and Politics: The Porto Alegre Experiment and Deliberative Democratic Theory." *Politics and Society* 29, no. 1: 43–72.

Berman, Sheri. 1997. "Civil Society and the Collapse of the Weimar Republic." *World Politics* 49 (April): 401–29.

Bonvin, Jean, and Miguel A. Martinez. 1998. "Preface." In Amanda Bernard, Henny Helmich, and Percy B. Lehning, eds., *Civil Society and International Development*. OECD Development Centre Studies. Paris.

Coleman, James. 1990. *Foundations of Social Theory*. Cambridge: Belknap, Harvard University Press.

Collier, Ruth Berins. 1999. *Paths toward Democracy: The Working Class and Elites in Western Europe and South America*. Cambridge: Cambridge University Press.

Crush, Jonathan, ed. 1995. *Power of Development*. London: Routledge.

Dahl, Robert. 1989. *Democracy and Its Critics*. New Haven: Yale University Press.

Deyo, Frederic C., ed. 1987. *The Political Economy of the New Asian Industrialism*. Ithaca: Cornell University Press.

Escobar, Arturo. 1995. "Imagining a Post-development Era." In Jonathan Crush, ed., *Power of Development*. London: Routledge.

Escobar, Arturo, and Sonia E. Alvarez, eds. 1992. *The Making of Social Movements in Latin America: Identity, Strategy, and Democracy*. Boulder: Westview.

Esping-Anderson, Gösta. 1990. *The Three Worlds of Welfare Capitalism*. Princeton: Princeton University Press.

Evans, Peter. 1995. *Embedded Autonomy: States and Industrial Transformation*. Princeton: Princeton University Press.

———. 1996. "Introduction: Development Strategies across the Public-Private Divide." *World Development* 24, no. 6: 1033–37.

Fals-Borda, Orlando, and Muhammad A. Rahman, eds. 1991. *Action and Knowledge: Breaking the Monopoly with Participatory Action Research*. New York: Apex.

Forbes. 2000. "Forbes World's Richest People: The Fourteenth Annual List of the World's Billionaires." <http://www.Forbes.com>.

Fortune. 2000. "Fortune 500, 2000." <http://www.fortune.com>.

Fox, Jonathan. 1992. *The Politics of Food in Mexico: State Power and Social Mobilization*. Ithaca: Cornell University Press.

———. 1994. "The Difficult Transition from Clientelism to Citizenship." *World Politics* 46, no. 2: 151–84.

———. 1996. "How Does Civil Society Thicken? The Political Construction of Social Capital in Rural Mexico." *World Development* 24, no. 6: 1089–1103.

Fritzsche, Peter. 1990. *Rehearsals for Fascism: Populism and Political Mobilization in Weimar Germany*. New York: Oxford University Press.

Gore, Charles. 2000. "The Rise and Fall of the Washington Consensus as a Paradigm for Developing Countries." *World Development* 28, no. 5: 789–804.

Grillo, R. D., and R. L. Stirrat, eds. 1997. *Discourse of Development*. Oxford: Berg.

Grindle, Merilee S. 1996. *Challenging the State: Crisis and Innovation in Latin America and Africa*. Cambridge: Cambridge University Press.

————. 2000. *Audacious Reforms: Institutional Invention and Democracy in Latin America*. Baltimore: Johns Hopkins University Press.

————, ed. 1997. *Getting Good Government: Capacity Building in the Public Sectors of Development Countries*. Cambridge: Harvard Institute for International Development and Harvard University Press.

Hall, Peter. 1986. *Governing the Economy: The Politics of State Intervention in Britain and France*. Oxford: Oxford University Press.

Harriss, John, Janet Hunter, and Colin Lewis, eds. 1995. *The New Institutional Economics and Third World Development*. London: Routledge.

Held, David, Anthony McGrew, David Goldblatt, and Jonathan Perraton. 1999. *Global Transformations: Politics, Economics, and Culture*. Stanford: Stanford University Press.

Heller, Patrick. 2001. "Moving the State: The Politics of Democratic Decentralization in Kerala, South Africa, and Porto Alegre." *Politics and Society* 29, no. 1: 131–63.

Houtzager, Peter P. 2000. "Social Movements amidst Democratic Transitions: Lessons from the Brazilian Countryside." *Journal of Development Studies* 36, no. 5: 59–88.

————. 2001a. "Collective Action and Patterns of Political Authority: Rural Workers, Church, and State in Brazil." *Theory and Society,* 30 no. 1: 1–45.

————. 2001b. "We Make the Law and the Law Makes Us: Some Ideas on a Law in Development Research Agenda." *IDS Bulletin* 32, no. 1: 8–18.

Houtzager, Peter P., and Marcus Kurtz. 2000. "The Institutional Roots of Popular Mobilization: State Transformation and Rural Politics in Brazil and Chile, 1960–95." *Comparative Studies in Society and History* 42, no. 2: 394–424.

Howell, Jude. 2000. "Making Civil Society from the Outside: Challenges for Donors." *European Journal of Development Research* 12, no. 1: 3–22.

Huntington, Samuel. 1968. *Political Order in Changing Societies*. New Haven: Yale University Press.

Johnson, Chalmers. 1999. "The Developmental State: Odyssey of a Concept." In Meredith Woo-Cumings, ed., *The Developmental State*. Ithaca: Cornell University Press.

Joshi, Anuradha, and Mick Moore. 2000. "Enabling Environments: Do Antipoverty Programmes Mobilise the Poor?" *Journal of Development Studies* 37, no. 1: 25–56.

Kasfir, Nelson. 1998. "Introduction: The Conventional Notion of Civil Society— a Critique." *Commonwealth and Comparative Politics* 36, no. 2: 123–49.

Katznelson, Ira. 1997. "Structure and Configuration in Comparative Politics." In Mark I. Lichbach and Alan S. Zuckerman, eds., *Comparative Politics: Rationality, Culture, and Structure*. Cambridge: Cambridge University Press.

Keane, John. 1988. "The Limits of State Action." In John Keane, ed., *Democracy and Civil Society*. London: Verso.

Kitschelt, Herbert. 1986. "Political Opportunity Structures and Political Protest: Anti-nuclear Movements in Four Democracies." *British Journal of Political Science* 16:57–85.

Koshar, Rudy. 1987. *Social Life, Local Politics, and Nazism: Marburg, 1880–1935*. Chapel Hill: University of North Carolina Press.

Krasner, Stephen. 1984. "Approaches to the State: Alternative Conceptions and Historical Dynamics." *Comparative Politics* 16, no. 3: 223–46.

Kumar, Krishan. 1993. "Civil Society: An Inquiry into the Usefulness of an Historical Term." *British Journal of Sociology* 44, no. 3: 375–95.

Laclau, Ernesto, and Chantal Mouffe. 1985. *Hegemony and Socialist Strategy: Towards a Radical Democratic Politics*. London: Verso.

Levi, Margaret. 1997. "A Model, a Method, and a Map: Rational Choice in Comparative and Historical Analysis." In Mark I. Lichbach and Alan S. Zuckerman, eds., *Comparative Politics: Rationality, Culture, and Structure*. Cambridge: Cambridge University Press.

Linz, Juan, and Alfred Stepan. 1996. *Problems of Democratic Transition and Consolidation: Southern Europe, South America, and Post-communist Europe*. Baltimore: Johns Hopkins University Press.

Lipset, Seymour. 1994. "The Social Requisites of Democracy Revisited." *American Sociological Review* 59, no. 1: 1–22.

Mahoney, James. 2000. "Path Dependence in Historical Sociology." *Theory and Society* 29, no. 4: 507–48.

Manzo, Kate. 1991. "Modernist Discourse and the Crisis of Development Theory." *Studies in Comparative International Development* 26, no. 2: 3–36.

March, James G., and Johan P. Olsen. 1984. "The New Institutionalism: Organizational Factors in Political Life." *American Political Science Review* 78, no. 1: 734–49.

Migdal, Joel. 1994. "The State in Society: An Approach to Struggles for Domination." In Migdal, Joel, Atul Kohli, and Vivienne Shue, *State Power and Social Forces: Domination and Transformation in the Third World*. Cambridge: Cambridge University Press.

———. 1997. "Studying the State." In Mark I. Lichbach and Alan S. Zuckerman, eds., *Comparative Politics: Rationality, Culture, and Structure*. Cambridge: Cambridge University Press.

Moore, Barrington, Jr. 1966. *Social Origins of Dictatorship and Democracy: Lord and Peasant in the Making of the Modern World*. Boston: Beacon.

North, Douglass. 1990. *Institutions, Institutional Change, and Economic Performance*. Cambridge: Cambridge University Press.

Nugent, Jeffrey. 1993. "Between State, Market, and Household: A Neoinstitutional Analysis of Local Organizations and Institutions." *World Development* 21, no. 4: 623–32.

O'Donnell, Guillermo. 1993. "On the State, Democratization, and Some Conceptual Problems: A Latin American View with Glances at Some Postcommunist Countries." *World Development* 21, no. 8: 1355–69. Reprinted in Guillermo O'Donnell, *Counterpoints: Selected Essays on Authoritarianism and Democratization*. Notre Dame: University of Notre Dame Press, 1999.

Pasha, Mustapha Kamal, and David L. Blaney. 1998. "Elusive Paradise: The Promise and Peril of Civil Society." *Alternatives* 23: 422–23.

Pierson, Paul. 2000a. "Increasing Returns, Path Dependence, and the Study of Politics," *American Political Science Review* 94, no. 2: 251–67.

———. 2000b. "Big, Slow-Moving, and . . . Invisible: Macro-social Processes in the Study of Comparative Politics." Paper presented at the meetings of the

American Political Science Association, Washington, DC, August 30–September 2.

Pierson, Paul, and Theda Skocpol. 2000. "Historical Institutionalism in Contemporary Political Science." Paper presented at the meetings of the American Political Science Association, Washington, DC, August 30–September 2.

Putnam, Robert. 1993. *Making Democracy Work: Civic Traditions in Modern Italy*. Princeton: Princeton University Press.

Roberts, Kenneth M. 1998. *Deepening Democracy? The Modern Left and Social Movements in Chile and Peru*. Stanford: Stanford University Press.

Rueschemeyer, Dietrich, Evelyne Huber Stephens, and John D. Stephens. 1992. *Capitalist Development and Democracy*. Cambridge: Polity.

Santos, Boaventura de Sousa. 1998. "Participatory Budgeting in Porto Alegre: Toward a Redistributive Democracy." *Politics and Society* 26, no. 4: 461–510.

Schneider, Ben Ross. 1999. "The *Desarrollista* State in Brazil and Mexico." In Meredith Woo-Cumings, ed., *The Developmental State*. Ithaca: Cornell University Press.

Skocpol, Theda. 1992. *Protecting Soldiers and Mothers: The Political Origins of Social Policy in the United States*. Cambridge: Belknap, Harvard University Press.

Skocpol, Theda, and Morris P. Fiorina, eds. 1999. *Civic Engagement in American Democracy*. Washington, DC: Brookings Institution Press.

Stepan, Alfred. 1988. *Rethinking Military Politics: Brazil and the Southern Cone*. Princeton: Princeton University Press.

Tarrow, Sindey. 1994. *Power in Movement: Social Movements, Collective Action, and Politics*. Cambridge: Cambridge University Press.

Tendler, Judith. 1997. *Good Government in the Tropics*. Baltimore: Johns Hopkins University Press.

Thelen, Kathleen, and Sven Steinmo. 1992. "Historical Institutionalism in Comparative Politics." In Sven Steinmo, Kathleen Thelen, and Frank Longstreth, eds., *Structuring Politics: Historical Institutionalism in Comparative Analysis*. Cambridge: Cambridge University Press.

Tilly, Charles. 1978. *From Mobilization to Revolution*. New York: McGraw-Hill.

———. 1997. "Parliamentarization of Popular Contention in Great Britain, 1758–1834." In *Roads from Past to Future*. Lanham, CO: Rowman and Littlefield.

Tocqueville, Alexis. 1945. *Democracy in America*. Vol. 1. New York: Vintage.

———. 1990. *Democracy in America*. Vol. 2. New York: Vintage.

UNDP. 2000. *UNDP Poverty Report, 2000: Overcoming Human Poverty*. New York: UNDP.

Varshney, Ashutosh. 2001. *Civic Life and Ethnic Conflict*. New Haven: Yale University Press.

Wade, Robert. 1990. *Governing the Market: Economic Theory and the Role of the State in East Asian Industrialization*. Princeton: Princeton University Press.

World Bank. 1998. *Beyond the Washington Consensus: Institutions Matter*. Washington, DC: World Bank.

————. 2000. *World Development Report, 2000–2001.* Oxford: Oxford University Press.

Young, Iris Marion. 1999. "State, Civil Society, and Social Justice." In Ian Shapiro and Casiano Hacker-Cordón, eds., *Democracy's Value.* Cambridge: Cambridge University Press.

2 Political Capabilities over the Long Run

Laurence Whitehead and George Gray-Molina

When we looked at the life histories of the people involved, we found that
most of them had previously participated in other, generally more
"radical" experiences of collective action. . . . It is as though the
protagonists' earlier aspiration for social change, their bent for collective
action, had not really left them even though the movements in which they
participated may have aborted or petered out.
—Albert Hirschmann

This chapter is a preliminary attempt to add to the political understanding of pro-poor policy-making in new democracies. We adopt the
view that pro-poor policies are about enhancing personal capabilities,
self-confidence, the capacity for community organization, and recognition of dignity, as well as about income generation and basic needs
fulfillment. In the long run, development of income generation capabilities, social endowments, and political capabilities are likely to be closely
interrelated and strongly reinforcing. Here we focus specifically on the
political capabilities of the poor, defined as the institutional and organizational resources as well as the collective ideas available for effective
political action. Opportunities for political action, we argue, arise
through the iterative construction and diffusion of political capabilities
during, and long after, the implementation of pro-poor policies.[1] We
explore the potential of a capabilities approach by assessing the forty-
year-long process of grassroots collective action that emerged between
the Bolivian Agrarian Reform and the most recent Popular Participation
Reform. As also noted by Ronald J. Herring in chapter 3, the cumulative
and long-run effects of the nature of agrarian reform are well suited to a
historical assessment of the trajectory of state-society relations.

A focus on political capabilities is intended to address what a long-
term and political approach could add to our understanding of pro-poor
policy-making. The approach borrows from Amartya Sen's multidimen-

sional conception of poverty and is extended to the political arena and the analysis of pro-poor policy-making. Both the instrumental and intrinsic usages of the capabilities approach draw attention to the subjective and contextual dimensions of poverty assessment. Perceptions and understandings of poverty are deployed alongside more general, comparable, and cross-country indicators. A capabilities approach also focuses on the long-term processes through which pro-poor policies interact and have an impact. The welfare-enhancing effects of land tenure reform, educational reform, and nutritional and health changes often take more than one generation to play out. Not surprisingly, the political effects of poverty reduction policies develop on a different time scale, one that is sharper and more visible in the short run but anchored to long-term foundational events or reforms. A capabilities approach may help to frame the question of pro-poor policies within a broader analytical perspective. It has become commonplace to accept that "politics matters" for the successful pursuit of pro-poor policies. But what kind of political analysis is needed to fill the gaps in our understanding?

We illustrate the potential of a political capabilities approach by discussing the politics of pro-poor policies in Bolivia between the 1950s and the present. The emergence and development of political capabilities within rural agrarian unions during the Bolivian land reform are traced through periods of populist inclusion, military rule, and more recent democratic reforms. We argue that the construction of political capabilities over four decades has allowed organizations of the poor to play a key role in the decentralization reforms of the 1990s. The Bolivian case also exemplifies our more general approach as the cumulative and heterogeneous development of political capabilities has, over several generations, bridged social trust and networks beyond the community level to the regional and national levels of decision making.

A POLITICAL CAPABILITIES APPROACH

The move from "Washington" to "post–Washington Consensus" debates in multilateral agencies, think tanks, and academia has highlighted a revival of politics within the development literature.[2] Renewed emphasis on engaging the poor in the policy-making process, moving from poverty targets to political agency, has pushed questions of what is required of the poor beyond individual entrepreneurship, human capital, and social solidarity. We adopt the view that an effective pro-poor approach to development policy should more explicitly acknowledge the political resources of the poor.[3] For this purpose, political capabilities are defined instrumentally to include those organizational and institutional resources as well as collective ideas used by the poor to influence the policy-making process. Conceptually, this view of political capabilities overlaps with the idea that individual political entrepreneurs can acquire "political capital" and the related idea that organizations of the poor can accumulate "social capital." However, the notion of political capabilities is more closely tied to the object of collective action—in this case, the process of pro-poor policy design, implementation, and feedback—than to the characteristics of individuals or organizations themselves. A focus on the policy-making process rather than individuals or organizations attempts to capture the political mechanisms by which actors become agents involved in deciding, lobbying, deliberating, and negotiating on pro-poor outcome. In this formulation, political capabilities, unlike political or social capital, are developed for a particular objective—pro-poor policy-making—and change as the object of collective action changes. A set of capabilities useful for claiming land, for example, is likely to be complemented with new capabilities when the poor participate in social service provision or monitoring.

A useful way to think about political capabilities is to focus on the intersection of three arenas driving pro-poor policy-making: the institutional characteristics of the state, which affect which social and political actors have access to political resources throughout the policy-making process; the organizational resources of the poor, through which broad-based alliances of the poor and nonpoor mobilize and frame their political action vis-à-vis the state; and the content of pro-poor policy-making itself, such as land, health, and education policy, through which the poor have a chance to influence and reshape the policy process. From this perspective, the development of political capabilities can be initiated in any of three ways (or combinations of the three): by the state, when policymakers and politicians within the state engage directly with organizations of the poor during the policy-making process; by organizations of the poor, lobbying, negotiating, or bargaining the state for pro-poor policy outcomes; and by third-party alliances with organizations of the nonpoor such as nongovernmental organizations (NGOs), churches, and other broad-based community associations involved in the all of the above. This approach of political capabilities is largely complementary to the polity-centered focus discussed by Peter P. Houtzager in chapter 4, as both analyze the construction of political space for pro-poor coalitions. While the polity-centered approach focuses on the institutional character of the state in inducing pro-poor coalitions, the capabilities approach focuses on the organizational and institutional resources of the poor themselves.

The analysis of political capabilities assumes national and subnational politics in new democracies with reasonably stable boundaries and relatively coherent systems of public policy-making and implementation. This screens out many of the most overwhelming impediments to pro-poor policy-making. We do not consider "failed states" or states threatened by secession, armed intervention, or civil war. Nor do we start from a baseline of kleptocracy or despotic rule. Our potential subset includes many newly democratized countries in Latin America as well as selected countries in Asia and Africa that have usable states and are engaged in democratic politics. They are countries with sufficient political and administrative autonomy to adopt coherent and sustained pro-poor policies, but they are also societies that must expect to contend with widespread and serious poverty for the indefinite future. In all cases, we believe we can only speak of coherent, sustained, and potentially cumulative pro-poor policies in countries where some minimum standards of national integration and policy-making capacity have been institutionalized and rendered durable.

SPATIAL FOCUS

A disaggregated reading of political capabilities calls attention to the discontinuous and disparate links between organizations of the poor, the non-poor, and the state across communities and regions. Unevenness in state presence; geographic patches of ethnic, clientelistic, or corporatist strength; and associative networks that link social movements of varying degrees of cohesion are starting points for assessing whether and how political capabilities develop.[4] Rather than departing from an idealized or monolithic description of the state or the policy-making process, we aim to describe how meeting points between state and society tend to be heterogeneous and cut across income-based thresholds. Under highly institutionalized and relatively stable political conditions, the development of political capabilities is likely to hinge on whether the poor are able to exercise existing political and civil rights and gain political influence over political parties, formal political institutions, and established government channels. In less institutionalized political settings, where political power is diffused among informal networks of ethnic, clientelistic, or other, more or less particularistic political institutions, political capabilities are likely to be linked to more informal strategies through which the poor associate, bargain, or otherwise influence policy-making. In both cases, the analysis of political capability development only makes sense in an evaluation of the particular political and historical context in which the poor organize and engage the state. Among the multiple approaches taken by organizations of the poor, some will be structured through alliances with organizations of the non-poor, alliances with state reformers, or more autonomous contestative action. Attention to heterogeneity across state-society relations provides a closer description of how the poor—or more frequently fragments of the poor—relate to decision-making centers and how this changes from one political setting to the next.

A complementary focus on political capability development over time is meant to call attention to the process of political learning that lies behind effective political action by the poor. The bridging role of ideas, identities, and collective self-awareness is particularly important as individuals and groups of individuals regenerate collective memories of past instances of collective action under new guises for future political change.[5] Action that took on a contestative and territorial form in one period may be rekindled under a functional and bargaining form in another. The fragmentation of many organizations of the poor—most prominently labor and peasant unions—in many new democracies, suggests that pro-poor political action is being reframed through increasingly heterogeneous alliances with the non-poor (see Peter Houtzager's detailed discussion of fragmentation of the organizations of the poor in chap. 4). Ethnic, regional, and single-issue political actions provide new cleavages for pro-poor policy-making and increasingly blur the lines between "poor" and "nonpoor" organizations. The collective memories that constitute a stock of political learning move from one arena of political action to the next, often across generations, as may be seen in the case of labor and peasant offshoots. This long-term focus means that we must consider not just changes of protagonists but of modes of analysis exemplified, for example, in the research shift in social movement literature from class-based to identity-driven politics that infuses new meanings and understandings for pro-poor political action. Pro-poor policies that were formulated in the idiom of, for example, the Alliance for Progress may revive in a different guise when the framing ideas are those of the Washington Consensus.

The analysis of political capabilities over time and space aims to provide a more realistic mapping of how state-society relations affect pro-poor policies over the long run. The focus on the political capabilities of the poor also takes on a more actor-centered approach. Traditional questions of institutional design (what sorts of political institutions promote pro-poor policies?) are complemented by new questions concerning the process of political engagement of the poor (what sorts of alliances empower the poor in context X and period Y, and how do they change in response to a given reform strategy Z?). Actors themselves change over time and emphasize different aspects of their political identity in a highly contextual and contingent manner. Peasants without land coalesce around the banner of unionism in one period but may emphasize ethnic claims in others. Protestant lay preachers in one setting become community organizers in another, revert to religious group organizations in a third, and so on. In most instances, multiple political identities are managed simultaneously: unionism with respect to the formal political system, community organizations with respect to local clientelist networks, and ethnic organizing for national or regional territorial claims. A disaggregated approach aims to capture as much of this variation as possible while still holding on to a common story line.

THE POOR

The "poor" constitute such a central category in our analysis that our approach to it requires brief elucidation. We refer to the political capabilities of the poor, organizations of the poor, and pro-poor policies. But who is to be included and how is this category to be constituted for the purpose of political analysis? Income and basic needs indices are often central to public policy debates about the poor. However, income and basic needs thresholds often include many disparate subgroups of the poor, including some that are not often able to organize or participate as political subjects precisely because of extreme indigence. A political analysis must not exclude the extremely poor whose claims to entitlements in a democracy may exert significant pressure on the design of public policies. But, whereas the state bureaucracy may view them as a homogeneous category and targeted object of policy, this is likely to be misleading as an account of how they understand themselves or how they enter into the political process. Both the very poor and broader strata of the poor tend to group themselves into highly diverse subgroups identified on dimensions quite different from the typical poverty yardstick. They carry historical memories and accumulated memories of their rights and grievances, which strongly influence the scope and limits of political expectations and alignments. From this perspective, indicators of income or basic needs deprivation need to be supplemented with a more contextualized and subjective account of poor political identities, even when these are being reconstituted by the experiences of democratic politics and interactions with the state and representative institutions.

Clearly this subjective identification may include many who barely qualify on income and basic needs indicators but who nevertheless add a substantial stock of political capabilities, and therefore leverage, to the pursuit of pro-poor policies. The organized poor may also strengthen incentives for the less poor, and even some nonpoor, to join in concerted political action. The possibility of "free riding," which is often perceived in an exclusively negative light, may in fact provide some benefits for the poorest of the poor in the course of pro-poor policy-making. In order to exercise sustained influence and achieve cumulative growth in capabilities, the poor need allies. One possibility is that such allies might be constituted vertically, through asymmetric patron-client ties, for example. Another is that allies might include horizontal linkages to nongovernmental or church organizations engaged in shaping or implementing pro-poor policies. A third possibility is, of course, that the poor may scale up collective action autonomously, as has been observed with peasant and labor unions, to bargain from a position of greater power. The subjective identification of who is an ally of the poor is decidedly time and space specific. Understood in tandem with more objective indicators of poverty, subjective identifications highlight the democratizing and dignity-enhancing aspects of pro-poor policy that besides reducing material deprivation also increase the social and political agency of broad sections of the population.

A BOLIVIAN CASE STUDY

Bolivia's history of popular mobilization and its long record of pro-poor policy-making make it an interesting case through which to examine the construction of the political capabilities of the poor. The period that runs between the Agrarian Reform of 1953 and the recent Popular Participation Reform of 1994 provides a four-decade stretch for the assessment of pro-poor policy-making.[6] Many of the results achieved during this period can be understood by reference to extensive and preexisting processes of learning and capability building. For the future, a long-term perspective will be needed to confirm their durability. Long considered the poorest country in Latin America, Bolivia is today classified by the World Bank as a lower middle income country based on its gross domestic product (GDP) per capita, estimated at U.S.$1,000 (or U.S.$2,820 at purchasing parity prices) in 2000.[7] Between 1950 and 2000, demographic changes have been significant. The population increased sharply, from 3.0 to 8.3 million, and the urban population share grew from 34 percent in 1950 to 62 percent in 2000. The only direct measure of well-being available for this fifty-year period is the literacy rate, which increased from 31 percent in 1950 to approximately 80 percent in 2000.[8] A more recent comparison, which uses education, health, and housing data from the 1976 and 1992 censuses, shows a sixteen-point drop in the "basic needs" poverty index, from 85 to 69 percent.[9]

   While the historical record provides a rich source of contextual materials on which to draw, the historical vignettes presented in this section aim only to provide the bases for an analytic narrative of the development of pro-poor political capabilities. Here we focus on three cases of political development that run through three successive periods of time: that of national revolutionary reform, of corporatist state building, and of neoliberal reform. A focus across time is disaggregated across space to account for the numerous paths through which capabilities have developed or had an impact on the poor.[10]

THREE PERIODS

National 1952–65 Revolution: The Poor as Protagonists

The Bolivian National Revolution of 1952 cast the rural and urban poor, at least in official discourse, as key protagonists of vast social and political change. Universal suffrage, nationalization of the mines, reform, and agrarian reform were the hallmarks of a Revolution driven by mass mobilization and characterized by political contestation.[11] The agrarian reform, in particular, was to be regarded as one of the most comprehensive land redistribution initiatives carried out in the region.[12] The expropriation of hacienda lands and redistribution to tenant farmers, smallholders, and campesino communities was accompanied by a continuous process of state-led rural mobilization. The creation of thousands of new agrarian unions promoted and supported by the ascendant Movimiento Nacionalista Revolucionario (MNR) would set the stage for a long period of corporatist state building and political clientelism. By 1956–60, the object of popular mobilization had shifted from land reclamation to political negotiation with a highly dispersed network of state patronage. Public works and food subsidization schemes managed through line ministries and departmental prefectures were channeled through networks of party sympathizers and militants, inducing atomization within the national peasant movement. By the early 1960s, the zeal of the initial period of revolution and reform had abated and given way to a more pragmatic realignment with the emerging developmental state.

Corporatist State Building, 1964–78: The Poor as Clientele

A second and contrasting period of policy-making arose with corporatist and clientelist politics. After twelve years of MNR rule, a 1964 coup initiated an eighteen-year period of military rule marked by interim periods of civilian government.[13] The diminished political power of MNR patrons and the political containment strategy of the military vis-à-vis radicalized miner and worker movements led to the establishment of a military-campesino pact, the Pacto Militar Campesino, which endured through the mid-1970s. The pact thus substituted for the MNR-union clientelistic ties, secured the continuity of land reform gains, and laid the foundations of a new corporatist and clientelistic political relationship.[14] The rural poor lost their organizational autonomy, and although they still exercised some capacity for political expression they were subject to a series of vertical controls organized through local garrison commands. The demobilization of the campesino union movement was to last only a few years. By 1968, calls for an independent and unaligned union leadership emerged after the Barrientos administration floated a policy proposal aimed at consolidating a single rural land tax.[15] The Banzer coup d'état of 1971 restricted the splintered campesino movement and restored the military-campesino pact until the mid-1970s. Price hikes decreed in 1974, however, fueled a bloody confrontation between military troops and campesino protesters in Tolata, reigniting a more radical mobilization period aimed at opposing the authoritarian regime and pushing toward a popular and democratic transition. The creation of a unified agrarian union confederation, Confederacion Sindical Unificada de Trabajadores Campesinos de Bolivia (CSUTCB), marked a political shift in the campesino movement in 1979, leading to a three-year stretch of active popular mobilization through the democratic transition of 1982.

Popular Participation, 1993–99: The Poor as Agents

A third scenario arises from the present period of democratizing state reforms. First-generation reforms that focused on economic stabilization and fiscal balance in the 1980s were followed by second-generation reforms focusing on decentralization; capitalization; and pension, educational, and judicial reforms in the 1990s. The most recent initiatives have aimed to reintroduce the poor as agents of public policy. The Popular Participation Reform is perhaps the most salient of the recent reforms as a result of its local political and institutional effects. Close to 200 new municipalities were created, and rural areas were included within municipal jurisdictions for the first time. Initially rejected by the campesino and indigenous leadership, Popular Participation was to gain momentum with the municipal elections of 1995, which for the first time included open and direct rural municipal elections.[16] Close to a quarter of the municipal councilors in 311 municipalities were self-identified campesino or indigenous candidates.[17] More important for the grassroots movement, however, was the institutionalization of participatory planning procedures involving some 16,000 campesino and indigenous and neighborhood organizations.[18] While the development of popular participation is widely regarded as being marked by an equal measure of "success" and "failure," the emphasis on territorially based grassroots organizations has redrawn the rules of the game for political intermediation and policymaking in rural areas. State patronage and political clientelism, which had relied on national-to-local networks of redistribution and reciprocity, today compete with newly established local networks, some building upon the political capabilities of a previous era and some newly adapted to the changed rules of political engagement. Richard C. Crook and Alan S. Sverrisson's discussion of decentralization in chapter 9 addresses the comparative importance of local-central political relations in determining elite capture, grassroots participation, and the prospects for pro-poor development in decentralized government systems.

THREE CASES

Central Cochabamba

Developing Capabilities

Central Cochabamba was at the heart of the 1953 Agrarian Reform. Between 1953 and 1993, the breakup of the hacienda system distributed close to twenty million hectares of land, benefiting some 550,000 smallholders and landless workers in the highlands and valleys.[19] The creation and mobilization of thousands of agrarian unions during the 1950s led to the development of strong campesino organizations endowed with a rich collective memory of mobilization and political activism. During the early reform years, agrarian unions emerged to claim hacienda land and oppose political and policy reversals.[20] The development of agrarian unions was by no means uniform. Radical and moderate political leaders vied for political power at the grassroots level and played off internal divisions with competing left-wing and right-wing factions of the MNR. The signing of the Agrarian Reform Law in August of 1953 united both factions under a departmental federation of agrarian unions that would later set the pattern for the establishment of campesino federations in the rest of the country.[21] The dynamic and iterative process of political engagement and negotiation behind agrarian reform allowed the broad-based development of political capabilities, harnessed by the union system but promoted by the governing party, that permitted organizations of the poor to gain political leverage over pro-poor policy-making.

Addressing Localism

The union system, which was organized pyramidically through departmental central and provincial subcentral hubs, played a larger political intermediary role both during and long after the corporatist state-building period of the early 1960s. The threat of political "localism," or isolation from policy-making networks, played a determining role in inducing union scaling up and pragmatic alliances with the MNR in the 1950s and the military in the 1960s. The zenith of campesino organizing in the valleys was reached during the 1960s with the military-campesino pact. A decade of reform and political mobilization also led to a demographic and generational shift in political leadership in the valleys. Union leaders of the 1950s became local politicians, national congressmen, and national campesino leaders in the 1960s. Although it was impoverished, union organizing provided a dense network of social and political power linked to state patronage and national decision-making influence.

The turning point for agrarian union influence was reached in 1974 after riots and blockades against the Banzer administration led to a massacre of union leaders in rural Cochabamba. For the following eight years, the agrarian union leadership would retreat from direct alliances with the state and the military and would itself splinter into independent and radical blocs. The breakdown of the corporatist state and the transition to democratic rule in the early 1980s signified a radical realignment of the agrarian union system. At first linked to the workers' Central Obreras Boliviana/Bolivian Labor Federation (COB) during the period of authoritarian breakdown, the campesino confederation was to chart a more independent path and pursue pragmatic alliances with international donor and nongovernmental organizations in the mid-1980s.

Again the threat of political localism led to closer ties with a vast web of NGOs acting as state surrogates for public investment, social service provision, and emergency aid during the 1980s. For the first time since the early Agrarian Reform period, union leaders joined the key political parties, mostly the Movimiento de Izquierda Revolucionario (MIR) and the Movimiento Bolivia Libre (MBL), that sustained the NGO boom. NGO-sponsored union leaders participated directly in credit, technical assistance, and rural development initiatives through the regional agrarian union system. The emergence of a flourishing coca-cocaine trade in the tropical Chapare region, in eastern Cochabamba, fueled an additional political front that had become radicalized by the late 1980s. Crop substitution, alternative development, and rural development programs financed by USAID were met with organized opposition within the regional agrarian union system.

Pro-Poor Outcomes

The Popular Participation Reform, launched in 1994, unified a relatively fragmented agrarian union system around a single territorial objective: participatory municipal planning. Today the Cochabamba central valleys boast the highest rates of electoral participation, the second-highest rate of grassroots mobilization for municipal planning, and the highest number of campesino and indigenous councilors in the country.[22] While the decentralization process is far from ideal and continues to be riddled with political conflict, Cochabamba municipalities have capitalized on the long-standing organizational power of the agrarian union system. Unions have scaled up political access to the departmental and national levels through pragmatic alliances with national reformist elites and regional nongovernmental and church organizations. They have also made inroads in political participation through grassroots alliances with progressive political parties. The Izquierda Unida (IU), Movimiento al Socialismo (MAS), and MBL are among the strongest rural political parties in the department, and they continue to open party slates to agrarian union leaders. In 1995, close to a hundred Cochabamba union leaders were elected to municipal office; and in 1997 five leaders were elected to the national congress.[23]

Northern Potosi

Developing Capabilities

A second and sharply contrasting case developed in northern Potosi in the Andean highlands. Here the breakup of hacienda lands into individually owned plots was overshadowed by the legal recognition of communally owned commons. Hundreds of Quechua and Quechua/Aymara-speaking indigenous communities legalized communal or pro-indiviso access to land in the highlands.[24] Unlike Cochabamba, which implemented the reform through a strong and relatively united agrarian union system, northern Potosi developed a dual system of rural grassroots organizations. Indigenous *ayllus,* organized through customary moieties, clashed with newly created agrarian unions throughout the region and exacerbated a long-standing town-countryside political divide. The top-down political appointment of union leaders by the MNR led to bloody confrontations between indigenous communities in Toro Toro and San Pedro de Buena Vista (1958).[25] By the late 1950s, the governing MNR had alienated most of the region's grassroots leadership through political confrontation and open territorial division. The fragmentation of grassroots leadership inhibited broad-based participation in policy reform and led to only isolated opportunities for the development of political capabilities. Confrontations between grassroots organizations and between these organizations and state institutions fed an iterative cycle of social and political fragmentation.

Addressing Fragmentation

The military-campesino pact ratified during the Banzer administration in 1971 furthered the territorial divide between unions and *ayllus,* but it also led to the construction of political clientelist bridges between the two.[26] The unions lobbied the corporate state and renegotiated regional political power with the ayllus. The agrarian union confederation of Potosi, based in Sacaca, allied itself with the military against the regional mining confederation, thus isolating the indigenous ayllu leadership from substantive decision making and public services. The distribution of political patronage and public employment revolved around the town leaders based in Llallagua, Uncia, Sacaca, San Pedro, Pocoata, and Ocuri and led to political infighting and fragmentation within the union system. By the late 1970s, the emergence of an independent campesino movement within the agrarian union system would turn the tables on the campesino-military alliance. A 1979 congress held in Chayanta broke with the military leadership and called for joint ayllu-union cooperation against the authoritarian regime. Despite growing ties between campesino and indigenous leaders, joint political mobilization lasted only three years, through the democratic transition and emergency relief operations following the 1982–83 drought.

The relief efforts, led by a Catholic Church organization (Radio Pio XII), drew attention to the new political role played by NGOs and private voluntary organizations in the region. NGOs linked to the MIR and later the MBL gained prominence in the provinces of Bustillos and Chayanta. The partial overlap of union and ayllu organizations added an additional political issue for development agencies and NGOs working in northern Potosí. The weak clientelist ties between town elites, agrarian unions, and indigenous ayllus in the 1980s ensured a highly fragmented political arena parceled out among unions, *ayllus*, NGOs, and political parties.

Pro-poor Outcomes

The Popular Participation Reform, introduced in 1994, built upon the political fragmentation and territorial disputes engulfing grassroots organizations in the region. For close to three decades, isolated instances of pro-poor policy-making initiatives floundered in a region beset by social and political strife. Northern Potosí today boasts the highest rates of infant and maternal mortality in Bolivia and in the Western Hemisphere. Literacy rates are among the lowest in the country and are accompanied by a deep gulf between indigenous-speaking communities and the Spanish-speaking school system. While most indicators are traceable to a long history of state neglect, many have remained stagnant through a prolonged period of political infighting. Northern Potosí also exhibits one of the highest rates of electoral absenteeism and one of the lowest levels of grassroots participation in municipal planning in the country. The disengagement of indigenous ayllus from local politics has been matched by the politicization of NGO staff members and rural teachers. "Surrogate" indigenous representatives today make up most of the municipal councils in northern Potosí.[27] The dispersion of the rural vote has also added to the political instability. Twelve out of thirteen municipalities in the region changed mayors at least once—six changed mayors every year—over a four-year period. Recent reviews of the decentralization process suggest a recursive cycle of grassroots disengagement, weak and opportunistic political alliances, disillusion, and political apathy at the local level.[28]

Northern Santa Cruz

Developing Capabilities

Lowland resettlement policy, agrarian unions, and developmental state agencies account for political capability development in northeastern Santa Cruz. Between 1967 and 1993, some three to five million hectares were distributed to approximately 800,000 families.[29] Most families emigrated from Cochabamba, Chuquisaca and Potosi in the early to mid-1960s, adapting the agrarian union system to the demands of colonization, agricultural expansion, and commercialization.[30] Spontaneous, state-supported, and partially supported (mainly through land grants) colonization programs took on different political colors, largely based on their degree of dependence on the MNR and its factions in the 1960s and more authoritarian groups during the 1970s, including those that later founded the Accion Democratica Nacional (ADN) in 1979. Colonization in northern Santa Cruz has changed the face of local politics in the region. The strong clientelist ties between agrarian unions, the MNR, and the ADN have been weakened by the more radical political fronts led by the Izquierda Unida until 1997 and the Movimiento al Socialismo in 1999.

Addressing Political Capture

San Julian, one of the most prominent state-supported colonization programs, exemplifies the transition between MNR-supported unions and more contestative and independent political mobilization. Founded in 1968, San Julian began with two state-supported and two spontaneous colonies. State support initially focused on land grants, titling, and organizational support through the Instituto Nacional de Colonizacion (INC). In 1972, the INC expanded the state-supported program to forty new colonies (*nucleos de colonizacion*) with the assistance of the United Churches Committee (CIU), which was made up of representatives of the Catholic, Methodist, and Mennonite churches. Between 1972 and 1978, San Julian grew exponentially and scaled up its agrarian union system to the provincial level through the Federacion Especial de Colonizadores de San Julian (FECSJ). Political clientelist ties between the Banzer administration (1971–78) and the union system ensured the steady expansion of road works, urban infrastructure, and social services during this period.[31]

By 1979, the INC-CIU agreement had ended and with it the state support that had sustained colonization since the late 1960s. Nongovernmental and religious organizations began to fill the vacuum in the early 1980s, together with a third wave of migration—this time mostly spontaneous—from Santa Cruz and the valleys. Today San Julian hosts 160 colonies, with as many unions organized by subcentral and central hub federations. The third wave of migration weakened the previous clientelistic links substantially and introduced a new style of politics based on regional links with other colonization areas in northern Santa Cruz. In local politics, the clientelistic ties between the MNR and the agrarian unions continue to thrive, although they are increasingly threatened by alternative movements such as the Eje Pachacuti, the Movimiento Bolivia Libre, and the Union Civica Solidaridad, each of which elected a councilor in 1995. In 1999, San Julian again elected an MNR candidate to the mayorship, but it also spread the vote to Accion Democratica Nacionalista and Union Civica Solidaridad.[32]

Pro-poor Policy Outcomes

More than thirty years have passed since the initial colonization settlements were established in lowland Santa Cruz. The migrants were from many of the poorest regions of the country, including northern Potosi, Chuquisaca, and southern Cochabamba. In two generations, colonization regions have almost doubled their literacy rates and lowered infant and maternal mortality rates to near urban levels. Since the implementation of the Popular Participation Reform, San Julian has regained influence in the region due to its organizational strength and the political opportunities it has to lobby for public investment regionwide. Although electoral absenteeism is relatively high, participation in municipal planning is among the strongest in the region, and the number of elected indigenous councilors is also one of the highest in Santa Cruz. In contrast to both Cochabamba and Potosi, San Julian thrives through grassroots political action aimed at agricultural expansion supplemented by strong demographic growth. In this highland enclave in the tropics, the colonization experience has produced a cohesive agrarian union system that plays by the rules of clientelist politics but aims for greater political autonomy in the region.

COMMON THEMES

Three themes emerge from a reading of the Bolivian experience with pro-poor policy-making. The first is the cumulative impact of long-term political learning. The agrarian reform had as a starting point the massive mobilization and empowerment of agrarian unions, most of which continue to play a central role in local politics. Nearly 70 percent of the sixteen thousand territorial grassroots organizations that are involved in participatory planning today are tied to the agrarian union system. The construction of political capabilities initiated during the agrarian reform can be regarded as a highly iterative process of grassroots organizational and ideological change. The broad-based and pyramidal system of community *sindicatos,* provincial centers, and departmental federations has survived and been transformed over long periods of demobilization, co-option, and assimilation into larger mass movements. The organizational capabilities of the union system changed from playing a largely redistributive role during the agrarian reform to a political bargaining role during the national revolutionary period and a proactive role in local politics at present. Political capabilities forged in one arena of collective action have migrated to others, often at the expense of community organizations themselves, as is suggested by the proliferation of single-interest and functional organizations in recent years.

The second theme is the local-national bridging effects of political capabilities. The means to address political localism, fragmentation, and elite capture in Bolivia have been diverse, but they have in common the construction of bridges in local and national spheres of politics and policy-making. While the cases of Cochabamba and Santa Cruz suggest some success in reaching beyond the confines of local power struggles, Potosí shows the opposite trend. The strained separation between national and local policy-making, as well as between central and local politics, adds to the perception that they constitute autonomous arenas. The long-term viability of pro-poor policies is likely to depend on the social and political ownership of reforms and on the ability to propose and defend gains at the local and national levels. The top-down focus on the sustainability of many first- and second-generation reforms in recent years requires complementary thinking on bottom-up and crosscutting strategies of participation, brokership, and continuous legitimation. In new democracies with spotty and discontinuous states, the "holes" left by state absence are often filled by regional, ethnic, or clientelist social networks in alliance with fragments of central government, NGO, or church presence. Despite the tendency toward centralized policy design, the successful implementation of agrarian reforms, education reforms, decentralization, and other institution-building initiatives depends on how local institutions perform and translate one-time demands into cumulative processes.

The third theme in the Bolivian experience is an acknowledgment of the contingency and discontinuity of pro-poor policy-making. Politics and policy after the agrarian reform were seldom as orderly and consistent as was initially intended. In the case of popular participation, the very process of creating new rules of the game for public investment and service delivery was battled out through local politics with dozens of different outcomes. Municipalities with strong grassroots organizations had the voice to propose and bargain with local elites. Procedures were modified to fit local circumstances or at least to define mutually agreeable rules for resolving disputes—and hence to build viable local institutions.

The "politicization" of the Bolivian decentralization reform played a key role in the creation of new rules and legitimacy around the process, not just the design, of state reform. In the future, local politics can be expected to shift away from rule making and move toward policy implementation, including the development of means of evaluating and overseeing more specific policies on education, health, and urban development.

In this light, the examination of the ups and downs between foundational or institution-changing events is as important as the analysis of the path-changing events themselves. In the Bolivian case, what is stable and what is contingent in the development of political capabilities are important and interesting questions, the answers to which vary from case to case. The path set forth by agrarian unions in central Cochabamba, for example, is more consistently empowering than those observed in the other two cases. Capacity building within the agrarian union system developed continuously throughout state-building and withering periods. In contrast, the process of policy change in Potosi and Santa Cruz was marked by short-term shifts that magnified the conflictive aspects of pro-poor alliances and ultimately weakened grassroots capacity building. Problems of social and political fragmentation in one case and political capture in the other forestalled a long-term learning process. A focus on the process of policy-making also calls attention to the changing strategies of participation or contestation used by the poor. In Potosi today, contingent alliances between rural community organizations and teachers and NGOs occur simultaneously with attempts to recapture local political power through "ethnic parties" such as the Eje Pachacuti, the Izquierda Unida, and the Movimiento al Socialismo. In Santa Cruz, long-standing clientelist relations with the MNR are traded for more pluralistic options at election time but are rekindled whenever the MNR wins the national elections. Little can be predicted—politically—from the demographic or ethnic profile of most grassroots communities today. The ongoing process of political engagement and disengagement is highly localized and contingent and continually changing.

CONCLUSIONS

The pro-poor policies reviewed in the Bolivian case studies all required high level, indeed presidential, commitment and legislative enactment. They were "political" in the narrow sense that they emerged from the decisions of top political officeholders and were implemented through formal political processes. However, the top-down component of the adoption of pro-poor policies should not be viewed in isolation from the distribution of political expectations and capabilities in the larger society.

If a popular participation law such as that adopted by Bolivia in 1994 were to be enacted in a different society, one unaccustomed to establishing inclusionary links with organizations of the poor, the outcome would probably be quite different. Indeed, the accumulated political capabilities of Bolivia's poor are as crucial for explaining the substantial and procedural effects of the reform as are the intentions of its official authors. Procedurally, Popular Participation introduced a new set of rules designed to both devolve power to local governments and empower community organizations at the grassroots level. Substantially, however, the Popular Participation Reform had a significant redistributive effect from urban to rural areas and resulted in a large increase in social spending as a proportion of total government expenditures. In Bolivia, the cumulative cycle of interactions between the central political authorities and local organizations of the poor determined the content of a pro-poor policy; neither side could secure its objectives without bargaining with the other. The Bolivian example can be generalized, but only within limits. We identified two key limits in the introduction: our analysis refers to reasonably secure new democracies with sufficient state capacity to generate and sustain effective pro-poor policies. Where such conditions exist, it is possible to implement reforms that do not merely entail pro-poor policies but can increase the long-term chances of building pro-poor initiatives. The implementation of such reforms is always likely to be an untidy and potentially conflict ridden process, but the existence of local political capabilities of the kind illustrated in this chapter can help to stabilize positive outcomes and over the long run set in motion a cumulative process of pro-poor development.

From a comparative perspective, the capabilities approach suggests a number of conceptual bridges linking academic and policy analysis on pro-poor politics. First, the Bolivian case study suggests the importance of viewing pro-poor policy-making in a long-term perspective. In fact, several generations may require consideration if one adopts a political capabilities approach. The World Bank and international donor community aim to halve the number of the poor by 2015, which is a specific, ambitious, and long-term goal. But children and teenagers currently suffering from malnutrition or lacking basic education will be less than halfway through their productive lives in sixteen years' time, and many of these problems will be passed on as disabilities to their children. The eventual success of pro-poor policies must therefore be considered not just over a single generation but over several. This is not the only way to evaluate pro-poor policies, but it is one necessary and possible way. It is particularly relevant when we consider the broader political dimensions of a pro-poor political strategy. Short-term emergency measures may have a substantial impact on certain manifestations of poverty, but for these gains to become cumulative and self-sustaining the beneficiaries will require self-organization, influence over policy-making, and the experience and confidence to use these advantages effectively. In other words, they will require an extended process of political learning, deliberation, and self-expression. A key theme of this chapter is that when they are large scale such processes need to be evaluated on a long-term horizon. For example, the asset redistribution component of a land reform cannot be fully assessed in isolation from its effects on the second and third generations of beneficiaries, nor can the consequences of a literacy campaign be evaluated solely in terms of its first-round effects.

The second conceptual bridge is the challenge posed by multidimensional poverty conceptions. Effective poverty alleviation can be usefully conceptualized over the long run as involving the establishment of income generation opportunities and capabilities, the cumulative development of social endowments, and the ongoing construction of political capabilities. In the long term, income generation promoted at the cost of social endowments or political capabilities is unlikely to be sustainable. Likewise, the development of political capabilities or social endowments at the expense of the other two is likely to flounder. In Bolivia, for example, chronic malnutrition coupled with widespread exposure to the debilitating Chagas' disease, low productivity in agriculture, and inadequate access to credit and technology in rural areas conspires against the best-organized agrarian union system. Given the continuous interaction between the three, we cannot view the long-term pro-poor outcomes envisioned by the current development common wisdom as the product of easily predictable and redistributive strategic choices alone. Such strategic choices are of course necessary but only if they are constructed with reference to ongoing feedback from the agents of pro-poor policies themselves. This goes beyond "consulting with the poor" to thinking about how the poor (or rather heterogeneous groups of the poor) redefine themselves with reference to available social endowments, changing state policies, fragile political alliances, and the very process of poverty exit. The Bolivian case includes periods of economic growth at the expense of political capabilities development (1972–79) as well as periods of political capabilities development at the expense of economic growth (1979–85). Political reforms and democratization since the 1980s appear to have created a better framework in which these competing policy objectives can be at least provisionally reconciled. In the long run, effective pro-poor policy-making will require the reinforcement of that framework.

Third, a capabilities approach acknowledges many of the contextual and contingent determinants of pro-poor policy-making. Even within a single-case study, long-run analysis can be comparative and intertemporal. In Bolivia, we find historically and socially derivable differences in political capabilities in different localities. The country, after all, is geographically large and diverse and so provides a good laboratory for investigating how national policies develop differentially in different settings and how such differences translate into positive or negative development outcomes. The agrarian reform of the 1950s, for example, was a powerful instrument for developing the political capabilities of the poor, but its effects were highly varied—between highlands, valley, and lowland but also within these broad categories. Our illustration of a sample of municipalities draws attention to the powerful self-replicating characteristics of different localities, despite a single national development project. There is a difficult balance to be struck here. Just as economic growth needs to be balanced with other dimensions of poverty alleviation, so centrally designed development strategies and policies need to be balanced against local initiatives, accountability, and learning processes. Centrally designed strategies—such as Agrarian Reform, Popular Participation, and others—may purport to offer a development gain that can be generalized across the whole society. However, a disaggregated and long-term focus draws attention to the highly differentiated consequences of each of these policies as they are experienced in different localities.

Fourth, and related to the last point, a capabilities approach draws attention to questions of social and political agency. As national strategies and policies translate into patchy and uneven responses across different localities, questions of political agency and process become central and modify the logic of institutional design. We should not expect linear progress or straight-line extrapolations if policies that are appropriate in some localities are repelled in others. Here the imperatives for policy feedback, democratic responsiveness, and political accountability overshadow issues of institutional design. In the course of reform initiatives, the object of pro-poor policy-making continuously changes as the organized poor discover new opportunities, redirect their efforts, and construct new alliances. The process of policy-making is highly iterative, not necessarily because of idealized participation but because pro-poor policies tend to spill over into new arenas and reshape the policy map accordingly. Our case studies suggest that this kind of feedback in policy-making is accompanied by a shift in the way the poor perceive and are perceived in the policy process, from objects of policy intervention to subjects of social and political agency. The capacity to engage the policy process autonomously and choose ends and means is of intrinsic value to the poor and complementary to a sustainable and long-run strategy to promote economic and social well-being.

NOTES

The authors wish to thank Peter Houtzager, James Putzel, Tony Atkinson, and Frances Stewart for helpful comments on preliminary drafts. All errors and omissions are our own. The quotation at the beginning of the chapter is from Hirschman 1984 (42–43).

1. Although this chapter concentrates on the conceptual aspects of a long-run political capabilities approach, it is the first step in a proposal to study political and economic capabilities comparatively in Latin America.

2. See Stiglitz 1998a, 1988b; and Gore 2000.

3. We borrow from Amartya Sen's work on capabilities (1999, 1997, 1985) and extend Sen's usage to the particular contexts of pro-poor policy-making in new democracies.

4. A growing literature on state-society relations in Latin America has focused attention on the effects that an uneven reach of the state has over citizenship claims, social movements, and policy-making. Key contributions include O'Donnell 1999, 1993; Fox 1996; and Chalmers et al. 1997. Analyses of ethnic politicization in Latin America include Yashar 1999; 1998; and Van Cott 2000, 1994.

5. This observation is hardly new. A voluminous literature on social movement framing, starting with the work of Tilly (1978) and Tarrow (1983a; 1994) and summarized by recent work on new social movements by Larana, Johnston, and Gusfield (1994), Johnston and Klandermans (1995); and McAdam, McCarthy, and Zald (1996), places ideas and collective self-awareness at the center of a converging consensus on social movement theory.

6. See Medina 1997b; Molina and Arias 1996; and Blanes and Ayo 1998 for historical analyses that link both reforms.

7. See World Bank 1999. Other lower middle income countries (defined by GDP per capita of U.S.$760 to $3,030) include Paraguay, Ecuador, Peru, Guatemala, El Salvador, Colombia, Cuba, and Belize. Haiti, Honduras, Nicaragua, and Guyana were ranked as low income countries (defined by GDP per capita of U.S.$760 or less).

8. Population and literacy figures for 1950 are quoted from Republica de Bolivia 1950. Year 2000 population and literacy estimates are quoted from UDAPE 2000.

9. See UDAPSO et al. 1993.

10. See Gray-Molina 2001, 2002 for an analysis of alternative reform pathways that existed under the Popular Participation Reform.

11. Early assessments of the National Revolution were made by Montenegro (1953); Alexander (1958); Peñaloza (1963); Zondag (1966); and Malloy (1970).

12. Assessments of the Agrarian Reform include Heath 1959; Carter 1965; Antezana and Romero 1968; Heath, Erasmus, and Buechler 1969; Dandler 1969; and Calderón and Dandler 1986.

13. See Whitehead 1986; Malloy and Gamarra 1988; and Dunkerley 1984 for political and historical accounts of this period.

14. See Rivera 1984; and Calderón and Dandler 1986.

15. See Lavaud 1986 (283–84). The Proyecto de Impuesto Unico proposal was revived through United States Agency for International Development (USAID) technical assistance by the Inter-American Committee on Development and the University of Wisconsin Land Tenure Center.

16. See Molina Monasterios 1997 for an account of the policy-making process behind the Popular Participation Reform. See also Gray-Molina, Perez, and Yañez 1999; Graham 1998; and Grindle 2000.

17. See Albó 1997; and Ayo 1997 on the emergence of indigenous candidacies and Calla and Calla 1996; and Rojas and Zuazo 1996 on the municipal elections of 1995.

18. On participatory planning, budgeting, and oversight, see Medina 1997a; and Gray-Molina 1997.

19. Land titles were maintained in a three-tiered tenure system, which recognized individual, communal, and pro indiviso (individual access communal land) tenure rights.

20. Although *sindicatos campesinos* (rural unions) had emerged throughout the 1930s (Dandler 1969) and had organized a national congress by 1947 (Dandler and Torrico 1986), their massive mobilization would only emerge in the wake of the 1952 National Revolution.

21. For testimonial research on the development of central Cochabamba unions, see Gordillo 1998.

22. See Gray-Molina 2000.

23. See Albó 1997 and Ayo 1997 (148–49).

24. See Platt 1982; Harris and Albó 1975; and Rivera 1984 on the development of agrarian reform in the region.

25. See Platt 1982 (148–72).

26. See Rivera 1992 on relations between *ayllu* and *sindicato*.

27. See Albó 1999 (50).

28. See Gray-Molina 2000.

29. Figures are drawn from Muñoz and Lavadenz 1997.

30. See Tendler 1983; and Painter et al. 1984 for detailed accounts of colonization and rural development in the San Julian region. See Gill 1987 for a more regional perspective on lowland migration and rural development efforts.

31. See Soria Martinez 1996 for a detailed comparison of colonization policies in the 1960s, 1970s, and 1980s.

32. See Gray-Molina 2000.

REFERENCES

Albó, Xavier. 1999. *Ojotas en el poder local: Cuatro años despues.* CIPCA 53. La Paz: CIPCA.

———. 1997. "Alcaldes y concejales campesinos/indígenas: La lógica tras las cifras." In *Indígenas en el poder local,* 7–26. La Paz: Ministerio de Desarrollo Humano, Secretaría Nacional de Participación Popular.

Alexander, Robert. 1958. *The Bolivian National Revolution.* New Brunswick: New Brunswick Press.

Antezana, Luis, and Hugo Romero. 1968. "Origen, desarrollo, y situacion actual del sindicalismo campesino en Bolivia." I–V. La Paz, CIDA, University of Wisconsin. Mimeo.

Ayo, Diego. 1997. "La elección del tres de diciembre de 1995: Análisis de las 464 autoridades indígenas y campesinas elegidas." In *Indígenas en el poder local,* 27–40. La Paz: Ministerio de Desarrollo Humano, Secretaría Nacional de Participación Popular.

Blanes, Jose, and Diego Ayo. 1998. "Participación social y modernización del estado: La sociedad boliviana y la oferta de participación estatal." La Paz, CEBEM. Manuscript.

Calderón, Fernando, and Jorge Dandler. 1986. *Bolivia: La fuerza histórica del campesinado.* La Paz: CERES and United Nations.

Calla, Ricardo, and Hernando Calla. 1996. *Partidos políticos y municipios: Las elecciones de 1995.* Debate Político 2. La Paz: Instituto Latinoamericano de Investigaciones Sociales.

Carter, William. 1965. "Aymara Communities and Agrarian Reform in Bolivia." Monographs in Social Science 24. Gainesville: University of Florida Press.

Chalmers, Douglas, Carlos Vilas, Katherine Hite, Scott Martin, Kerianne Piester, and Monique Segarra. 1997. *The New Politics of Inequality in Latin America: Rethinking Participation and Representation.* Oxford: Oxford University Press.

Dandler, Jorge. 1969. *El sindicalismo campesino en Bolivia: Los cambios estructurales en Ucureña (1935–1952).* Mexico City: Instituto Indigenista Interamericano.

Dandler, Jorge, and Juan Torrico. 1986. "El congreso nacional indígena de 1945 y la rebelión de Ayopaya (1947)." In Fernando Calderón and Jorge Dandler, eds., *Bolivia: La fuerza histórica del campesinado,* 135–205. La Paz: CERES and United Nations.

Dunkerley, James. 1984. *Rebellion in the Veins: Political Struggle in Bolivia (1952–1982).* London: Thetford.

Fox, Jonathan. 1996. "How Does Civil Society Thicken? The Political Construction of Social Capital in Rural Mexico." *World Development* 24, no. 6: 1089–1103.

Gill, Leslie. 1987. *Peasants, Entrepreneurs, and Social Change: Frontier Development in Lowland Bolivia.* Boulder: Boulder Press.

Gordillo, Jose. 1998. *Arando en la historia: La experiencia politica campesina en Cochabamba.* La Paz: Plural, Ceres. and UMSS.

Gore, Charles. 2000. "The Rise and Fall of the Washington Consensus as a Paradigm for Developing Countries." *World Development* 28, no. 5: 789–804.

Graham, Carol. 1998. *Private Markets for Public Goods: Raising the Stakes in Economic Reform.* Washington, DC: Brookings Institution Press.

Gray-Molina, George. 2002. "The Politics of Popular Participation in Bolivia, 1994–1999." D.Phil. diss., Nuffield College, Oxford University.

———. 2001. "Exclusion, Participation, and Democratic State-Building." In J. Crabtree and L. Whitehead, eds., *Towards Democratic Viability: The Bolivian Experience.* London: St. Martin's.

————. 2000. "Three Reform Pathways," chapter 3 of "The Politics of Popular Participation in Bolivia, 1994–1999," D.Phil. diss., Nuffield College, Oxford University.

————. 1997. *Participación popular: Construyendo políticas públicas locales en Bolivia*. La Paz: Unidad de Análisis de Políticas Sociales.

Gray-Molina, George, Ernesto Pérez de Rada, and Ernesto Yañez. 1999. "Economía política de reformas institucionales en Bolivia." IDB Research Network Papers R350. Washington, D.C.: Inter-American Development Bank.

Grindle, Merilee. 2000. *Audacious Reforms: Institutional Invention and Democracy in Latin America*. Baltimore: Johns Hopkins University Press.

Harris, Olivia, and Xavier Albó. 1975. *Monteras y guardatojos: Campesinos y mineros en el Norte de Potosí*. La Paz: Centro de Investigación y Promoción del Campesinado.

Heath, Dwight. 1959. "Land Reform in Bolivia." *Inter-American Economic Affairs* 12, no. 4: 3–27.

Heath, Dwight, Charles Erasmus, and Hans Buechler. 1969. *Land Reform and Social Revolution in Bolivia*. New York: Praeger.

Hirschman, Albert. 1984. *Getting Ahead Collectively: Grassroots Experiences in Latin America*. Elmsford, NY: Pergamon.

Johnston, Hank, and Bert Klandermans. 1995. *Social Movements and Culture*. London: University London College Press.

Laraña, Enrique, Hank Johnston, and Joseph Gusfield. 1994. *New Social Movements: From Ideology to Identity*. Philadelphia: Temple University Press.

Lavaud, Jean Pierre. 1986. "Los campesinos frente al estado." In Fernando Calderón and Jorge Dandler, eds., *Bolivia: La fuerza historica del campesinado* 277–313. La Paz: CERES and United Nations.

Malloy, James. 1970. *Bolivia: The Uncompleted Revolution*. Pittsburgh: Pittsburgh University Press.

Malloy, James, and Eduardo Gamarra. 1988. *Revolution and Reaction. Bolivia, 1964–1985*. New Brunswick, NJ, and Oxford: Transaction.

McAdam, Doug, John McCarthy, and Mayer Zald. 1996. *Comparative Perspectives on Social Movements: Political Opportunities, Mobilizing Structures, and Cultural Framings*. Cambridge: Cambridge University Press.

Medina, Javier. 1997a. *Poderes locales: Implementando la Bolivia del próximo milenio*. La Paz: Fondo Editorial FIA/Semilla/CEBIAE.

————. 1997b. "La participación popular como fruto de las luchas sociales." In *El pulso de la democracia: participación ciudadana y descentralización en Bolivia*. Caracas, Venezuela: Nueva Sociedad.

Molina, Sergio, and Iván Arias. 1996. *De la nación clandestina a la participación popular*. La Paz: Centro de Documentación e Información.

Molina Monasterios, Fernando. 1997. *Historia de la participación popular*. La Paz: Ministerio de Desarrollo Humano, Secretaría Nacional de Participación Popular.

Montenegro, Carlos. 1953. *Nacionalismo y coloniaje*. La Paz: Editorial Los Amigos del Libro.

Muñoz, Jorge, and Isabel Lavadenz. 1997. "Reforming the Agrarian Reform in

Bolivia." HIID Development Discussion Papers 589. Cambridge: Harvard University Department Discussion: 289.

O'Donnell, Guillermo. 1999. "Polyarchies and (Un)Rule of of Law in Latin America." In J. Mendez, G. O'Donnell, and P. S. Pinheiro, eds., *The (Un)Rule of Law and the Underprivileged in Latin America,* 303–37. Notre Dame: University of Notre Dame Press.

———. 1993. "On the State, Democratization, and Some Conceptual Problems: A Latin American View with Glances at Some Postcommunist Countries." *World Development* 21, no. 8: 1355–69.

Painter, Michael, Carlos Perez-Crespo, Marta Llanos, Susan Hamilton, and William Partridge. 1984. "Colonizacion y desarrollo regional: Lecciones de San Julian, Bolivia." Binghamton, NY, Cooperative Agreement on Settlements and Natural Resource Systems Analysis.

Peñaloza, Luis. 1963. *Historia del Movimiento Nacionalista Revolucionario, 1941–1952.* La Paz: Los Amigos del Libro.

Platt, Tristan. 1982. *Estado boliviano y ayllu andino: Tierra y tributo en el Norte de Potosí.* Lima: Instituto de Estudios Peruanos.

Republica de Bolivia. 1950. *Censo Demografico de 1950.* La Paz: Ministerio de Hacienda y Estadistica, Direccion General de Estadisticas y Censo.

Rivera, Silvia. 1992. *Ayllus y proyectos de desarrollo en el Norte de Potosí.* La Paz: Editorial Aruwiyiri.

———. 1984. *Oprimidos pero no vencidos: Luchas del campesinado aymara y quechua en Bolivia (1900–1980).* La Paz: HISBOL-CSUTCB.

Rojas, Gonzalo y Moira Zuazo. 1996. *Los problemas de representatividad del sistema democrático boliviano: Bajo el signo de la reforma del Estado.* Debate Político 1. La Paz: Instituto Latinoamericano de Investigaciones Sociales.

Sen, Amartya. 1999. *Development as Freedom.* London: Knopf.

———. 1997. *Inequality Re-examined.* Oxford: Oxford University Press.

———. 1985. *Commodities and Capabilities.* Amsterdam: North-Holland.

Soria Martinez, Carlos. 1996. *Esperanzas y realidades: Colonizacion en Santa Cruz.* Cuadernos CIPCA 49. La Paz: Centro de Investigación y Promoción del Campesinado.

Stiglitz, Joseph. 1998a. "More Instruments and Broader Goals: Moving toward the Post–Washington Consensus." Washington, DC, World Bank. <www.worldbank.org/html>

———. 1998b. "Towards a New Paradigm for Development: Strategies, Policies, and Processes." Prebisch Lecture at UNCTAD, 1998, Washington, DC, World Bank. <www.worldbank.org>

Tarrow, Sidney. 1994. *Power in Movement: Social Movements, Collective Action, and Politics.* Cambridge: Cambridge University Press.

———. 1983a. *Struggling to Reform: Social Movements and Policy Change during Cycles of Protest.* New York and Ithaca: Center for International Studies and Cornell University.

Tendler, Judith. 1983b. *What to Think about Cooperatives: A Guide from Bolivia.* Rosslyn, VA: Inter-American Foundation.

Tilly, Charles. 1978. *From Mobilization to Revolution.* Reading, MA: Addison-Wesley.

UDAPE. 2000. "Estrategia para la reduccion de la pobreza." La Paz: Unidad de Análisis de Políticas Sociales.

UDAPSO, UDAPE, INE, and UPP. 1993. *Mapa de pobreza: Una guia para la accion social.* La Paz: Unidad de Análisis de Políticas Sociales.

Van Cott, Donna Lee. 2000. *The Friendly Liquidation of the Past: The Politics of Diversity in Latin America.* Pittsburgh: University of Pittsburgh Press.

Van Cott, Donna Lee, ed. 1994. *Indigenous Peoples and Democracy in Latin America.* Washington, DC: Inter-American Dialogue.

Whitehead, Laurence. 1986. "Bolivia's Frustrated Democratic Transition, 1977–1980." In Guillermo O'Donnell, P. Schmitter, and L. Whitehead, eds., *Transitions from Authoritarian Rule: Prospects for Democracy.* Baltimore: Johns Hopkins University Press.

World Bank. 1999. *World Development Report, 1999–2000.* Washington, DC: World Bank.

Yashar, Deborah. 1999. "Democracy, Indigenous Movements, and the Post-liberal Challenge." *World Politics* 52 (October): 76–104.

———. 1998. "Contesting Citizenship: Indigenous Movements and Democracy in Latin America." *Comparative Politics* 31, no. 1.

Zondag, Cornelius. 1966. *The Bolivian Economy 1952–1965.* New York: Frederick Praeger.

3 Beyond the Political Impossibility Theorem of Agrarian Reform

Ronald J. Herring

AGRARIAN POLITICAL ECONOMY AS DISMAL SCIENCE: VENERABLE CONCEPTS, NEW COALITIONS

It is commonly said that the rural poor have been excluded by dominant paths of development. More accurately, the terms of inclusion have been adverse; when states and the elites that run them have needed labor, taxes, or soldiers, the poor were included. That agrarian reforms have periodically altered the terms of inclusion for the rural poor in substantial ways is widely recognized. Genuine agrarian reform sets the stage for new social dynamics and thus opens possibilities for alternative trajectories. The long-term consequences of rural asset redistribution at critical historic junctures illustrate the importance of a path-dependent view of development policy.

Despite what seems to be a clear case in logic and history, agrarian reform has been slighted of late in discussions of pro-poor policy. The political impossibility theorem carries some but not all of the explanatory burden. The theorem states that, despite demonstrated merits of agrarian reform in terms of growth and social justice, it is politically impossible and thus not a policy choice. Though accurate for a wide range of times and places, the theorem is doubly dubious as a general forecasting tool. First, its narrow conceptualization of agrarian reform omits much that may be relevant to understanding potential coalitions. Second, it misses the rural property component underlying many contemporary struggles waged in other terms. Reports of the demise of agrarian reform on the ground are premature—empirically, analytically, and prescriptively.

Asset distribution is at the core of relative poverty and wealth as well as political capabilities; the rich understand this and invest extensively in preserving and extending rules that protect and enhance concentrations of property. Yet official and academic discourse about the poor has moved away from this most fundamental conclusion of political economy. The developmental paths of South Korea, Japan, and Taiwan are widely held to have been enabled by fairly radical agrarian reform.[1] Yet when it comes to consideration of the poorest people in the poorest places in the contemporary world, redistribution recedes into silence. If there is genuine interest in poverty alleviation, this is a curious silence.

Despite historical evidence of the costs of failure and the benefits of success, recommendations of agrarian reform are often met with the response that beneficial policies are, alas, politically impossible—and thus unworthy of further consideration. The impossibility theorem rests on good political economy. Land confers power in agrarian systems; reform policy must work through that very system of power to restructure its base (Herring 1983). Conceptualization of agrarian systems as integrated nets of multidimensional social and economic control would predict not only compromised policy but, just as important, faulty implementation: power is expressed at all levels of the political system, from agenda setting to administration. The theorem is buttressed by the long history of failed agrarian reforms. Exceptions prove the rule; these have occurred through rare historical conjunctures—communist revolution (China), external intervention (Japan), or effective social democratic mobilization of the poor majority (Kerala State in India). When the landless are economically dependent and politically powerless, and sometimes consequently ideologically incorporated, the theorem is robust. Even in agrarian systems lacking dominant landlordism of classic form, redistribution is blocked by intermediate and relatively privileged classes—for example, by what the Rudolphs (1987) call "bullock capitalists" in India. Limited redistribution continually creates veto blocs opposed to further redistribution—an unvirtuous ratchet. Having moved up, substantial farmers want to pull up the ladder after them: a dependent work force is in their interest, and their own limited prosperity seems paltry in comparison with urban extravagances of wealth. Their power vis-à-vis governments is structural if not directly political: "the nation" needs ever increasing production from agriculture, and uncertainty about changes in property systems may suppress investment (Herring 1983, chap. 8). Moreover, a political coalition for pro-poor reform is unlikely and for well known reasons: problems of collective action among dispersed actors without resources, economic dependency, multiple crosscutting political interests among the poor, diffusion of interests by entrepreneurial political parties, and the hostility of powerful classes with privileged access to state operatives.[2]

But surely theorems do not drive politics. The waning, then end, of the cold war reduced the political motivation for removing the agrarian base of communist movements. The proponent, funder, and architect of many agrarian reforms in poor countries, the United States moved in its development assistance agenda from fighting local communists to a confused and often contradictory set of nominal objectives—human rights, gender equity, empowerment, humanitarian assistance, and democratization (McHugh 2001)—and then to nation building, marketization, and suppression of terrorism. Poverty discourse within powerful institutions turned to expanding the pie rather than redistributing it, despite a broad consensus that growth and agrarian reform are compatible, even complementary. William Thiesenhusen (1995) emphasizes debt crises and structural adjustment as reasons for dropping agrarian reform from the agenda; Alison Brysk (2001) makes this case explicitly for Ecuador. Market solutions to poverty largely replaced concern with redistributive policy in the 1980s. In the 1990s, as Peter Houtzager's introduction to this volume makes clear, the discussion moved away from large-scale political organizations and institutions in general to decentralization, disaggregated empowerment, and institutions of civil society. The impossibility theorem is consonant with the worldviews of powerful actors on the international stage. Governments that fund multilateral assistance and international financial institutions—and their clients—seldom depend on a power base that favors redistribution of assets.

The impossibility theorem, then, explains only partly the decline of agrarian reform in poverty discourse and is itself part of a larger silence on redistribution. Yet, even if the analytical core of the theorem rings true, its very rootedness in a specifically agrarian political economy suggests reasons for rethinking it. Perhaps most obviously, the declining importance of agriculture throughout the poor world reduces the political power of landed oligarchies nationally. Educated youth abandon agriculture in droves. Urbanization and economic diversification simultaneously reduce the political salience of agricultural landownership. In Jeffrey Paige's model of agrarian conflict (1975), the necessity of the political control of land—and thus suppression of the citizenship rights of the landless—was rooted in the absence of economic alternatives for landed elites. Political controversies surrounding agrarian reform and overhanging residues of unenforced legislation combine with economic change to shift the political salience of land control; it is increasingly prudent, and possible, for agrarian elites to diversify or divest.

From the other side of the class structure, technological change in agriculture, with or without the promised miracle seeds of biotechnology, should in principle continually lower the subsistence threshold size of holding while expanding options for small farmers (Conway 1997). One result is that the scale of necessary redistribution is reduced and therefore more politically feasible. The extent to which new technologies, including transgenics, benefit the poor will depend heavily on property systems—in land, water, and patents—as well as supportive institutional reforms in credit, marketing, and other ancillary services. Reforms in the property structure of agriculture become more complex, and compelling, even as traditional obstacles decline in importance.

Considerations of the impossibility theorem to this point have assumed the conventional frame of agrarian political economy and land reform discourse. To understand the contemporary political opportunity structure, we need to reconceptualize agrarian reform—from agriculture to land use in development generally. Most obviously, the science of ecology has penetrated the species learning curve. It is increasingly recognized that terrain is not simply agricultural land, or potential agricultural land, but the base of complex agro-ecological systems (see Uphoff 2002). Policies intended to address environmental crises and recognition of both services of ecological systems and the public goods embodied in biodiversity create structural bases for new proreform coalitions motivated by both "deep" and social ecology. The poor, for example, may prove to be better managers of ecological systems than the state (Kothari 1997; Kothari et al. 1996). Social forestry and collaborative management of forests redistribute access, power, and opportunities, often reforming the local state in train (Buck et al. 2001). Refocusing on land as landscape—not simply as agricultural capital—is necessary because environmental degradation produces and is fed by poverty (Blaikie and Brookfield 1987); public goods beyond production and justice are at stake. Privatization of landscapes has historically spawned significant conflict between states pursuing developmental objectives and marginal peoples whose livelihoods are premised on access to nature and its products (e.g., Peluso 1992; Guha 1989; Herring 2001d). Although concern for ecologies is often termed an elitist enterprise, the first victims of environmental degradation are the poor. Environmental integrity, then, is not a luxury nor a separate desideratum but must be a core developmental concern.

The historically deep macrocontroversy over owning nature is now joined by a growing conflict over the distribution of microlevel property rights in biota. There is, then, a pressing question of the appropriate balance of public interest and distributed rights in these resources.

Genetic engineering enables ownership of the most basic building blocks of life. A global system of property rights in biota is in formation. For this system to support the poor requires property reform similar to that of traditional agrarian reform; there are potentially new partners for a reform coalition. Natural systems have historically provided living laboratories, counterintuitive insights, and raw materials for remarkable innovations (Weiss and Eisner 1998; Reid 1996). Even those who protest against genetically engineered foods have been quiescent on pervasive applications to pharmaceuticals; insulin is not simply ingested, it is injected. Indeed, a new agro-pharmaceutical industry is emerging, called "pharming" in the United States, to produce enzymes such as trypsin for pharmaceutical production. Getting the biosafety regime right internationally is a daunting challenge, as is the co-optation of new property rights by multinational firms, but there are urgent questions in the emergent nature regime for the poor.

It is impossible to enter here the intense debates around poverty, property, and the integrity of natural systems. It does seem clear, however, that social justice in land systems is not incompatible with environmental protection and regeneration. Putting agrarian reform back on the pro-poor agenda would require attention to at least three issues: (1) *resurrection of the commons:* experiments in restructuring command and control systems to include joint property and state-society collaboration at a very local level may overcome some of the political inequality that corrodes the governance of nature and deepens poverty; (2) *ecologically sensitive land reform:* pressures for expanding cultivation destructively to ever more marginal land can be alleviated by rationing productive land and redistributing it away from rentiers and speculators (e.g., Adger 1997); (3) *establishing and distributing intellectual property rights in biota:* as biotechnology enhances the prospects of commercializing genetic materials, those who have foregone the opportunities to exploit their environments destructively deserve, and sometimes demand, intellectual property rights and the benefits that flow therefrom (Gupta 1996, 1998). Taking these issues seriously expands the coalition for reconfiguring landed rights.

Traditional agrarian reform discourse was largely gender blind (Agarwal 1992, 1997). Recognition of property-differentiated deprivations opens new policy space for assessing control of rural assets. Increased mobilization of women potentially adds a political force for redistribution.[3] International and domestic nongovernmental organizations (NGOs) committed to this cause increasingly recognize the roots of gender disability and powerlessness in property distributions. Bina Agarwal argues that not just agrarian reform but poverty programs in general assume that money or benefits going to the male "head of household" reach the household. She finds that to the extent women have resources outside the family—in the civil society and economy—their position inside the family is improved.[4] Gender-sensitive agrarian reform could thus improve intrafamily outcomes and smooth out intertemporal crises. Carmen Diana Deere's (1997) study of fourteen Latin American countries indicates progress in gaining access to land through agrarian reform legislation influenced by the activism of women's groups. Property ownership is more important than entitlements, which depend on a fickle public moral economy and fiscal health.

The work of Bina Agarwal also reflects growing recognition (e.g., 1992, 186; 1997) of the intersection of common property institutions, nature, and poverty: the commons provides an income source, and thus bargaining strength, independent of men, although the typical commons is a crucial resource for everyone with a low opportunity cost of labor. Privatization of commons, which is a global phenomenon, reduces the supports—and reservation wage—of the most vulnerable. Contemporary agrarian reform cannot be limited to correcting inequities in private land distributions but must address the privatization or degradation of common lands—or, more proactively, resurrecting the commons as a property form (Herring 1990) and regenerating its natural resource base. Regeneration of "wastelands," for example, is both labor intensive and restorative of security and opportunity for weaker sectors, given an appropriate property structure.

Democratic transitions, though often fragile, also open new possibilities for reform. In cases such as those of South Africa, the post-Marcos Philippines, and Zimbabwe, agrarian reform emerged as a pressing political issue.[5] In newly opened systems, political entrepreneurs seek new bases of support; constraints on mobilization simultaneously decline. New nations, such as Eritrea, consider alterations in rural property from the perspective of nation building and economic growth.

An enabling factor affecting all of the dynamics sketched here is the proliferation of NGOs and their legitimation by the international development assistance community. By means of their presence in both rural communities and national and international institutions, these organizations can alter the political environment in which the rural poor attempt to mobilize for new rights. These actors represent a force for exposing those denials of human rights and political freedom that have often blocked effective collective action by agrarian movements.[6] There is a numbing consistency in the finding that human rights abuses involve those without standing or economic autonomy in the agrarian underclass; the phenomenon is almost naturalized. The impossibility theorem slights overt repression, but it has been a major factor in quashing rural movements for justice.

This enumeration of developments from the local to the global levels that affect the potential balance of power is by no means exhaustive. One idiosyncratic example may be considered. The *New York Times* of December 18, 1996, contained an article entitled "Turning Colombia's Drug Plots over to Peasant Plowshares," by Diana Jean Schemo. New legislation authorized the seizure of drug dealers' assets; the Minister of

Agrarian Reform was sanguine that such seizures could ease the plight of landless peasants.[7] Seizure of assets of criminals engaged in land-based illegal activities offers an untapped pool of resources; international pressure on activities such as drug trafficking adds to the political weight for redistribution. It is not that drug growers are always rich and powerful, nor that the power of those who are is easily broken; it is the accumulation of similar pressures that underlines the need to rethink the political possibility of land redistribution.

To argue that new coalitions are possible, new openings are emerging, and new conceptualizations are useful is not to bury the honored tradition of land reform as an intellectual and political project. As long as there are regionally concentrated incidences of increasing landlessness, land concentration, underutilized land, and underemployed rural people, the traditional model rings true as policy desideratum.[8] The forces that historically have moved agrarian reform persist, with their familiar regionally and temporally uneven character; likewise, even failed reforms often form nodes around which politics may precipitate.

REPORTS OF THE DEMISE OF AGRARIAN
REFORM ARE PREMATURE

In a small space, it would be impossible to review the contemporary agrarian politics surrounding land reform. Yet even a cursory survey indicates that traditional issues of social justice and redistribution are by no means unimportant in the mobilization of the poor throughout the world. There is no reason to expect that these pressures will disappear. There is every reason to expect that mobilization will be unevenly developed and episodic. Nevertheless, poor people have not forgotten the centrality of land to livelihood, even if for the moment development economists have.

First, even dead land reforms are not dead. Promises unkept keep movements alive; past failures in implementation are not forgotten. Both become focal points for new politics. The slogan "forty acres and a mule"—referring to the promise of land for former slaves in the American South after the Civil War—became the rallying point for demands for reparations in the 1990s. The Consent Decree of Judge Paul Friedman (April 19, 1999) acknowledging the role of racism in the U.S. Department of Agriculture and the subsequent loss of African American farms prominently refers to the failed land reform of the 1860s. In 2001, claims for reparations premised on the abuses of slavery and the failure of redress totaled $2.7 billion; some $30 million in unauthorized reparations payments have been made by the U.S. Treasury. The most common claim for reparations was $43,209, a figure calculated as the current value of the forty acres and a mule originally promised in 1865 (Johnston 2002).

Nancy Abelmann (1996) examines the social and political activism of the 1980s in South Korea through the lens of the Koch'ang Tenant Farmers' Movement. In the turbulent "summer of protest" of 1987, North Cholla Province farmers organized to protest against the Samyang Corporation's ownership of tenant plots that should have been distributed in the 1949 land reform. Potts and Mutambirwa (1997) document the continuing conflicts in moral economy caused by promised land redistribution and pressures for commercialization of redistributed plots in Zimbabwe. Century-old land settlements and unequal treaties with indigenous peoples in North America are now being contested in courts, often with large findings for Native Americans. Nicaragua's tumultuous land reforms under the Sandinistas redistributed more than one million hectares—about a third of the nation's arable land—to about 200,000 families, setting in train controversies over permanent titles that were resolved only in December 1997 with conferment of rights to beneficiaries.[9] Vietnam's land reforms were the core of controversy in that country's civil war;[10] reconstruction continues to rearrange landed rights in the direction of longer term security of holdings for individuals and groups (Haque and Montesi 1997).

The uneven results of agrarian reforms derive in part from their origins. Land restructuring is often a statist project. This dilemma is acute: without state cues, organizational support, and adequate legal backstopping, participation of the rural poor is less likely. But state domination of the process often substitutes goals of political entrepreneurs and bureaucrats for those of the unorganized poor. State socialism's global collapse introduced a "third wave" of reforms, restructuring land rights long held by nondemocratic states (Swinnen et al. 1997; Griffin 2001). Donald Williams (1996) argues that land reforms in Africa have likewise often increased state power and patronage in ways inconsistent with traditional reform objectives. Powelson and Stock (1990) make this claim globally. Writing on South Africa, Henry Bernstein (1998, 28) warns against "the seductions of voluntarism, whether of statist (substitutionist) or populist ('communitarian') varieties." Bernstein captures the central dilemma of advocacy of agrarian reform: popular forces are seldom sufficiently formed, or powerful enough, to drive political change; yet substitution of state officials for popular forces may result in despotism, complicity with local elites, or irrelevance for lack of local roots. The brief explication of the case of former slaves in the United States that follows both confirms and modifies Bernstein's caution: without the substitutionist power of the state, beginnings of agrarian reform may subject dependent populations to continued or enhanced oppression. It is wrong to write off the central state, whatever its class composition.[11] Property law is after all typically subject to national legislation and interpretation by national courts. Agrarian reform opens one more dimension of the urgent reform of the state and offers one mechanism. Surely no one thinks that national reconstruction in Afghanistan can avoid coming to terms with the landed prerogatives of regional warlords.

There is obviously no guarantee that states can or will respond to rural mobilization, whether of the traditional or new variety. South Africa offers a case of cumulative political pressures for agrarian reform driven both by traditional agrarianism based on dispossession and reverberations of promises made during mobilization against apartheid. Land control overlaps significantly with gender inequalities (Meer 1997). As in Zimbabwe, past promises of land reform present current political and economic dilemmas for newly democratic governments. Uncertainty for current holders depresses investment, communal arrangements and chiefly prerogatives present unique complications, and discretionary authority on the ground presents political contradictions.[12] Financing compensation in poor states remains an obstacle to reform. Newly popular advocacy of "market-based" land reforms may in some cases facilitate redistribution, but it is more elixir than solution (Riedinger, Yang, and Brook 2001). For all the repackaging of old wine in a more marketable bottle, market-based reforms have to come to terms with the fundamental fact of rural life: if the poor could buy farms, they would. If the government is to acquire and redistribute land, it needs money, although many land reforms historically have had an element of confiscation grounded in arguments of social justice. There is no market magic that bypasses these fundamental problems in agrarian reform.

Not all contemporary politics of agrarian reform are based on residues of past failures and mobilizational promises. New peasant movements are born; James Petras (1997) writes of "the resurgence of the left" generally in Latin America, particularly in the countryside. The Movimiento dos Trabalhodores Rurais Sem Terra (Movement of Rural Landless Workers, MST) in Brazil emerged from a coalition of redistributive forces in the 1980s to become the principal exponent of agrarian reform; among social movements it has been described as "the best organized, and the most effective, with a record of concrete achievements and considerable support" (Veltmeyer 1997, 154). Important for the dynamism of the MST— and for understanding the new coalitional possibilities for agrarian reform—is the "eruption of a new generation of young women militants" (Petras 1998, 132). Likewise important in considering new political environments for social movements, financial assistance from the European Community and international religious organizations (Charitas, Bread for the World, and others) aided significantly. The MST was able to transform itself from a militant sectoral agrarian reform movement of the classic form into a national movement with broader political and developmental objectives: literacy programs for adults, consumer cooperatives, small agricultural industries, and about a thousand primary schools (Foweraker 2001). Success in redistribution has been, however, more the result of militant land occupations than of altered government policies. Success has also been geographically uneven, as one would expect. Although the nation-state remains the typical unit of analysis in development studies, such variations are of great analytical importance (see Putzel 1992; and Heller 2001). Decentralization of political authority—much touted by development assistance agencies—may offer on balance more local and regional potential for agrarian reform movements and their success, where movements have more local power than national, but there is risk of further empowering local elites (Mamdani 1996).

"New" peasant movements use different idioms and have more ambiguous ties with established political parties, but they exhibit continuities of analysis and personnel with previous struggles, even while representing creative political practice under new circumstances. Veltmeyer's (1997, 139) survey of resistance to neoliberal policies in Latin America concludes that "new peasant movements" constitute the "most dynamic forces." Armed struggle in Chiapas illustrates Veltmeyer's point; putting agrarian reform back on the policy agenda was a predictable response by the Mexican state (Johnson 1995), although to date that response has been limited (Diaz 2001). Both Veltmeyer and Petras stress neoliberal policies as a focal point for new political movements in Latin America. Alison Brysk (2001) illustrates concretely the fusions of which they write with an analysis of new niches for identity politics in the face of new deprivations induced by structural adjustment in Ecuador. Mandated cuts in social programs, and deceleration of land reform, threatened rural progress and security; specifically agrarian issues were joined to and expanded by concern with national development strategy writ large, built on a mobilizational base of "Indian" ethnicities. More generally, contrary to primordialist understandings, political identities, including "ethnic" identities, are not only fluid and situationally contingent (Herring and Esman 2001) but are overlapping, as oppression and exclusion frequently conjoin social indignity with class subordination (Herring 2001b).

The legitimation of neoliberal policies in a pro-poor developmentalism is that economic expansion is a surer route to material well-being than clumsy government programs. Simultaneously, marketizing and globalization produce (unevenly) new grounds for mobilization. Since growth discourse often silences redistributive discourse, it is important to ask whether this silence is legitimate.

WHAT IF A RISING TIDE RAISES ALL BOATS?

All politically difficult, fiscally burdensome, and administratively complex interventionist schemes for the poor are called into question if mere
economic growth eliminates poverty across the board. The growth-first
perspective reduces the importance of the state and its policies—as Peter
Houtzager's introduction to this volume emphasizes—and shifts attention away from the politically fraught question of redistribution. To be
more concrete, in one nation that contributes disproportionately to the
world's absolute poor, the World Bank's study of poverty reduction in
India (1997a) concluded that economic growth has been the major factor.
Liberalization was held to be the major reason for growth. Growth
would provide resources for public safety nets and investment in human
capital that round out the desirable poverty reduction scenario. The prescription is growth encouragement as the major antipoverty mechanism;
the rest (safety nets, human capital development) is desirable if afford-
able.

Although India is often considered a failed development state (Herring
1999), there is great regional variation in both growth (Sinha 2000) and
poverty reduction (Harriss, this volume; Dreze and Sen 1996). Since there
is great variance, a sensible analytic strategy would be to see what conditions characterize states doing well in reducing poverty, holding constant
regime-level policies and pathologies. Kerala State has been especially
successful in reducing poverty; agrarian reforms have been significant in
this accomplishment. Although the World Bank is ambivalent about
agrarian reform in India, and gives it only passing reference, about 80
percent of India's poverty is rural poverty. By class, agricultural workers
are especially likely to be poor; landlessness remains the major cause of
poverty. The absolute numbers of poor continue to increase in India as a
whole: by World Bank estimates, from 164 million in 1951 to 312 million
(about 35 percent of the population) in 1993–94. Consistent with contemporary celebration of the "Kerala model,"[13] the World Bank noted that
Kerala's progress in lowering the head count index of poverty (2.4 percent per year, on average, between 1957–58 and 1993–94) was "more than
120 times that of Bihar and more than four times that of Rajasthan"
(1997a, v). A compelling question arises: what is special about the Kerala
case? It is not growth; Kerala's growth rate has been quite anemic
(Tharamangalam 1998). The World Bank's conclusion, centering growth
as the solution for poverty, is therefore puzzling based on the interstate
comparisons within India.

Agrarian reforms in Kerala have been radical. The government abolished an especially oppressive rentier landlordism integrated with
agrestic serfdom in a period of Indian history dominated by inaction on

the agrarian question (Herring 1983). Agrarian labor legislation established entitlements anomalous for the poor world and radical by the standards of rich nations. Social democratic distribution and market taming characterize other sectors of the economy as well (Heller 1999). The conditions for this broadly entitled polity include coalitional mobilization of the weakest sectors of society, a political party with roots in those movements and a sufficiently adaptive strategy to ride the whirlwinds of political conflict successfully, and the integrity to stay the course. Kerala produced what was arguably the first elected communist government in the world in 1957, and it remains—contrary to the global pattern—an electoral stronghold of leftist politics.[14] There may be a growth penalty, but the case remains unproved. Many economies with low levels of industrialization and poor natural resource endowments have grown slowly without the imputed burdens of social democracy and redistribution.

Despite public presentation of great confidence in the efficacy of marketization leading to growth leading to poverty alleviation, there are clearly "holes in the consensus" (Lipton 1997). Whatever the empirically and theoretically contested causes and effects of anomalously high or low growth rates, there will be a role for public intervention meant to alleviate particular forms of poverty and to address people passed over or harmed by economic change.[15] States employing public intervention that caters to unreconstructed elite dominance are less likely to play those roles well compared to states reacting to a field of power in which there is more strength at the bottom of the class structure. Growth alters the distribution of political power; advocates for the poor are naive if they lean on the reed of altruism of the new rich. The notion that growth creates the financial conditions for "safety nets" presupposes political dynamics sympathetic to those needing nets; the strengthening of vested interests opposed to redistributive transfers is at least as likely an outcome. Given these uncertainties, direct and knowable results should have precedence; agrarian reform has a strong track record in terms of the trajectories of states that have grown rapidly and with some equality (e.g., South Korea, Japan, and Taiwan).[16] Not all growth paths have equal implications for the poor. There are good reasons to believe that poverty-alleviating growth works better in relatively egalitarian settings, which are themselves more amenable to growth (Lipton 1997).

Contemporary Kerala has the type of political institutions that are often desiderata but seemingly impossible choices for other societies. The electorate is informed, extraordinarily participatory, alert, and assertive; political parties are representative and competitive; the state is responsive; and political behavior matters. As a consequence, political institutions work (Heller 1999). Yet these parameters of the political system are the product of a long process of evolution, of struggle, and of reforms—

social and economic. They were born not entirely of policy choice but through popular reaction to repression and exclusion: landlordism, the caste system, the degradation of women, slavery, and untouchability (Herring 2001b).

There is a serious "chicken or egg" problem embedded in this association: asset redistribution also enables social democracy, which enables distribution. Although social democracy is not a direct policy choice— there is a lot of historical contingency at work—policy choices do matter. One of the means through which these institutions were developed in Kerala was popular responses to state initiatives and state failures on the ground in agrarian reform, beginning in the late nineteenth century (Herring 1988). A reach exceeding the state's grasp encouraged mobilization of newly benefited groups seeking to make legislated de jure rights operational de facto rights. Ratchet politics was able to bring in new classes without losing the old precisely because of the need for local power to enforce legislated rights. Creating coalitions for the poor necessitated a political party with the capacity to learn from local grievances and support local agitations even as it projected broader long-term goals. Without this political praxis, reaching across traditional social barriers and continually extending the scope of reform would have been impossible. Some policies reconfigure incentives and capacities for the poor more than others do. Whether political actors will take advantage of the niches so created is another question. The timing of these policy interventions contributes to branching paths of social change, hence the importance of exploring path dependence as a developmental concept.

THE UNITED STATES AND SOUTH INDIA:
LOST HISTORICAL MOMENTS

Democracy may not be the best political system for the poor, as Mick Moore and his colleagues argue in this volume. There are certainly no guarantees. As a citizen of a very rich country, I cannot help but notice that neither growth nor democracy in the United States has adequately provided for the poor. Nevertheless, democracy itself is a developmental goal of the excluded; just as important, political rights and meaningful competition offer a significant potential for both redress of injustice and response to economic change. That there is a substantial historical relationship between agrarian reform and democratic development seems almost self-evident. As the subtitle for his *Social Origins of Dictatorship and Democracy* (1966), Barrington Moore Jr. chose *Lord and Peasant in the Making of the Modern World*. Moore made sweeping claims about the political importance of breaking landed aristocracies in the interest of democratic development based on the historical paths of particular nations, including the United States and India. In Rueschemeyer, Stephens, and Stephens 1992, Moore's early findings were confirmed across a broad range of cases (though with little attention to Asia), with special emphasis on the additional strategic importance of the working class. Prosterman and Riedinger (1987) make a sustained argument on the relationship between land reform, citizenship, and democratic development. This literature depends on an essential tenet of political economy: concentrations of economic power enable, and sometimes necessitate, concentrations of political power. Landlessness, in a reciprocal dynamic, enables dependency, political inequality, and sometimes subjugation (Dube 1998).

These dynamics are illustrated by the divergent paths of agrarian underclasses in the United States and Kerala. Comparing Kerala to less effective states within India—Bihar, for example (see Jannuzi 1974 in contrast to what follows)—is one way to highlight the potential effects of agrarian reform on governance and poverty. But comparison with historic failures in the United States is more instructive. John Echeverri-Gent (1993) has made a bold and reasoned comparison of the agrarian structure of rural India with that of the American South in order to tease out the impact of policy on the poor. He finds in the Depression era U.S. case a castelike system of political-economic oppression and marginalization; high rates of dependency among laborers, share tenants, and marginal farmers; small-scale, labor-intensive agriculture; extortionate sharecropping; credit exploitation; and extensive poverty. Politics was characterized by "elite domination, intra-party factionalism, agrarian populism" (76). This comparative frame reminds us of the utility of thinking beyond static and overly aggregated categories—for example, the "third world"—and focuses instead on processes of change given similar developmental problems.

How did so rich and nominally democratic a country as the United States come to perpetuate conditions in its South so parallel to those of rural India? After the Civil War, the nation confronted the great challenge of integrating former slaves, freed during the war, into the body politic. What would be the terms of inclusion? "Radicals" in the Congress tried to impose a social transformation that came to be called Reconstruction (1865–77).[17] In 1864, the American Freedmen's Inquiry Commission was appointed by Secretary of War Stanton to make policy recommendations; the commission concluded that "No such thing as a free, democratic society can exist in any country where all lands are owned by one class of men and cultivated by another" (Stampp 1965, 124). There was an immediate political problem: the freed slaves who were to benefit from the transformation could in no way constitute a political force. The president was opposed to the program of the radicals, and it was already clear that local elites could block it. Northern capitalists worried about the loss of a labor reserve, and many congressmen believed that land reform was a dangerous attack on the principle of private property. Nevertheless, agrarian reform was promoted by the radicals in Congress as a means of punishing the landed aristocrats who had waged war on Washington and as a means of constituting the freed slaves as a political force and economic engine of recovery. The rumored/promised land reform came under the slogan "forty acres and a mule."

Congress finally did not legislate the agrarian reform; an attempt to extend the power of the Freedmen's Bureau to expand land distribution was vetoed by the president, who also reversed some of the more important policies of the bureau. Experiments in land redistribution in the South were dismantled. Land reform under martial law—which worked fairly well in Japan after World War II—was abandoned.[18] Not only did redistribution not become law, but even preferential distribution of public lands in favor of freedmen (as opposed to railroad companies) failed as well (Foner 1989, 451). With the departure of federal troops, Southern elites reestablished rule with terror, fraud, intimidation, and economic power. Because the (white) landed elite retained economic power, and eventually returned to rule, efforts to resurrect a subject class had no base. In the aftermath of failed reconstruction, backsliding in land policy—then entirely in the hands of the state governments—became the norm. The failure of Reconstruction left in place an agrarian political economy of subjugation and dominance, largely coterminous with race. Testimony before the U.S. Congress Committee on Reconstruction produced evidence of vagrancy laws and extralegal coercion "to force Negroes back into agricultural labor under strict discipline" (Stampp 1965, 123).

When the radical agrarian populism of the 1890s subsequently swept through the South (Goodwyn 1976), African Americans were not politically available for a biracial coalition, which might have altered the national developmental path. Eric Foner (1989, 604) argues that the failure of Reconstruction led directly to one-party (and white) dominance in the "Solid South," which "helped define the contours of American politics and weaken the prospects not simply of change in racial matters but of progressive legislation in many other realms." After the failure of Reconstruction, the rights of nominally freed slaves were steadily eroded: restrictions on the rights of former slaves to vote, to be admitted to equal public schools, or to fully participate in dominant institutions of public or civil society. Prosterman and Riedinger's comparative study of land reform concludes more generally that reforms "provide a village-level underpinning that reinforces the national-level freedoms rather than contradicts them" (1987, 232). Of special importance for the long trajectory of poverty, human capital development was restricted; social safety nets and educational facilities remained comparatively underdeveloped in the South generally, especially for African Americans, into the contemporary period.

The failure to break local landed power in the South had the further pernicious consequence of creating suspicion in regional voting publics of any policy from Washington and a blind allegiance to local rule. Antipathy to intervention by the federal government was so intransigent that military force was required in the 1950s to enforce court orders to enroll African Americans in public schools. The irony of contemporary development thinking is that a premature celebration of the local valorizes precisely the decentralized structure that kept racial dominance alive in the southern United States.[19]

Agrarian reform by itself would not have solved the economic, much less the social and political, problems of former slaves, but there is evidence that it would have made a difference. Foner (1989, 109) notes that "well into the twentieth century, blacks who did acquire land were more likely to register, vote, and run for office than other members of the rural community." Subsequent evidence indicates that the counterfactual argument is strong. Lester Salamon's work on the effects of New Deal experiments in land distribution demonstrates that landless African American tenants who benefited from very limited land distribution in the 1930s created "a permanent middle class that ultimately emerged in the 1960s as the backbone of the civil-rights movement in the rural South" (1979, 129). In an interview with one of the displaced African American farmers who brought a successful suit against the U.S. Department of Agriculture (Bullard 1999), Gary Grant said of the New Deal distribution: "The black landowners have been the thorn in the side of the political power in Halifax County, North Carolina ever since, because we have not been dependent on them for our survival." The relationship between structural reform and an autonomous civil society capable of pursuing further reform seems clear.

Thaddeus Stevens, leader of the radicals in Congress during Reconstruction, used a comparative argument to move his opponents: even the emperor of Russia gave the serfs homesteads when they were emancipated.

> The whole fabric of southern society *must* be changed and never can it be done if this opportunity is lost. How can republican institutions, free schools, free churches, free social intercourse exist in a mingled community of nabobs and serfs? (quoted in Stampp 1965, 126)

Lost historical moments foreclose some options, select for others, and shift social trajectories. As radicals in the Congress prophetically feared, education was systematically denied to former slaves. Educational qualifications were then used as tests for the eligibility to vote. The subjugated position of African Americans in the half-free society reinforced racist stereotypes. Eric Foner (1989, 604) writes that "Reconstruction's demise and the emergence of blacks as a disenfranchised class of dependent laborers greatly facilitated racism's further spread, until by the early twentieth century it had become more deeply embedded in the nations's culture and politics than at any time since the beginning of the antislavery crusade and perhaps in our entire history." To the extent that racism (or caste) explains some of poverty's persistence, the implications are profound and durable.[20]

Historical struggles for agrarian reforms in Kerala likewise confronted extraordinary subjugation in the form of agrestic slavery and serfdom, persisting into the 1960s in local understandings of the social system (Herring 2001b). Agrarian reform had a significant impact on the transformation of subjects into citizens. This transformation put pressure on the political system for redistributive public policy, not all of which is unambiguous in terms of long-term poverty reduction but in no sense is as decisively destructive of growth as critics claim (e.g., Tharamangalam 1998). Kerala is a social democracy on a subnational scale, with all the warts and messy politics of any democracy but without the control of fiscal, monetary, or trade policy that characterizes nation-states. That democracy owes its form in large part to decades of pursuit and final implementation of fairly radical agrarian reforms.

The long process began with peasant insurrections—the Moplah uprisings—to which a traumatized colonial state responded incrementally with conservative agrarian reform. In ratcheted episodes of reaction to agrarian reforms that existed more on paper than on the ground, beginning with the Malabar Tenancy Act of 1929, those involved in agrarian mobilization made connections with other reformist groups in society. It was always two steps forward, one back. Agrarian reform was one of the focal points around which social mobilization occurred. The core of Kerala's agrarian reforms—legislated in 1959, defeated by machinations in Delhi, and finally implemented in the 1970s—was the abolition of landlordism as a system of social control and exploitation (Herring 1988).

What the Kerala experience highlights but does not really resolve is the problem of the most awkward class—the agricultural laborers.[21] Income gains from more rapid growth in agriculture are uncertain, lagged, and unevenly distributed among households and over time. Problems of the laborers in Kerala were addressed through the distribution of homestead/garden plots for many, which are intensively used and quite important both nutritionally and commercially. If it is politically impossible to redistribute land, it is still possible to formalize the obligations that traditionally legitimated landownership (the obligation to take care of the landless) and redistribute the product of the land via higher wages and pensions. In Kerala, old age pensions funded through farmer surpluses were mandated by the Agricultural Workers Act of 1974. When this proved politically and administratively impossible, the state took up the fiscal burden.[22] Security of employment ("permanency") was the second method, enforceable minimum wage legislation was the third, and institutionalized bargaining over the terms of employment was the fourth.

Poverty reduction in Kerala has been achieved via land reforms, labor reforms, and transfer payments. All three presupposed an effective political and administrative system and popular pressure on the state (Heller 1999). The result was objective measures of human welfare—mortality, longevity, literacy, and the male-female population ratio—anomalous for the level of per capita income (below the mean for India) and for the rate of growth in agricultural production (also below the mean for India).[23] Any purposive alleviation of poverty presupposes governance. Kerala is often considered a model due to its success in human welfare, but just as important is a political system that works. Education and ration shops are two examples often cited. The common abuse of the educational system by absentee teachers and phony schools, for example, would be extraordinarily difficult to perpetrate on Kerala's citizens. Gaiha and Kulkarni (1998) give a number of examples. Ration shops are far more successful in Kerala than in most other states precisely because both politicians and bureaucrats know that they face monitoring and retribution from an anomalously alert and active citizenry. Citizens with secure rights are more likely to demand results. Antipoverty values are now embedded in real institutions, guarded and refreshed by political participation. In the absence of these conditions, public programs often degenerate into boondoggles for the middle class, rent subsidies for the bureaucracy, and patronage for politicians (see Bardhan 1995). Strong local institutions and broad-based leftist coalitions in government enabled experiments in new relationships between decentralized democracy and economic development (Tornquist and Tharakan 1996). Because of popular mobilization and agrarian reforms, this experiment is unlikely to lead to elite co-optation of local control, a familiar consequence of decentralization in unreformed rural systems.

It is quite wrong to romanticize the "Kerala model," as is too commonly done. It is equally wrong to overlook its liberating potential. Every social system, every institutional matrix, every policy has its warts; the crucial question is always "compared to what?" Within the Kerala model, agrarian reforms provide negative as well as positive lessons (Herring 2000), but the implications for the poor have been impressive in comparative terms. In ethical terms, the Kerala model is quite defensible; democratic development and poverty alleviation have substantially improved the prospects of the most vulnerable people through direct and predictable public policy. The contrast to the American South is telling.

RETHINKING THE IMPOSSIBILITY THEOREM

Both analytically and normatively, impossibility theorems are dubious propositions. Predicting political possibilities requires either extraordinary hubris or better social theory than we have. At one time, the overthrow of both apartheid and Soviet regimes seemed politically impossible. Economic liberalization in India was likewise considered by many to be politically impossible, as bureaucrats and politicians were codependent on discretionary authority in the permit *raj*. That an extraordinary historical conjuncture enabled liberalization in India (Herring and Mohan 2001) does not diminish the wisdom of introducing some modesty into claims of system-reproducing analysis. It is not obvious that the coalitions and regime imperatives that have driven historic agrarian reforms will be the only or most telling ones in the future. More important, the same opposition that thwarts agrarian reform is likely to mock the dubious assumption that alternative pro-poor policies are somehow politically less difficult. If agrarian reform is impossible, how possible are alternatives? Alternative proposals also make strong assumptions about either effective states or, increasingly, "communities." The World Bank's *World Development Report* (1997b) centered the capable state. If growth itself is dependent on the capable state, much more so is poverty alleviation that is efficient and effective. Yet the evolution of an efficacious and representative political system derives from unique historical conjunctures and subsequent path dependence. What assumptions can be ethically made about the malleability of political dynamics?

Entitlements offer one route to poverty alleviation. External policy advice increasingly moves away from politically feasible, universalistic programs to more politically difficult, targeted programs on efficiency grounds (Bardhan 1995). But mass publics prove to be fickle and politicians can count: retreat from welfare in the United States in the last two decades has coincided with a marked conservatizing of the political party traditionally cognizant of poverty. The political problem is sustaining a public belief that the deserving are benefiting, the undeserving are not, and a public norm of capitalist society is not too extensively undermined: if you don't work, you don't eat (absent inheritance). To sustain any universalistic welfare scheme, moral economies bound by time and place must be reliably grounded in either uncontestable cases (the blind are deserving) or empathetic possibility: it could happen to anyone (disaster relief, unemployment insurance). These are strong assumptions when applied to the settings in which the majority of the world's poor live.

Interventionist alternatives to asset redistribution fall into two broad categories: market rigging and political rigging. Market rigging (price supports, minimum wage legislation, "handicraft" subsidies, etc.) has been so extensive in currently rich nations that it is naive or simply ideological to argue that growth cannot be built on an interventionist political economy. Yet there are observable problems with market rigging, from enforcement costs and rent seeking to distortion of incentives with unintended consequences. Political rigging assumes that the poor will not fully benefit even from targeted programs nor get their share of general entitlements and development projects absent reconfiguration of local power. India's revision of local governance (*panchayati raj*) in 1993 represents one end of the continuum: mandated special representation for traditionally outcaste groups and tribals and a quota for women. Reconstruction in the southern United States attempted political rigging without redistributing economic power and largely failed. In India, village councils still often represent the interests of the locally affluent, who use poor retainers as pawns through formal institutions (Gaiha and Kulkarni 1998; Gaiha, Kaushik, and Kulkarni 1998). Capture of local institutions is a common outcome of devolution and decentralization, now almost totems of development discourse.

Rural public works promise something for everyone. Elites have little cause to oppose or obstruct such programs. In India, Maharashtra State's Employment Guarantee Scheme is an archetype: developmental public works provide wages for the poor, means tested by the difficulty of the work and distance from the village. Infrastructural improvement placates those who own rural Maharashtra, financed by the convenient cash cow of Mumbai (Bombay) in a reversal of "urban bias" dynamics (Herring and Edwards 1983). Although landowners reap the lion's share of benefits and some projects are useless and attract corruption, the benefits to the poor are considerable, most importantly a guarantee of employment. But the costs of such entitlements are high, and sustainability is problematic. Echeverri-Gent's (1993) critique of the Employment Guarantee Scheme (EGS) is that it fails to mobilize and involve the rural poor on a trajectory of political development.

Transfer payments, public works, and antipoverty schemes in India frequently engender corruption and miss their targets or approach them inefficiently (World Bank 1997a, xix). A large part of this problem is the lack of accountability of the state to the citizenry. It is likely that all pro-poor policies will over time work better in a system of inclusive citizenship than in one of widespread destitution and dependency. The thresh-

old cost of agrarian reform is higher than more politically attractive alternatives—hence the rarity of genuine reform—but it is not clear that the
long-term costs are greater. Ethically justifiable policy prescriptions must
somehow separate the effects of any discrete change on poverty outcomes
amid the myriad of factors affecting household well-being. Our understandings are crude and approximate, whatever the heroic precision of
policy prescriptions. Useful criteria for ethical choice would seem to
include two dimensions: how certain and how direct is the pro-poor
effect?

By these criteria, agrarian reform looks better than many of the more
fashionable prescriptions, despite its recent fall from favor. Offering
immediate and direct benefit to the rural poor, agrarian reform more
importantly can serve both as a symbol for the mobilization of powerless
people and a means of furthering political development. Agrarian reform
is therefore sturdier and more enduring than many alternatives; it takes a
longer view. This argument is buttressed by comparative consideration of
the historical experience of the United States. Promised land reforms to
rehabilitate former slaves as citizens after the Civil War in the nineteenth
century were abandoned; the result was an agrarian structure, and attendant political economy, that perpetuated abject dependency. Poverty not
only persisted in the population of former slaves for generations but it
remains disproportionate. In contrast, Kerala State in India abolished
agrestic serfdom and slavery in a compressed historical time, with
notably salubrious effects on human welfare despite growth rates below
the Indian mean.

Regardless of whether pro-poor policy promotes more or less state
intervention, agrarian reform remains one means of restructuring the
field of power to which state functionaries respond, and therefore enables
a more effective and responsive state, without which all other antipoverty
options—including growth—are reduced in efficacy. Contemporary evidence suggests that classic agrarian reform is neither dead nor irrelevant;
its dual contributions to direct relief of poverty and democratization
remain potentials worthy of consideration. Although there are other
roads to purposive poverty alleviation, all are subject to distortions
induced by social inequality, a major component of which is the skewed
distribution of landed property.

The leader of the radicals in the Congress of the United States during
Reconstruction, Thaddeus Stevens, presciently noted the importance of
historical conjuncture for path dependence. In a speech delivered on
December 18, 1865, he said: "If we fail in this great duty now, when we
have the power, we shall deserve and receive the execration of history
and of all future ages."[24] This chapter has argued that there is much truth
in the emphasis on historical conjuncture and agrarian reform suggested

by Thaddeus Stevens. The political impossibility theorem states that such moments of power at critical turning points are historically rare, but perhaps this is not so true as is commonly believed. The venerable conceptualization of agrarian reform and its politics is too limiting, both in its politics and its economics. The customary political focus on agrarian classes organized around agricultural production needs broadening to incorporate new forces motivated by the social correlates of land-based inequality—"new social movements" and their domestic and international allies. These elements include not only environmental integrity and regeneration but women's rights, cultural survival, human rights, and democratization. The range of the "politically possible" is in principle unknown, reflecting more ideology and speculation than knowledge, as Mick Moore argues in the concluding chapter of this volume. More important, possibilities are subject over time to purposive public policy that shapes political development. The customary economic focus in agrarian reform on the intersection of landed rights and agriculture needs broadening to incorporate technological change enabled by the biological revolution and the importance of ecological systems that support both agriculture and the survival strategies of the poor. Both conceptual broadening and a hard look at the assertion of political impossibility are important for adequate evaluation of agrarian reform, particularly if our normative focus is a development path that includes the poor on terms consistent with human dignity and opportunity.

NOTES

I am indebted to Dia Mohan and Malinda Seneviratne for invaluable research assistance and discussions. This version of the essay from which this chapter branches has also benefited from the comments of Terry Neale, Manoj Srivastava, John Harriss, Judith Tendler, Mick Moore, James Putzel, Manuel Diaz, Chuck Geisler, Richard Bensel, Monica Dasgupta, Peter Houtzager, and conference colleagues too numerous to list. An earlier version was published without the author's permission as Herring 2001c.

   1. Keith Griffin (2001) considers these cases in conjunction with agrarian reforms in China and Vietnam, noting convergence over time, although the collectivist "detour" in the latter cases stalled development. On Korea specifically, see Shin 1998; on the broader developmental argument, see Lipton 1993.
   2. From very different methodological stances, both Dube (1998) and Siddiqui (2000) illustrate important strands of this argument in India and Bangladesh.
   3. Recognizing the gendered nature of property is not sufficient, however. Ambreena Manji's treatment of the Commission of Inquiry into Land Matters in Tanzania confirms concretely Agarwal's generalizations about deeply embedded

gender bias even among reformers. Political obstacles that preclude assuming women's activism as a powerful force for agrarian reform include "urban bias" and class divisions in activist groups (Manji 1998, 664–65). Her analysis also demonstrates that there is no necessary connection between progressive stances on women's issues internationally and within the domestic state. Nevertheless, from everything we know about oppression, exclusion, and opportunity, redressing gendered inequalities in much of the world must include property reform.

4. For example, Sri Lanka and Kerala do better on four factors that affect female bargaining power and also have the highest ratio of females to males in Agarwal's analysis. This ratio discrepancy is especially marked in comparison with Northwest India, where the females are notoriously missing from the demographic data (1992, 201–2).

5. The Philippines presents an important caveat: weak political parties organized for patronage with few local organizational roots proved ineffectual in furthering reforms after the fall of Ferdinand Marcos (Riedinger 1995). Nevertheless, the politics of transition reinvigorated land reform politically. More recent experience shows "relatively vibrant land redistribution" despite continuing troubles in agriculture as a sector (Borras 2001). The troubles introduced by reform in Zimbabwe and the minimal progress to date in South Africa underline the serious difficulties in reform conceptualization and effective administration that have plagued other land reforms historically.

6. Hendrix (1996–97) argues that the causes of many domestic conflicts and human rights abuses considered by international agencies seeking reconstruction and reconciliation reside in land tenure conflicts, which are typically ignored by international agencies.

7. Schemo noted that about 250 people who had been forced off their parcels by a nearby landowner and drug dealer "were camping at government agencies in Bogota, seeking protection, after several of their number were killed and others threatened."

8. James Putzel's work on the Philippines (1992, chaps. 1 and 11) makes an archetypal case for one society. El-Ghonemy (1990) makes the general case that the increasing concentration of holdings and growing landlessness—agrarian degeneration—still necessitate land reform; he argues that countries that have undertaken land reform do better on a range of development indicators than unreformed countries do (chaps. 6 and 7).

9. Enriquez 1991. The *Economist* of December 28, 1997 (31–32) reports that titles will be conferred on urban dwellers who received one hundred square meters or less and rural people who received thirty-five hectares or less. Larger properties are subject to review before a title is granted.

10. See Tom Bethell's quirky "Land Reform Lost Vietnam" (1995) for a view of antagonists in the U.S. policy debates.

11. Bernstein is concerned with "decentralized despotism," in consonance with Mamdani's work on "citizen and subject" (1996). The pernicious effect of celebrating the local will be discussed subsequently; see also Crook and Sverrisson, this volume.

12. The *Economist* of June 24, 1995, quoted Nelson Mandela—who had received some land in his own village—as saying: "You have to be on good terms

with your chief, and fortunately the chief in my home is my nephew." Not everyone is so well connected. The African National Congress (ANC) has been understandably reluctant to tackle the issue of "traditional" forms of authority and the resultant concentrations of local political and economic power.

13. For a representative range of positive and critical commentary, see Drèze and Sen 1989 (221ff.); Parayil 1996; Heller 1999; Mencher 1980; Herring 1980; Tharamangalam 1998; and Jeffrey 1993.

14. Atul Kohli (1987) finds similar conditions in his comparative study of Indian states. John Harriss, in this volume, concurs but adds that populist mobilization may likewise prove effective in poverty reduction.

15. Although the World Bank's study (1997a) concludes that its results "clearly refute any presumption of 'immiserizing growth,'" Gaiha and Kulkarni's panel data from Maharashtra (1998, table 1) indicate significant fractions of village populations who were either poor and became poorer or nonpoor and became poor despite aggregate growth. It seems unlikely that the Bank has sufficiently disaggregated and reliable data with which to make the sweeping claim just described. There are always victims of economic change, whatever the net vector sum.

16. See Herring 1983 (chaps. 9 and 10) for the logic. Besley and Burgess (1998) present evidence that land reforms explain some differences in poverty reduction across states in India; although they arrive at what seems to be the obvious right answer, their data and method are not convincing.

17. This section relies on Woodward 1951; Franklin 1961; Simkins 1939; Stampp 1965; Foner 1989; Oubre 1978; and Bensel 1990.

18. Following the Civil War, General Sherman, via Special Field Order 15, began distributing lands to slaves in areas where the federal armies were in control, although the titles were temporary and none was for more than forty acres. Army mules were provided to work the land. President Johnson did not sustain this policy (Stampp 1965, 124) but instead pardoned the rebellious landowners and restored their lands. For a view that former slaves made a better adjustment as farmers than the dominant literature allows, see Simkins 1939. Richard Bensel (personal communication) reminds me that the explicit bargain was for Republicans to rule in the South during Reconstruction in return for a national development policy favoring manufacturing interests in the North over the sectional interests of the South. See also Bensel 1990.

19. Pranab Bardhan (1996) terms the advocates of this celebration "anarcho-communalists," displacing responsibility from bad states to good communities; see also Herring 2001a.

20. Gaiha and Kulkarni found in their empirical work in India (1998) that caste had an important impact on escaping poverty. In addition to the authors' reasoning on mechanisms, it must be true that caste affects distribution of connections; it is easier to get a job, a loan, or any advantage if one has caste fellows in positions to help.

21. See Krishnaji 1979; Mencher 1980; and Herring 1980; compare Lerche 1998 on Uttar Pradesh. McReynolds (1998) finds unambiguously that beneficiaries of land reform in El Salvador hired more labor, improving rural job prospects in the aggregate, as the economic theory of land reform predicts (Herring 1983, chap. 9).

22. Herring 1989; Gulati 1990. Old age pensions also improved intrahouse-

hold income distribution for the most vulnerable sections of the most vulnerable class, as families recognized that nonworking members were an economic asset, even if small.

23. This claim is not meant to ignore the points about history raised in the debate between Amartya Sen and Surjit Bhalla (Srinivasan and Bardhan 1988); certain improvements in social welfare predate land reform. Land reform was the culmination of a process that included caste reform, educational reform, altered priorities in social welfare spending, and labor reform.

24. Speech posted by The American Revolution: An HTML Project at <http://odur.let.rug.nl/~usa/D/1851–1875/reconstructio/steven.htm>.

REFERENCES

Abelmann, Nancy. 1996. *Echoes of the Past, Epics of Dissent.* Berkeley: University of California Press.

Adger, N. 1997. "Property Rights, Nature Conservation, and Land Reform in South Africa." In F. Smith, ed., *Environmental Sustainability: Practical Global Implications,* 213–31. Boca Raton, FL: St. Lucie.

Agarwal, Bina. 1992. "Gender Relations and Food Security: Coping with Seasonality, Drought, and Famine in South Asia." In L. Beneria and S. Feldman, eds., *Unequal Burden: Economic Crisis, Persistent Poverty, and Women's Work,* 181–218. Boulder: Westview.

———. 1997. "Environmental Action, Gender Equity, and Women's Participation." *Development and Change* 28:1–44.

Bardhan, Pranab. 1996. "Research on Poverty and Development: Twenty Years after Redistribution with Growth." Supplement to *World Bank Economic Review* 1996. Washington DC: World Bank.

Baviskar, Amita. 1995. *In the Belly of the River: Tribal Conflicts over Development in the Narmada Valley.* Delhi: Oxford University Press.

Bensel, Richard. 1990. *Yankee Leviathan: The Origins of Central State Authority in America, 1859–1877.* Cambridge and New York: Cambridge University Press.

Bernstein, Henry. 1998. "Social Change in the South African Countryside? Land and Production, Poverty, and Power." *Journal of Peasant Studies* 25, no. 4: 1–32.

Besley, Timothy, and Robin Burgess, eds. 1998. *Land Reform, Poverty Reduction, and Growth: Evidence from India.* Development Economics Discussion Paper. London: London School of Economics.

Bethell, Tom. 1995. "Land Reform Lost Vietnam." *American Spectator* 28, no. 6: 16–18.

Blaikie, Piers, and Harold Brookfield. 1987. *Land Degradation and Society.* London: Methuen.

Borras, Saturnino M., Jr. 2001. "The Philippine Agrarian Reform: Relatively Vibrant Land Redistribution amidst Less-Than-Dynamic Agricultural Transformation." In Horacio R. Morales, Jr., and James Putzel, eds., *Power in the*

Village. Quezon City: Project Development Institute and University of the Philippines Press.

Brysk, Alison. 2001. "Indian Market: The Ethnic Face of Adjustment in Ecuador." In M. J. Esman and R. J. Herring, eds., *Carrots, Sticks, and Ethnic Conflict: Rethinking Development Assistance*. Ann Arbor: University of Michigan Press.

Buck, Louise E., Charles C. Geisler, John Schelhas, and Eva Wollenberg, eds. 2001. *Biological Diversity: Balancing Interests through Adaptive Collaborative Management*. Boca Raton, FL: CRC Press.

Bullard, Robert D. 1999. "No Forty Acres and a Mule: An Interview with a Displaced Black Farmer." Environmental Justice Resource Center, June 25, 1999. Posted on <http://www.blackradicalcongress.org>.

Conway, Gordon. 1997. *The Doubly Green Revolution: Food for All in the Twenty-first Century*. New York: Penguin.

Cousins, B. 1997. "How Do Rights Become Real? Formal and Informal Institutions in South Africa's Land Reform." *IDS-Bulletin* 28, no. 4: 59–68.

Deere, Carmen Diana, and Magdalena León. 1997. *Women and Land Rights in the Latin American Neo-liberal Counter-reforms*. East Lansing, Michigan: Women in International Development, Michigan State University.

Diaz, Manuel. 2001. "The Impact of Agrarian Reform in Mexico." In Horacio R. Morales, Jr., and James Putzel, eds., *Power in the Village*. Quezon City: Project Development Institute and University of the Philippines Press.

Drèze, Jean, and Amartya Sen, eds. 1989. *Indian Development: Selected Regional Perspectives*. Delhi: Oxford University Press.

———. 1996. *Indian Development*. New Delhi: Oxford University Press.

Dube, Siddarth. 1998. *In the Land of Poverty: Memoirs of an Indian Family, 1947–1997*. London: Zed.

Echeverri-Gent, John. 1993. *The State and the Poor: Public Policy and Political Development in India and the United States*. Berkeley: University of California Press.

El-Ghonemy, M. Riad. 1990. *The Political Economy of Rural Poverty: The Case for Land Reform*. London: Routledge.

Enriquez, Laura J. 1991. *Harvesting Change: Labor and Agrarian Reform in Nicaragua, 1979–1990*. Chapel Hill: University of North Carolina Press.

Foner, Eric. 1989. *Reconstruction: America's Unfinished Revolution, 1863–1877*. New York: Harper and Row.

Foweraker, Joe. 2001. "Grassroots Movements and Political Activism in Latin America: A Critical Comparison of Chile and Brazil." *Journal of Latin American Studies* 33, no. 4 (November): 839–65.

Franklin, John Hope. 1961. *Reconstruction: after the Civil War*. Chicago and London: University of Chicago Press.

Gaiha, Raghav, P. D. Kaushik, and Vani Kulkarni. 1998. "Jawahar Rozgar Yojana, Panchayats, and the Rural poor in India." *Asian Survey* 38, no. 10: 928–49.

Gaiha, Raghav, and Vani Kulkarni. 1998. "Is Growth Central to Poverty Alleviation in India?" *Journal of International Affairs* 52:145–80.

Goodwyn, Lawrence. 1976. *Democratic Promise: The Populist Moment in America*. New York: Oxford University Press.

Griffin, Keith. 2001. "Poverty and Land Distribution: Cases of Land Reform in Asia." In Horacio R. Morales, Jr., and James Putzel, et al., eds., *Power in the Village*. Quezon City: Project Development Institute and University of the Philippines Press.

Guha, Ramachandra. 1989. *The Unquiet Woods: Ecological Change and Peasant Resistance in the Himalaya*. Delhi: Oxford University Press.

Gulati, Leela. 1990. "Agricultural Workers' Pension in Kerala." *Economic and Political Weekly* 35, no. 6 (February): 339–43.

Gupta, Anil K. 1996. "Technologies, Institutions, and Incentives for Conservation of Biodiversity in Non-OECD Countries: Assessing Needs for Technical Cooperation." Paper presented at Investing in Biological Diversity, the Cairns Conference of the Organization for Economic Cooperation and Development, Cairns, Australia.

———. 1998. "Rewarding Local Communities for Conserving Biodiversity: The Case of the Honey Bee." In L. D. Guruswamy and J. A. McNeely, eds., *Protection of Global Biodiversity: Converging Strategies*, 180–89. Durham: Duke University Press.

Haque, T., and L. Montesi. 1997. "Tenurial Reforms and Agricultural Development in Vietnam." In *Land Reform, Land Settlement, and Cooperatives*, 66–77. Rome: Food and Agriculture Organization of the United Nations.

Heller, Patrick. 1999. *The Labor of Development: Workers and the Transformation of Capitalism in Kerala, India*. Ithaca: Cornell University Press.

Hendrix, Steven. 1996–97. "Pride of Ownership: Land Tenure and Conflict Resolution." *Harvard International Review* 19, no. 1: 40–43.

Herring, Ronald J. 1980. "Abolition of Landlordism in Kerala: A Redistribution of Privilege." *Economic and Political Weekly* 15, no. 26 (June 28): A59–A69.

———. 1983. *Land to the Tiller: The Political Economy of Agrarian Reform in South Asia*. New Haven: Yale University Press.

———. 1988. Stealing Congress Thunder: The Rise to Power of a Communist Movement in South India. In Peter Merkl and Kay Lawson, eds., *When Parties Fail*. Princeton: Princeton University Press.

———. 1989. "Dilemmas of Agrarian Communism." *Third World Quarterly* 11, no. 1 (January): 89–115.

———. 1990. "Resurrecting the Commons: Collective Action and Ecology." *Items* 44, no. 4 (newsletter of the Social Science Research Council, New York) (December): 64–68.

———. 1999. "Embedded Particularism: India's Failed Developmental State." In M. Woo-Cumings, ed., *The Developmental State*. Ithaca: Cornell University Press.

———. 2000. "Political Conditions for Agrarian Reform and Poverty Alleviation." IDS Discussion Papers 375. Institute for Development Studies, Sussex, U.K., June.

———. 2001a. "Authority and Scale in Political Ecology: Some Cautions on Localism." In Louise E. Buck, Charles C. Geisler, John Schelhas, and Eva

Wollenberg, eds., *Biological Diversity: Balancing Interests through Adaptive Collaborative Management*. Boca Raton, FL: CRC Press.

———. 2001b. "Contesting the 'Great Transformation': Local Struggles with the Market in South India." In James C. Scott and Nina Bhatt, eds., *Agrarian Studies: Synthetic Work at the Cutting Edge*. New Haven: Yale University Press.

———. 2001c. "Beyond the Impossibility Theorem of Agrarian Reform." In Horacio R. Morales, Jr., and James Putzel, eds., *Power in the Village*. Quezon City: Project Development Institute and University of the Philippines Press.

———. 2001d. "State Property Rights in Nature (with Special Reference to India)." In John F. Richards, ed., *Land, Property, and the Environment*. Oakland, CA: Institute for Contemporary Studies.

Herring, Ronald J., and Rex M. Edwards. 1983. "Guaranteeing Employment to the Rural Poor: Social Functions and Class Interests in the Employment Guarantee Scheme in Western India." *World Development* 11, no. 7 (July): 575–92.

Herring, Ronald J., and Milton Esman. 2001. "Projects and Policies, Politics and Ethnicities." In Milton Esman and Ronald J. Herring, eds., *Carrots, Sticks, and Ethnic Conflict: Rethinking Development Assistance*. Ann Arbor: University of Michigan Press.

Herring, Ronald J., and N. Chandra Mohan. 2001. "Economic Crisis, Momentary Autonomy, and Policy Reform: Liberalization in India, 1991–1995." In Amita Shastri and A. J. Wilson, eds., *The Post-colonial States of South Asia: Democracy, Development, and Identity*. London: Curzon.

Jannuzi, F. Tomasson. 1974. *Agrarian Crisis in India: The Case of Bihar*. Austin: University of Texas Press.

Jeffrey, Robin. 1993. *Politics, Women, and Well Being: How Kerala Became a Model*. Delhi: Oxford University Press.

Johnson, Natalia. 1995. "Rural Reforms Fail to Take Root." *Business Mexico* 5, no. 3: 24ff.

Johnston, David Cay. 2002. "I.R.S. Paid Millions in False Claims for Slavery Credit." *New York Times*, April 14, 22.

Kannan, K. P., and K. Pushpangadan. 1998. "Agricultural Stagnation in Kerala." *Economic and Political Weekly* 23, no. 39: A120–28.

Kohli, Atul. 1987. *The State and Poverty in India*. Cambridge: Cambridge University Press.

Kothari, Ashish. 1997. *Understanding Biodiversity: Life, Sustainability, and Protected Areas*. New Delhi: Orient Longman.

Kothari, Ashish, Neena Singh, and Saloni Suri. 1996. *People and Protected Areas*. New Delhi: Sage.

Krishnaji, N. 1979. "Agrarian Relations and the Left Movement in Kerala." *Economic and Political Weekly* 14, no. 9 (March): 515–21.

Lerche, Jens. 1998. "Agricultural Labourers, the State, and Agrarian Transition in Uttar Pradesh." *Economic and Political Weekly* 33, no. 13 (March 28): A29–35.

Lipton, Michael. 1993. "Land Reform as Commenced Business: The Evidence against Stopping." *World Development* 21, no. 4: 641–58.

————. 1997. "Poverty: Are There Holes in the Consensus?" World Development 25, no. 7: 1003–7.

Mamdani, M. 1996. Citizen and Subject: Contemporary Africa and the Legacy of Late Colonialism. Cape Town: David Phillip.

Manji, Ambreena. 1998. "Gender and the Politics of the Land Reform Process in Tanzania." Journal of Modern African Studies 36, no. 4: 645–67.

McHugh, Heather S. 2001. "USAID and Ethnicity: An Epiphany?" In M. J. Esman and R. J. Herring, eds., Carrots, Sticks, and Ethnic Conflict: Rethinking Development Assistance. Ann Arbor: University of Michigan Press.

McReynolds, S. A. 1998. "Agricultural Labour and Agrarian Reform in El Salvador: Social Benefit or Economic Burden?" Journal of Rural Studies 14, no. 4: 459–73.

Meer, S. 1997. "Gender and Land Rights: The Struggle over Resources in Post-apartheid South Africa." IDS Bulletin 28, no. 3: 133–44.

Mencher, Joan P. 1980. "The Lessons and Non-lessons of Kerala: Agricultural Labourers and Poverty." Economic and Political Weekly 15:41–43.

Moore, Barrington, Jr. 1966. Social Origins of Dictatorship and Democracy: Lord and Peasant in the Making of the Modern World. Boston: Beacon.

Oubre, C. F. 1978. Forty Acres and a Mule: The Freedmen's Bureau and Black Land Ownership. Baton Rouge: Louisiana State University Press.

Paige, Jeffrey. 1975. Agrarian Revolution: Social Movements and Export Agriculture in the Underdeveloped World. New York: Free Press.

Parayil, Govindan. 1996. "The 'Kerala' Model of Development: Development and Sustainability in the Third World." Third World Quarterly 17, no. 5: 941–57.

Peluso, Nancy. 1992. Rich Forests, Poor People: Resource Control and Resistance in Java. Berkeley: University of California Press.

Petras, James. 1997. "The Resurgence of the Left." New Left Review 223:17–47.

————. 1998. "The Political and Social Basis of Regional Variation in Land Occupations in Brazil." Journal of Peasant Studies 25, no. 4: 124–33.

Polanyi, Karl. [1944] 1957. The Great Transformation. Boston: Beacon.

Potts, Deborah, and Chris Mutambirwa. 1997. "The Government Must Not Dictate: Rural-Urban Migrants' Perceptions of Zimbabwe's Land Resettlement Programme." Review of African Political Economy 24, no. 74: 549–66.

Powelson, John P., and Richard Stock. 1990. The Peasant Betrayed: Agriculture and Land Reform in the Third World. Washington, DC: Cato Institute.

Prosterman, Roy L., and Jeffrey M Riedinger. 1987. Land Reform and Democratic Development. Baltimore: Johns Hopkins University Press.

Putzel, James. 1992. A Captive Land: The Politics of Agrarian Reform in the Philippines. London and New York: Catholic Institute for International Relations, Monthly Review Press.

Reid, Walter V. 1996. "Gene Co-ops and the Biotrade: Translating Genetic Resource Rights into Sustainable Development." Journal of Ethno-Pharmacology 51:75–92.

Riedinger, Jeffrey M. 1995. Agrarian Reform in the Philippines: Democratic Transitions and Redistributive Reforms. Stanford: Stanford University Press.

Riedinger, Jeff, Wan-Ying Yang, and Karen Brook. 2001. "Market-Based Land Reform."

Rudolph, Lloyd, and Susanne Rudolph. 1987. *In Pursuit of Lakshmi: The Political Economy of the Indian State.* Chicago: University of Chicago Press.

Rueschemeyer, Dietrich, Evelyne Huber Stephens, and John Stephens. 1992. *Capitalist Development and Democracy.* Chicago: University of Chicago Press.

Salamon, Lester M. 1979. "The Time Dimension in Policy Evaluation: The Case of the New Deal Land-Reform Experiments." *Public Policy* 27, no. 2 (spring): 129–83.

Shin, Gi-Wook. 1998. "Agrarian Conflict and the Origins of Korean Capitalism." *American Journal of Sociology* 103, no. 5 (March): 1309–51.

Siddiqui, Kamal. 2000. *Jagatpur: 1977–1997.* Dhaka: University Press Limited.

Simpkins, Francis B. 1939. "New Viewpoints of Southern Reconstruction." *Journal of Southern History* 5 (February): 49–61.

Sinha, Aseema. 2000. "Divided Leviathan: Comparing Subnational Developmental States in India." Ph.D. diss., Cornell University.

Sinha, Subir, and Ronald J. Herring. 1993. "Common Property, Collective Action, and Ecology." *Economic and Political Weekly* 28 (3–10 July): 1425–32.

Srinivasan, T. N., and Pranab K. Bardhan, eds. 1988. *Rural Poverty in South Asia.* New York: Columbia University Press.

Stampp, Kenneth M. 1965. *The Era of Reconstruction, 1865–1877.* New York: Vintage.

Swinnen, Johan F. M., Allan Buckwell, and Erik Mathijs, eds. 1997. *Agricultural Privatization, Land Reform, and Farm Restructuring in Central and Eastern Europe.* Aldershot, England: Ashgate.

Tharamangalam, Joseph. 1998. "The Perils of Social Development without Economic Growth: The Development Debacle in Kerala." *Bulletin of Concerned Asian Scholars* 30, no. 1: 23–34.

Thiesenhusen, William C. 1995. *Broken Promises: Agrarian Reform and the Latin American Campesino.* Boulder: Westview.

Tornquist, Olle, and P. K. Michael Tharakan. 1996. "Democratization and Attempts to Renew the Radical Political Development Project of Kerala, India." *Political and Economic Weekly XXXI*, no. 28, 29, 30 (June 13): 1847–58.

Uphoff, Norman, ed. 2002. *Agroecological Innovations.* London and Sterling, VA: Earthscan.

Veltmeyer, Henry. 1997. "New Social Movements in Latin America: The Dynamics of Class and Identity." *Journal of Peasant Studies* 25, no. 1: 139–69.

Weiss, Charles, and Thomas Eisner. 1998. "Partnerships for Value-Added through Bioprospecting." *Technology and Society* 20:481–98.

Williams, Donald C. 1996. "Reconsidering State and Society in Africa: The Institutional Dimension." *Comparative Politics* 28, no. 2: 207–24.

Woodward, C. Vann. 1951. *Reunion and Reaction: The Compromise of 1877 and the End of Reconstruction.* Boston: Little, Brown.

World Bank. 1997a. *India: Achievements and Challenges in Reducing Poverty.* Washington, DC: World Bank.

———. 1997b. *World Development Report: The State in a Changing World.* New York: World Bank.

4 Coalition Building from Below

Peter P. Houtzager (with Jonathan Pattenden)

In low- and middle-income democracies, social groups loosely classified as poor are typically in the majority, but their political participation seldom influences national policy. There are many explanations for this. Some are familiar: the malfunctioning of democratic institutions in these countries, the class bases of liberal (bourgeois) democracy itself, and Olsonian obstacles to collective action such as the free-rider problem. The fragmentation and "localism" of most organizations representing the poor, considered by some polycentrists (see chap. 1) to be the carriers of radical (direct) democracy, is a less familiar but growing concern. The concern stems from an apparent paradox. Widespread adoption of formal democratic institutions and marked increase in civil society activism in the last two decades have coincided with a decline in the state's responsiveness to social claims and the adoption of marketizing economic policies, which have produced increasing inequality and few visible signs of poverty reduction.[1] Scholars such as Castells (1996–98) and Roberts (1998) find that the community groups, nongovernmental organizations (NGOs), and other civic groups that have proliferated during this period "are often isolated and disconnected from each other, in part because of their insistence on political autonomy; and they generally focus on immediate, particularistic needs or partial demands that do not have generalized appeal" (70–71). These localized forms of organization are, as a result, unable to challenge dominant structures of power and influence state behavior.

Fragmentation and "localism" have become particularly salient concerns because of the apparent decline of organized labor—the historic carrier of broad social rights—in many middle-income countries: the weakness of party systems in many Third Wave democracies, which offers little opportunity to the poor for interest aggregation and representation; and the inability of transnational networks of activists, NGOs, and social movements to pressure either national governments or international bodies into adopting significant distributive and redistributive policies.

Under what conditions are local organizations representing poor social groups able to coalesce into broad coalitions, and when are these coalitions able to influence national policy-making centers? One can address these questions in different ways. In chapter 2 of this volume, Whitehead and Gray-Molina take a long-term view and argue that the political capabilities that enabled Bolivian peasant groups to gain from the recent Popular Participation reform were constructed over a forty-year period, in an iterative cycle of pro-poor policy-making and popular mobilization. They explore three such cycles and illustrate how particular types of state interventions created new opportunities for peasant groups to extend their political capabilities—that is, to "become agents in deciding, lobbying, deliberating and negotiating on pro-poor outcome." This chapter takes a different approach. It extends the polity approach set out in the introduction to this volume and, for analytic reasons, focuses on a single cycle, or episode, in what Whitehead and Gray-Molina correctly point out are iterative, path dependent sequences of state-society interactions.

The chapter presents a comparative analysis of two episodes of coalition building from below that, between the mid-1980s and early 1990s, succeeded in overcoming localism and for a time acquired access to key policy-making centers. The first episode was that of the Congress for a People's Agrarian Reform (CPAR) in the Philippines, an NGO-brokered coalition of peasant organizations; the second was the women's *comedores* (community kitchen) movement in Peru, a coalition of community-based kitchens in poor urban areas. The term *NGO-brokered* is used to highlight NGOs' central role in the emergence of the CPAR coalition without assuming direct leadership or control.[2] Coalitions brokered by NGOs are of special interest because, in national contexts characterized by poorly institutionalized party systems, they have become partial "functional equivalents" of progressive parties. While CPAR was part of a foundational moment that set in motion a new sequence of state-society interactions, the *comedores* coalition represents at least a second episode in such a sequence.

Even in the relatively brief period examined here, both the Philippines and Peru experienced profound political-institutional shifts that had substantial effects on both coalition building and efforts to shape public policy. High degrees of political-institutional flux reflect the fact that, unlike the relatively stable, high-income (Western) democracies, many low- and middle-income democracies remain marked by high levels of political conflict over the basic parameters of the political system and hence by frequent institutional change at the levels of the national political regime and state.

The chapter extends the polity framework in order to capture the impact of these political-institutional shifts. It focuses on the effects national patterns of political authority—constituted by the state, the national political regime, and the political alliances that breathe life into those institutions—have on coalition building from below and on the relationship between such coalitions and political elites that produce policy influence (Houtzager 2001). Relations between coalitions and elites, the polity approach suggests, are shaped in large measure by (1) the level of intraelite conflict over the pattern of political authority, (2) the geography of state-society relations, and (3) the strength of the social bases of poor people's organizations. The task, as Epsing-Andersen (1990, 29) observes in his work on the origins of the welfare state, "is to identify salient interaction-effects" among such factors.

The approach helps highlight one finding in particular. The coalitions had the most influence when they faced a relatively coherent state (with a professional bureaucracy) whose authority was broadly accepted. This allowed organizations of the poor and agents of the state to build relatively stable working relations. When state authority was heavily contested or state bureaucratization was low, wielding substantial influence was difficult if not impossible. Relatively profound political-institutional change made sustaining coalitions and access to state decision-making centers particularly difficult.

One often reads and hears of the influence organizations and movements (representing whatever set of ideas, identities, or interests) wield in particular contexts. But what do we mean by *influence* and by *policy influence* in particular? Policy influence is a multidimensional concept that is, foremost, relational and has important temporal elements. It acquires analytic utility only upon some form of specification. This specification can take a variety of forms, but for the purposes of this chapter the four dimensions that Kitschelt (1986, 66–67) and Kriesi et al. (1995, chap. 9) define impose a particularly valuable analytic sharpness. The four types are as follows.

- *Procedural* influence alters aspects of the policy-making process and includes recognition of previously excluded organizations as legitimate political actors and the opening of new political channels to those actors.
- *Substantive* influence results in a change in policy.
- *Structural* influence leads to the transformation of political institutions and/or national political alignments.
- *Sensitizing* influence entails favorable alterations in either the attitude of particular actors toward a coalition's goals or in public opinion more generally.

The temporal quality of influence is more difficult to address. The effects of a series of activities such as a lobbying campaign will vary over time as relations between actors in the political arena alter. Anticipating or theorizing these variable effects is, to say the least, difficult. In the Philippine case, legislation that resulted at least in part from CPARs' efforts was not implemented under one government, yet it became a cornerstone of the policies for a successor government, and for a new episode of state-society interactions, even though CPAR itself had ceased to exist. In Peru, new legislation for which the *comedores* fought was enacted but has yet to become practice. As the introduction to the volume points out, temporal effects will depend in part on whether an event (such as a lobbying campaign) helped initiate a new causal path, which then reproduces its impact over time, or whether it occurred as part of a process of "change within paths." In the latter case, influence will be more incremental and perhaps less visible.

EXTENDING THE POLITY APPROACH

If our concern is the ability of organizations of the poor to affect state behavior, then relations between the poor and elite groups stand at the center of our analytical framework. Coalitions of the poor make claims on political elites, and elite response determines the type and degree of influence they acquire. The level of intraelite conflict over the pattern of political authority and the relative strength of a movement's social base condition the opportunities for claim making and the ways in which elites will respond to movement claims. When coalitions succeed in acquiring structural influence, the pattern of political authority itself changes. Although they are critically important, this chapter will not address the grassroots dynamics of collective action nor the bases of organizational strength (or leverage) of the poor. These are explored in great detail in the literature on social movements and collective action (McAdam 1982; McCarthy and Zald 1977; Melucci 1996; Oberschall 1973; Tarrow 1998; McAdam, McCarthy, and Zald 1996; McAdam, Tarrow, and Tilly 2001). It will give considerable attention to the institutions that link state and society, such as the party system and other political institutions on the one hand and structural (administrative, legal, and policy) links on the other. One goal of this chapter is to explore in more detail one of the core claims of the polity approach: that political institutions facilitate certain types of claim making and coalition building while inhibiting others.[3]

Elite Conflict. The level of intraelite conflict shapes the ways in which elite groups respond to the activities and demands of coalitions of the poor. When intraelite conflict is low, elite actors are more likely to ignore or repress movements of the poor. Middling levels of conflict entail a significant degree of elite contestation but within previously accepted boundaries of a democratic political arena such as in highly competitive multiparty systems. In such instances, elites are likely to forge new alliances with subordinate social actors. In cases of high levels of conflict, such as in democratic transitions, contestation is over the pattern of political authority itself—that is, the basic contours of the political arena. Elites will seek out new allies and in some cases may act as institutional hosts for entirely new actors.[4]

Allies. One of the central questions among actors in (and students of) civil society is how, and what kind of, autonomy organizations of the poor should develop from political parties, elite groups, and agents of the state. There are those who advocate strong forms of autonomy (to avoid co-optation, goal displacement, and worse), others who favor engagement while maintaining relative autonomy, and then those who support entry into stable alliances. If an actor's goal is to influence policy, rather than self-provisioning, then the strong autonomy position is the least tenable. Furthermore, there is growing agreement among students of development that the ability of organizations of the poor to influence policy is greatly enhanced by alliances with reformist elements within the state (Fox 1992, 1996; Evans 1996; Tendler 1997). More generally, an array of scholars suggests that historically it has been in instances in which broad coalitions of the poor succeeded in attracting the support of critical elite and nonelite allies and engaging the state that they have succeeded in acquiring influence along the dimensions outlined earlier (Esping-Andersen 1990; Hanagen 1998).

When organizations of the poor join alliances or integrate themselves into larger movements or parties, they inevitably surrender some degree of autonomy. In the case of alliances with political parties, one of the fears many activists and students of civil society carry is the subordination of the organization's goals to broader party objectives. This fear has foundation, but Hanagen (1998, 3, 28) argues convincingly that in the past 125 years in Western and Central Europe "incorporation of left-wing social movements into political parties has often resulted in persistence of movement activities *within* party structures and . . . incorporated social movements have exerted enduring influence on social policy." Furthermore, he suggests that "parties have proved more enduring and resourceful than independent SMOs (social movement organizations). . . . While less rewarding, at least the subordinate incorporation of movements into parties has provided routine political access denied to independent movements." Molyneux (1998), in her analysis of contemporary women's movements, reaches a similar conclusion.

If we accept the need for sustained alliances, then an important ancillary question is raised. How close are a coalition's allies to the centers of state power? Allies who are senior partners in the governing coalition or occupy influential positions within the state significantly enhance a coalition's capacity to influence policy, whereas allies who are marginalized from power do not.[5]

State. Influencing public policy means influencing the state. Although critical areas of public policy are increasingly constrained by international institutions and actors, the state remains the primary target for actors seeking to influence policy-making. How the state is organized, and particularly where authority resides, have a profound impact on the issues around which organizations of the poor organize and build coalitions, the form these coalitions take, and the strategies they pursue.

The degree to which state authority is contested within a national territory is particularly important. On the one hand, the modern state eliminates rival centers of authority over large geographic areas and populations and creates a new normative order to legitimize its authority. This provides the basis on which social groups can organize on a national scale and construct collective identities that cut across diverse geographic regions and social strata (Tilly 1984; Migdal, Kholi, and Shue 1994).[6] On the other hand, whether or not social groups mobilize to influence the state depends in part on whether they believe the state has the authority and capacity to meet their demands. Where state authority is tenuous or heavily contested, such as in war-torn regions or areas with guerrilla activity, one would not expect to find a significant amount of collective action by the poor targeting the state.

The degree to which the state has bureaucratic coherence—that is, a professional civil service and effective coordination among units—influences the types of relations organizations of the poor can establish with the state. Similar to the claim that Evans (1995, 63) makes about the conditions in the information technology (IT) sector, under which government and private actors are able to establish "regularized ties" that make "administrative guidance" possible, close working relationships around substantive issues are difficult to establish when the state has a weak bureaucracy and is run along personalistic and/or patronage lines. The degree of bureaucratization of the state also conditions its capacity to respond to the demands of the poor.

Structural Linkages. Structural linkages are the administrative and legal institutions through which the state exercises its social, productive, and regulatory functions (Houtzager and Kurtz 2000). These can include the rural corporatist institutions Whitehead and Gray-Molina discuss in their chapter and systems of social welfare and land tenure. Such linkages reflect the state's role in economic and social spheres and play a significant role in defining the boundaries of the political arena. Coalitions of the poor, and political contestation more generally, tend to crystallize around structural linkages. Such linkages help define which issues are open to legitimate contestation and provide points of access to the state. Organizations of the poor lower the costs of collective action and increase the likelihood of success by mobilizing around such linkages, seeking to politicize them. It is, for example, far more costly for elite groups to ignore or repress movements that are widely perceived to be making legitimate claims on the state. It is for this reason that, as Herring notes in his discussion of unfulfilled agrarian reform in this volume (chap. 3), even unkept promises can "become nodes around which politics precipitate." The extent of state intervention in social and economic life therefore has important implications for the forms and levels of organizing activity.

Party System. The organization of the party system affects the nature of representation, how public policy is made, and the state's capacity to implement policy. As Mainwaring (1999, 13) points out, parties are the first and foremost route to state power and "virtually monopolize access to elected positions in most democracies." In particular, parties monopolize the process of enacting legislation, a valued goal of most coalitions.[7] Party systems shape the behavior of nonparty actors, including movements of the poor, in basic ways (15). In particular, if a party system offers diverse actors significant opportunities to make claims in the political system (i.e., high access), coalitions are likely to emerge around political parties and invest significantly in electoral politics. In cases in which party systems are relatively closed to movements of the poor, parties will play a far less important role (Kriesi et al. 1995; Kitschelt 1986).

Party systems vary in myriad ways, but in order to assess how they may influence organizations of the poor it is helpful to identify three dimensions. Sartori (1976) suggests two: the number of parties and the level of ideological polarization. In the case of Third Wave democracies, Mainwaring (1999) argues, a third dimension can usefully be added: level of institutionalization. Weakly institutionalized party systems are those that suffer instability in the patterns of party competition, have parties that are comparatively weakly rooted in society, and have weak formal organizations.

Access to party systems is greatest in a multiparty system with ideologically diverse and well-institutionalized parties. In such systems, electoral competition is most likely to push parties to seek alliances with newly constituted collective actors. Moreover, it also gives such actors the most leverage vis-à-vis parties. Party systems with two dominant but incoherent and poorly institutionalized parties offer the least access to nonparty actors. Personalism and clientelism undermine the capacity of movements to establish substantive ties to parties. Many Third Wave democracies have multiparty systems that are weakly institutionalized and have a narrow ideological spectrum. These systems, such as those in Brazil and the Philippines, offer relatively low levels of access.

THE CASES

The following analysis of CPAR in the Philippines and the *comedores* movement in Peru is organized to facilitate comparison across the five sets of factors identified in the previous section. The factors are summarized in table 1. The *state* is disaggregated along two dimensions: the extent to which its authority is accepted and the degree of its bureaucratic coherence. *Party systems* are disaggregated along three dimensions: number of parties, degree of polarization in the system as a whole, and level of institutionalization of the parties themselves. Not included in the table are *structural linkages.*

The five sets of factors are of course a heavy causal burden for two cases to carry. For this reason, each case is divided into two periods that correspond to distinct constellations of the five political factors. This gives us four cases and makes possible "within case" comparisons that capture a part of the temporal dimension of influence alluded to earlier. Nonetheless, the range of variation is still insufficient to allow a careful sorting of the causal weight of each set of factors. The following analysis therefore relies on process tracing to identify common causes (or combinations of causes) that contribute to coalition building and influence in the Philippines and Peru.

Table 1 provides a limited but useful summary of what lies ahead. The scores for each of the variables are admittedly subjective and intended only as a means of identifying variation within and between the two cases analyzed here.

CONGRESS FOR A PEOPLE'S AGRARIAN REFORM, THE PHILIPPINES

CPAR was an ideal, typical, NGO-brokered coalition. Rural development NGOs, along with the hierarchy of the Catholic Church and other groups, brought diverse peasant movements together and orchestrated the formation of CPAR.[8] It became the broadest and most enduring national peasant coalition in the history of the Philippines (Goño 1997, 15; Putzel 1998, 90). The CPAR exercised a substantial degree of procedural and sensitizing influence during the period when it was active (1987–92) but little substantive influence. In the 1993–96 period, after CPAR's dissolution, that procedural and sensitizing influence contributed to important, if limited, substantive gains in agrarian reform. The subsequent episode in the iterative interaction between peasant coalitions, this time organized in PARRDS (Partnership for Agrarian Reform and Rural Development Services), and state agents took place on the foundations laid during the CPAR episode.

The timing of CPAR's emergence and the form it took were strongly influenced by the nature of the state and party system, which in several ways made the coalition-building process more difficult. Access to the state, and the state's capacity to act, were severely limited. The Philippines of the 1986–92 period scores very low on state authority and bureaucratic coherence. The new democracy inherited a patrimonial state that suffered a bureaucratic apparatus permeated with the private interests of regional clans, Marcos's cronies, and a powerful and highly politicized military (Thompson 1995). The Department of Agrarian Reform, created by Marcos in the 1970s and the principal agency responsible for implementing reform, was not an exception. It had four different secretaries between 1987 and 1992, some lasting as little as four months, and suffered various corruption scandals (Borras 1998).

Furthermore, the state's authority was severely contested by various groups during the 1980s. Thompson (1995) in fact argues that the Philippines was on the edge of a revolutionary precipice in the mid-1980s. Between 1985 and 1992, sectors of the military initiated nine coup attempts, in the south the Moro National Liberation Front fought for

TABLE 1. FACTORS CONTRIBUTING TO COALITION BUILDING AND INFLUENCE IN THE PHILIPPINES AND PERU

	Philippines		Peru	
	1986–92	1993–96	1985–91	1992–96
Actors				
Elite conflict	High	Mid/low	Mid	High
Allies' proximity to power	Mid/low	Mid/high	High	Low
State				
Authority	Low	Mid	Low	Mid
Bureaucratic coherence	Weak	Mid	Weak	Weak/mid
Party System				
Number of parties	High	High	Mid	
Polarization			High	
Institutionalization	Low	Low	Mid	
Outcomes				
Coalition	CPAR	—	Comedores movement	Comedores movement
Influence	Procedural and sensitizing	Substantive	Procedural, sensitizing, and substantive	—

independence, and at the local level warlords exercised considerable authority (Lara and Morales 1990, 148; Thompson 1995, 168–70). Most important, however, was the mounting challenge of the Communist Party of the Philippines (CPP) and its armed wing, the National People's Army (NPA). Through the NPA, the Communist Party created a parallel base of authority in substantial parts of the countryside. In areas under its control, the NPA played an important law and order role, provided services such as medical training and adult education, and ran a "rudimentary" local administration, often more effectively than either the local or central governments. The NPA even launched its own agrarian reform, which included reduction in land rents, limits on usury, and in some instances outright redistribution (Putzel 1992, 122; Riedinger 1995, 60).[9]

The party system was not a viable channel through which to make demands in the political arena and, at least for coalitions of the poor, failed to provide access to the critical decision-making centers within the state. It was a weakly institutionalized multiparty system in which parties were based primarily on personalities and were dominated by regional clans (Anderson 1988; Thompson 1995, 1996). In the 1990s, a new type of personalistic electoral politics emerged alongside the traditional pattern—that of personalities who lacked strong ties to traditional clans but who created parties as electoral vehicles and relied heavily on the mass media (Canlas 1988, 73–74). The only ideologically coherent mass-based party was the CPP, which opted for a clandestine existence. In large measure, due to the CPP's dominant position on the Left, no center-leftist party emerged during the democratic transition.[10]

The challenge of the CPP/NPA to the state in the 1986–92 period had a profound impact on peasant sector coalition-building efforts. The CPP/NPA was the largest and best organized sector of the Left and occupied a key political space in the countryside. Its popular organizing efforts were central in creating a mass base that made CPAR possible, but its dominant position made extremely difficult any efforts to build broad-based coalitions that could engage the state and work through formal political institutions. The party had influence over an array of popular organizations, including several of the large peasant federations in what became known as the "national democratic" camp.[11] It did not participate in the transition, being opposed to the authority of the state, and its "protracted people's war" combined armed struggle with a political united front (Putzel 1992, 1995).

Two factors were critical to the emergence of CPAR. The first was the high level of elite conflict and the accompanying transition to democracy. The transition occurred by collapse. Marcos was forced from power in a sudden combination of insubordination by segments of the armed forces, popular protest of the "people power revolution," and elite political maneuvering in which the United States government played an important role (Thompson 1995). As a result, the new Aquino government upon taking office had substantial power and room to maneuver; it discarded both the Marcos constitution and the Congress. A new Congress would only be seated in mid-1987. Aquino's legitimacy came in large measure from her role in the "people's revolution" and expectations ran high that she would tackle major social reforms. This expectation was reinforced when the government opened negotiations with the CPP/NPA. Furthermore, peasant groups had important potential allies within the state after 1986. Aquino came to power on the shoulders of a broad coalition that included traditional political elites that had been marginalized under Marcos, sectors of the armed forces, the middle class, NGOs, and popular organization (PO) leaders who represented the aspirations of the people's revolution. This latter group received prominent cabinet appointments, including those of executive secretary, labor secretary, presidential spokesperson, and social welfare secretary (Clarke 1995, 72). Finally, there was the prospect of writing a new agrarian reform program into law with the redrafting of the constitution.[12]

The other factor was the large and well-organized NGO sector in the Philippines. During the 1980s, there was dramatic growth in the number of NGOs and associations in the Philippines, making it one of the largest and most highly organized civil society sectors in the developing world (Clarke 1995, 67). A number of important rural development NGOs emerged during this period. Among the most important was PhilDHRAA, which had supported Aquino and stood at the center of a network of organizations on the Left that formed the principal counterweight to the CPP/NPA (National Democratic Front). The NGOs' organizational strength, programmatic orientation, and autonomy from clan politics contrast markedly with that of political parties.[13] Their strength and relative autonomy from domestic actors, however, was in large measure a result of resource dependence on Northern European and North America donors.[14]

The network of rural development NGOs served in a limited sense as the functional equivalent of a center-leftist party. That is, NGOs took the lead in bringing competing peasant federations together in a broad coalition, mediating their conflicts, helping give the coalition direction, and securing access to financing (Goño 1997, 20–21; Putzel 1998). They also played an important role in providing access to the state, albeit not in an institutionalized fashion; various NGO activists found positions within the executive branch, including the Department of Agrarian Reform (DAR), and on congressional committees. The NGOs' efforts led to the creation of a new national peasant federation, PAKISAMA, in 1986 and culminated in the formation of CPAR in 1987.

Facilitating this process was the existence of structural linkages in the area of agrarian reform. Although state-society links were tenuous in most rural areas, in the 1970s Marcos had launched an agrarian reform program that kept the issue on the national agenda and legitimized claim making in this area during the transition. Marcos first declared the entire country subject to land reform and then restricted reform to tenanted rice and corn lands. In practice, only 13,590 tenants had received official land titles by 1986 (Putzel 1992, 124, 137). Nonetheless, Marcos frequently touted reform as the basis of his New Society. The existence of the agrarian reform law (Presidential Decree 27) and a bureaucracy dedicated to reform (the DAR) facilitated organizing and coalition building around the issue.

Under these political conditions, CPAR brought together two of three broad and ideologically highly differentiated peasant groups. These were the national democrats linked to the CPP (the single largest organized bloc) and the social democratic and democratic socialist peasant federations with strong ties to rural development NGOs and progressive sectors of the Catholic Church (Borras 1998, 30). The NGOs made a concerted effort to bring the national democrats into the coalition. Despite its size, the CPP was not dominant.[15]

The CPAR succeeded in having a substantial degree of procedural and sensitizing influence. It obtained recognition as a legitimate national political actor almost immediately and, through its lobbying, collective action, and participation in congressional debates, helped create a political climate favorable to agrarian reform. It kept the issue at the top of the national agenda at a time when the government had little interest in reform. Perhaps the clearest indication of CPAR's sensitizing influence was the widespread media support for its agrarian reform amendment to the constitution.

The efforts of the peasant coalition to change government policy, however, were blocked by the weakness of the state and the closed nature of the party system, which ensured that conservative, antireform groups dominated both the executive and legislative branches of government. The coalition sought to influence policy by focusing its energies first on the executive branch, second on the legislature, and finally through a campaign for a popular constitutional amendment. The first efforts of CPAR, which were undertaken with the support of its allies in the executive branch, attempted to influence the drafting of an executive order on agrarian reform before Aquino would have to contend with a newly elected Congress, which was expected to be conservative. The organization combined a substantial mobilization campaign with direct negotiations with the cabinet. The cabinet included supporters of reform, and there was widespread popular support for decisive action on the issue.

The dominant elements within the Aquino government, however, were sectors of the armed forces, conservative business leaders, and traditional elites that had been marginalized under Marcos (Putzel 1992, 176–79).[16] Furthermore, the increasing threat to the state by rebel groups within the armed forces and the CPP/NPA pushed the government further to the right. The influence of the military, which was strongly opposed to agrarian reform and to working with popular organizations, grew significantly after 1987 (260–61).[17] The executive order that Aquino signed in 1987 deferred key questions to the newly elected Congress after all.

CPAR shifted its attention to the legislature, where it sought to influence the writing of the Comprehensive Agrarian Reform Law (CARL). Here it faced other obstacles. The frail, and essentially "closed," nature of the party system and the absence of a leftist party ensured that the coalition's efforts in this area would be defeated. Public demonstrations organized by CPAR were combined with the lobbying of legislators and active participation in the process of drafting a progressive reform bill in the Technical Committee of the House Committee on Agrarian Reform. Traditional political clans, however, dominated the Congress elected in 1987. Of 200 seats in the lower house of the Congress elected in 1987 (which would legislate a new agrarian reform law), 130 were won by members of "traditional political families" who had played a central role in the pre-1971 period and another 39 were won by relatives of these families (Anderson 1988, 27). Proreform congressmen numbered fewer than 50. The bill that passed in 1988 was widely considered to favor landowners, and CPAR's rejection of it was unequivocal. After the law's passage, the Department of Agrarian Reform made little headway in implementing it because proreform officials were isolated within the weak bureaucracy and lacked presidential support (Borras 1998, 24–25).

In response to its legislative defeat, the coalition launched a campaign to replace CARL with its own agrarian reform law, PARCODE, under a provision of the new constitution that allowed for "people's initiatives," that is, popular constitutional amendments. To become law, an initiative had to secure the signatures of 3 percent of the voters in each legislative district, approximately three million signatures. Despite media support for the amendment, the signature campaign never gained momentum and CPAR abandoned it in 1991.[18]

Consolidation of State Authority and Agrarian Reform, 1993–96

Table 1 indicates that in the 1993–96 period several dimensions of the Philippine political system changed. The state consolidated its authority to a substantial degree, and particular public agencies were strengthened, including the Department of Agrarian Reform. The level of intraelite contestation declined significantly with the gradual, if partial, consolidation of democratic institutions (Thompson 1995, 176). Challenges to state authority decreased markedly as the CPP/NPA declined as a military force, peace talks with the Moro National Liberation Front progressed, and the wave of military coup efforts ended. Fidel Ramos, once he assumed the presidency in 1992, forged a more cohesive coalition than Aquino had. Ramos did not come from the old landed elite, and as the threat of the CPP/NPA declined so did the role of the armed forces in the governing coalition. As a result, he was able to push through a number of measures to strengthen the state apparatus. These reforms made possible significant advances in agrarian reform on the foundations laid by CPAR in the earlier period.

Although the party system remained much the same as in the previous period, the strengthening of the DAR, albeit with a smaller budget, and the decline of the CPP/NPA opened the door for progressive forces to establish new ties with the state. One measure of the DAR's enhanced capacity was the remarkable increase in the number of agrarian reform cases it adjudicated, which increased from 53 to 95 percent of the total, even though the absolute number of cases increased more than fourteenfold.

Perhaps most importantly, the new head of the DAR sought closer ties with proreform groups, including peasant federations, and was an influential cabinet member with direct access to Ramos.[19] He encouraged the federations to pressure the state from the outside and also sought to institutionalize their access to the policy process so that proreform groups could "penetrate the state" and "push . . . from within."[20] When CPAR collapsed in 1992, its opposition to CARL gave way to efforts by various peasant federations to work with the DAR in implementing its more progressive features.[21] In the post-CPAR period, most peasant federations combined their efforts to ally themselves with proreform groups within state agencies, with substantial pressure from below (Borras 1998, 33–39). Although peasant groups lost the unity enjoyed under CPAR, their ability to forge stable substantive ties with the DAR compensated for this loss and played a significant role in accelerating reform. The earlier activities of CPAR laid part of the foundation for the post-1992 relationships that were built.

Although CARL was widely seen as a defeat, it represented an improvement over previous agrarian reform laws and provided the legal basis for an acceleration of reform after 1992 (quite likely CARL would have been considerably weaker without CPAR's campaign). By the end of 1997, the government had distributed no less than 4.61 million hectares of land, meeting 57 percent of the revised program target set in 1988 under the legislation of 8.04 million hectares (Borras and Franco 1998). This represents a significant improvement over the record of the 1970s and 1980s, although both the Aquino and Ramos governments focused primarily on the less contentious provisions of CARL, such as the distribution of public lands, voluntary offer to sell, and voluntary land transfers (Borras and Franco 1998).

The structural influence of CPAR was very limited in both periods. For example, despite its efforts through the United Rural Sector Electoral Council to coordinate electoral activity during the 1992 elections, no coherent rural electoral base emerged as a result of its work. It did spawn the Nationwide Coalition of Fisherfolk for Aquatic Reform (NACFAR) in 1990, which has become a nationally acknowledged actor in its own right and has outlived CPAR.[22]

THE WOMEN'S *COMEDORES* MOVEMENT, PERU

The women's *comedores* movement was considered one of the most dynamic sectors of the Peruvian women's movement during the 1985–91 period. Composed of various federations representing community kitchens, including the Comision Nacional de Comedores (CNC), it moved beyond the *comedores'* traditional localized survival strategies and sought to influence national social policy.[23] The movement was the second episode in a sequence of state-society interactions set in motion during military rule in the late 1970s. The *comedores* won recognition as national actors, exercised a significant degree of sensitizing influence, and had a limited degree of substantive influence, including the enactment of new social legislation. Along with other popular movements in Peru, they also had a structural impact by building local-level solidarity among poor women and increasing their politicization. In the second period (1992–96), the movement effectively abandoned its political role and reverted to its pre-1985 focus on local survival strategies. Although the *comedores* remain, their influence at the national level has virtually disappeared. The CNC ceased to exist in 1996.

The Peruvian military surrendered power in 1980, and by mid-decade elite conflict was at a middling level, relative to both the 1986–92 period in the Philippines and the early 1990s in Peru. Alain García won the presidential election in 1985 with 53 percent of the vote and enjoyed overwhelming popular support in Lima. His party, the American Popular Revolutionary Alliance (APRA), held absolute majorities in both houses of Congress. The party system, for all its defects, effectively bounded political conflict. The civil-military relations were complex and difficult but did not threaten the stability of the new democratic regime.

Peru inherited a far more coherent and effective state apparatus in the 1980 democratic transition than the Philippines had after its transition.[24] Between 1985 and 1992, however, the Peruvian state experienced a gradual erosion of bureaucratic capacity and authority. When Alain García took office in 1985, he had an arguably middling to weak state bureaucracy at his command. As was the case in the Philippines, clientelist networks and patronage politics were pervasive in Peru. The centralization of power in the executive branch increased steadily after 1985 and further weakened other sectors of the state; it also limited social groups' access to policy-making centers. Although the state's authority faced a growing challenge from the Shining Path Maoist guerrilla movement in rural areas, particularly in the southern highlands, it was uncontested in urban areas until the end of the 1980s.

The state, however, did have extensive structural links to sectors of the urban poor. These included in particular the Programa de Apoyo Directo (PAD), a program created in 1986 to provide shanty towns with social services from primary health care to sports complexes. It also provided assistance to *comedores* with food donations, kitchen equipment, help with constructing buildings, and credit (Graham 1992, 178; van Wesemael-Smit 1988, 28). Government-sponsored *comedores* were organized under the control of PAD, which was itself administered directly from the presidential palace (Mujica 1994, 6; Blondet and Montero 1995, 262).

These new linkages developed at least in part because of the pressures that electoral competition placed on the populist ruling party, APRA. Peru during the 1980s had a highly competitive and polarized multiparty system. Although party leadership was personalized and, with a few exceptions, heavily reliant on patronage, the two dominant parties—APRA and the principal opposition party United Left (IU)—were among the few political institutions with mass-based legitimacy.[25] Roberts (1998, 202) observes that "after the transition to democratic rule (in 1980) Peru boasted the strongest and most successful electoral left in South America for most of the 1980s." Both parties had strong ties to the women's movement, although these ties differed substantially in nature and represented powerful potential allies for the movement. Many members of the movement were also active in party politics. The IU and APRA competed for the same urban constituencies, and the votes of the urban poor women were particularly important (Radcliffe 1988). The competition for this constituency led APRA to initiate PAD after García took office in 1985. In contrast to CPAR in the Philippines, therefore, electoral competition played a vital role in the emergence of the *comedores* coalition.

The APRA and IU had different strategies vis-à-vis poor urban women. The IU played a central role in creating a coalition among *comedores autogestionarios* (self-managed community kitchens), which stood at the center of the national *comedores* coalition.[26] The party sought to integrate itself into the daily lives of urban communities and develop densely networked, self-governing, grassroots organizations (Roberts 1998, 226). Its ties to such organizations, including the *comedores auto-*

gestionarios, were explicitly political and politicizing. In contrast, APRA established more paternalistic vertical ties to *comedores.* Unlike the IU and the NGOs that worked with the *comedores autogestionarios,* APRA exercised considerable control over the community groups it sponsored. The PAD was particularly important in this respect. It provided funds to *comedores* in exchange for loyalty to the party. Party cadres working for APRA acted as intermediaries between the *comedores* and the government and excluded other grassroots organizations from participating in the social program.

The availability of nonparty allies such as the Catholic Church, the women's movement, and NGOs also contributed to the emergence of the coalition. Church organizations and NGOs in particular provided the *comedores* federations with important support, including resources, training courses, and advice on various policy proposals that sought food subsidies, the elimination of food imports, and the organization of agricultural production in the river valleys near Lima (Barrig 1990, 379). In 1986, members of the feminist wing of the women's movement became involved in supporting the emerging coalition, which many considered to be part of the "popular wing" of the women's movement. Drawing partly on funds from overseas NGOs, they sought to educate members of the popular wing about women's rights. However, such efforts at coordination between the feminist and popular wings of the women's movement were episodic and stopped short of formulating a clear common agenda around which to make demands in the political arena (Blondet 1995, 265).

In 1986, the same year in which President García launched PAD, the *comedores* began to multiply their horizontal linkages. In fact, PAD provoked a concerted drive on the part of the movement to centralize its organization in order to assert its autonomy from the state and enter the political arena. One of the consequences of the new government program was that resources that would otherwise have been received by *comedores autogestionarios* were diverted to PAD *comedores* (Barrig 1990, 379). With the help of the IU and other groups, federations were formed first at the neighborhood level, then the district level, and finally at the metropolitan and national levels. The highest-level organization was the CNC. In this process, the *comedores autogestionarios* in particular sought to establish their autonomy from political parties, the middle-class institutions that supported the *comedores,* neighborhood organizations (primarily male dominated), and families (Barrig 1988, 107).

The movement grew, and in 1989 there were 62 *comedores* federations in Lima, bringing together hundreds of smaller organizations (Barrig 1988, 107).[27] By 1991, there were 5,112 *comedores* in Lima alone providing subsidized meals, with 200,000 women participants (Blondet 1995, 150; Vargas and Villanueva 1994, 582).[28] Supported by its allies, assisted by access to parties, and galvanized by APRA's vertical approaches to the grass roots, the *comedores* became political actors.

The influence of the coalition, as in the case of CPAR, was perhaps strongest at the procedural and sensitizing levels. The role of poor women in social reproduction was brought into the public domain and women who were subordinated economically, socially, and politically on the grounds of their gender won access to public forums, where they could, and did, articulate demands and question the status quo. The government and other political actors recognized the *comedores* movement as a national actor in the late 1980s. This recognition was put on legal footing in 1991, when legislation proposed by the CNC and its congressional allies (the IU in particular) was passed with broad support. Law 25307 called on the state to grant *comedores* legal status as "social base groups" and to create a fund to support them.[29] The CNC also influenced the "designing, planning and proposing of national food policies and social programs, and became the officially recognized representative of communal kitchens across the country" (Mujica 1994, 12). It participated, for example, in the design of the government's Social Emergency Program (PES), which targets the urban poor. One of its central demands has been the inclusion of all "poor" women—not just those with connections to the ruling party—in welfare programs.

The *comedores* had an impact on local power relations in the shanty towns and by extension a degree of structural influence. They "brought about changes in the private sphere by increasing the negotiating power and authority of women within their families" (CESIP 1987, cited in van Wesemael-Smit 1988) and contributed significantly to building solidarity among women. The networks of community kitchens provided opportunities to forge relationships with other women or, for some, to find an independent source of income. These networks represented a particular form of "social capital" that enhanced poor women's value as an electoral constituency.

Erosion of the State and Political Arena

A number of processes set in motion in the mid-1980s came to a head at the end of the decade to substantially alter the political environment in which the coalition operated. These changes, along with a savage economic recession, forced federations such as the CNC to retreat from their overtly political role and refocus on more localized survival strategies. The declining bureaucratic capacity of the state and the growing challenge to its authority from the Maoist guerrilla movement, the Shining

Path, in the late 1980s in particular placed substantial limits on the coalitions' substantive influence. This is reflected most vividly in the fact that in practice levels of funding for the kitchens actually fell.

State capacity had declined significantly by the late 1980s as a result of the concentration of power in the executive branch and APRA's reliance on patronage politics to maintain itself. The resulting erosion of policy-making capacity turned an economic recession into a national crisis. Wise (1997, 98), for example, observes that state financial institutions were marginalized from the policy-making process and the government abandoned "any pretence at national planning," relying heavily on "patronage and the meager expertise of those with close personal ties to the executive. By 1990 per capita public spending had shrunk by eighty-three percent compared to 1975, not least because the tax base had shrunk inexorably." High inflation turned into hyperinflation in 1988, and "a series of adjustment programs produced the most violent economic contraction in national history. . . . Per capita domestic product shrank by nearly thirty percent over the course of the 1980s, falling back to the level of 1960" (Roberts 1998, 236–7). Furthermore, by the end of the 1980s the Peruvian state had also lost its monopoly over the use of violence. Its authority was contested by the Shining Path in rural and urban areas, by the Tupac Amaru Revolutionary Movement (MRTA), and by right-wing death squads and civilian self-defense groups. All of these groups claimed the legitimate use of violence (Sagasti and Hernandez 1994, 24).

Elite conflict rose significantly and, together with mounting popular discontent and mobilization, culminated in a presidential coup in 1992. The ire of the business community and upper middle classes had been provoked in 1987 with the government nationalization of the banking system. Together with Popular Action and the PPC, these sectors began a virulent anti-APRA campaign. Peruvian author and presidential candidate Mario Vargas Llosa launched his own neoconservative assault, challenging "the organizations, platforms, and policies that grew from the state-centered matrix of the 1930s, blaming all political actors equally for Peru's decline" (Cotler 1995, 347). Civil-military relations became increasingly conflictual as well. The domestic war against the guerrilla movements increased the power of the military, which was made responsible for "emergency areas" that covered almost half of national territory. Political interference, tight budget constraints, and the growth of insurgent movements produced profound conflict between the military and the civil government as well as serious divisions within the military itself (342).

The Shining Path's expansion into urban areas after 1990 had a significant demobilizing effect on the *comedores* movement. The growth of the guerrilla movement was made possible in part by the weakness of the state, by the post-1986 rift between the government and the military, and by the severity of the economic crisis. The Shining Path sought to neutralize the self-managed organizations of the shanty towns, which it viewed as a significant obstacle to its revolutionary work. It made substantial inroads into the *comedores* movement, and dozens of community activists were assassinated, including those with strong ties to the IU (Obando 1998, 389–94).

Furthermore, the party system virtually collapsed in the period leading up to the 1990 presidential election. Ideological cleavages within the IU and APRA's declining popularity due to the widespread view that it was responsible for the economic and political crises which enveloped the country left the party system in disarray. The IU split in 1989 as the "guerrilla insurgency . . . drove IU moderates toward the political center at the same time that it reinforced the radicals' search for an alternative revolutionary project in civil society" (Roberts 1998, 263). APRA suffered severe internal polarization as well; it had supporters of the armed revolutionaries of both the MRTA and the counterrevolutionary paramilitary death squads of the Comando Rodrigo Franco (Graham 1992). The Peruvian people, reeling under the weight of a severe economic crisis and disenchanted with established parties, all of which were tainted by APRA's failings, voted in Alberto Fujimori under the party banner "Cambio 90"—more a collection of individuals than a political party.

The deep recession also contributed to the collapse of the party system and to building Fujimori's support among the urban poor (Cameron 1997, 37).[30] The economic crisis shifted significant segments of the working population into the informal sector. This process fragmented and destabilized political and community identities. The loyalties and identities of the informal sector workers, unlike the unionized and nonunionized factory workers of the late 1970s, were highly mobile. Informal workers were immersed in smaller socioeconomic networks and tended to make individual assessments when voting (Roberts 1998, 237–43). This undermined both APRA and the IU.

The state's institutional decline was reversed to some degree under Fujimori, who strengthened the state apparatus while cutting back its size and scope of activity. Fujimori fired thousands of state bureaucrats who allegedly owed their positions to party patronage in the 1980s, reformed the tax system and customs offices, and co-opted the military high command (Wise 1997, 98; Obando 1998). The government's structural adjustment policies, however, led to a significant decline in funding for social projects, stalled implementation of Law 25307 granting *comedores* legal status as "social base groups" altogether, and weakened the state-society linkages established during the 1980s. Furthermore, the presidential coup in 1992 led to an extreme concentration of power in the executive branch. After Fujimori disbanded regional governments and restructured the Congress and judiciary to guarantee the dominance of the executive, "the office of the presidency claimed a near monopoly over public works projects" (Roberts 1998, 267). The party system did not recover under these conditions.

In this context, the ability of the CNC and other federations to influence policy was very limited. The number of *comedores* continued to rise to counteract the food price increases and wage cuts brought about by structural adjustment, the removal of subsidies, and falling wages. Their efficacy as a national political actor, however, suffered a marked decline. On the one hand, the *comedores* had little access to the state as a result of the centralization of power in the executive branch, the collapse of the party system, and, after the 1992 presidential coup, the semi-democratic character of the regime. Its allies in the party system were greatly weakened and distant from power. Roberts (267) in fact suggests that the "once formidable Left . . . essentially disappeared as a national political force." On the other hand, the high levels of political violence and severe economic conditions put a stop to many of the *comedores'* political initiatives as they faced an "unprecedented demobilization" (Tanaka 1998).

CONCLUSION

The episodes of coalition building in the Philippines and Peru discussed here illustrate some of the processes through which collective actors emerge to represent poor social groups and some of the conditions under which such coalitions acquire national policy influence. The polity approach deployed to analyze the episodes highlights the contingent nature of these processes: that different combinations of political factors can lead to favorable opportunities for coalition building and that such opportunities do not always overlap with opportunities for influencing policy. It also reveals that virtually all of the factors highlighted by the approach underwent substantial change in the relatively short (ten-year) period examined (see table 1).[31] This high degree of flux reflects the fact that, unlike the relatively stable Western democracies, many of the Third Wave democracies are marked by high levels of political conflict over the basic parameters of the political system and hence by significant institutional change. The implications of this for the scope and types of change that enhance the opportunities for poor social groups to acquire leverage in national policy-making are manifold.

Two such implications deserve special attention. The first is that such flux profoundly affects the ability of such groups to negotiate and institutionalize their relationships with the state. CPAR and the *comedores* show that strengthening state authority, including the ability to maintain the rule of law and increased levels of bureaucratic coherence, helps to "empower" organizations of the poor. Coalitions representing poor social groups wielded the most substantive influence when state authority and bureaucratic coherence were at least middling. The relationship between coalition building, state authority, and bureaucratic coherence is more ambiguous. In the Philippines it appeared to have made little difference, perhaps because of countervailing factors such as the well-organized NGO sector and the dynamics associated with the democratic transition. In Peru, the decline of state authority and bureaucratic coherence contributed significantly to the coalition's retreat from high politics.

Engineering bureaucratic coherence writ large is a monumental task in both political and technical terms, and it is likely to require a dramatic and difficult break with the past. However, it is possible, through relatively incremental change, to create havens of bureaucratic capacity or, more ambitiously, islands of efficiency. In settings of relatively low bureaucratic coherence, political leaders often seek to "protect" particular state agencies from clientelist and other political pressures.[32] As Evans (1995, 61) observes, presidential protection plays a decisive role in keeping these islands from being flooded by waves of clientelism or other forms of political meddling. The survival of such islands is therefore contingent to a significant extent on the will of particular national leaders. The DAR in the Philippines was certainly not an island of efficiency, but under Ramos it did enjoy a degree of insulation from the political interventions that had undermined the agency's administrative capacity in prior years.[33] The consequences for the ability of peasant federations to negotiate and shape agrarian reform policy, discussed previously, were considerable.

The second implication is that high levels of political-institutional change influence the opportunities for coalitions to acquire elite allies, including allies within the state. There appears to be a curvilinear relationship between the level of elite conflict and the opportunities of poor groups to secure allies. Substantial elite conflict that is bounded by democratic political institutions—such as competitive party systems—creates important opportunities. This was the case in Peru between 1995 and 2000, when competition between APRA and the AD helped provoke a process of electoral bidding and community organizing. Very low levels of conflict may work to exclude poor claimants, but very high levels can produce regime breakdown, as occurred in Peru under Fujimori, producing exclusion of a different, perhaps harsher type.

NGO-brokered coalitions have become increasingly common in Third Wave democracies, particularly in national contexts such as the Philippines where party systems are poorly institutionalized. The CPAR example illustrates that NGOs can link disparate groups into broad coalitions and have helped formulate programmatic agendas. As Putzel (1998, 83–84) notes, such nonparty arrangements permit "more autonomous development vis-à-vis both the state and political organizations [and] facilitate access to foreign and government funds and provide expertise." In the case of CPAR, the coalition escaped the threat of having its goals displaced by broader party goals. However, it pressured for a narrow, if very important, set of issues and failed to create the organizational structures and collective identities necessary to keep the coalition intact over time (CPAR dissolved after less than six years) and to institutionalize access to policy-making centers. The latter is critical to ensure that short-term gains will become long-term policy and to lower the cost of future efforts to influence national policy. The CPAR experience in particular suggests that NGO-brokered coalitions have important limits as the functional equivalents of progressive parties.

The polity approach developed in this chapter points to two important areas for future research. The creation of structural linkages in particular policy areas is a short-term change within paths that can, under certain conditions (some of which are identified in this chapter), contribute to group formation and coalition building. As Whitehead and Gray-Molina find in Bolivia, and Herring notes in his chapter, structural linkages in the Philippines and Peru served as an important political axis around which the poor attempted to build alliances and make claims.[34] The Philippine peasant federations forged a broad coalition around Marcos's agrarian reform legislation and institutions. The *comedores* movement in Peru built a series of federations, including the CNC at the national level, around the social program, PAD. Structural linkages not only provide a readily apparent target for claim making, but they also determine which issues are subject to public policy and hence are objects of legitimate contestation in the political arena. We know that linkages do not produce the crystallization of coalitions and public demand making. What we need to learn more about is what types of linkages (in what policy areas and under what political conditions) may facilitate them.

The approach also suggests the need to explore how neoliberal state reforms—in particular, deregulation, privatization, and decentralization—may affect collective action and coalition building by the poor. Such reforms explicitly aim to move issues off the political agenda and into the marketplace, thereby depoliticizing them and narrowing the political arena. They reduce the density of structural linkages around which mobilization and coalition building can occur. The leverage of the poor in the marketplace, where material wealth determines outcomes, is of course very limited. There may be real efficiency gains to be achieved in pursuing such a strategy, but more research is needed on its potential to "disempower" the poor.

NOTES

The authors thank Mick Moore, Marcus Kurtz, James Putzel, Jun Borras, Cielito Goño, Virginia Vargas, Peter Newell, and Sarah Lister for providing much good advice.

1. World Bank (2000, 23) data indicate that between 1987 and 1998, a period when implementation of marketizing economic models was well advanced in many regions of the world, the share of people living in absolute poverty (under one dollar a day) rose slightly in Latin America and the Caribbean, from 15.3 to 15.6 percent, and in sub-Saharan Africa fell slightly from 46.6 to 46.3 percent. The countries of the former communist bloc saw a significant rise in absolute poverty, from 0.2 to 5.1 percent. World Bank data show that the share of population living in poverty is far higher if a poverty line of one-third of a country's average consumption level is used. The share of the population living below this poverty line in 1998 was: 51.4 percent in Latin America, 50.5 in sub-Saharan Africa, and 25.6 percent for the former communist countries.

2. Coalitions brokered by NGOs are of special interest because they have emerged in a number of the Third Wave democracies that are characterized by poorly institutionalized party systems, where political parties have generally failed to provide channels through which movements of the poor can influence state action.

3. This claim comes from the new institutionalism. See Hall 1986; Krasner 1984 (225); Kitschelt 1986 (61–62); Skocpol 1992 (54); and Thelen and Steinmo 1992 (8).

4. While allies support existing movements, institutional hosts attempt to create new movements by drawing disparate peoples into their organizational and ideological fields and redefining them as social groups. Hosts in effect seek to remake the political cleavages and reorient political contestation by organizing new actors. Unlike allies, hosts contribute in a critical way to the local social networks, organizational resources, and ideological frameworks needed to overcome the obstacles to collective action. The notion of the institutional host is developed in Houtzager 2000, 2001.

5. See, for example, Collier and Collier 1991; and Kitchelt 1986.

6. The most obvious example is the current widespread organizing around citizenship rights in the Third Wave democracies (Foweraker and Landman 1997).

7. Institutionalizing one's demands through legislation, Tilly, for example, observes, is "the ultimate touchstone of the value of political action" (cited in Tarrow 1998, 50). The reason is simple: legislation does "at a sweep what myriad of strikes, demonstrations, absenteeisms, featherbeddings, sit-ins, marches, assassinations, and prayer meetings [can] not, precisely because the latter [are] inevitably local or regional, episodic, and without legal force" (Anderson 1996,

13). The assumption is that laws are enforced across national territory with reasonable impartiality. This presumes an effective state organized along Weberian lines.

8. Thirteen Philippine peasant federations and a similar number of NGOs formed CPAR. The federations are Aniban ng Manggagawa sa Agrikultura (AMA), Pambansang Pederasyon ng Kababaihang Magbubukid (AMIHAN), Bahanggunian ng mga Maliliit na Mangingisda sa Lawa ng Laguna, Katipunan ng Bagong Pilipina (KABAPA), Kapatiran ng Malalayang Maliliit na Mangingisda ng Pilipinas (KMMMP), Kalipunan ng mga Samahang Mamamayan (KASAMA-FPO), Kilusang Magbubukid ng Pilipinas (KMP), Lakas ng Magsasaka Manggagawa at Mangingisda ng Pilipinas (LAKAS), Lakas ng Magsasakang Pilipino (LMP), National Federation of Sugar Workers and Food and General Trades (NSW-FGT), Pambansang Kilusan ng mga Samahang Magsasaka (PAKISAMA), Pambansang Lakas ng Kilusang Mamamalakaya ng Pilipinas (PAMALAKAYA), and United Farmers-Fishermen Association of the Philippines (UFFAP).

9. The dramatic growth of the NPA during the 1980s is directly related to the weakness of the state's military wing, the Armed Forces of the Philippines; the state's inability to deliver better services and public goods to rural communities; and the lack of formal political channels for making claims on the Marcos regime (Anderson 1988; Putzel 1992; Riedinger 1995).

10. The CPP made a halfhearted attempted to form such a party in 1986, the Partido ng Bayan (PnB), but it failed to attract the support of social democrats and democratic socialists, who saw it as an instrument of the CPP. The party's poor performance in the elections and the collapse of peace talks with the government that same year shut down the CPP's electoral experiment.

11. Tancangco (1988, 99) estimates that national democratic groups "totaled 50,000 full-time organizers operating in two-thirds of the country's provinces."

12. The commission formed by the government to produce a new constitution included a number of popular leaders, including Jaime Tadeo of the KMP, the peasant federation tied to the CPP.

13. The NGOs, however, were themselves not apolitical. Many, including those involved in the creation of CPAR, were tied to different political blocs (national democrats, different segments of the social democrats, and other leftist and center-leftist groups), which saw in CPAR a channel through which to pursue a broader political agenda.

14. One estimate put at $20 million the volume of money flowing to NGOs annually by 1991. Clarke (1995, 70) points out, however, that the influx of foreign donor money and the 1991 decentralization law that gave local officials discretion . . . led to a proliferation of NGOs created by "politicians, local government units, [and the] military" (Clarke 1995, 69, n. 14). See also Putzel 1998 (85).

15. The four national democratic organizations that participated in CPAR accounted for over half of the 1.5 million members it claimed to represent. They had strong reservations about joining the coalition but did so to ensure that they would not become further isolated after the CPP's 1986 election boycott fiasco and as a part of a united front strategy. Not included were conser-

vative federations that had had close ties to the Marcos regime (Goño 1997, 24).

16. Aquino herself was a member of one of the largest landowning families in the Philippines and had little personal inclination toward land reform.

17. The United States, which had long influenced government policy in the Philippines, was split on reform but generally favored conservative groups and strong counterinsurgency measures against the CPP/NPA (Putzel 1992, chap. 9).

18. The campaign's failure is at least in part attributable to the decision by the KMP and other national democrat organizations to launch their own nationwide land occupation campaign and by and large ignore the "people's' initiative."

19. I am indebted to Jun Borras for bringing to my attention Ernesto Garilao's influential position in the cabinet. Garilao headed the government's social reform agenda and was one of only two cabinet members to complete his full six-year term.

20. Ernesto Garilao, personal communication, August 1, 1999.

21. The collapse of CPAR had several causes. A number of federations opposed its efforts to strengthen its organization by reproducing the coalition at the regional and local levels. Its efforts to play a direct role in the presidential and congressional elections of 1992 created profound partisan divisions. Perhaps most importantly, the national democrats, facing declining influence among peasant groups even as that of the CPAR grew, "appeared to work actively to wind down the organization" (Putzel 1998, 96). Efforts by state agencies in the 1990s to institutionalize peasant representation by sponsoring their own peasant umbrella organizations also contributed to CPAR's dissolution. In order to gain access to state resources and decision makers a number of CPAR's federations participated in these new organizations.

22. Today NACFAR has eight federations and approximately 600,000 members.

23. The kitchens originally focused primarily on managing and distributing food donations from state agencies, church organizations, and international donors.

24. Military rule in Peru (1968–80) had strengthened the historically weak state, increased public expenditures, and promoted social rights and the organization of workers and peasants along corporatist lines (Cotler 1995, 333).

25. Other major parties included Popular Action (AP), which governed between 1980 and 1985, and the rightist Popular Christian Party (PPC). The 1979 Constitution granted the vote to all adults, including for the first time illiterates, and set the voting age at eighteen. These changes enfranchised the substantial Indian peasantry and significantly expanded the electorate (ibid., 337–38).

26. The IU was in reality an electoral coalition of several leftist parties. Of these, the Partido Unificado Mariateguista (PUM) was the most active in organizing community groups in urban lower-class neighborhoods (Roberts 1998, 229–30).

27. The CNC was set up at a conference held by the Episcopal Commission for Social Action (CEAS) where the central issue was autonomy vis-à-vis the state.

28. Unification of the community kitchens made negotiations for food sup-

plies, cooking equipment, and health campaigns for children more successful. It also increased the availability of educational workshops, which were "available in a myriad of subjects at the NGOs, through the central and local government, and in Catholic and other churches" (Barrig 1988, 107). In 1991, community kitchens served close to 1.5 million meals a day (106).

29. Law 25307 obliged the state to cover the expense of 65 percent of the food distributed by the *comedores,* to institutionalize *comedores'* access to the state through new Management Committees made up largely of representatives of the social-base organizations, and to create the Programa de Apoyo a la Labor Alimentaria de Las Organizaciones Sociales de Base (Cendoc, n.d.; Barrig 1998, 108).

30. The share of the population living below the poverty line rose to over 50 percent, and by 1991 real wages had dropped to 38.7 percent of their 1980 level.

31. Only the party system in the Philippines remained essentially unchanged during this period.

32. These are agencies that national leaders perceive as vital to the functioning of government or implementation of their agendas.

33. The DAR's enhanced capacity to act after 1992 was related at least in part to the strong relationship between its head and President Ramos. Ramos appointed a close associate and reformer as secretary of the DAR (Clarke 1995; Borras 1998, 26–27; Borras and Franco 1998).

34. For examples from Brazil and Chile, see Houtzager and Kurtz 2000.

REFERENCES

Anderson, Benedict R. 1988. "Cacique Democracy in the Philippines: Origins and Dreams," *New Left Review* 169:3–29.
———. 1996. "Elections and Participation in Three Southeast Asian Countries." In R. H. Taylor, ed., *The Politics of Elections in Southeast Asia.* Cambridge: Woodrow Wilson Center Press.
Barrig, Maruja. 1988. *De Vecinas a Ciudadanas: La Mujer en el Desarollo Urbano.* Lima: Sumbi.
———. 1990. "Women and Development in Peru: Old Models, New Actors." *Community Development Journal* 25, no. 4: 377–85.
———. 1998. "Female Leadership, Violence, and Citizenship in Peru." In J. Jaquette and S. Wolchik, eds., *Women and Democracy: Latin America and Central and Eastern Europe.* Baltimore: John Hopkins University Press.
Blondet, Cecilia. 1995. "Out of the Kitchens and onto the Streets: Women's Activism in Peru." In Amrita Basu, ed., *The Challenge of Local Feminisms: Women's Movements in Global Perspective.* Boulder: Westview.
Blondet, Cecilia, and Carmen Montero. 1995. "La Situacion de la Mujer." Study 68, Instituto de Estudios Peruanos, Lima.
Borras, Jun, and Jenny Franco. 1998. "A Critical Review of CARP and Its Accomplishments." *Philippines International Review* 1, no. 2.
Borras, Satumino M. 1998. "The Bibingka Strategy to Land Reform and Implementation: Autonomous Peasant Mobilizations and State Reformists in the Philippines." Working Paper 274, Institute of Social Studies, The Hague.

Cameron, Maxwell. 1997. "Political and Economic Origins of Regime Change in Peru: The Eighteenth Brumaire of Alberto Fujimori." In Maxwell A. Cameron and Philip Mauceri, eds., *The Peruvian Labyrinth: Polity, Society, and Economy*. University Park: Pennsylvania State University Press.

Canlas, Mamerto. 1988. "The Political Context." In Mamerto Canlas, Mariano Miranda Jr., and James Putzel, eds., *Land, Poverty, and Politics in the Philippines*. London: Catholic Institute for International Relations.

Castells, Manuel. 1996–98. *The Information Age: Economy, Society, and Culture*. 3 vols. Oxford: Blackwell.

Cendoc, Mujer. N.d. "Warmi: 25 anos de informacion sobre la mujer en la prensa escrita, 1970–1996." CDRom, Centro de Documentacion sobre la Mujer, Lima, Peru.

Clarke, Gerard. 1995. "Non-governmental Organisations (NGOs) and the Philippine State, 1986–93." *South East Asia Research* 3, no. 1: 67–91.

Collier, Ruth Berins, and David Collier. 1991. *Shaping the Political Arena: Critical Junctures, the Labor Movement, and Regime Dynamics in Latin America*. Princeton: Princeton University Press.

Cotler, Julio. 1995. "Political Parties and the Problems of Democratic Consolidation in Peru." In Scott Mainwaring and Timothy R. Scully, eds., *Building Democratic Institutions: Party Systems in Latin America*. Stanford: Stanford University Press.

Esping-Andersen, Gøsta. 1990. *The Three Worlds of Welfare Capitalism*. Princeton: Princeton University Press.

Evans, Peter. 1995. *Embedded Autonomy: States and Industrial Transformation*. Princeton: Princeton University Press.

———. 1996. "Government Action, Social Capital, and Development: Reviewing the Evidence on Synergy." *World Development* 24, no. 6: 1119–32.

Foweraker, Joe, and Todd Landman. 1997. *Citizenship Rights and Social Movements: A Comparative and Statistical Analysis*. Oxford: Oxford University Press.

Fox, Jonathan. 1992. *The Politics of Food in Mexico: State Power and Social Mobilization*. Ithaca: Cornell University Press.

———. 1996. "How Does Civil Society Thicken? The Political Construction of Social Capital in Rural Mexico." *World Development* 24, no. 6: 1089–1103.

Giugni, Marco. 1999. "How Social Movements Matter: Past Research, Present Problems, Future Developments." In Marco Giugni, Doug McAdam, and Charles Tilly, eds., *How Social Movements Matter*. Minneapolis: University of Minnesota Press.

Goño, Cielito C. 1997. *Peasant Movement–State Relations in New Democracies: The Case of the Congress for a People's Agrarian Reform (CPAR) in Post-Marcos Philippines*. Quezon City: Institute on Church and Social Issues.

Graham, Carol. 1992. *Peru's APRA: Parties, Politics, and the Elusive Quest for Democracy*. Boulder: Lynne Rienner.

Hall, Peter. 1986. *Governing the Economy: The Politics of State Intervention in Britain and France*. New York: Oxford University Press.

Hanagan, Michael. 1998. "Social Movements: Incorporation, Disengagement, and Opportunities—A Long View." In Marco G. Giugni, Doug McAdam, and

Charles Tilly, eds., *From Contention to Democracy*. Lanham, CO: Rowman and Littlefield.

Houtzager, Peter P. 2000. "Social Movements amidst Democratic Transitions: Lessons from the Brazilian Countryside." *Journal of Development Studies* 36, no. 5: 59–88.

———. 2001. "Collective Action and Patterns of Political Authority: Rural Workers, Church, and State in Brazil." *Theory and Society* 30, no. 1: 1–45.

Houtzager, Peter P., and Marcus Kurtz. 2000. "The Institutional Roots of Popular Mobilization: State Transformation and Rural Politics in Brazil and Chile, 1960–95." *Comparative Studies in Society and History* 42, no. 2: 394–424.

Kitschelt, Herbert P. 1986. "Political Opportunity Structures and Political Protest: Anti-nuclear Movements in Four Democracies." *British Journal of Political Science* 16:57–85.

Krasner, Stephen. 1984. "Approaches to the State: Alternative Conceptions and Historical Dynamics." *Comparative Politics* 16, no. 3: 223–46.

Kriesi, Hanspeter, Ruud Koopmans, Jan Willem Duyvendak, and Marco G. Giugni. 1995. *New Social Movements in Western Europe*. Minneapolis: University of Minnesota Press.

Lara, Francisco, and Horacio R. Morales Jr. 1990. "The Peasant Movement and the Challenge of Rural Democratisation in the Philippines." *Journal of Development Studies* 26, no. 4: 145–62.

Mainwaring, Scott. 1999. *Rethinking Party Systems in the Third Wave of Democratization*. Stanford: Stanford University Press.

McAdam, Doug. 1982. *Political Process and the Development of Black Insurgency, 1930–1970*. Chicago: University of Chicago Press.

McAdam, Doug, John D. McCarthy, and Mayer N. Zald, eds. 1996. *Comparative Perspectives on Social Movements: Political Opportunities, Mobilizing Structures, and Cultural Framings*. Cambridge: Cambridge University Press.

McAdam, Doug, Sidney Tarrow, and Charles Tilly. 2001. *Dynamics of Contention*. Cambridge: Cambridge University Press.

McCarthy, John D., and Mayer N. Zald. 1977. "Resource Mobilization and Social Movements: A Partial Theory." *American Journal of Sociology* 82:1212–41.

Melucci, Alberto. 1996. *Challenging Codes: Collective Action in the Information Age*. Cambridge: Cambridge University Press.

Migdal, Joel S., Atul Kohli, and Vivienne Shue, eds. 1994. *State Power and Social Forces: Domination and Transformation in the Third World*. Cambridge: Cambridge University Press.

Molyneux, Maxine. 1998. "Analysing Women's Movements." *Development and Change* 29:219–45.

Mujica, M. 1994. "Meals, Solidarity, and Empowerment: Communal Kitchens in Lima, Peru." Working Report 246, University of Massachusetts.

Obando, Enrique. 1998. "Civil-Military Relations in Peru, 1980–1996: How to Control and Coopt the Military (and the Consequences of Doing So)." In Steve Stern, ed., *Shining and Other Paths: War and Society in Peru, 1980–1995*. Durham: Duke University Press.

Oberschall, Anthony. 1973. *Social Conflict and Social Movements*. Englewood Cliffs, NJ: Prentice-Hall.

Putzel, James. 1992. *A Captive Land: The Politics of Agrarian Reform in the Philippines*. London: Catholic Institute for International Relations.

———. 1995. "Managing the 'Main Force': The Communist Party and the Peasantry in the Philippines." *Journal of Peasant Studies* 22, no. 4: 645–71.

———. 1998. "Non-governmental Organizations and Rural Poverty." In G. S. Silliman and L. G. Noble, eds., *Organizing for Democracy: NGOs, Civil Society, and the Philippine State*. Honolulu: University of Hawai'i Press.

Radcliffe, Sarah. 1988. "Asi es Una Mujer del Pueblo: Low-Income Women's Organisations under APRA, 1985–1987." Centre of Latin American Studies, University of Cambridge.

Riedinger, Jeffrey M. 1995. *Agrarian Reform in the Philippines: Democratic Transitions and Redistributive Reform*. Stanford: Stanford University Press.

Roberts, Kenneth M. 1998. *Deepening Democracy? The Modern Left and Social Movements in Chile and Peru*. Stanford: Stanford University Press.

Sagasti, Francisco, and Max Hernandez. 1994. "The Crisis of Governance." In J. Tulchin and G. Bland, eds., *Peru in Crisis: Dictatorship or Democracy*. Boulder and London: Lynne Rienner.

Sartori, Giovanni. 1976. *Parties and Party Systems: A Framework for Analysis*. Cambridge: Cambridge University Press.

Skocpol, Theda. 1992. *Protecting Soldiers and Mothers: The Political Origins of Social Policy in the United States*. Cambridge: Belknap Press of Harvard University Press.

Tanaka, M. 1998. "From Movimientismo to Media Politics: The Changing Boundaries between Society and Politics in Fujimori's Peru." In J. Crabtree and J. Thomas, eds., *Fujimori's Peru: The Political Economy*. London: Institute of Latin American Studies.

Tancangco, Luzviminda G. 1988. "The Electoral System and Political Parties in the Philippines." In Raul P. de Guzman and Mila A. Reforma, eds., *Government and Politics of the Philippines*. Singapore: Oxford University Press.

Tarrow, Sidney. 1998. *Power in Movement: Social Movements and Contentious Politics*. Cambridge: Cambridge University Press.

Tendler, Judith. 1997. *Good Government in the Tropics*. Baltimore: Johns Hopkins University Press.

Thelen, Kathleen, and Sven Steinmo. 1992. "Historical Institutionalism in Comparative Politics." In Sven Steinmo, Kathleen Thelen, and Frank Longstreth, eds., *Structuring Politics: Historical Institutionalism in Comparative Analysis*. Cambridge: Cambridge University Press.

Thompson, Mark R. 1995. *The Anti-Marcos Struggle: Personalistic Rule and Democratic Transition in the Philippines*. New Haven: Yale University Press.

———. 1996. "Putting 'People Power' Back Together Again: Some Puzzles from the Philippines." *Research on Democracy and Society* 3:397–415.

Tilly, Charles. 1978. *From Mobilization to Revolution*. New York: McGraw-Hill.

———. 1984. "Social Movement and National Politics." In Charles Bright and Susan Harding, eds., *Statemaking and Social Movements: Essays in History and Theory*. Ann Arbor: University of Michigan Press.

———. 1999. "From Interaction to Outcomes in Social Movements." In Marco

Giugni, Doug McAdam, and Charles Tilly, eds., *How Social Movements Matter*. Minneapolis: University of Minnesota Press.
van Wesemael-Smit, Lillian. 1988. *Communal Kitchens in Peru: Women's Groups Pursuing Their Interests in the Face of Interference*. Amsterdam: Free University, Institute of Cultural Anthropology and Sociology of Development.
Vargas, Virginia, and Victoria Villanueva. 1994. "Between Confusion and the Law." In B. J. Nelson and N. Chowdhury, eds., *Women and Politics Worldwide*. New Haven: Yale University Press.
Weir, Margaret, Ann Shola Orloff, and Theda Skocpol, eds. 1988. *The Politics of Social Policy in the United States*. Princeton: Princeton University Press.
Wise, Carol. 1997. "The Institutional Backdrop: Whither Civil Society? The Limits to a Strong-Executive, Weak-State Approach." In Maxwell A. Cameron and Philip Mauceri, eds., *The Peruvian Labyrinth: Polity, Society, and Economy*. University Park, PA: Pennsylvania State University Press.
World Bank. 2000. *World Development Report, 2000–2001*. Oxford: Oxford University Press.

5 Grounds for Alliance?

OVERLAPPING INTERESTS OF POOR
AND NOT SO POOR

Joan M. Nelson

Peter Houtzager's introduction to this volume advocates a polity-based approach to the politics of inclusion. An important component of that approach is the complex interaction between the state and public policy, on the one hand, and the evolving capability of groups in society to develop their own identity, organize, and make political alliances. This chapter focuses on the possibilities for public policy to encourage, and to be sustained by, a specific kind of pro-poor alliance, one based on shared interests between some among the poor and some slightly higher on the income ladder. The potential of such alliances may be growing in many countries, as democratization spreads and lower middle class groups become more organized and vocal.

Pro-poor reformers tend to be suspicious of such alliances. Since resources are limited (the more so, the poorer the country), it makes sense to target programs tightly to those most in need. Moreover, especially in less than wealthy countries, broad-gauged programs ostensibly serving much of the population often shortchange the poor. Therefore, for the past two decades much of the international development community has strongly favored tightly targeted programs as the major direct approach to poverty reduction. This chapter argues for a reappraisal of these assumptions. More encompassing or universal programs are often easier to launch and sustain and may attract more generous local funding. Under such circumstances, pro-poor reformers should consider a wider menu of options, including augmenting and modifying the design of broad programs or embedding targeted components in them rather than thinking largely or solely in terms of tightly targeted but more vulnerable approaches.

The argument rests on two sets of propositions. The first set is political and concerns the relative political influence of poor versus middle strata and the politics of tightly targeted versus broader economic and social programs. The second set concerns the degree to which the poor share needs and interests with the not so poor. The first and second sections of this chapter discuss these issues in turn. The third section briefly explores the relevance of alliances between the poor and the middle strata for different kinds of policies and programs.

A major caveat should be stated at the outset. The terms *poor* and *middle strata* are used in this discussion as shorthand. As the next section discusses, using income statistics to define both categories is arbitrary. The boundary between the categories is artificial, and there is a great deal of movement across that line and indeed among all income groups. Moreover, the political logic of the chapter rests on assumed correlations between relative and absolute income, on the one hand, and social and political relations, attitudes, and behavior on the other. But both low-income and slightly better off strata are highly heterogeneous in most countries. Broad qualitative generalizations are risky. Despite these caveats, the chapter points to patterns that can be observed in many countries, with important implications for the politics of poverty-reduction efforts.

THE POLITICAL LOGIC OF ALLIANCES
BETWEEN POOR AND MIDDLE STRATA

DEFINITIONS AND CONCEPTS

The concepts of "poor" and "middle" strata are central to this discussion. But they are difficult concepts to pin down. Definitions based on national official poverty lines are arbitrary. Are the poor those whose incomes are half the median income of all citizens? Three-quarters? Are they those who must spend half of their income on food? Two-thirds? Eighty percent? Because definitions are arbitrary, groups designated as poor vary tremendously in living standards and social and political character, even across countries with similar per capita incomes.

Moreover, the concept of the poor refers not only to degrees of material deprivation but to nonmaterial correlates such as education, social status, and dependence. Indeed, for this chapter absolute income levels are much less important than social and political characteristics that indicate how different groups relate to the larger communities and national societies in which they are embedded and their accompanying attitudes and predispositions toward political action. Despite wide variations across countries in the status and characteristics of the lowest income groups, and despite heterogeneity within any one country, there is almost always a correlation between low absolute and relative income (especially durable or long-term as distinct from transitory poverty), levels of education, social status, and social relationships. In almost all societies, those near the bottom of the income scale tend to feel politically ineffective, dependent, or alienated. They often view politics as irrelevant, incomprehensible, or threatening. They are rarely well informed and organized for political action. They are difficult for political parties to mobilize. When they attempt—as individuals or groups—to express opinions or press for solutions to their problems, local officials and elites tend to pay little attention or directly or indirectly to suppress the attempts.

The concept of "middle strata" is even more ambiguous. The term is used here to avoid the connotations of *middle class,* which in developing countries often designates people in the top 10 or 20 percent of the income distribution. Middle strata are somewhat better off and less insecure materially than the poor. They are more likely to be literate and to have completed primary school; they enjoy more respect in their communities. But, as with the poor, their character varies tremendously across and within countries. In Latin American cities, the middle strata include much of what is sometimes labeled the "urban mass." Many of the poor eke out a living as day laborers or itinerant peddlers and rent a room, or part of a room, in a tenement. In contrast, many of the middle strata are semiskilled manual workers in medium or large industries or service establishments or licensed vendors with a permanent sidewalk or market stall; they may "own" a house in a squatter settlement. In much of rural India, the bulk of the poor are the landless and those with scraps of land too small to feed their families. Middle strata generally include those with barely enough land to feed their families, plus some of the nonfarming artisans. As countries gradually become richer, more urban, and less agricultural, middle strata tend to meld into more familiar (though almost as vague) designations of "working class" and "lower middle class."

Neither national official poverty lines nor standardized cross-national measures of poverty necessarily—or even probably—mesh with this more qualitative concept of the poor. To illustrate, in 1993 Poland defined poor households as those with monthly per capita expenditures less than 77 percent of the national average. That definition drew a high line: it included 37.5 percent of all households. In Estonia in 1995, the poverty line was much lower, at 39 percent of average monthly per capita expenditures. Only 2.8 percent of households met this description (Milanovic 2000, 2, 21). Yet gross national product (GNP) per capita for Poland and Estonia were similar (World Bank 1997, 215),[1] and Estonia's income distribution (in 1995) was less egalitarian than Poland's in 1992 (Gini coefficients of 35.4 and 27.2, respectively).[2] Estonian households just above the (very low) poverty line may not fit the qualitative socioeconomic concept of middle strata sketched earlier. The reverse holds in

Poland, where many of those classified as poor probably have connections, attitudes, and behavior that correspond to the concept of middle strata.

Standardized absolute measures of poverty—for instance, poverty lines defined as less than one (or sometimes two) dollars per day per person, with money and estimated nonmoney income adjusted for purchasing power parity across nations—also have no consistent relationship with the sociopolitical correlates of class described here. In some countries (mainly in sub-Saharan Africa), more than half the population subsists on less than a dollar a day. In the early 1990s, according to World Bank data, 87 percent of Indians, 58 percent of Chinese, a surprising 55 percent of Costa Ricans and Czechs, and as high or higher percentages in many other countries were estimated to be living on less than two dollars a day (World Bank 1997, 66–68, table 2.7).[3] One strongly suspects that many of these people correspond more closely to the sociopolitical description of middle strata than poor in terms of their relations in their communities and their political attitudes and behavior.

One further observation is extremely important in thinking about the concepts and relationships of poor and middle strata. Neither category is static: typically, there is considerable movement into and out of the category defined as poor. Data for the United States show that about half of families with incomes in the lowest fifth in 1967 had moved to higher income brackets by 1979 and almost half of those in the poorest fifth in 1979 were better off by 1991. In both time periods, about 22 percent of those initially in the second quintile had fallen into the bottom fifth by the end of the period, while just over half had risen into higher income categories (Fields 2000, 107). In Peru, survey data indicate that roughly a fifth of respondents remained poor between 1991 and 1996, while another two-fifths were never poor. But during these five years a quarter moved up out of poverty and another 15 percent slid into poverty (Graham and Pettinato 1999, app. C–1). In terms of the experience of a great many individuals and households, the boundary between poverty and nonpoverty is not only fuzzy but highly permeable. Indeed, much of the middle strata at any time may have been poor earlier, and many may feel vulnerable to sliding into poverty in the future. I return a little later to some of the probable political implications of that fact.

RELATIVE POLITICAL INFLUENCE AND SHARED VERSUS COMPETING INTERESTS

For this discussion, the key point is that middle strata are, in general, less powerless politically than the poor—probably the long-term poor in particular. Middle strata tend to be less dependent, more self-confident, better informed, and better connected. They are more likely to belong to various kinds of associations, including some, like squatters', vendors', or parents' associations, set up in part to interact with local officials. For all of these reasons, middle strata are more likely than the poor to be politically articulate and active.

More tentatively: in many poor and middle income countries middle strata may have been gaining in political influence in the past several decades. This trend is reinforced by urbanization, education, and the spread of civil society. Political liberalization in much of the developing world during the 1980s and 1990s may well have further boosted political participation by middle strata in a greater degree than by the poor. Where elections are somewhat competitive, political parties give at least some attention to middle strata demands. More generally, growing middle strata sophistication and activism create incentives for political elites to heed their needs.[4]

Given that middle strata usually have more political weight than the poor, are they potential competitors or allies? There is no simple answer. One can think about the question from several different standpoints. One approach focuses on the goals and concerns of individuals and households that flow from the ways in which they earn their livelihoods and the circumstances of their daily lives: housing, risks of crime or fire, and access to services and facilities. Sometimes livelihood and living circumstances generate conflicts between poor and middle strata. For example, vendors with licensed market stalls may seek to restrict or ban poorer itinerant vendors from the area. Or poor and middle-strata residents of separate but nearby neighborhoods may compete for priority in extending water or electricity lines. But under other circumstances interests may converge. Landless labor and sub-subsistence farmers share an interest in low food prices. Poor and middle-strata neighbors in mixed income neighborhoods have common interests in better roads, water supplies, electricity, or clinics. The second section considers more systematically some of the factors that determine conflicting or overlapping interests.

The considerable mobility into and out of poverty mentioned earlier provides a second perspective on shared concerns of the poor and not so poor. Here the central point is a common sense of vulnerability. High mobility means that many in the middle strata feel vulnerable to sliding into poverty sometime in the not too distant future. Indeed, in a recent essay Pritchett, Suryahadi, and Sumarto (2000) estimated vulnerability to poverty. They measured variation in household expenditures over time and calculated the proportion of the population facing a fifty-fifty chance of falling into poverty over varying periods of time. Defining a poverty line such that 20 percent of the population is poor, they used data from panel surveys of household expenditures in one hundred Indonesian towns and villages in the late 1990s and concluded that more than half the surveyed population faced even odds of becoming poor in the following three years. Their estimates are of course subject to a great many caveats regarding data and would also vary if they were calculated for different parameters (e.g., for time period). Nonetheless, the findings are striking: the vulnerable population, as they had defined it, was more than double the currently poor.

In hard times, larger numbers slide into poverty. (The data Pritchett and his coauthors use were collected in the midst of Indonesia's depression in the late 1990s and probably reflect unusually high income variability and risks of downward mobility.) Memories of hard times, and the influence of such memories on politics, may linger long after the crisis is past. The experience of the Great Depression of the 1930s shaped the thinking and attitudes of at least one generation in the United States. Hyperinflation in Germany after World War I seared not only those who lived through it but their children as well. Argentine hyperinflation in the late 1980s and early 1990s may have similarly long-lived effects. Thus, even in fairly good times the behavior, including specific political reactions, of much of a country's population may be shaped partly by echoes of the past. It seems plausible that those middle strata most vulnerable to sliding into poverty in hard times may continue to worry about vulnerability even when objective risks diminish. Therefore, they may be particularly interested in programs and policies that reduce risks or offer safety nets.

Similar goals and concerns among poor and middle strata do not necessarily generate political alliances. As noted earlier, they may compete for limited resources available to address their common problems. For example, in poor countries schools and clinics are inadequate or lacking in many rural areas. Allocation of funds for education and health is often influenced by political patronage or community pressure, and the poorest areas are likely to lose out to the slightly better off. Sometimes, however, poor and middle strata do form alliances to press for programs serving their shared needs or politicians or technocrats devise such programs and succeed in winning broad-gauged political support. This discussion seeks to direct more attention to this last possibility.

THE POLITICS OF TARGETED VERSUS BROAD PROGRAMS

Policies or programs targeted at the poor alone rarely attract broad and sustained political support. There are obvious exceptions to this generalization. Major parties' ideological traditions may lead them to favor significant pro-poor measures, as Social Democratic and Christian Democratic parties in many West European and some Latin American countries have done. For instance, since the early 1970s Costa Rica has funded (from payroll taxes) a special Investment Fund and an institute focused on poverty reduction. The design of specific pro-poor initiatives also affects prospects for adoption and survival. Measures narrowly focused on the deserving or appealing poor (e.g., poor or ill children) are often more politically feasible and sustainable than programs targeted at the poor more generally. For example, in the United States during the 1980s and 1990s the Head Start Program directed to disadvantaged preschool children continued to be supported despite the broader anti-welfare trend.

Despite these exceptions, even in wealthy democracies where resource constraints are much less binding, programs targeted at the poor alone are often regarded with suspicion. They are often funded meagerly from the outset and are vulnerable to cutbacks when fiscal pressures mount. In contrast, more encompassing programs that also significantly benefit the poor, such as social security or national health insurance programs, have proved extremely resilient politically. Even in those countries where social programs are shaped by strong Social Democratic or Christian Democratic traditions, the bulk of spending is channeled to broad programs such as education, health, and social security. Many of the universal social insurance programs that form the core of the Western European and Anglo-American welfare states have also proved highly effective in reducing poverty, though frequently at high cost.[5] Similarly, Costa Rica and Uruguay, with their extensive social insurance and assistance programs, have been very successful in reducing poverty and inequality.

The history of attempts to target rice subsidies in Sri Lanka makes a similar political point. During World War II, rice subsidies had been introduced for the entire population. The fiscal burden soon mounted, but efforts to trim the program proved to be politically disastrous until the late 1970s. Then several factors coincided to permit change. In a context of prolonged economic stagnation and political turmoil, a reformist government was elected with a strong majority. Opposition parties were in disarray. Favorable weather and international prices provided some leeway. Politically influential rice farmers supported reform. In 1978, the government successfully discontinued the rice subsidy for the top half of the population. The following year it converted the remaining subsidies to a food stamp system. Then, and again in 1985, it tried to target the benefits more tightly to the poorest third. Those attempts failed. In democratic Sri Lanka, under unusually favorable circumstances, it was feasible to convert a universal to a broadly targeted program but not to cut benefits for the middle sectors in order to increase benefits for the poor.[6]

More generally, universal or broad-based social insurance programs address the problems of mobility and vulnerability much more effectively than targeted programs do. Universal health services and workmen's compensation programs reduce the risks or costs of illness and accidents, which often push households into poverty (Graham and Pettinato 1999). Similarly, universal unemployment compensation, or in poorer countries work relief programs that not only reach the destitute but are available and acceptable to unemployed middle strata, may prevent the exhaustion of family resources that can convert a temporary rough patch into a long-term disaster.

The broad lesson is clear: politically, universal programs or those that serve both poor and middle strata are likely to be easier to launch and sustain than are more tightly targeted measures. Targeted measures embedded within broader programs may also be more feasible, politically, than similar measures on a stand-alone basis. For example, nutrition programs directed at poor mothers and infants are often embedded in broader programs intended to expand and improve clinic facilities in poor rural and urban areas. The clinics serve a broad swathe of the population, but only those mothers and infants found to be mal- or under-nourished are given nutritional supplements.

As the example suggests, many programs are in fact broadly targeted to somewhat less well off groups rather than tightly focused on the poor, precisely because the politics (and often the administration) are easier. The central proposition in this chapter is not that such programs can or should constitute an adequate poverty-reduction strategy in and of themselves. The suggestion is more modest: the political advantages of the approach recommend it for more frequent and explicit attention by policymakers and external aid agencies.

ADVANTAGES AND DRAWBACKS OF ENCOMPASSING PROGRAMS AND POLICIES

As a partial poverty-reduction strategy, there are several clear advantages to pursuing broader programs or embedding pro-poor measures in programs that serve a broader swathe of the public. First, broad programs with wide political support are less vulnerable to attrition or abandonment than tightly targeted programs. The latter are often put in place by a dedicated pro-poor minister or other official and/or at the urging and with the support of external aid agencies. Frequently such programs are orphaned when their original local sponsor is pushed from or leaves that particular position or when the outside agency that initially provided support (and often guidance) moves on to other projects.

Second, targeting is often difficult and costly to achieve in practice. Means testing to determine eligibility for a benefit, whether administered by officials or local community committees, demands considerable time and effort and often arouses controversy. Moreover, many people who are not eligible will look for ways to evade the requirements, and they are likely to become increasingly sophisticated and successful.[7] Leakage to the nonpoor is sometimes so great that only a small fraction of benefits reaches those for whom they are intended. "Embedding" pro-poor measures in broader programs automatically eases the problems of determining and enforcing eligibility, although there will remain problems of ensuring that the poor receive a reasonable share of benefits.

Third, the rationale for targeting is primarily financial. Where resources are limited (or, more precisely, where total budgets are assumed fixed), targeting channels funds to the places where they are most needed. But there is a political counterargument. Legislatures, and politicians in general, may be willing to approve much larger budgets for popular broad programs than for targeted ones. The difference in expenditures may be so great that the poor will draw more benefits from their limited share of the big programs than from the entire budget of targeted programs. That possibility is well recognized among poverty reduction specialists. The theoretical parameters have been developed in some detail.[8] Yet the possibility is seldom considered in discussions of concrete poverty reduction strategies or programs.

Fourth, more encompassing programs are more compatible with social solidarity. They are less likely to stigmatize the poor and encourage mentalities disparaging them among the better off. Moreover, low-income people are more likely to seek out and use services and programs that do not set them off from other citizens. Quality standards are also likely to be higher when programs are not directed solely to the poor.

Notwithstanding these advantages, broader programs, with or without embedded, specific pro-poor features, also have major drawbacks. Most obviously, they cost more. In low-income countries, many of the needed measures are out of reach financially, even with partial funding from user fees. The choice may lie between extremely partial and modest measures spread across a broad clientele and somewhat more adequate measures targeted at those most in need.

Looser targeting reduces the costs of identifying those eligible for benefits, and universal programs eliminate such costs. But these approaches are likely to exacerbate a related problem: the risk that the poor will be shouldered aside in the actual allocation of benefits for which both poor and not so poor are eligible. When benefits are directly allocated to individuals or households (usually in the form of subsidies or direct assistance or sometimes microcredit), the somewhat better off are often more aware of opportunities, better connected and informed regarding procedures to be followed, and more persistent in overcoming bureaucratic glitches than are the poor. In principle, these advantages could be counterbalanced by special efforts to reach the poor to inform

them of their rights and opportunities. In practice, this rarely happens. At
the level of collective community benefits available to all—for instance,
piped water, electricity, feeder roads, or schools—a similar problem
emerges. Since resources are always limited, government agencies determine the allocation of such collective goods to specific regions, districts,
cities, or neighborhoods. At this level, too, those with better information,
connections, and confidence are more likely to go to the head of the
queue. Organized collective action and citizens' pressures may also
influence the allocation of collective benefits; middle strata are more
likely than the poor to form such organizations and exercise such pressures.

These drawbacks suggest that a strategy of seeking and addressing
overlapping needs of poor and middle strata is a partial strategy, not a
replacement for more conventional approaches. But the substantial
advantages of the strategy, for some goals and in some contexts, suggest
the value of explicitly considering the approach as part of a larger menu
of pro-poor options. Indeed, as noted earlier, because of the political
advantages, programs that benefit middle strata along with some among
the poor are not unusual. But explicit attention to the approach as part
of the anti-poverty arsenal is less common, and therefore such programs
often are not selected and designed so as to optimize their potential for
reducing poverty, while preserving their greater political robustness.[9]

WHAT FACTORS DETERMINE THE SCOPE OF OVERLAPPING INTERESTS OF THE POOR AND MIDDLE STRATA?

How much scope is there for a strategy of poverty reduction through
broad rather than tightly targeted programs? Since broader programs are
usually more costly than those focused on the poor, national (or state or
local) fiscal constraints partly determine the scope of the approach. Still
more fundamental is the extent and nature of overlapping needs and
interests among poor and middle strata.

A word of clarification: some overlap is consistent with considerable
divergence. The ten or twelve most important needs or problems con-
fronting a sample of poor households will almost surely differ from a list
drawn up by middle strata households. (There would also be substantial
variation in the priorities of different poor households. A bit less obviously, different members of the same household—men and women,
young and old—might draw up rather different lists.) The key question
for the purposes of this discussion is whether certain issues or problems
affect the welfare both of many poor households and many middle strata
households without necessarily having the same priority in both.

We can guess that the extent and character of overlapping needs and concerns vary widely, both among nations and in different regions and settings within each nation. Despite the scarcity of useful empirical data (discussed a little later in this section), we can offer educated guesses about the characteristics in an economy and society likely to generate shared interests among poor and middle strata. In general, overlap is likely to be greater where the following conditions exist.

1. The gap between the incomes and lifestyles of many of the poor and much of the middle strata is modest. If poverty lines were drawn in rough accord with the social and political characteristics already discussed, this could be expressed as an income distribution concentrated just above and just below the poverty line rather than being more widely dispersed or polarized.
2. Poor and middle strata are intermingled geographically.
3. Poor and middle strata have complementary rather than competing patterns of income generation.
4. Ethnic, religious, and other group identities cut across rather than coincide with income categories.

CONCENTRATED RATHER THAN DISPERSED PATTERNS OF INCOME DISTRIBUTION

Income alone does not adequately define poverty, but households with similar incomes (adjusted for the size and age composition of households) are likely to have partly similar needs. Income distribution profiles vary even among countries with similar average per capita incomes. For the question of overlapping or diverging interests, the most important feature of the income distribution profile is not overall inequality (e.g., as measured by the Gini coefficient) but whether a sizable fraction of the population has incomes closely clustered somewhere toward the lower end of the distribution rather than flatter or more polarized patterns. If we knew that a country's official poverty line roughly coincided with the kinds of sociopolitical groups described earlier, we could measure how much of the population had incomes within a band from (say) 25 percent below to 25 percent above the poverty line. Other things being equal, exploiting overlap as a poverty reduction strategy will be more relevant in countries where a sizable fraction of the population falls within that band.

SPATIAL INTERMINGLING OR SEGREGATION

The geographical distribution or spatial location of the poor and middle strata also affects the extent and nature of overlapping interests. Where both groups live in the same fairly small communities or the same urban neighborhoods, both are affected by the quantity, quality, and costs of public services and facilities for the locality: water and electricity, roads and public transport, schools and clinics, and police and fire protection. Whether poor and middle strata live and work intermingled or segregated reflects factors such as landholding and cultivation patterns or the pace and process of urbanization. A rural region with many smallholders and some landless labor is more likely to mix poor and middle strata than a rural region dominated by large estates. Residential districts in some towns and cities are far more segregated by income group than others. In some countries, many of the poor are concentrated in particular geographical regions; in others they are more evenly distributed.

Spatial segregation makes programs targeted at the poor easier to design and administer. But spatial segregation may also reduce the odds that improvements for poor neighborhoods or communities are approved, adequately financed, and sustained. There are always choices to be made regarding precisely where to locate any new or improved public facility or service. Sharp income segregation increases the probability that areas where middle or higher strata dominate will exercise more political clout and crowd out the needs of largely poor areas. Conversely, where many of the poor live interspersed with middle strata, alliances are far more likely.

The point applies at all levels of aggregation, from locating water outlets in a neighborhood to allocating central funds among states or regions. However, in general the smaller the scale of the geographic unit the more likely it is that the poor will really benefit from programs or facilities directed to both poor and middle strata. Many national governments make some effort to redistribute resources in favor of poorer regions, at least in part to improve equity. But regional elite and middle classes as well as middle strata usually dominate the actual utilization of such funds, so that the poor get little or nothing (Lipton and Ravallion 1995). In contrast, at the level of the urban neighborhood sheer geographical proximity makes it difficult to exclude the poor from the benefits of improved facilities or services.[10]

EARNINGS AND CONSUMPTION PATTERNS

The extent and content of overlapping interests among poor and middle strata are also affected by earnings and consumption patterns. As was discussed earlier, many lower middle-strata workers share with most of the poor the vulnerability that results from unstable incomes. In addition, poor and middle-strata workers engaged in similar economic activities may share specific livelihood-related interests. For example, landless rural laborers are concerned with agricultural wages and low food prices. Marginal farmers, who do not grow enough food to meet their needs, usually favor low food prices. They are often also interested in higher agricultural wages, since they do not hire help and are likely to augment precarious farm incomes by working as wage laborers. Usually, neither group is particularly interested in subsidies for farm inputs, since marginal farmers are unlikely to purchase many of them. Thus, landless laborers (the poor) and marginal farmers (the slightly better off) may share an agenda quite different from the goals of small and larger farm owners who seek higher prices for crops in general, lower input prices, and low wages for labor.[11]

But the economic, social, and institutional details of specific localities and crops may generate different configurations of interests. In parts of India, for instance, Green Revolution technology increases output even on marginal farms more than enough to compensate for the costs of purchased inputs. Thus, marginal farmers may share their richer neighbors' interest in reduced prices for inputs and be ambivalent regarding increased producer prices for food. Moreover, social status interests also influence behavior. "A landholder, however marginal, may simply choose to identify with the landed classes rather than the landless" (Varshney 1995, 131). The opportunities for livelihood-based alliances between poor and middle strata therefore depend on highly specific and sometimes complex details.

ETHNIC, RELIGIOUS, OR OTHER SOCIAL TIES

Ethnic, religious, and other nonclass identities may reinforce or cut across divisions between poor and middle strata. The reluctance of many Indian marginal farmers, themselves net food purchasers, to align themselves politically with the landless is strongly reinforced by the fact that most agricultural laborers are Dalits (former untouchables) or come from other extremely low caste groups (Varshney 1995, 135). In other settings, ethnic or "home place" ties may have the opposite effect of strengthening the ties between the poor and the somewhat more fortunate. In many African cities, poor and better-off migrants who have come from a particular rural area to the same city belong to tribal or home place associations that help newcomers and poorer members meet job, housing, and other needs. Home place associations also often provide a basis for political organization.

To summarize, structural features largely determine the extent and nature of overlapping interests between poor and middle strata. Income distributions concentrated just below and above an "appropriate" poverty line will be associated with more overlap than income distributions that are more widely dispersed or polarized. Spatial distributions that mix rather than segregate poor and middle strata will generate more overlap of interests. So will complementary rather than competing patterns of income generation. Overlapping interests will be reinforced by ethnic and other group identities that cut across rather than coincide with income categories. Overlap in turn is hypothesized to affect the political ease or difficulty of introducing and sustaining measures that benefit the poor jointly with middle strata. Other factors obviously intervene at this second stage. For example, given two countries with similar degrees of overlapping interests, political institutions may encourage building political alliances between poor and middle strata in one but discourage such alliance building in the other.

SOURCES OF INFORMATION ON OVERLAPPING INTERESTS

The propositions just sketched strongly suggest that there are substantial overlapping interests between the poor and not so poor in most countries, even though the extent and character of overlap will vary widely. Researchers and reformers have given little attention to overlapping interests. To actually pursue the lines of strategy and program design suggested in this chapter requires detailed knowledge of living and earning conditions, access to services and facilities, and perceived priorities among different groups toward the lower end of the income scale. In some countries, at least some relevant data are available. In others, data would have to be collected, but it is not difficult to envisage how to do so.

In a fair number of countries, national household surveys provide data that could help to identify the similarities and contrasts in life situations among the poor and the slightly better off. Household surveys typically collect data on household composition, sources of income and nature of employment, and patterns of expenditure. They are also likely to inquire about access to public services and status with regard to education, health, and housing. The data can be arrayed by income categories and disaggregated by urban versus rural location to provide a fair idea of contrasts between households in the lowest income (or expenditure) brackets and those a step or two better off.

Household surveys, however, do not provide information on the subjective or perceived priorities that people in different income categories assign to various issues. In principle, opinion surveys can provide this complementary information. While the use of well-designed and well-executed opinion surveys is spreading, two problems limit their utility for identifying overlapping interests among the poor and middle strata. First, opinion surveys are less likely than household surveys to provide data on income. Sometimes they include data that permit constructing estimated or proxy indices of wealth, but some uncertainty remains about the accuracy of the estimates.[12] Second, attitude surveys do not usually include questions about respondents' own problems and priorities in forms that would be useful for assessing overlap between poor and middle strata. Surveys often include questions about "the most important problems the country faces" or "the most important problems the government should address." Questions framed this way give only very general indications of people's perceived needs, but they can nevertheless provide some information on which issues are a high priority for those at all (or almost all) income levels: common examples are employment, high prices (inflation), crime, and unfair or corrupt law enforcement and systems of justice.

LatinoBarometro, an annual survey conducted in almost all Latin American countries, asks respondents what they view as the most important problem in the country. Replies in 1998 were examined for four countries—Bolivia, Chile, Costa Rica, and Peru. In all four, unemployment and education were mentioned most frequently. There are sizable contrasts among the countries in the emphasis given to these and other issues. However, within each country respondents' socioeconomic status rarely had a clear and systematic influence on the problems they viewed as most severe at the national level. In Chile, roughly 18 percent of the total sample cited unemployment as the biggest problem; that proportion varied only slightly across five categories of (estimated) income and socioeconomic status. In Bolivia, a remarkably uniform 25 to 29 percent of respondents in the five income categories named education as the country's biggest problem.[13] These surveys may well fail to represent the views of the full range of income categories. Representativeness of the samples is gauged at only 48 percent for the Bolivian sample, ranging up to 67 percent for the Chilean sample.[14] The poorest are those most likely to be missed. More generally, opinion surveys rarely ask the more precise questions that would be most useful for assessing overlapping needs, such as "What are the most important problems your family (or your neighborhood or community) faces now?" and "What are the most pressing needs the government could help with?"

Ethnographic studies of rural communities or urban neighborhoods can provide useful supplementary information about different income groups' lifestyles, and about relations among different income, ethnic, and other social groups. Aid agencies, NGOs, and government agencies occasionally sponsor consultative forums and focus groups, which are additional sources of information on felt needs and priorities. The World Bank's ambitious multicountry project Voices of the Poor, which was conducted in 1999 and 2000, is one illustration.[15] It is hard to gauge precisely what income levels and groups such forums represent, and specific localities may or may not be typical of larger areas. Nonetheless, these sources can be extremely useful because they capture nuances, suggest linkages, and explain perceptions in ways that more rigidly structured surveys cannot.

In sum, reformers and researchers who wish to test the extent and nature of overlapping interests between the poor and middle strata can find at least some information in a fair number of (particularly middle-income) countries. In countries where there are ongoing periodic household and/or opinion surveys, it would be simple to commission additional questions to gather better information on specific kinds of needs or concerns. Special surveys are, of course, a further possibility, but they would be much more costly and difficult than piggybacking new surveys on established programs.

DESIGNING PROGRAMS AND PROJECTS TO ADDRESS OVERLAPPING INTERESTS

Different underlying structural features generate different patterns of overlapping interests. Where the poor and middle strata live in intermingled neighborhoods, for instance, they are likely to share interests in better infrastructure and services for the community as a whole. Therefore, it may be feasible to engage much of the community in a drive for such facilities. But if, in that same neighborhood, there are substantial differences in incomes and living standards between the poor and middle strata, their interests may diverge on many specifics, such as the acceptability of user fees for certain services. Nor would the neighborhood be united on issues that did not concern neighborhood facilities, for instance, the priority assigned to price controls for food staples. In short, the extent and character of overlapping needs and interests establish the goals and parameters of political alliances between middle strata and poor.

This chapter has argued that two major drawbacks of broadly targeted or universal benefit programs as vehicles for poverty reduction are (1) fiscal costs and (2) the tendency of the somewhat better off to claim the great bulk of benefits. "Universal" programs available to all citizens avoid the second problem but are generally very costly. (There may of course be exceptions that particularly benefit poor and middle-strata households, like the free textbook program introduced in the early 1980s in Sri Lanka.) However, measures that reduce market prices for items that loom large in poor and middle-strata household budgets, not through subsidies but through legal and regulatory changes, offer the advantages of universal access at only modest public sector costs. In some countries, for instance, the production and distribution of textbooks is a monopoly. Introducing competition can considerably lower prices at little cost to the government other than enforcement of appropriate quality regulations. Greater scope for the distribution of generic drugs offers similar benefits in some countries. Still more fundamentally, measures that expand output, stabilize supply, and reduce the costs of basic food staples offer the equivalent of significant income increases for both poor and middle-strata households. The benefits of lowered prices for specific items are universal and nonrival, that is, access by some users does not diminish access and benefits for others. Indeed, wider markets may encourage lower prices.

The principle of nonrival consumption or benefit applies also to community or neighborhood facilities and services. Universal access to basic public facilities is a widely accepted goal or norm. A basic list includes schools and clinics, improved roads, access to electricity, public telephones (particularly for emergency use), and (in urban areas) hookups to city water and sewerage systems and improved fire and police protection. Such services and infrastructure tremendously improve the quality and security of life, even though they may not be captured in data on the incidence of poverty or the distribution of income.

In contrast, subsidized programs that allocate benefits to specific individuals or households (and therefore unavoidably exclude others) are particularly strongly affected by the linked problems of high public costs, limited supply, and probable competition between the poor and middle strata. Examples of such programs include scholarships, microcredit loans, land redistribution, and subsidized housing. If such programs are to be effective poverty-reduction measures, they may indeed require tight targeting. That is, they may not be promising candidates for the kind of cross-class alliances this chapter seeks to encourage.

In short, different kinds of poverty-reduction measures have varied intrinsic features that make some programs more likely candidates than others for broad targeting. Both the inherent features of different measures and the kind and degree of overlapping interests among the poor and middle strata jointly determine the feasibility and scope for broad targeting in particular countries.

The political desirability of broad targeting (or universal programs) depends on the relative political influence and capacities of the poor and middle strata. This chapter starts from the hypothesis that while the political capabilities of the poor are probably growing in much of the world, the capabilities and influence of the middle strata are greater and in some countries may be increasing more rapidly. Strategies that build on shared needs are likely to become increasingly attractive to politicians and political parties. Pro-poor technocrats and reformers would do well to give more serious attention to the possibilities for broad targeting, not as a sole strategy but as an important addition to the range of politically sustainable approaches to poverty reduction.

NOTES

I would like to thank those who helped shape this chapter through conversations or comments on earlier drafts: Carol Graham, Rebecca Grynspan, Peter Houtzager, Jacob Meerman, Guy Pfefferman, Lant Pritchett, and Sylvia Saborio.

1. Data are from 1995.

2. Data for Poland are from 1992 and for Estonia from 1995.

3. Data are based on surveys conducted in different years in the early and mid-1990s for different countries.

4. Carol Graham points out that counterforces may be at work, perhaps particularly in some Latin American countries (personal communication). Austerity and structural adjustment programs have affected some of the middle strata particularly directly through public sector layoffs and contracting public services. In some countries (such as Peru and Venezuela), political parties, which tend to represent middle-strata interests much more than those of the poor, are playing reduced roles in politics. Labor unions have been weakened in most countries. Therefore, in some cases it is not clear that middle-strata influence in politics has been increasing at all or more rapidly than that of the poor.

5. For examples drawn from the United States, the United Kingdom, and Australia, see Skocpol 1991; Goodin and Le Grand 1987 (especially the introduction and chap. 10); and Hanson 1987.

6. For more details and Sri Lankan references, see Nelson 1992 (241–42).

7. After Sri Lankan rice subsidies were officially withdrawn from the more affluent half of the population, many relatively comfortable households reported less than their real incomes and members of Parliament pressured officials not to challenge declared incomes. Later studies showed that roughly 30 percent of households in the upper half of the income distribution were receiving food stamps while about the same proportion of poor households were not receiving the stamps. Somewhat similarly, in Poland in 1993, 35.5 percent of households receiving social assistance intended for the poor were not in fact eligible. In several other postcommunist countries examined in the same study, even higher proportions of social assistance were "leaking" to the nonpoor (Nelson 1992; Milanovic 2000, 4, 11, 22).

8. See, for example, Lipton and Ravallion 1995 (2616); Van de Walle 1995 (605–6, 609–10); and especially Gelbach and Pritchett 1997.

9. In some countries with strong traditions of universal or broad-based social programs, the merits and problems of this approach as a strategy for reducing poverty may indeed be explicitly discussed. In Costa Rica, for example, the two large political parties traditionally differ regarding broad-based versus more targeted approaches; the government in power in 1994–98 made broad-based approaches an explicit element of its Social Program, and the concepts enter into campaign and legislative debates (Rebecca Grynspan, personal communication).

10. Of course, there are exceptions. Especially where there are ethnic or caste differences between the poor and middle strata, powerful cultural traditions and/or the threat of force may exclude the poor from use of ostensibly public facilities. Dalits in Indian villages, for instance, risk deadly violence if they try to use wells or other facilities. Much more commonly, the location of water taps, paved streets, clinics, or other public benefits favors the better off in neighborhoods or villages, but generally the effect is to reduce convenience rather than excluding the poor from benefits.

11. Varshney 1995 (chap. 5) provides a careful analysis of the patterns of shared and divergent interests among rural people in India.

12. For example, the annual LatinoBarometro surveys conducted in Latin American countries do not ask respondents to state their income. However, they are asked several questions about material possessions (color television, freezer, computer, washing machine, telephone, car, home, second holiday house) and housing utilities (drinking water, hot water, sewerage). The Brookings Institution Center on Social and Economic Dynamics used the replies to these questions to construct a wealth index that divides respondents into five estimated income categories.

13. I am grateful to Carol Graham and Stefano Pettinato of the Center for Social and Economic Dynamics at the Brookings Institution for providing this information based on LatinoBarometro 1998 data and the index of income they derived from them.

14. Stefano Pettinato, personal communication.

15. For a detailed description of that project and its findings, see Narayan et al. 2000.

REFERENCES

Fields, Gary S. 2000. "Income Mobility: Concepts and Measures." In Nancy Birdsall and Carol Graham, eds., *New Markets, New Opportunities? Economic and Social Mobility in a Changing World*. Washington, DC: Carnegie Endowment for International Peace and Brookings Institution Press.

Gelbach, Jonah B., and Lant H. Pritchett. 1997. "More for the Poor Is Less for the Poor: The Politics of Targeting." Updated version of World Bank Policy Research Working Paper 1523. Washington DC: World Bank.

Goodin, Robert E., and Julian Le Grand. 1987. *Not Only the Poor: The Middle Classes and the Welfare State*. London: Allen and Unwin.

Graham, Carol, and Stefano Pettinato. 1999. "Assessing Hardship and Happiness: Trends in Mobility and Expectations in the New Market Economies." Working Paper 7. Center on Social and Economic Dynamics, Brookings Institution, Washington, DC.

Hanson, Russell L. 1987. "The Expansion and Contraction of the American Welfare State." In Robert Goodin and Julian Le Grand, eds., *Not Only the Poor: The Middle Classes and the Welfare State*. London: Allen and Unwin.

Lipton, Michael, and Martin Ravallion. 1995. "Poverty and Policy." In J. Behrman and T. N. Srinivasan, eds., *Handbook of Development Economics*. Vol. 3. Amsterdam: Elsevier Science.

Milanovic, Branko. 2000. "The Role of Social Assistance in Addressing Poverty." In J. Braithewaite, C. Grootaert, and B. Milanovic, eds., *Poverty and Social Assistance in Transition Countries*. London: St. Martin's.

Narayan, Deepa, Robert Chambers, Meera K. Shah, and Patti Petesh. 2000. *Voices of the Poor: Crying Out for Change*. New York: Oxford University Press for the World Bank.

Nelson, Joan M. 1992. "Poverty, Equity, and the Politics of Adjustment." In Stephan Haggard and Robert R. Kaufman, eds., *The Politics of Economic Adjustment*. Princeton: Princeton University Press.

Pritchett, Lant, Asep Suryahadi, and Sudarno Sumarto. 2000. "Quantifying Vulnerability to Poverty: A Proposed Measure with Application to Indonesia." Manuscript, Washington, DC.

Skocpol, Theda. 1991. "Universal Appeal: Politically Viable Policies to Combat Poverty." *Brookings Review* 9, no. 3 (summer): 29–33.

Van de Walle, Dominique. 1995. "Incidence and Targeting: An Overview of Implications for Research and Policy." In Dominique van de Walle and Kimberly Nead, eds., *Public Spending and the Poor: Theory and Evidence.* Baltimore: John Hopkins University Press.

Varshney, Ashutosh. 1995. *Democracy, Development, and the Countryside: Urban-Rural Struggles in India.* Cambridge: Cambridge University Press.

World Bank. 1997. *World Development Report.* Washington, DC: World Bank.

6 The Boundaries of Antipoverty Policy

ECONOMIC IDEAS, POLITICAL COALITIONS,
AND THE STRUCTURE OF SOCIAL PROVISION
IN CHILE AND MEXICO

Marcus J. Kurtz

In an era in which international economic integration is accelerating and "market forces" are seen as the inevitable if not the ideal arbiters of distribution, many scholars have highlighted the increasing costs even to wealthy states of attempting to pursue expansionist policies (e.g., Williamson 1994; Garrett 1996). But others have suggested that there might indeed still be quite a lot of room for maneuver for poorer nations even in a world of substantial capital mobility, with respect to both industrial policy (Evans 1995) and social provision (Weiss 1998). There have also been hopeful signs of new and innovative antipoverty strategies in Latin America, despite a continentwide turn to market-based economic organization and a dramatic worsening of poverty levels during much of the 1980s and 1990s. This raises the question of when the possible—poverty relief even in a neoliberal world—becomes the probable.

In this chapter, I examine social welfare outcomes in three cases characterized by competitive political systems[1]—Chile before military rule (1932–73); Mexico (1988–2000); and Chile after its return to democracy (1989–2000). The latter two cases were selected because they evidence wide variation on the dependent variable—social welfare outcomes—but take place in similarly outward-oriented economic systems. The period of inward-looking development in Chile (1932–73) is included as a control that serves to highlight the broad limits that open economy policies place on welfare regimes. Explicit comparison with the period of military rule in Chile or that of unquestioned one-party dominance in Mexico is avoided since the political dynamics accounting for social policy outcomes in those contexts are likely to be quite different from those under competitive conditions. What is the range of variation to be explained, and what accounts for it? To begin, policies that benefit the poor are disaggregated by target. Are they oriented toward the production process, or are they subsidies to consumption? Production-side policies are further disaggregated into those that focus on the redistribution of assets and those that focus on the correction of market failures. Consumption-support policies are divided into benefits of a highly targeted (or "means tested") variety and those that are more universalistic in applicability.

Different combinations of antipoverty policies can be found in the three cases under consideration in this study (see table 1). In Chile, both before and after the period of military rule, universalistic (or broad-based) consumption subsidies have been important parts of the social welfare policy. Production-oriented policies focused on asset redistribution in the pre-1973 period. Not only was a large state sector created, but by 1967 a substantial land reform was launched. This would eventually redistribute most of the large farms in the country. After democratization in 1989, production-side policy was refocused on efforts to correct market failures. On the consumption side, policy became quasi-universal in scope. Benefits were raised—though not to the level of the first case—and extended to a broad swath of society, not simply the "very poor."[2]

In Mexico production-side policies have focused on correction of market failures, while consumption-side policies have, since the late 1980s, been more strictly targeted at the poor. After the election of Carlos Salinas in 1988, tentative moves toward democracy were coupled with decisive moves toward a neoliberal economic strategy, culminating in the North American Free Trade Agreement (NAFTA), and a massive and controversial social welfare effort gathered under the rubric of the Programa Nacional de Solidaridad (PRONASOL). This program included both targeted consumption supports and substantial funds for the betterment of human, physical, and social infrastructure among poor communities and marginal producers on the production side.

How are we to account for these very different patterns of policy? I argue that they are a result of coalitional dynamics situated within a par-

TABLE 1.   PATTERNS OF SOCIAL WELFARE POLICY IN CHILE
AND MEXICO

	Development Strategy	Consumption-side Policy	Production-side Policy
Chile, 1932–73	ISI	Universal provision	Asset redistribution
Chile, 1989–2000	Neoliberal	Quasi-universal	Limited efforts to correct market failure
Mexico, 1988–2000	Neoliberal	Targeted	Extensive efforts to correct market failure

ticular developmental model and its ideological underpinnings. Structural features of the developmental model can be economically inconsistent with some antipoverty policies, placing wide but strict boundaries on policy. They demarcate an arena that has room for wide variations in policy outcomes but nevertheless does preclude strategies that transcend its boundaries. More important, development models are accompanied by "development ideologies" that narrow options in a more substantial way. They frame the very definition of the problem of poverty and thus the political terrain within which solutions are debated. Antipoverty approaches that clash with ideological presuppositions, whether potentially efficacious or not, will tend to be marginalized from the political and planning process.

Within the arena defined by developmental model and ideology, however, antipoverty policies are political outcomes. The coalitional basis of consumption and production-side outcomes is shaped by, among other factors, (1) the degree of organization of the poor, (2) patterns of political alliance, and (3) the competitiveness of the party system. While a variety of combinations of these factors are logically possible, I examine only those relevant to the cases at hand. Where the poor organize and ally with middle-sector political actors, the antipoverty effort will be greater and more universalistic. When based in broad multiclass constituencies, policies providing benefits to all members are easiest to implement.[3] Targeted efforts would tend to divide such coalitions. Policy will also tend toward consumption supports over production-side interventions since the needs of the poor have a means of entry onto the national political agenda and a sizable coalition can be assembled behind transparently redistributive policies. In party systems in which more than one reformist party competes for the support of the poor, a bidding dynamic may ensue, leading to social welfare provision even in advance of direct pressure from below (with respect to agrarian reform in Chile, see Kaufman 1972; and Loveman 1976). Where the poor are not well organized and the level of political competition is lower, antipoverty efforts will tend toward smaller, more targeted, and merely palliative forms. Moreover, efforts will take on a more production-side character that avoids obviously redistributionist outcomes and can simultaneously provide resources to the poor and middle-sector interests through which resources can be channeled.

The implications of these processes are twofold. First, they call for greater catholicism among decision makers when evaluating strategies for combating poverty and an attentiveness among international organizations to the political and ideological externalities of the broad development models that they promote. That is, the system of ideas that comes with particular economic strategies constrain the range of antipoverty policies that local decision makers consider. Second, they reinforce the point that self-organization and the construction of political coalitions can be as important as democratization itself in terms of placing the needs of the poor on the national agenda.

HOW DEVELOPMENT IDEOLOGIES AFFECT ANTIPOVERTY OUTCOMES

Development models are overarching choices typically taken prior to the elaboration of a coherent antipoverty strategy. At the broadest level, commitment to a development model—in the cases examined here either a neoliberal or an import-substituting one—puts concrete economic boundaries on the range of policy outcomes in subsidiary areas such as social welfare. These structural limits are, however, quite loose. More important is the fact that differing development models tend strongly to be accompanied by "developmental ideologies." That is, in addition to a technical economic package to overcome underdevelopment they comprise a set of a priori beliefs that condition policy outcomes in other areas. These can include perspectives on nationalism versus internationalism, the relative value of public action, the efficacy of markets as allocative mechanisms, and the appropriate boundaries of private property relations. These ideational constraints are substantially more limiting than the strict but wide boundaries imposed by the logic of the developmental model itself. For policymakers they function as something akin to ideological blinders that preclude empirical evaluation of certain policy strategies, leaving blind spots that can undermine efforts to ameliorate poverty.[4]

Consider the logic of import-substituting (inward) and neoliberal (outward) developmental models. Under the former, the goal is to promote industrialization, at least initially (and in practice over the longer term) targeted at the domestic market. The source of investment is typically national, and the state itself is often an entrepreneur. Since the market for manufacturers is domestic, the model depends for its survival on the existence of a fairly substantial middle sector and "privileged" working class whose incomes are sufficient to make them a consumer base for the protected industries (Hirschman 1968, 12). Because of inefficiencies and a typically overvalued exchange rate, the sale of manufactures in foreign markets is precluded (Bates 1981). As a consequence, social welfare policy will have a tendency to favor the "middle"—that is, it will tend to transfer income to this large middle and working class of consumers who are the engine of growth. Typical losers in this scenario are both the wealthy, oligarchic classes and the mass of urban informal workers and peasants, who are unable to obtain the comparatively scarce but privileged jobs in the urban industrial sector. Of the range of social welfare policies outlined in this chapter, few are precluded, but highly targeted aid is unlikely because of the structural biases of import-substituting industrialization—targeting expends resources in ways not consonant with the promotion of growth.

Neoliberal strategies, because they depend for their success on access to international markets, impose stricter and different constraints. Since the locus of investment is much more strongly foreign, some forms of production-side antipoverty policy are precluded. Specifically, efforts to redistribute productive assets are unlikely. The negative externalities that such policies would induce—by threatening the absolute character of property rights and raising perceptions of risk among foreign investors—would make them risky in an outward-looking development model. Similarly, any credible search for foreign investment requires a commitment to "sensible" macroeconomic policies and thus puts strong constraints on the ability of states to pursue expansionary fiscal policies (Waterbury 1999, 324; Williamson 1994). The policy consequence of this would be fiscal pressure in the direction of smaller and more targeted consumption supports.

It should be recognized, however, that these are simply boundaries. Politicians and states have quite a lot of room to maneuver within the structural confines produced by development strategies. But if antipoverty strategies are constructed they will emerge from within the idea systems that decision makers bring to government.

How do development ideologies shape antipoverty strategy? Coherent development strategies bring with them important assumptions about the nature of economic activity, the structure of international interactions (e.g., positive sum and anarchic, or hierarchical and zero sum), the efficacy of public intervention, and the efficiency of markets. These idea systems represent comparatively durable commitments and can become institutionalized in the relevant public bureaucracies.[5]

The emergence of import-substituting (ISI) strategies in Latin America after World War II and the associated structuralist perspectives on economic development, for example, were rooted in two particular beliefs: that international markets were systematically biased against producers of primary products; and that, under free market conditions, neither local nor international investors could or would initiate a process of industrialization (see, e.g., Prebisch 1959). In ideational terms, this produced several consequences: (1) it undermined faith in the efficacy of a reliance on market forces, (2) it valorized the role of public intervention, and (3) it prioritized industrialization over the production of primary products. Since in Latin America the production of the latter was typically tightly held in the hands of either foreigners or local oligarchs, ISI tended to bring with it nationalist and antioligarchical forms of politics.[6] In intellectual terms, the wave of dependency thinkers of the 1960s and

1970s provided the ideational underpinnings of inward-looking developmental strategies.

Explaining the turn to neoliberal developmental strategies in both Chile and Mexico is beyond the scope of this chapter.[7] But in both instances the change in developmental model occurred in the context of economic crisis and limited state resources. A consequence of the crisis was the fundamental reevaluation of the inward-looking developmental model and the assumptions that had undergirded it: the efficacy of public intervention and the risks involved in dependence on foreign markets.

PRO-POOR POLICIES IN TWO CHILES: FROM REDISTRIBUTION OF WEALTH TO WELFARE

The change of social welfare regime across the two periods in Chile could hardly have been more dramatic. In the first period (1932–73), highly competitive politics, mobilized popular sector constituencies, and a nationalist developmental ideology combined to produce a universalistic welfare state geared to the redistribution of wealth and income. In the second period, following seventeen years of military rule, a free market developmental ideology, interparty cooperation, and social quiescence produced an austere but broad-based welfare system aimed at mitigating the worst aspects of the open economic strategy. In this section, I elaborate the political and ideational foundations of the current neoliberal form of social provision, seen against the backdrop of the redistributive statism that was its democratic antecedent.

THE BACKGROUND CASE: DEVELOPMENT IDEOLOGY, POLITICS, AND POVERTY ALLEVIATION IN PRE-COUP CHILE

The statist and redistributive mode of social provision began in earnest in Chile under the Popular Front administrations (1938–52) and included substantial spending on housing, health, and education; price controls on basic necessities; and explicit income policies. Under the Christian Democratic Party (PDC) Frei government of the 1960s this expanded still further, lifting public spending from 36 to 47 percent of the gross domestic product (GDP) between 1965 and 1970 (Vergara 1986, 86). The socialist Allende administration (1970–73) did not so much change this model as intensify it, especially in the areas of consumer subsidies and price controls. Its form is telling: increases in consumption standards were provided through the universalization of social benefits formerly limited to the middle sectors and urban working classes and through the encouragement of broad-based trade unionism. Explicitly for the Christian Democrats, the incorporation of the poor into social welfare and labor regimes was aimed at broadening the internal market, which by this time had begun to reach its limits. Moreover, on the production side public intervention increased, and in 1967 Christian Democratic President Frei enacted a massive land reform.

The ideological foundations of this approach to poverty alleviation were linked to the nationalist and inward-looking development strategy. These tendencies are clearest in the primary export sector—mining. Here Frei, forcing joint ownership on U.S. multinationals, launched a process of "Chileanization." Later an outright nationalization of the copper mines was accomplished as one of the first acts of the incoming Allende administration. Lest this be thought of as simply the product of a Marxist president elected by only a narrow margin, it should be remembered that the copper nationalization was approved unanimously in the Parliament. Nationalism and the suspicion of foreign investors in key sectors of the national patrimony ran deep even among Allende's arch enemies on the political Right. But precisely this sort of policy is what one would expect given the ideological underpinnings of ISI. The devalorization of market forces (especially international trade) and the need to expand domestic markets were intellectually consonant with antipoverty strategies that stressed asset redistribution (in agriculture) and nationalization (in mining).[8] Moreover, consumption-side policies focused on universalism in part because market broadening for domestic manufactures was a high priority and in part because fiscal balance was comparatively less important. There was limited foreign investment, and much domestic consumption was not obviously or directly linked to the availability of foreign exchange.

Another part of the explanation of the expanding reach of the redistributive state in pre-coup Chile can be found in the mobilized and competitive politics that characterized the period. Since the 1930s, Chilean politics had been characterized by a multiplicity of competing reformist/progressive parties—initially communists, socialists, and radicals and later also Christian Democrats. Particularly by the 1950s and 1960s the expanding Christian Democratic Party explicitly targeted the poor as it sought (successfully) to establish an electoral presence (Scully 1992, 141). Once the PDC attained the presidency in 1964, it vigorously embarked on efforts to organize and support its constituencies among the poor (Valenzuela 1978, 36). But rather than build a new national consensus this forced the Left to respond with ever more radical positions, many of which were incorporated into policy after the election of Allende in 1970.

Pressure from below, from an increasingly organized and mobilized popular sector, helped to propel further redistributive reform. In agriculture, strike activity rose from a mere 54 disputes in the 1960–64 period to 1,821 between 1967 and 1969, as promotional efforts by the PDC and a new labor law launched a reinforcing dynamic between mobilization and policy enactment (on strikes, see Scully 1992, 153). This turned even more militant after 1970 when land invasions became prevalent (Marín 1972). Similar mobilizational and organizational activity characterized the urban formal and informal sectors as strikes and property seizures became more widespread there. While the PDC made efforts to gain clientelistic control over the organizations of the poor (especially in the urban areas), opposition from both Left and Right guaranteed the autonomy of popular organizations and their continued political importance (Scully 1992, 161).

PRO-POOR POLICY IN CHILE AFTER REDEMOCRATIZATION

The conventional wisdom with respect to Chilean social policy in the postmilitary era (1989–2000) is that in many respects it follows the "targeted" logic developed during the military's neoliberal transformation of the economy. While the center-leftist democratic governments of Aylwin (1989–93) and Frei (1993–2000) certainly increased spending on poverty relief, most analysts have argued that it remains narrowly aimed at the very poor (e.g., Vergara 1994, 248). In contrast, careful scrutiny of governmental sources indicates a substantial broadening of the recipient base of social welfare policies (e.g., MIDEPLAN 1991, 17). This change is linked to the process of democratization and the attendant changes in the dynamics of political competition. This produced a shift in focus to quasi-universalistic consumption-side policy outcomes and the emergence for the first time since 1973 of serious production-side welfare efforts.

The model of social provision implemented during the second democratic period in Chile differed dramatically from the first case considered here—the period before the coup of 1973. The pre-1973 Chilean welfare state was, if anything, regressively organized before the transformations of the neoliberal era. Benefits were generally structured as universal entitlements, but enforcement and implementation were more established among middle sector and unionized formal sector workers than among the poor concentrated in the countryside and urban informal sectors. During the course of military rule, targeted (and much less generous) forms of welfare replaced almost all these entitlements.[9]

With the return of democracy, however, the commitment to targeting diminished, and social provision took on a quasi-universalistic character. Table 2 presents the scope and character of social welfare policy across the two periods of interest. We see that once the neoliberal model was entrenched in the social policy arena in the early 1980s targeted forms of provision became the norm. With democratization, however, dramatic expansions were made in more universalistic aspects of poverty relief— especially increases in the family allowance (a subsidy paid on a per child basis to, principally, formal sector workers) and the minimum wage.[10]

The point is not that targeted programs were abolished or that non-means-tested programs expanded dramatically. Rather, the aggregate of poverty-targeted and broad-based subsidies amounted to a basically universal system, albeit one fragmented into many programs. While obviously the Chilean government did not wholly abandon targeted social spending after the democratic transition, it also did not deepen the process of targeting. While the value of means-tested welfare transfers (SUF) was increased, the program's size had been capped in 1986 and coverage declined thereafter as recipients leaving the program were not replaced. Moreover, the program is a complement to the family allowances scheme, which covers only those citizens affiliated with a private or public pension system (almost exclusively formal sector, urban workers). Considered together, these means tested and family allowance subsidies are of comparable size and are granted to complementary constituencies; collectively they are nearly universal. The only area in which substantial targeting is evident is in the value of the poverty pension, which expanded more rapidly than the average civilian pension. By contrast, fully 50 percent of the new social development revenues raised in the 1990 tax reform went to the somewhat regressive and broadly distributed family allowance and pension increases (Vergara 1996).

TABLE 2. THE TRANSFORMATION AND RETRANSFORMATION OF SOCIAL WELFARE IN CHILE (PESOS PER MONTH, 1990 PRICES)

	Targeted Assistance				Universal Assistance			
	Cash Transfers (SUF)		Welfare Pensions		Family Allowance		Real Minimum Wage Index (1970 = 100)	Civilian Pensions (avg. value)
Year	Recipients	Value	Recipients	Value	Recipients	Value		
1970			0	0			2,429	100.0	31,354
1974			0	0			2,547	108.3	16,184
1977			66,000	6,989			2,118	119.3	17,964
1981		2,031	156,200	9,819	3,962,000	1,987	138.7	24,528
1983	527,000	1,604	229,400	9,901	3,929,000	1,564	109.5	26,229
1986	1,086,000	1,246	324,700	9,059	4,024,000	1,119	85.8	26,072
1989	896,000	951	292,900	7,840	3,817,000	696	88.9	27,724
1991	879,000	1,155	289,100	9,430	4,021,000	903	103.4	30,065
1996	766,082	1,164	326,447	10,326	3,200,000	895[a]	128.0	

Source: For pensions, SUF recipients, family allowances from 1970 to 1991: Raczynski and Romaguera 1995 (297); for 1996, Ministerio de Planificación y Cooperación (MIDEPLAN) 1998 (12–20); for value of SUF to 1991: MIDEPLAN 1992 (246); for real minimum wage, all years, Bravo and Vial 1997 (151).

[a]The average of three rates; subsidies are phased out at the highest income levels.

Production-side investment with an antipoverty component has taken
two principal forms in Chile. The most explicit is the social investment
fund (FOSIS), which is aimed at encouraging human capital formation,
supporting microenterprises, and improving infrastructure in marginalized areas. It also directly incorporates the goal—though not necessarily
the reality—of increasing organizational capacity in civil society. Fondo
de Solidaridad e Inversión Social (FOSIS) funding, as an experimental
program, has been largely constant at roughly U.S.$50 million since the
program's inception (Vergara 1996; Wurgaft 1993). In addition, there are
the decentralized regional and local development funds (Fondo Nacional
de Desarrollo Regional [FNDR] and Inversión Sectorial de Asignación
Regional [ISAR]) and the agricultural assistance program for small farmers administered through Instituto de Desarrollo Agropecuario (INDAP)
and the Ministry of Agriculture.[11] Here the aim is investment for development, but the infrastructure needs of marginal areas are given substantial priority. It is in the latter category that posttransition spending
has increased most notably.

While the regional development funds (FNDR) have been in existence
since 1976, they did not rise substantially until democratization (see table
3). Over the period 1989 to 1994, spending increased by 178 percent in real
terms, while overall public investment rose by 80 percent. Unlike the case
for demand-side assistance, which was often applied to very broad constituencies, these funds have increasingly incorporated antipoverty criteria in their goals.

NEOLIBERALISM, THE CONCERTACIÓN, AND QUIESCENCE:
THIN BUT BROAD WELFARE PROVISION

I have characterized the social policy of the governing Concertación
alliance (1989–2000) in Chile as one of limited universalism on the consumption side and market-failure correction on the production side. This
is not identical to the outcome in the first case (Chile before 1973), as policy does not involve asset redistribution, nor is it as universalistic and
generous in its benefits. An important part of this outcome can be

TABLE 3. DECENTRALIZED SOCIAL AND INFRASTRUCTURAL
INVESTMENT IN CHILE (THOUSANDS OF PESOS, 1986 PRICES)

Source of Funds	1989	1990	1991	1992	1993	1994
Decentralized	12,777	12,058	15,305	27,536	33,562	35,631
FNDR	12,777	12,058	15,305	17,177	21,483	21,922
ISAR	0	0	0	10,358	12,080	13,709
Overall Public Investment	101,132	95,399	118,641	147,980	164,216	182,287

Source: Serrano 1996 (69–79).

explained by the way in which new ideas about the state and its relationship with society and market developed alongside the free-market development model. It also involved the posttransition alliance between center and leftist parties as well as the political parameters agreed on as part of the democratization process itself (see Houtzager and Kurtz 2000).

In Chile, free market ideas began to make headway after the 1973 coup. The best-developed local supporters were led by a group of Chilean economists trained at the University of Chicago, which had a long-standing relationship with the Catholic University in Santiago. The new neoliberal developmental model that began to emerge in the 1970s was in large measure designed by these individuals, and public policy increasingly prioritized market forces and operated under the principle of state subsidiarity.[12] Market forces came to be valorized by those on the Right as "neutral" and "efficient," while public action became vilified as inherently inefficient and "bureaucratic."

With this change in the developmental model, the statism inherent in the former universalistic form of social provision became ideologically untenable. It entailed redistribution deemed at once inefficient and unjust by the Chicago School economists who shaped the military's economic policy (see Piñera 1991; and Büchi Buc 1993). On the production side, then, most intervention was halted except in the form of the restitution of previously redistributed property. Indeed, the only coherent form of social welfare produced by the military government was on the consumption side, where broad-based entitlements were replaced with highly targeted forms of public assistance. Ideologically, this had the benefit of targeting resources only at those individuals deemed unable to participate in the broader market economy. It placed little burden on the public purse, in keeping with neoliberal norms about low tax and spending levels, and did not substantially redistribute income.[13]

This well-known and highly targeted form of social welfare provision was not "caused" by neoliberal ideology, though it was framed by it. Even under authoritarianism, ideology only shaped public action in accordance with political circumstances. Thus, during military rule, when pressure from mobilized constituencies was weak, social provision took on a minimalist, targeted form. With the transition to democracy, the rise to power of reformist center-leftist governments, and the emergence of previously pent-up demands, both the level and scope of antipoverty spending increased. Thus, taxes were substantially increased, and the newly available resources were applied to programs benefiting a vast array of sectors from the indigent to the upper middle classes. It is interesting to note, however, that it was still framed by the neoliberal development ideology (now shared by the center and most of the left) and remained consonant with its outlines.[14]

Finally, any more explicitly redistributive or statist approaches would leave political leaders open to charges of attempting to reintroduce "failed" policies from the past—judged guilty by association with ISI. In an intellectual environment that asserted the primacy of markets and the inefficiency of states, political debate could center only on the level of spending and the degree of targeting. Qualitative changes involving a redefinition of the state's role in society or an end to private provision lack a widely shared intellectual foundation in Chilean society.

Since the democratic transition, Chile has been governed by a coalition of Christian Democratic and Socialist parties (the Concertación de Partidos por la Democracia, or Concertación). This coalition mirrors the bipolar democratic/authoritarian cleavage that has become central to Chilean politics (see Agüero and Tironi 1999). It is reinforced by an electoral law that places a premium on cross-party cooperation.[15] Changes in social policy have as a consequence been negotiated at the highest levels of the party leadership. This has served to insulate leaders from the pressures of the Concertación's own organized social constituencies. As a result, no electoral "bidding" dynamic—the competitive expansion of the welfare state driven by political conflict between center and Left that characterized the 1960s and early 1970s—has emerged. Competition among reformist parties has been replaced by a competition between a "responsible" center-leftist alliance emphasizing fiscal probity and a neoliberal right promoting minimalist government. Lacking political traction, the organized social constituencies and competitive political dynamics that historically shaped welfare policy have declined substantially. In particular, the Concertación alliance has moderated the policy proposals of the Socialist Left and has implemented only gradual increases in social spending, distributing them widely across its constituencies in the middle and lower classes.[16] Thus, a large proportion of the increase in social spending after democratic transition went to the broadly applied (though recently more progressive) family allowance, benefiting all but the highest income categories (Vergara 1996).

The comparatively austere approach taken by posttransition governments is evident in the data on sources of income in table 4. While poverty declined quite dramatically over the period 1987–96, this was not due to dramatic increases in the incidence of government transfer payments in the incomes of the poor (on poverty declines, see León 1994; and Mejía and Vos 1997). Indeed, even for the poorest quintile government transfers as a percentage of total income declined by nearly 50 percent. Clearly, public payments (for all quintiles) lagged well behind the growth in earnings in the private sector. The independent political weight of public welfare beneficiaries in Chilean politics is so limited that even under center-leftist governments relative parity in the incidence of public assistance in income has not been maintained. While it could be argued that the decline in public assistance reflects the success of growth-mediated poverty reduction, it must be remembered that the poor in Chile have only recently reestablished the living standards they had in 1970, while overall inequality has increased dramatically. Consequently, one would expect a substantial desire for continued and expanded efforts to repay the social debt of neoliberalism.

Further evidence of the moderating effects of the present bipolar party system or political competition can be found in the list of issues explicitly removed from the political agenda before President Aylwin took office and in the program of government of the Concertación (Houtzager and Kurtz 2000). The latter includes a commitment to the broad outlines of the neoliberal model and the agrarian counterreform. Pension, health, and industrial privatizations were not only left to stand, but they were expanded. While not all of these concessions were to the liking of the alliance, particularly of the Socialist faction, alternatives were limited.

Thus, what we see are broad but moderate policy reforms. Indicative of the fiscal restraint implicit in a neoliberal developmental model is the fact that the largest real increases in the incomes of the poor came through the minimum wage (on the minimum wage, see Bravo and Vial 1997). This is a policy that affects large swathes of income earners in Chile and costs the treasury little. Direct transfers increased in value, although overall spending increased only moderately as coverage declined. The entire increase in the welfare family allowance (SUF) between 1989 and 1996 amounted to little more than U.S.$1 per month. This was in contrast to a long period of decline but was substantially less than the 44 percent real increase in the minimum wage over the same period.

The character and level of antipoverty activity is also intimately linked to the amount of leverage that the poor themselves can directly apply to

TABLE 4. PUBLIC SUBSIDIES AS A
PERCENTAGE OF CASH INCOME, BY
INCOME QUINTILE, CHILE

Income Quintile	1987	1990	1996
1	22.6	15.5	11.3
2	7.1	4.4	4.0
3	3.9	2.2	2.0
4	2.0	1.1	0.7
5	0.7	0.4	0.1

Source: 1987, 1990: calculated from MIDEPLAN 1992 (247); 1996: calculated from MIDEPLAN 1998 (30).

the political system. We saw earlier how this was partly structured by party system dynamics—particularly the level of competition and the presence of more than one reformist faction. But it also reflects the power that the popular sector has as an actor in its own right or as an ally with others. Two issues impinge here; how organized are the poor and what political alliances have they struck?

When the poor as a group are mobilized and capable of allying themselves with other major actors, they can overcome the disadvantages of a less competitive party system. But this requires the representation of popular sector interests by powerful intermediaries that are valuable allies for middle-class actors and are capable of punishing politicians who fail to keep their promises. Unfortunately, the most disadvantaged sectors of society—the informal sectors in the peri-urban areas and the peasantry—are also those least likely to have strong organizational intermediation. Moreover, in Chile, they lack political connections to the Right and have only weak organizational linkages to the center-left. As a consequence, these groups are largely captive constituencies of the Concertación.

Why is this the case, and what can be done about it? Much of the organizational weakness of the popular sectors can be attributed to the social effects of the neoliberal developmental model pursued since the late 1970s. Indeed, one of the key aims of many of the reforms of the military era—particularly in social provision, labor law, and the pension system—was the disarticulation of what had formerly been exceedingly powerful beneficiary coalitions (see Piñera 1991). Individualization was the watchword, as the state largely ceased to have direct responsibility for levels of benefit or the terms of labor agreements. In addition, systematic political repression coupled with extremely "flexible" labor markets (and two waves of severe unemployment and recession) served to undermine most organized actors in civil society (see Garretón 1983). But this atomization disproportionately affected the poorest elements of society, as organization in the countryside all but disappeared.[17] Even the briefly hopeful signs of organization among the urban popular sectors in the mid-1980s quickly evaporated (Oxhorn 1995).

Thus, while the national peasant (Confederación Nacional Campesina [CNC]) and labor (Central Unico de Trabajadores [CUT]) confederations are directly tied to the governing parties of the Concertación alliance, their ability to affect policy decisions is weak and contrasts markedly with the situation that prevailed in the 1960s and early 1970s. Indeed, the peasant sector has had virtually none of its key demands addressed, despite ten years of governance by political allies. The labor movement has been slightly more successful, but it has obtained only minor changes in the labor code and has been marginalized from discussions over the minimum wage.[18]

The production-side investments of the posttransition governments have some potential to mitigate this problem. The FOSIS program in particular has had as one of its several goals the reconstruction of a more vibrant associational life among marginalized sectors; it thus represents an effort at both human and social capital formation. Undertaken on a sufficiently ambitious scale, this has the potential to produce a virtuous cycle of expanding organization and ever more solid political bases for further and deeper antipoverty efforts.

Politically the FOSIS program is structured around a cross-class alliance, and this underlines its stability across time. First, it deliberately involves the private sector. The fund undertakes no projects directly, operating instead through private firms or organized social groups. It provides microenterprise funding, especially for peasants and indigenous groups, but it does this largely by offering credit indirectly through the private financial system by subsidizing banks, savings and loan institutions, and nongovernmental organizations (NGOs). Second, its community development activities are channeled through, and promote, the creation of local development committees. It is explicitly hoped that these will survive after the initial seed money provided by FOSIS disappears, leading to improvements in local governance and increased capacity to articulate and promote interests. Unfortunately, the program has remained quite small. Since its inception, it has been funded at a level of around U.S.$50 million, making it more of an experimental project than a focus of public policy (Wurgaft 1993, 59).

MEXICO: RISING POLITICAL COMPETITIVENESS, NEOLIBERALISM, AND THE SHIFT TO PRODUCTION-ORIENTED AND TARGETED POVERTY ALLEVIATION

Antipoverty policy in Mexico experienced dramatic transformations as the country was beset by twin shocks—catastrophic economic crisis and the sudden decline in the Institutional Revolutionary Party's (PRI) traditional political hegemony. After decades of inattention to poverty, punctuated only in the 1970s by a return to land redistribution, pro-poor policies finally took center stage under the presidency of Carlos Salinas (1988–94). National political competition became in part organized around welfare provision—but now under the leadership of a president trained in neoclassical economic thought and committed to international integration.[19] As politics became competitive—much more so than in the first two posttransition elections in Chile[20]—and disquiet from below mounted, a highly targeted but extensive production and consumption side response was initiated.

The debt crisis of 1982 delivered a blow to the prevailing statist developmental model from which it would never recover. Initially, despite a dramatic upsurge in poverty, austerity was the watchword of the day, not a transformation of social welfare. The existing form of social provision based on universal consumption subsidies (especially for basic foods) quickly became fiscally unsustainable. Indeed, during the presidency of Miguel de la Madrid (1982–88) social development spending contracted by 6.2 percent per year (Friedmann, Lustig, and Legovini 1995, 344–46). It declined more steeply than government revenues, as resources were redirected to payment of external debt.

These first six years of crisis were a period of political redefinition along several axes, culminating in the election of Carlos Salinas in 1988, and the establishment of a new model of poverty alleviation. Two aspects of this redefinition were critical: it was the first truly competitive presidential election since the Revolution early in the twentieth century,[21] and it marked the ascendance of the technocratic wing of the ruling PRI. Salinas's antipoverty strategy, embodied in the National Solidarity Program known as PRONASOL, was designed to make social spending compatible with neoliberal adjustment strategies. It was to target social programs directly at those most in need and bypass corporatist and clientelist institutions that had formerly been central channels of state-society interaction (Consejo Consultivo del Programa Nacional de Solidaridad 1994, 11–12). Salinas also hoped it would rebuild support for the severely weakened governing party (see Ward 1993). This very ambitious program reoriented Mexican antipoverty policy into highly targeted forms on the consumption side and, on the production side, market failure corrections, human and social capital formation, and microenterprise finance. Table 5 presents a breakdown of the very considerable resources allocated to this program. Between 1989 and 1994, this single program accounted for between 6.6 and 7.7 percent of all central government consumption, an amount equivalent to roughly 1 percent of GDP in 1994.

The participation of local social groups in the design and execution of projects was a key aspect of PRONASOL. The basic mode of operation was through the local solidarity committees. During the six-year life of the program, some 250,000 committees were at least officially operational (SEDESOL 1994, 23). The political independence and "bottom-up" character of these committees varied a great deal, but the principle of using social welfare funds to alleviate poverty and create the basis of local social capital simultaneously was at least sometimes a meaningful consequence of the program (see Fox 1994). Importantly, unlike the earlier Companía Nacional de Subsistencias Populares (CONASUPO) and Sistema Alimentaria Mexicana (SAM) programs, PRONASOL was market friendly, involving neither price controls nor direct competition with the private sector (Cornelius, Craig, and Fox 1994, 10–11).

Like so many grand projects in Mexico, PRONASOL came to an end in the midst of economic crisis and the election of a new president, Ernesto Zedillo, in 1994. While Zedillo retained much of the policy orientation of PRONASOL, the administration of social welfare funds was restructured dramatically. Instead of allocating funds through solidarity committees linked directly to the federal government, states and municipalities were for the first time given an important role in the conduct of national antipoverty policy. The federal government was officially relegated only to defining broad goals (see Poder Ejecutivo Federal 1995, 124).

Table 6 outlines the spending patterns for social welfare and infrastructure under Zedillo. In inflation-adjusted terms, actual spending had declined since the heyday of PRONASOL. This was due to the peso crisis of 1995 and the subsequent fiscal tightening in 1997–98, which was also partly to a decline in funds derived from privatization. By 1999, more than 77 percent of funds were being managed by state and local governments.

NEOLIBERAL IDEOLOGY, POLITICAL COMPETITION, AND CIVIL SOCIETY: THE LIMITS OF POVERTY ALLEVIATION

The very features that made poverty relief initially more substantial in scope in Mexico than in Chile (greater competitiveness in the party system but little linkage between the poor and reformist parties) eventually undermined its survival. While the general boundaries of policy were defined in similar ways by the overarching developmental ideology, there were substantial differences in the domestic political dynamics that shaped the policies. Crucially, while the momentary threat to PRI dominance in 1988

TABLE 5. PRODUCTION AND CONSUMPTION-ORIENTED SPENDING IN MEXICO'S PRONASOL PROGRAM, 1989–94 (THOUSANDS OF NEW PESOS, 1989 PRICES)

	1989	1990	1991	1992	1993	1994
Consumption-side Supports (includes education, health, housing, and food aid)	1,266,919	1,953,475	2,526,213	3,431,617	3,817,502	2,683,053
Production-side Supports	1,050,668	1,772,892	2,343,264	2,672,277	2,729,020	1,998,801
Regional Development Infrastructure	(613,314)	(893,854)	(1,488,259)	(1,520,684)	(1,474,748)	(1,197,045)
Direct Aids to Production	(437,354)	(879,038)	(853,062)	(1,153,594)	(1,254,271)	(801,766)

Source: Data from SEDESOL 1994 (176–90) adjusted by the December to December variation in consumer prices as reported by the Bank of Mexico.

brought a large policy response via PRONASOL, it was a response designed to simultaneously improve living conditions and undermine dissent (i.e., oppositional popular sector organizations). Since the autonomous organizational capacity of the poor was low—or undermined by the presence of official organizations—the popular sector was unable to keep its needs squarely on the national agenda. Nor was it able to form strong linkages to democratic, reformist forces on the Left (the Party of the Democratic Revolution [PRD]) or the Right (the National Action Party [PAN]) that might make it a locus of political competition rather than a captive of the PRI. Policies remained highly targeted on the consumption side, in both political and socioeconomic terms, and generous funding could not be sustained from one presidential period to the next.

In Mexico, as in Chile, the implementation of a neoliberal developmental model marked a dramatic break with the past. The first moves in this direction occurred under President de la Madrid (1982–88), whose constitutional reforms (Article 25) at once strengthened the state's role in the economy but transformed its intended function from an engine of growth to a regulator of the private sector (Trejo and Jones 1993, 181). While neoliberalism as a development ideology may not be as widely accepted across the Mexican political spectrum as it is in Chile, the historical alternatives—nationalism, populism, and import substitution—have been thoroughly discredited.

Indeed, the emergence of an ideological commitment to neoliberalism can be seen in the willingness of Mexican presidents to challenge the sacred cows of the revolutionary legacy. Reforms to Article 27 of the constitution and the passage of the 1992 Agrarian Law ended the land reform and brought a guarantee of property rights to private landowners. Similarly, any pretense to the nationalism historically so central to regime

TABLE 6. ANTIPOVERTY SPENDING IN MEXICO UNDER PRESIDENT ZEDILLO, 1995–98 (MILLIONS OF CURRENT PESOS)

	1995	1996	1997	1999[a]
Federal Spending	10,002	12,114	13,313	4,078
Decentralized Spending (FSM, FDSM, FAIS)[b]	5,612	7,150	8,223	13,934
Total	15,614	19,264	21,536	18,012

Source: For 1995–97 federal spending, SEDESOL 1999a; for 1999, SEDESOL 1999b; for decentralized spending, SEDESOL 1999c.

[a]These represent funds budgeted but not actually spent.

[b]For 1995, this represents the Municipal Solidarity Fund (FSM); for 1996–97, the Municipal Social Development Fund (FDSM); and for 1999 the Fund to Support Social Infrastructure (FAIS).

legitimacy was abandoned in the ratification of the North American Free Trade Agreement. Just as important as the economic effects that these changes wrought, however, was the transformation of development ideology that they embodied. The combination of tariff reduction, privatization, and guarantees of property rights amounted to a public (and almost irreversible) renunciation of a strong state role in economic guidance. In addition, NAFTA insured that it would be foreign markets (for capital and products) that would in future guide the Mexican political economy.

In ideological terms, a commitment to neoliberalism meant a rethinking of state-society relations that would result in changes to the regime of social provision. As efficiency criteria began to govern state action and an emphasis on market price signals became axiomatic, antipoverty policies were pushed in a more targeted (and means tested) direction (Gordon 1996, 249–50). This squared an important ideological and political circle: it permitted the state to intervene to mitigate poverty but intellectually justified it in terms of nineteenth-century notions of social liberalism rather than the claims of broad-based distributive justice that had formerly prevailed (Gortari and Ziccardi 1996, 226). In intellectual terms, policy also borrowed from the Chilean approach to rendering social and economic policy consistent by utilizing private agents where possible (e.g., private pensions) and emphasizing the objective of perfecting the functioning of market (e.g., FOSIS and PRONASOL). Some have gone so far as to suggest that the creation of this neoliberal form of social welfare was largely an external imposition, linked to the implementation of liberal economic policies and propelled politically by the International Monetary Fund (IMF) (Ward 1993, 628).

But the neoliberal development ideology, shared with contemporary Chile, does not explain the differences in social policy across these two countries. Here the crucial variables are located in the political system. In Chile, before the authoritarian interlude, politics had always been a highly competitive affair, with all tendencies having a meaningful chance of assuming national executive power. Moreover, society, even its poorest segments, had become well organized by the 1960s (see Loveman 1976; and Petras 1969). The dynamic in Mexico, while it did not involve the brutal authoritarianism of the Pinochet dictatorship, has been quite different. Since the Revolution, a single political force—the PRI—has dominated government. While after the 1988 presidential elections party politics became substantially more competitive, with the leftist (PRD) and rightist (PAN) oppositions winning gubernatorial elections, no alternation of national executive power occurred until the PAN candidate won the presidential elections in 2000.

Their previous dominance placed the Mexican governing party in a somewhat different position from that of its Chilean counterparts. With the historic blending of state and party resources, it has typically responded to incipient dissatisfaction in an ad hoc fashion rather than via institutionalized welfare channels. The continuing viability of corporatist social institutions (labor unions, peasant confederations, and popular sector organizations) that date from the 1930s has kept its position secure in the absence of a powerful, autonomous, and organized opposition. When such autonomous mobilization among the poor did develop, public welfare efforts were used to reestablish regime legitimacy and political quiescence.[22]

This dynamic was apparent in the 1980s. When de la Madrid first faced the debt crisis, the response was austerity and even a disproportionate decline in antipoverty spending. Pro-poor policies suffered dramatic reductions, and real wages shrank between 7.7 and 10.5 percent per year between 1983 and 1988, while implicit unemployment reached 20.3 percent by 1985 (Friedmann, Lustig, and Legovini 1995, 334–41). This was possible precisely because up until this time the PRI's political hegemony was unchallenged.

The consequences of this catastrophe were, however, left to the next president, Salinas, who faced a powerful and organized political threat from the Left in the form of Cuauhtémoc Cárdenas and the PRD. Rising political competitiveness provoked a response: Salinas launched a massive new program of poverty relief (PRONASOL) that was also very centrally a political strategy. Resources were to be targeted not simply by degree of poverty but also to areas of opposition strength. In this fashion, he sought to relegitimize the government and turn back the opposition threat (see Horcasitas and Weldon 1994). Indeed, by the 1991 midterm elections, PRI support had rebounded to 61 percent of the vote. This was a remarkable feat, indeed, especially given the scope of the economic catastrophe of the 1980s. The continued dominance of the PRI in the countryside—despite the concentration of poverty there—was also achieved in part through the use of PRONASOL resources.[23]

The effect of the partiality of Mexican democratization on antipoverty policies could be mitigated were the poor able to organize and act autonomously on a large scale. And addressing this historical organizational weakness in civil society was a stated goal of the PRONASOL strategy. By targeting its resources through local solidarity committees, which often included independent local organizations, it was hoped that local instances of citizen participation would emerge to take advantage of available funds and would persist after this period of "seed money" ended. It was also designed to build support for the PRI and co-opt more radical forms of opposition.

At this point, the linkage between political competitiveness and autonomous organization becomes crucial. For PRONASOL to have embodied a truly effective form of social and human capital formation, it would have to have been severed from the discretionary political control of the PRI. Unfortunately, the governing party was incapable of this degree of neutrality. In a move that emphasized its political character, the PRONASOL program was actually administered directly out of the office of the president (Ward 1993, 626).

Consequently, the solidarity committees and the effort at social recapitalization they in part represented did not survive the end of the PRONASOL program. By the time Ernesto Zedillo took office in 1994, most of the over 250,000 committees had ceased to have a meaningful existence. And it is precisely this civil society component that was missing from the Zedillo approach to poverty alleviation. Without extensive efforts to support popular organization, it is unlikely to occur. First, one must remember that many of the effects of free market transformation have been decidedly atomizing and demobilizing, just as in Chile. This is further complicated by the fact that much of the political space for popular representation is already occupied by the PRI-controlled corporatist peasant and labor confederations. Unlike Chile, where the advent of democratization led directly to the reemergence of authentic (if dramatically weakened) intermediaries for peasant and worker interests, in Mexico this political terrain is already occupied. Any actors in civil society seeking to represent these interests must overcome the dual barriers of an atomized and fragmented society and competition from (quasi-)official organizations that monopolize most of the available political space.[24]

The profound weakness of rural civil society in particular may help to explain the discontinuities in Mexican antipoverty policy.[25] Unlike Chile, there has been no sustained alleviation of poverty, nor has there been a sustained strategy for its alleviation. This is in part due to the reduced level of political competition, making such efforts less important, and in part due to the absence of organized intermediaries connected to political parties that might press social demands in an ongoing way. If the Chilean efforts at poverty alleviation have been cautious and broadly targeted, the Mexican efforts have been intermittent and usually politically targeted. While neither represents the best of all possible worlds, at least in Chile the shift toward universal entitlements has made possible sustained and increased public spending on the poor.

Each case, however, ultimately has lessons for the other. Autonomous organization and participation in cross-class alliances have sustained the modest and quasi-universal antipoverty effort in Chile. But the advent of more substantial initiatives would require a more competitive political environment than that faced by the first two Concertación administrations.[26] In Mexico, in contrast, once the PRI's near death experience appeared to have passed, few organized actors could protest the dismantling of the briefly formidable and potentially innovative antipoverty effort of the Salinas presidency. The recent opposition presidential election victory is from this perspective a hopeful occurrence.

CONCLUSIONS

What do the experiences of Chile and Mexico tell us about the conditions that undergird different programs of poverty eradication? First and foremost, development strategies and ideologies place boundaries on the range of possible approaches to poverty relief that are politically viable. Second, political competition and conflict in the context of democracy are critical in determining policy within these limits, but democracy should be thought of in terms of degrees. In comparatively uncompetitive contexts, states may well engage in poverty relief, but their efforts have tended to take the form of means (and politically) tested efforts to combat short-run problems and reduce the potential for dissent. On the other hand, the establishment of open democratic competition by itself is insufficient to drive an antipoverty agenda, even when the impoverished population is numerous. Rather, party system dynamics and the level of competitiveness (the quality of democratic practice) are crucial mediators of policy outcomes. Where several reformist parties compete with each other, poor voters cannot be held as a captive constituency and antipoverty efforts and political accountability are likely to be highest, as in Chile before 1973. Where only one political party has as part of its goals serious antipoverty efforts, the latter can more easily be subordinated to other goals and responsiveness to actors in civil society is reduced. They have few other political options.

Finally, it has also been recognized that the recent shift toward more free market forms of economic organization have an atomizing effect on civil society, indeed, disproportionately on the more marginalized sectors of civil society. But if the formation of coalitions supporting a pro-poor agenda is to occur the popular sectors must generate autonomous representative organizations. Thus, antipoverty programs that support the organization of the poorer sectors of civil society—that is, those that support social capital formation, especially on the productive side—will have a greater likelihood of sparking a virtuous cycle. If an initial effort results in the generation of more powerful representatives of the poor in national politics, these same social actors become increasingly attractive as coalition partners and will be more able to sustain the antipoverty efforts that gave birth to them.

NOTES

This chapter is an adapted version of an article first published as "Understanding the Third World Welfare State after Neoliberalism: The Politics of Social Provision in Chile and Mexico," *Comparative Politics* 34 (April 2002): 293–313. It has been reprinted here in revised form with the permission of *Comparative Politics*. It could not have been completed without the help and support of a large number of individuals. Those to whom I owe a special debt of gratitude for having read many drafts of the manuscript are Peter Houtzager and Andrew Schrank. Ken Greene, Mick Moore, Ken Shadlen, and the many commentators at the conference arranged by the Institute for Development Studies and the Department for International Development in the United Kingdom were also invaluable to the improvement of this work. Whatever errors and omissions remain are the fault of the author.

1. I use *competitive* here rather than *democratic* out of a recognition that electoral competition has not always been fully "free and fair" in the cases in question. Nevertheless, all were characterized by a substantial level of competition among alternative political forces.

2. During the course of military rule (1973–89), the Chilean economy was reorganized along free market lines. Simultaneously, social welfare efforts were dramatically reduced and left in the form of highly targeted transfers to the very poorest strata of society. Former health, pension, and labor entitlements were abolished.

3. This is commonly argued in the American case. See Weir, Orloff, and Skocpol 1988; and Wilson 1996.

4. I do not wish to ascribe to the emergence of development models or ideologies excessive degrees of internal consistency and intentionality but only to consider the way in which they tend to shape outcomes through the elective affinities they entail (for an insightful discussion of the way in which such a development ideology can emerge, see Waterbury 1999).

5. Good examples of the importance of idea systems can be found in Weir and Skocpol's (1985) discussion of responses to economic depression in Sweden, the United States, and the United Kingdom. Critical to the adoption of demand stimulus policies in the first two cases was the relative absence of an intellectual commitment to orthodox economic policies such as was true of the Treasury Department in the United Kingdom. Hirschman (1968, 9) notes the emergence of a nationalist "developmentalist" ideology during the period of Brazilian import substitution.

6. The classic discussion of this is, of course, Cardoso and Faletto [1967] 1979.

7. For an examination in the case of Chile, see Kurtz 1999a.

8. Nationalization can be (and was) seen as both a developmental and antipoverty strategy, since by removing expatriated private profits it released funds for both reinvestment and redistribution.

9. This is particularly clear in the rural areas, where agricultural extension aid to smallholders became the hallmark of policy, in marked contrast with the land redistribution of the 1967–73 period.

10. The minimum wage is complex. I classify it as universalistic, as for large segments of the economy it is not effectively enforced. It obviously has application at the bottom rungs of the formal sector labor force, but it serves as more of a guideline for the large informal sector. Thus, as it is not in the Chilean context aimed at the poorest, and because its effects are felt in a broad swath of the income distribution it is more accurately thought of as "universalist" in orientation than "targeted."

11. Examples include the subsidized crop insurance available to all producers (Seguro Agrícola), which comes with a maximum benefit cap, and the agricultural extension services (Servicio de Asesoría Local), which are limited to only the smallest farmers (INDAP 2002).

12. For a book-length treatment, see Valdés 1989.

13. Indeed, even the pension system took on this individualized and welfare-based form: largely employer funded entitlements were replaced with a compulsory (for formal sector workers) private savings scheme that required no employer participation (Vergara 1994). Moreover, only a very small "poverty pension" scheme was to be financed by the state itself, via general tax revenues, and was aimed at those workers whose private savings were inadequate for retirement.

14. On the conversion of the bulk of the Chilean Left to free market economic ideas, see Roberts 1995.

15. The binomial electoral system consists of a series of two-member districts. In these districts, the first- and second-place finishers receive seats, unless the first-place list receives double the votes of the second-place list (in the Chilean context, this is rare). Especially in Chile, where the Left is slightly weaker than the center or Right, this is a powerful incentive keeping the Socialists in the Concertación alliance. The formerly important Communist Party maintained its autonomy and commitment to statism, and as a consequence it has no legislative presence whatsoever.

16. Agüero and Tironi (1999, 161) show that in class terms the Concertación wins overwhelmingly among the lower classes, is competitive in the middle sectors, and is decidedly unpopular among the upper classes.

17. On the sector-specific aspects of social and political disarticulation, see Kurtz 1999b.

18. Initially, the Concertación saw the minimum wage as an issue for corporatist bargaining between the Chamber of Commerce (CPC) and the labor confederation (CUT). The CPC quickly withdrew from the process, and recently the government has preferred to unilaterally impose minimum wage increases without coming to an agreement with the CUT. The government has shown little flexibility, and it has not been punished for this stance.

19. Carlos Salinas received his Ph.D. from Harvard University in 1978 and consolidated the trend toward a new generation of "technocratic" presidents that began with his predecessor, Miguel de la Madrid.

20. I do not mean to say that Mexico is more democratic than Chile. Rather, I contend that the likelihood of opposition victory in Mexico was greater than the likelihood that the Right could seriously challenge the Concertación's presidential candidates in Chile in 1989 or 1993.

21. Many observers wonder whether the leftist opposition candidate, Cuauhtémoc Cárdenas, was denied victory by fraud. In any event, it was the narrowest margin of any PRI candidate, with Salinas officially garnering only 50.3 percent of the vote.

22. A good example of this is the brief return to serious agrarian reform under President Echeverría (1970–76) in response to rising unrest in the early 1970s (see Bartra 1992).

23. See Myhre 1998 on the mechanisms of credit provision to the peasantry. Gibson (1997) emphasizes the importance of the rural base to the continued viability of the PRI.

24. This is not a claim that full-fledged corporatist control has been maintained. Rather, I suggest that the mere existence of quasi-official groups in a particular political field produces even greater barriers to autonomous organization than are produced by the severe collective action problems attendant upon neoliberal restructuring alone.

25. This claim may appear to be belied by the presence of the Zapatista rebels in Chiapas, Mexico. Given the massive economic disruptions that have particularly affected the rural sector since the 1980s, what is surprising is the small scale and isolated character of rural resistance. The Zapatista movement remains confined to an extremely remote part of Chiapas, one that is characterized by unique social conditions (recent colonization, very strong ethnic identification, and limited connection to the broader economy) (see Harvey 1998). While certainly internationally prominent, this movement has nowhere near the scope of many earlier bouts of rural insurrection in Mexico. The remainder of the countryside is, in contrast, deafeningly quiet.

26. From this perspective, the narrow margin of victory of Socialist Ricardo Lagos in the recent presidential election (51.3 percent against the right's 48.7 percent) is a hopeful sign. Conservative inroads into popular sector communities can only raise their importance to the governing coalition.

REFERENCES

Agüero, Felipe, and Eugenio Tironi. 1999. "Sobrevivirá el Nuevo Paisaje Político Chileno?" *Estudios Públicos* 74 (autumn): 151–68.

Bartra, Armando. 1992. *Los herederos de Zapata: Movimientos campesinos posrevolucionarios en México*. Mexico City: Ediciones Era.

Bates, Robert. 1981. *Markets and States in Tropical Africa*. Berkeley: University of California Press.

Bravo, David, and Joaquin Vial. 1997. "La fijación del salario mínimo en Chile: Elementos para una discusión." *Colección Estudios CIEPLAN* 45 (June): 117–51.

Büchi Buc, Hernán. 1993. *La transformación económica de Chile: Del estatismo a la libertad económica*. Barcelona: Grupo Editorial Norma.

Cardoso, Fernando, and Enzo Faletto. [1967] 1979. *Dependency and Development in Latin America*. Translated by Marjory Matting. Berkeley: University of California Press.

Consejo Consultivo del Programa Nacional de Solidaridad. 1994. *El Programa Nacional de Solidaridad: una visión de la modernización de México*. Mexico City: Fondo de Cultura Económica.

Cornelius, Wayne, Ann Craig, and Jonathan Fox. 1994. "Mexico's National Solidarity Program: An Overview." In Wayne Cornelius, Ann Craig, and Jonathan Fox, eds., *Transforming State-Society Relations in Mexico: The National Solidarity Strategy*. San Diego: Center for U.S.-Mexican Studies.

Evans, Peter. 1995. *Embedded Autonomy: States and Industrial Transformation*. Princeton: Princeton University Press.

Fox, Jonathan. 1994. "The Difficult Transition from Clientelism to Citizenship: Lessons from Mexico." *World Politics* 46 (January): 151–84.

Friedmann, Santiago, Nora Lustig, and Arianna Legovini. 1995. "Mexico: Social Spending and Food Subsidies during Adjustment in the 1980s." In Nora Lustig, ed., *Coping with Austerity: Poverty and Inequality in Latin America*. Washington, DC: Brookings Institution.

Garretón, Manuel. 1983. *El proceso político Chileno*. Santiago: Facultad Latinoamericana de Ciencias Sociales.

Garrett, Geoffrey. 1996. "Capital Mobility, Trade, and the Domestic Politics of Economic Policy." In Robert O. Keohane and Helen Milner, eds., *Internationalization and Domestic Politics*. Cambridge: Cambridge University Press.

Gibson, Edward. 1997. "The Populist Road to Market Reform: Policy and Electoral Coalitions in Mexico and Argentina." *World Politics* 49, no. 3 (April): 339–70.

Gordon, Sara. 1996. "Entre la eficiencia y la legitimidad: el Pronasol como política social." In Rosalba Casas Guerrero, ed., *Las políticas sociales de México en los años noventa*. Mexico City: UNAM, FLACSO, and Playa y Valdés.

Gortari, Hira, and Alicia Ziccardi. 1996. "Instituciones y clientelas de la política social: Un esbozo histórico, 1867–1994." In Rosalba Casas Guerrero, ed., *Las políticas sociales de México en los años noventa*. Mexico City: UNAM, FLACSO, and Playa y Valdés.

Harvey, Neil. 1998. *The Chiapas Rebellion: The Struggle for Land and Democracy*. Durham: Duke University Press.

Hirschman, Albert. 1968. "The Political Economy of Import-Substituting Industrialization in Latin America." *Quarterly Journal of Economics* 82 (February): 1–32.

Horcasitas, Juan, and Jeffrey Weldon. 1994. "Electoral Determinants and Consequences of National Solidarity." In Wayne Cornelius, Ann Craig, and Jonathan Fox, eds., *Transforming State-Society Relations in Mexico: The National Solidarity Strategy*. San Diego: Center for U.S.-Mexican Studies.

Houtzager, Peter, and Marcus Kurtz. 2000. "The Institutional Roots of Popular Mobilization: State Transformation and Rural Politics in Brazil and Chile, 1960–95." *Comparative Studies in Society and History* 42, no. 2 (April): 394–424.

INDAP [Instituto de Desarrollo Agropecuario]. 2002. "Seguro Agrícola and Servicio de Asesoría Local." Available at <http://www.indap.cl> (accessed January 31, 2002).

Kaufman, Robert. 1972. *The Politics of Land Reform in Chile, 1950–1970*. Cambridge: Harvard University Press.

Kurtz, Marcus. 1999a. "Chile's Neo-liberal Revolution: Incremental Decisions and Structural Transformation, 1973–89." *Journal of Latin American Studies* 31, no. 2: 339–428.

———. 1999b. "Free Markets and Democratic Consolidation in Chile: The National Politics of Rural Transformation." *Politics and Society* 27, no. 2 (June 1999): 275–301.

León, Arturo. 1994. "Urban Poverty in Chile: Its Extent and Diversity." Democracy and Social Policy Working Paper 8. Notre Dame, IN, Kellogg Institute.

Loveman, Brian. 1976. *Struggle in the Countryside.* Bloomington: Indiana University Press.

Marín, Juan Carlos. 1972. *Las tomas.* Santiago: ICIRA.

Mejía, José, and Rob Vos. 1997. "Poverty in Latin America and the Caribbean: An Inventory, 1980–95." Working Paper I–4. Washington, DC, Inter-American Development Bank.

Ministerio de Planificación y Cooperación [MIDEPLAN]. 1998. *Distribución e Impacto Distributivo del Gasto Social en los Hogares.* Santiago, Chile: MIDEPLAN.

———. 1992. *Programas sociales: su impacto en los hogares chilenos.* Santiago, Chile: MIDEPLAN.

———. 1991. *Evolución de las Políticas Sociales en Chile, 1920–1991.* Santiago: MIDEPLAN.

Myhre, David. 1998. "The Achilles' Heel of Reforms: The Rural Finance System." In Wayne Cornelius and David Myhre, eds., *The Transformation of Rural Mexico: Reforming the Ejido Sector.* San Diego: Center for U.S.-Mexican Studies.

Oxhorn, Philip. 1995. *Organizing Civil Society: The Popular Sectors and the Struggle for Democracy in Chile.* University Park: Pennsylvania State University Press.

Petras, James. 1969. *Politics and Social Forces in Chilean Development.* Berkeley: University of California Press.

Piñera, José. 1991. *El cascabel al gato: La batalla por la reforma previsional.* Santiago: Zig-Zag.

Poder Ejecutivo Federal. 1995. *Plan Nacional de Desarrollo, 1995–2000.* Mexico City: Secretaría de Hacienda y Crédito Público.

Prebisch, Raúl. 1959. "Commercial Policy in the Underdeveloped Countries." *American Economic Review* 49 (May): 251:73.

Raczynski, Dagmar, and Pilar Romaguera. 1995. "Chile: Poverty, Adjustment, and Social Policies in the 1980's." In Nora Lustig, ed., *Coping with Austerity: Poverty and Inequality in Latin America.* Washington DC: The Brookings Institute.

Roberts, Kenneth. 1995. "From the Barricades to the Ballot Box: Redemocratization and Political Realignment in the Chilean Left." *Politics and Society* 23, no. 4 (December): 495–519.

Scully, Timothy. 1992. *Rethinking the Center: Party Politics in Nineteenth- and Twentieth-Century Chile.* Stanford: Stanford University Press.

SEDESOL. 1999a. *La Política Social y el Combate a la Pobreza en México.* Mexico City: Unpublished document.

———. 1996b. *Estrategia de Combate a la Pobreza y Resultados por Programa.* Mexico City: Unpublished document.

———. 1999c. *Infraestructura Social Básica 1999*. Mexico City: Unpublished Document.

———. 1994. *Solidaridad: Seis Años de Trabajo*. Mexico City: SEDESOL and Solidaridad.

Serrano, Claudio. 1996. "Gobierno regional e inversión pública descentralizada." *Colección Estudios CIEPLAN* 42 (June).

Trejo, Guillermo, and Claudio Jones. 1993. *Contra la pobreza: Por una estrategia de política social*. Mexico City: Editorial Cal y Arena snf Centro de Investigaciones para el Desarrollo.

Valdés, Juan Gabriel. 1989. *La escuela de Chicago: Operación Chile*. Buenos Aires: Grupo Editorial Zeta.

Valenzuela, Arturo. 1978. *The Breakdown of Democratic Regimes: Chile*. Baltimore: Johns Hopkins University Press.

Vergara, Pilar. 1996. "In Pursuit of 'Growth with Equity': The Limits of Chile's Free Market Social Reforms." *NACLA Report on the Americas* 29, no. 6 (May–June).

———. 1994. "Market Economy, Social Welfare, and Democratic Consolidation in Chile." In William C. Smith, Carlos Acuña, and Eduardo Gamarra, eds., *Democracy, Markets, and Structural Reform in Latin America*. New Brunswick, NJ: Transaction.

———. 1986. "Changes in the Economic Functions of the Chilean State under the Military Regime." In J. Samuel Valenzuela and Arturo Valenzuela, eds., *Military Rule in Chile: Dictatorship and Oppositions*. Baltimore: Johns Hopkins University Press.

Ward, Peter. 1993. "Social Welfare Policy and Political Opening in Mexico." *Journal of Latin American Studies* 25: 613–28.

Waterbury, John. 1999. "The Long Gestation and Brief Triumph of Import-Substituting Industrialization." *World Development* 27, no. 2: 323–41.

Weir, Margaret, Ann Orloff, and Theda Skocpol. 1988. "The Future of Social Policy in the United States: Political Constraints and Possibilities." In Margaret Weir, Ann Orloff, and Theda Skocpol, eds., *The Politics of Social Policy in the United States*. Princeton: Princeton University Press.

Weir, Margaret, and Theda Skocpol. 1985. "State Structures and the Possibilities for 'Keynesian' Responses to the Great Depression in Sweden, Britain, and the United States." In Peter B. Evans, Dietrich Rueschemeyer, and Theda Skocpol, eds., *Bringing the State Back In*. Cambridge: Cambridge University Press.

Weiss, Linda. 1998. *The Myth of the Powerless State*. Ithaca: Cornell University Press.

Williamson, John. 1994. "In Search of a Manual for Technopols." In John Williamson, ed., *The Political Economy of Policy Reform*. Washington, DC: Institute for International Economics.

Wilson, William J. 1996. *When Work Disappears: The World of the New Urban Poor*. New York: Vintage.

Wurgaft, José. 1993. *Fondos de inversión social en América Latina*. Santiago: PREALC and OIT.

7 *Polity Qualities*

HOW GOVERNANCE AFFECTS POVERTY

Mick Moore (with Jennifer Leavy and Howard White)

This chapter employs some basic statistical analysis to address a question that has not been asked before. The question sounds complex and jargonistic: what explains the different efficiencies with which national political economies convert national material resources into mass welfare (i.e., human development)? It is actually a way of throwing new light on an old and familiar question: how does the quality of governance affect poverty? At the highest level of generality, the answer seems obvious: well-being will spread when governments are able to enforce the rule of law, suppress banditry and crime, collect enough taxes to finance a public education system, and do the other things that feature in any commonsense list of the functions of the state. Since public authorities in many poor countries currently fail to perform many of these tasks, it seems highly likely that improvements in governance will help reduce poverty. Serious disagreement begins when we ask more precisely *how* the very wide differences in the patterns of governance found in contemporary poor countries affect the welfare of their poorer people. There is no consensus on the answer but rather a diversity of views that in part reflects deep-rooted philosophical and ideological differences about the nature and functions of government. It is the role of social scientists to confront these kinds of preconceptions with evidence. At present, evidence is especially important in the field of international development because most aid donors and international financial institutions have been propagating a set of ideas about governance and poverty that are rooted more in ideology than in evidence, are certainly too standardized and simplified, and may be substantially awry. The essence of the donor consensus has been that market-conforming economic policies and liberal democratic governance reforms are mutually supportive and jointly represent the best way to reduce poverty. The statistical analysis reported here, which is based on analyzing cross-sectional variations among contemporary developing countries (only),[1] suggests that this consensus is wrong in important ways.

Our statistical results are robust and significant. We have done nothing fancy but used only straightforward data sets and basic analytic techniques. The first conclusion is essentially methodological, but it is no less important for that. We demonstrate the usefulness of a new and relatively simple measure of the performance of national polities in relation to poverty. Relative income conversion efficiency (RICE) is defined as the relative efficiency of national political economies in converting national material resources into human development. Crudely, how much education and good health is generated per dollar of gross national product (GDP)? This measure should have wider application, for it cuts through many of the complexities of statistically assessing how the quality of governance relates to poverty reduction. Our more substantive conclusions relate to the factors that explain, in a statistical sense, variations among countries in the RICE score. Two of these—population density and West African location—are incidental to our immediate interests. The three main political explanatory factors are, however, very germane to the broad concerns of this volume. They individually or jointly (1) throw serious doubt on the donor consensus on good governance summarized earlier and (2) support the meta-assumption behind this volume that nationally rooted differences in political institutions and state-society relations help explain differences in patterns of poverty and in the political possibilities for tackling it. The three findings, in ascending order of significance, are the following

- In common with related inquiries, we find no evidence that electoral democracies do any better in reducing poverty than other regime types.
- We find that governments that are heavily dependent on mineral resources for revenues tend to perform particularly badly in terms of poverty reduction. This finding is consistent with a growing body of research findings on the malignant effects of mineral wealth on governance and contributes to an emerging understanding of the broad causes of poor governance in the developing world.
- Our findings undermine the credibility of one of the most popular official measures of the quality of governance in poor countries: the ratings accorded governments for responsiveness to the needs of international investors and lenders—the International Country Risk Guide measures. Governments rated highly on these ICRG measures consistently perform badly in poverty reduction. If these ICRG measures do indeed gauge accurately

differences in the extent to which governments pursue market-conforming policies in general, then we must question how consistent such policies are with "pro-poor" outcomes. If instead the ICRG indicators gauge something narrower—the attractiveness of countries to foreign investors and lenders—then we cannot honestly use them to measure "good government" in a broad sense. We are rather edged toward a more traditional conclusion: that there is an element of direct conflict between policies that favor (international) capital and policies that favor the poor.

The next section deals in general terms with the problem of researching the link between governance and poverty through statistical comparisons of the recent experiences of developing countries. It is intended to explain why the apparently indirect analytic method adopted here is so useful. The main point is that alternative ways of testing the connections between governance and poverty suffer severe limitations. Readers can skip this section and still understand our analytic procedure and the results. The succeeding sections explain our statistical procedures; summarize the main results; and assess their implications.

GOVERNANCE-POVERTY CONNECTIONS:
EXPLORING THE TERRITORY

Governance, poverty reduction, and the relationship between the two are currently at the forefront of the programs and policy statements of international aid and development agencies. The allocation of development assistance is being shaped by judgments about how committed governments of poor countries are to reducing poverty and improving governance. There are strong pressures to measure (changes in) poverty and the quality of governance on a cross-national basis, to test for statistical associations between the two variables, and to derive broad policy conclusions. If statistically minded social scientists refuse to engage, then untested assertions about the connections between poverty and governance may rule the day. Yet statistical analysis of the poverty-governance connection on a cross-national basis is fraught with problems. The two central concepts—poverty reduction and good governance—are both broad and abstract. For operational purposes, each can be defined and measured in a variety of ways. There are few data bases that provide us with reliable measures of these concepts for poor countries. Those data bases that do exist tend to be recent, to have little historical depth, to be subject to much questioning on grounds of accuracy, and consistently to underrepresent the poorest countries. We discuss these issues in this section, avoiding technical detail and focusing on key points about concepts and method. Our first objective is simply to demonstrate the wide diversity of approaches that might be used and therefore to encourage readers to be skeptical and critical of apparently general research "conclusions" about the governance-poverty connection. The second objective is to explain why it is difficult to draw any conclusions from what might appear to be the obvious approach: examining how differences in governance impact changes in the per capita incomes of the poor. We pursue these objectives by dealing with three major questions of method.

- How practically to define and measure "poverty"?
- How practically to define and measure "quality of governance"?
- How practically to define, measure, and assess the causes of "poverty reduction"?

DEFINING AND MEASURING POVERTY

Purely material or money-metric concepts of poverty are not popular these days. Most of us prefer a broader concept of poverty—something like "ill-being," "deprivation," or "lack of capabilities." We can sidestep the arguments about precisely how broad our definition should be by limiting ourselves to those alternative conceptions of poverty that are measurable. There are at least four broad notions of poverty that are accurately measurable on a cross-national basis now—or could conceivably be in the near future. They are listed in ascending order, starting with the most basic notion of poverty as absence of basic human needs and progressing toward higher level conceptions of poverty as the absence of "capabilities."

- *Undernutrition*
- *Income*—understood here as shorthand for some broad concept encompassing income, expenditure, and consumption.
- *Longevity/mortality*—or some broader concept such as disability-adjusted life years—that is, the number of years of good health that a baby can expect at birth.
- *Education/literacy*

Not only do we have four different, broad, measurable concepts of poverty, but each can be defined in a different way. We could define *undernutrition* according to some combination of wasting and stunting among different age groups. *Income* could refer to income, consumption, or expenditure; we could refer to private income or include the use of publicly provided resources (roads, famine relief, education, etc.). The concepts of *longevity/mortality* and *education/literacy* each have many potential faces. Having decided on operational definitions, there are further questions and decisions. First, do we accept the data series we have available or begin to make adjustments to them because we know, for example, that the operational definition of *literacy* is strict in some countries and lax in others? How, then, can we be sure that our adjustments are both technically appropriate and likely to command general acceptance? Second, should we combine some of the separate measures of poverty into a composite poverty index? If we do, we then have to make a choice about how to weight the various components in relation to each other. Once again, our technical decisions have to command widespread professional acceptance if the results of statistical analysis based on them are to be credible. In sum, there are literally hundreds of different ways in which one could conceivably measure poverty. Conversely, and especially in relation to the poorer countries, we often have a very limited choice of data series.

DEFINING AND MEASURING QUALITY OF GOVERNANCE

This contrast—between an abundance of conceivable definitions and a dearth of actual usable data series—is greater in the case of governance. The first problem is that, within political science and political philosophy, there is a deep-rooted and continuing fundamental difference between two views of the state.[2] Liberals view state power primarily as a (potential) threat to the well-being of citizens and define *good governance* primarily in terms of legal, constitutional, and other arrangements that protect against this threat. They want to constrain the state, and warm to terms like *accountability, democracy,* and *participation.* By contrast, statists see the state primarily as a means of aggregating power and resources that may be used for the collective good. States provide order and security, protect commerce, build infrastructure, and create the conditions under which citizens can cooperate and transact peacefully. Statists view the weakness of government—manifested as disorder, vulnerability to external threat, or failure to provide collective goods—as the prime potential problem. They therefore tend to interpret good governance in terms of arrangements that promote the coherence and effectiveness of the state. They warm to terms like *authority, order,* and *capability.*

One can solve this problem in principle by incorporating into one's conception of good government both the liberal and the conservative perspectives. Indeed, no sensible theorist could do anything else: in a world of states, some compromise between these two sets of values constitutes the essence of good government. But at what point is the compromise to be made? We know that the strongest national contenders for contemporary good governance prizes look very different from one another and that there is no consensus on their ranking: Botswana, Costa Rica, Japan, Singapore, Sweden, Switzerland, the United States have all had their promoters and opponents in recent years. There is wide scope to dispute the weight to be given to different components of good government and to disagree about how to deal with tensions and conflicts between them.

This is, however, only the beginning of the measurement problem. We then have to decide how far to assess governance according to (1) *processes* (i.e., the way government is conducted), (2) *policies,* or (3) *outcomes.* These are contentious issues that lie at the heart of much current international dispute. For example, governance in China is generally ranked poorly by Western and global organizations with respect to processes and policies; but the outcomes, especially economic growth rates, are impressive. Suppose we resolve these issues and agree on a list of, for example, the major processual dimensions of good government: effective public service, rule of law, democracy, constitutionalism, effective mechanisms for making public policy, and the ability of the state to exercise its authority throughout its territory. The moment we start to try to find measures of these abstract processes we realize that we have to use a much larger number of variables. For example, more operational measures of a notion like "an effective public service" might include to what extent public servants are recruited on the basis of merit and without strong political or social bias, how effective budgetary and auditing mechanisms are, how well public offices are equipped, and what protections exist to protect public servants against corruption and the arbitrary use of power. Most of these things are very difficult to measure. Scarcely any have been measured on a cross-national basis. We have little empirical idea how the different measures relate to one another.

In principle, if a concept is highly disputed it is much better for purposes of statistical analysis to have a range of alternative measures. There are apparently a large number of potential indicators of the quality of governance available on an international basis. Many have been produced recently in response to the concerns reflected in this chapter. However, Steven Knack and Nick Manning have lately applied to them five basic tests of reliability, relevance, and coverage and found that almost all the data series failed the test.[3] In sum, when we look for cross-national data bases on quality of governance, we have (1) no consensus about what we should be measuring and (2) a choice limited to a few data sets that at best measure only one dimension of governance.[4]

DEFINING, MEASURING, AND ASSESSING THE CAUSES OF POVERTY REDUCTION

Conceptually, pro-poor outcomes (i.e., poverty reduction) come in two different forms.

- The first is an average improvement in the conditions of all people living in a poor environment (or country), for example, an increase in GNP per head in Bangladesh, in nutritional status in Bolivia, or in longevity in Burundi.

• The second is a pro-poor bias in outcomes within a particular jurisdiction, for example, an increased share of national income for the poor in Bangladesh ("pro-poor growth"); a "dispropor-tionate" improvement in nutritional status for the poor in Bolivia; or an especially large extension of life expectancy for the poor in Burundi.

Given the high levels of income inequality in many poor countries, there is a strong general case for taking intranational distributions of welfare explicitly into account and therefore for preferring the second of these two concepts of pro-poor outcomes. If we take that option, we then have to decide which section of a national (or other territorially defined) population is to be categorized as "the poor": the poorest 20 percent, 40 percent? Once we have sorted those questions of definition—and one should generally be comprehensive and try several—we appear to be on the right terrain. Surely the best indicator of a pro-poor outcome is changes over time in the relative welfare of the poor or in their relative access to resources. In principle, this is true. However, there are serious practical problems. We simply do not have sufficiently accurate data series for poor countries to enable us to track over time changes in the degree to which the poor, *relative* to the nonpoor, enjoy good nutrition, health, education, or literacy. The only extensive data sets we have relate to the distribution of incomes. But these are problematic for three distinct reasons.

• The first is that the data we have available on changes in intranational income distribution are unreliable. Even for rich countries with relatively good statistical services, different data sources paint very different pictures. These basic warnings, although repeated regularly, tend routinely to be ignored in the scramble to produce research results.[5]
• The second problem is that over the short and medium terms changes in income distribution in poor countries may reflect factors that are effectively "random" from the perspective of governance—notably, changes in price ratios over which public authorities have very little control. Almost all data series on income distribution are based on periodic household sample surveys. Over a five-year period, for example, poverty might fall appreciably in Pakistan because of a fall in the real cost of basic food staples. But those price effects might reflect (1) pure market forces, national or international (e.g., large-scale imports of cheap American wheat); (2) effective, intentional government

policy, or (3) some combination of the two. It is very difficult
to sort out the truth, especially because we cannot take the
declared intentions of governments as reliable indicators of successful intervention to modify market processes.

• The third problem in drawing conclusions from changes over
time in income distribution is similar but more general. Many
complex, interrelated influences affect changes in the incomes of
poor people, and it is very difficult to isolate the influence of
governance. We can be fairly certain that the primary explanation for changes in the incidence of poverty lies in rates and patterns of national economic growth (Dollar and Kraay 2000). But
what determines those? How far does governance contribute?
And how far can governance influence the pattern as well as the
rate of national economic growth? We do not know. Recent
cross-national statistical analysis has identified dozens of different variables that correlate with variations in rates of national
economic growth (Sala-I-Martin 1997). We have neither the data
nor the statistical techniques to determine, with any degree of
confidence, which of them are causally significant. We can be
fairly sure that rates of economic growth reflect the complex
interaction of a lot of factors. But we do not know which ones
or in which combination.[6]

More could be said on this subject, but the bottom line is clear: the
most "obvious" route to assessing the impact of governance on poverty
reduction is not open. We are unable to throw light on the contribution
of governance to poverty reduction by undertaking cross-national statistical analysis of the determinants of either rates of national economic
growth or changes in income distribution over time. We have few reliable
data series and many complex potential explanatory factors, some of
which might vary randomly over the medium term. It is not possible to
test for the impact of governance on poverty reduction by first determining the degree to which changes over time in poverty can be explained by
means of "purely" economic variables and then exploring how far governance variables can explain the residual.

The approach used here obviates these problems. We accept the
impossibility of drawing any robust conclusions about the impact of governance by trying to explain changes over time in poverty variables
within poor countries. We rather make cross-sectional comparisons
among countries using a simple but robust, inclusive, and stable measure
of the apparent "pro-poorness" of states: the extent to which national
economic resources are converted into "human development" for the
mass of the populations over which these states (formally) rule.

TESTING GOVERNANCE-POVERTY CONNECTIONS

National political economies vary considerably in their capacity to turn their material resources—gross domestic product (GDP) or GNP per head of the population—into human development outputs (the welfare of the mass of the population). We can measure the pro-poorness of a polity by its relative efficiency at this task. Our dependent variable is defined in principle as the relative efficiency of national political-economic systems in converting national material resources into human development. For simplicity, we will label as RICE both this underlying concept and our operational measure of it. The procedure followed to arrive at our operational measure of RICE is quite straightforward.

For some years the United Nations Development Program (UNDP) has been calculating what is known as the human development index (HDI) for all countries. The index is a composite measure, with three equally weighted components.[7]

- Life expectancy.
- Educational attainment, which is in turn composed of two sub-components: (1) adult literacy rates (given a two-thirds weighting); and (2) combined primary, secondary, and tertiary school enrollments (with a one-third weighting).
- Real GDP per capita.

Taking the 1995 HDI figures, we recalculated a modified HDI by omitting the GDP component. Following UNDP practice, we call this HDI*, which therefore comprises two equally weighted components: life expectancy and educational attainment. We then regressed HDI* on the natural logarithm of GNP per capita (purchasing power parity, 1995) to generate an operational measure of RICE. Technically, RICE is the residual of the regression of HDI* on the logarithm of income per capita. It is defined and measured for each country in the sample as the ordinary least squares (OLS) difference between (1) actual HDI* for 1995 and (2) the HDI* level that was predicted for that country in the regression equation on the basis of 1995 per capita GNP (purchasing power parity). Put more simply, RICE is the difference between (1) the actual level of the human development indicator for a country and (2) the level that one would predict for that country on the basis of its income per head and the typical relation of income and human development for the total sample of countries. RICE is either positive (i.e., the country performs better than predicted in terms of human development indicators) or negative. The RICE figures for our sample of countries are given in the second column of table A1 in the appendix at the end of this chapter.

This procedure for defining the dependent variable is unlikely to be

contentious. We know that levels of national income are powerful determinants of levels of human development (education, literacy, health, and
longevity).[8] The deviations of actual from projected human development
are prima facie good measures of the concept we are reaching for: the relative efficiency of national political-economic systems in converting
national material resources into human development. We used these HDI
data to estimate RICE because they are available and have received
sufficient attention and scrutiny that their reliability is to some degree
assured. Accepting the general approach followed here, one can raise
questions about whether RICE is the best way to measure our underlying
concept, that is, the relative efficiency of national political-economic systems in converting national material resources into human development.
We do not find any of these questions very worrying.[9] In sum, while we
are hungry for better measures of our dependent variable, we are not des-
perate.[10] In the case of the explanatory variables, the situation is less satisfactory.

The analysis was from the beginning driven by an explicit theory. We
were attempting to help test a set of ideas, explained in more detail later
in this section, about the ways in which sources of government revenue
shape patterns of public policy. However, we were aware that our measures of these revenue variables, and some of a wide range of other variables also likely to affect RICE, were indirect and unsatisfactory. To
some degree, we have to use whatever data series (1) are available, (2)
appear to be reliable, and (3) have some potential to throw light on plausible explanatory hypotheses. We decided to work with as large a sample
of poor countries as possible. Our universe was all countries defined by
the World Bank as low or middle income. We excluded countries from
the analysis only if data were not available. We ended up with sixty-one
countries. We did not use some other available data series that would
have necessitated a substantial reduction in sample size. The poorest
countries are generally particularly badly represented in incomplete
cross-national data series. Working with a smaller number of countries
would have led to severe underrepresentation of the poorest and would
have frustrated our objective of explaining differences among the full
range of countries with low- and lower-middle incomes.

In general, our explanatory variables are less satisfactory than our
dependent variable (RICE) in the sense that they are often indirect proxies for the things we would like to measure. Given these limitations, it
was something of a surprise that several turned out to be statistically
significant and that they jointly explain up to 55 percent of the observed
intercountry variance in RICE.

Our models all incorporate a time lag: it seems self-evident that the
level of human development relative to income in country X at a given
moment will reflect events and processes in preceding decades more than

it reflects immediate circumstances.[11] The dependent variable, RICE, relates to 1995. The explanatory variables are in most cases measured as an average for the 1980s (1980–89).[12]

Most of the explanatory variables that we have used in our preferred regression model derive from the underlying hypotheses we were testing or from inspection of early regression results. However, we used a clustering process to select from a wide range of potential explanatory variables that are political in the narrow sense of the term. First, we identified fourteen potentially interesting political variables from two main cross-national political data sets: nine from Polity III[13] and five from ICRG.[14] Fourteen is still a large number. Because some of them are likely to be highly intercorrelated, it would not be sensible to enter them all into a regression equation: the resulting multicollinearity would reduce the measured statistical significance of the resulting coefficients. Hence we tested for association between these fourteen political variables, grouped them into related clusters, and finally chose three variables to enter into our regression equation: democracy (DEMOC) and centralization of state authority (CENT) from the Polity III variables and a composite measure of all five of the ICRG variables measuring the quality of government institutions (QUALPOL).[15]

In more detail, the variables actually used in the regression analysis are the following.

POPULATION DENSITY (POPDENSE)

It seemed plausible that population density would contribute to RICE through two separate mechanisms. On the supply side, a denser population makes it both cheaper and easier for public authorities to provide (effective) education and health services. It is not simply that, for a given level of expenditure on services, the average distance from physical facilities to households is less and service uptake is greater. Actual provision of supplies, supervision, and so on is also easier and cheaper. There are economies of scale and scope. There is at least some evidence, notably from the cases of exceptionally high levels of human development relative to income (e.g., Kerala State in India and Sri Lanka), of a complementary demand-side relationship: dense population facilitates political mobilization and thus increases the political pressure for effective, widespread service provision.[16] POPDENSE is measured as the average number of people per square mile during the 1980s.[17]

DEMOCRACY (DEMOC)

The measurement of democracy is a complex business with an indifferent record for product quality. We do not have a single, comprehensive, international data series that is generally accepted as reliable and as measuring the right things. One main axis of dispute has deep theoretical and ideological roots. Should democracy be conceived and measured basically in *electoral* terms, that is, according to the extent to which (national) governments are chosen through free elections held under universal adult suffrage, or should one also to take into account "deeper" indicators of the existence of (egalitarian, institutionalized) popular control of governments, for example, the existence of constraints on peaceful political activity; the influence of unelected civil and military bureaucracies; the extent of electoral and other kinds of political participation; and the degree to which members of different population categories have effective access to elected office? Another main axis of dispute is related but often takes on a more pragmatic cast. Is democracy best scored in binary terms (i.e., a country is either a democracy or it is not) or do we have the data, the judgment, and the conceptual basis to produce reliable continuous measures, that is, scoring countries on a scale of zero to ten or the like? There is a variety of international data bases founded on different procedures. Most of them correlate fairly closely at the aggregate level but sometimes provide very contrasting scores for particular countries in any given year.[18]

We tried to deal with this problem by using two different data series based on contrary principles. The democracy indicator used in our reported results (DEMOC) is from the Polity III data base. It is a relatively complex composite variable directly measuring three indicators of democracy: competitiveness of political participation; the openness of executive recruitment; and the constraints on the chief executive. The scale is zero to ten, and our score is an average for each year in the 1980s. We also used two variants of an alternative, binary measure of democracy from a data series that goes back to 1950 for many countries (Alvarez et al. 1996). We also took advantage of this historical depth to test the proposition that the influence of democracy on RICE is observable only over a longer time period than the one we have otherwise used in this analysis. We formulated this alternative measure of the DEMOC variable in two different ways: as the number of years that countries had been scored as democracies (1) over the ten-year period 1980–89 and (2) over the twenty-six-year period 1965–90.

REVENUE SOURCES (MINERALS AND AID)

The main hypothesis that we set out to test initially was that RICE would be significantly influenced by the main sources of the revenue of individual governments. This hypothesis stems from ongoing work by an increasing number of scholars on the ways in which the fiscal dimension of state-society relations shapes variations in the quality of governance in poor countries. Empirically, interest in this subject is sparked by the fact that, while the governments of rich countries depend almost entirely on taxes levied on their own citizens, many governments of poor countries are independent of citizens in this sense and derive much of their income from control over concentrated mineral resources (especially oil) or from foreign aid. Moore (1998, 2001) expresses this concern in terms of the degree to which states are dependent on income that is "earned" from their perspective (mainly taxes) or "unearned" (mainly oil revenues and aid). State income is earned to the extent that the state has to devote some organizational and political effort to working with citizens in order to get its money. This particular formulation is an attempt to capture the essence of a new and fast-growing body of research that indicates strong causal linkages between poor governance and high state dependence on mineral or aid sources.[19] There is a range of ideas about the precise nature of these linkages. Most can be summarized in the propositions that high dependence on "unearned income" (minerals or aid but especially the former) tends, all else being equal, to

- Give governments little direct interest in the welfare of their citizens
- Provide governments with an unusually powerful resource base, including military capacity, in comparison with citizens
- Provide governments with strong incentives and opportunities to build up coercive rather than consensual state apparatuses and modes of rule
- Undermine the potential influence of elected legislatures
- Provide little incentive to build up effective civil bureaucracies or exercise effective rule over many spatially or politically marginal populations

It appears that, for a range of reasons, dependence on oil or mineral revenue has more malignant consequences for the quality of governance than does dependence on aid.[20] It is only in relation to mineral dependence that cross-national statistical evidence has begun to emerge. Both Michael Ross (2001) and Leonard Wantchekon (2000), using large samples of countries, have recently found strong negative associations between oil or mineral dependence (defined as the ratio of oil or mineral exports to total exports) and (1) democracy (both cases) and (2) observance of the rule of law (Wantchekon 2000). Ades and Di Tella (1999) found a positive connection between mineral exports and levels of corruption.

There are various ways in principle of further testing this general proposition about the consequences of alternative sources of state revenue by examining the effects on RICE. It seems very plausible that high dependence of states on "unearned income" would tend to result in low RICE outcomes. All the more direct and obvious specifications of the relationship require data that simply are not available for many countries: reliable figures on sources of government income and/or patterns of expenditure. The poorer the countries, the worse the data coverage.[21] And high fiscal dependence of governments on minerals or aid is itself associated with poor public accounting (see Ascher 1999, esp. 16–17). One cannot in practice use data series on public finances to test propositions about the quality of governance because most cases of poor governance drop out of the sample for lack of data. We tested the fiscal dependence argument using indirect indicators of the degree of revenue dependence of governments on (1) minerals and (2) aid. There is no way of obtaining a cross-national data series on the contribution of minerals to government income.[22] We have used the best proxy: the percentage contribution of the mining and quarrying sector to GDP, averaged over the 1980s (United Nations 1992).[23] The variable is called MINERAL. We measured aid dependence (AID) in terms of the ratio of aid to GNP, averaged over the period 1980–89 (World Bank 1998). It would have been preferable to measure the ratio of aid to government income or expenditure, rather than to GDP; that is, the relationship implied by our underlying hypotheses. The lack of adequate data on government income and expenditure for poorer countries closed off that avenue.

THE QUALITY OF GOVERNMENT INSTITUTIONS (QUALPOL)

The International Country Risk Guide provides a set of measures of the quality of public institutions that has been used extensively for quantitative research. All are based on "expert judgement."[24] They are produced for international investors and lenders. Two of their component measures—government corruption (scaled zero to six) and bureaucratic quality (zero to six)—purport to measure the quality of government performance in general. Three others relate more directly to contract enforcement and thus the concerns of international investors: Risk of expropriation (zero to ten); rule of law (zero to six, measuring the extent to which there are established peaceful mechanisms for adjudicating disputes); and risk of repudiation of contracts by government (zero to ten). The five components are highly intercorrelated. When they (average for each year, 1980–89) were used as separate variables in early regressions, they were not generally statistically significant. We then followed Knack and Keefer (1995) and combined them into one composite measure, on a scale of zero to ten.[25] We call this QUALPOL—the general quality of government institutions. The higher the score, the better the quality.

CENTRALIZATION OF GOVERNMENT
DECISION MAKING (CENT)

As explained earlier, this variable was used in part because it was not correlated with others in the Polity III data base. It formed a separate "cluster." While it was positively related to RICE and appeared significant in early regressions (i.e., more centralization, higher RICE), its effects evaporated when other variables were added. It appears to be a poor measure of actual centralization: the scores are determined by formal administrative arrangements, with no allowance for differences in country size.

THE "AFRICA-RELATED" DUMMY
(AFRICA, FRAFRICA, DEPEND, WAFRICA)

Visual inspection of the data in table A1 and examination of early regression results suggested that there was something we were not picking up in our hypotheses and regression model. It manifested itself most clearly in the fact that a high proportion of countries with the lowest RICE scores were in francophone Africa. We used four different "Africa-related" dummy variables to try to capture this effect. The countries that are covered by each alternative formulation are shown in table A2.

- Africa: *simply being in AFRICA.*
- *Dependent:* in accordance with the ideas sketched out earlier in this chapter about the political consequences of alternative state revenue sources, we hypothesized that international political and military dependence might be a significant factor here. To the extent that governments can rely on political and military support from a former colonial power, they have less incentive to treat citizens well or to cultivate internal political support. This would likely lead to low RICE scores. Nine countries, all African, were classified as being dependent in this sense (DEPEND).[26]
- *Francophone Africa:* FRAFRICA.
- *West Africa:* WAFRICA.

The following is a complete list of the variables that were used at various points in regression analysis.

Y = Three different formulations of the dependent variable: RICE, RICE-LONG (relating only to the longevity component of HDI*), and RICE-ED (relating only to the literacy/education component of HDI*).
X_1 = AID (aid as a percentage of GNP).
X_2 = MINERAL (the mining sector as a percentage of GNP).

X_3 = QUALPOL (index of the general quality of government insti-
tutions).
X_4 = POPDENSE (population density).
X_5 = Four different formulations of the Africa-related dummy
variable: DEPEND, AFRICA, FRAFRICA, and WAFRICA.
X_6 = DEMOC (democracy, measured in three different ways).
X_7 = CENT (centralization of government).
X_8 = DLAC (dummy for Latin America and the Caribbean).
X_9 = DASIA (dummy for Asia).

For a sample size of sixty-one, regression equations of the form $Y = \alpha$
$+ \text{ß}_i X_i + \varepsilon$ were specified and estimated using ordinary least squares,
where $i = (1 \ldots 9)$. Explanatory variables X_6 to X_9 were dropped when
early regression equations and examination of partial residual plots indicated that they were statistically insignificant. This gave us our "preferred model," which was reestimated with (1) five explanatory variables,
X_1 to X_5, including the four different definitions of X_5 (the "Africa/loca-
tion" dummy); and (2) three different definitions of the dependent variable. Partial residual plots suggested that, in the case of the AID and
MINERAL variables, there were clusters of influential points ("outliers")
that could be exerting substantial influence on the results. The model was
estimated with and without these clusters of influential points.[27]

STATISTICAL RESULTS

The results of nine multiple regression equations are summarized in table
A3. We have already explained that some of the independent variables
proved to be statistically insignificant. The main significant findings are
as follows.

1. The coefficients on population density (POPDENSE) were consistently positive and significant, around 2 to 3 percent. As predicted, high
population densities were strongly associated with higher RICE scores,
probably because of the causal sequences summarized earlier: dense populations reduce the unit cost of providing health and education services
and may increase the effective political demand.

2. The coefficients on MINERAL were negative and even more statistically significant. This implies that, as predicted, dependence of governments on mineral revenues generates low RICE scores. However, we have
to examine the data more carefully before reaching this conclusion, for
there were five MINERAL "influential points," that is, observations that
appeared to drive the conclusion that MINERAL is a significant determinant of RICE. These were Botswana, Gabon, Saudi Arabia, Oman, and
Angola. When they were removed from the data set (regression 3), leaving
a sample size of fifty-six, MINERAL was no longer significant. However,

we do not believe they should be removed. They are an important part of the story about the effect of high mineral dependence. The coefficient on the MINERAL variable comes through as being significantly negative in regressions 1 and 2 due to the very low RICE performance of this group of highly mineral dependent economies. There are enough mineral "influential points" to demonstrate that it is not merely a case of a couple of exceptions driving the results. There is good evidence here that mineral dependence leads to low RICE scores. This evidence is consistent with the finding, reported previously, that mineral dependence is associated with low levels of democracy and the rule of law.

3. The AID variable was negatively related to RICE and significant in some cases, that is, there is some evidence that the dependence of governments on aid revenues tends to reduce RICE scores. However, it was evident from the graphical scatterplot of the residuals from the regression that two particular outlier observations were significantly driving this result. These were the observations relating to the Gambia and Guinea-Bissau, two very small countries with the highest aid levels in the sample—37 and 46 percent of GNP, respectively. These observations were removed from the data set and the model reestimated ($N = 59$). AID was no longer a significant explanatory variable, even at the 10 percent level. We have presented our regression results both including and then excluding these two influential points (table A3). We can conclude that very high levels of aid dependence are associated with low RICE scores but that this relationship does not hold over the range of aid dependence: low aid dependence does not imply high RICE scores.[28] Overall, these results imply that there may be some validity in the hypothesis that (high) aid dependence leads to low RICE scores via the causal processes sketched out earlier, but the case is not proven.

4. Our variable measuring the quality of government institutions—QUALPOL—generated a surprise. We found that it was consistently, significantly, but negatively correlated with RICE: the higher government institutions are scored by the International Country Risk Guide, for the information of international investors and lenders, the worse the governments perform in converting national income into human development. It came as no great surprise that QUALPOL was not positively related with RICE: the priorities of international investors and lenders, and the ways in which states respond to them, are different from the priorities of poor people and generally involve different processes and different parts of the state apparatus. That there should be a significant negative relationship between the two was, however, unexpected.

5. All four alternative definitions of the Africa-related dummy variable were negatively related to RICE and statistically significant but at very different levels. The Africa location (AFRICA) and dependency

(DEPEND) definitions were significant at around 6 to 7 percent. The francophone (FRAFRICA) definition was more significant. But the West Africa definition (WAFRICA) was significant to a very high degree (more than o.1 percent). In other words, a West African location itself is associated with a reduction in the efficiency with which material resources are converted into human welfare. All else being equal, one needs a higher level of national income in West Africa than elsewhere to achieve a given level of human development. One possible explanation for this result is that the West African environment, to a greater extent than most areas of the world, is characterized by endemic tropical diseases.[29] A West African location, like having a sparse population, may be a structural handicap to the process of converting material resources into human welfare.[30]

6. None of the three alternative measures of the degree or existence of democracy (DEMOC) was at all related to RICE in a statistical sense. We are not satisfied with these or any of the alternative democracy data series. We cannot at this point entirely reject the possibility that democracy might exercise some positive influence on RICE scores. Note, however, that we are not satisfied with the way in which we have been able to measure most of the explanatory variables. The fact that nevertheless some of them turned out to be statistically (very) significant is an indication that democracy is certainly not a strong determinant of RICE.

IMPLICATIONS

How do these statistical results extend or amend our knowledge about the connections between patterns of governance and mass welfare? To answer that question, we need first to specify clearly the type of knowledge with which we are dealing and its boundaries:

- We have been trying to explain variations among countries in welfare defined in terms of a combination of life expectancy, education, and literacy. While this is a broader and more useful concept of popular welfare than is any measure of income, it is less broad than one would like. In particular, there is accumulating evidence that physical insecurity, crime, and repressive or exploitative policing are major causes of ill-being for many poor people (Narayan et al. 2000, chap. 8). Were we able to rank countries according to measures of policing and security, we would find, almost by definition, an even stronger connection between the quality of governance and mass welfare.
- We have been looking at a particular set of low- and lower-middle-income countries. There is much less variation within this set, with respect of the kinds of factors we have been examining, than there is for "whole world" samples, which also

include upper-middle-income and Organization for Economic Cooperation and Development (OECD) countries. It is correspondingly more difficult to find statistically significant patterns within our subset of countries. Such patterns are, however, particularly useful from a policy perspective: relatively small differences in achievement between poor countries are more likely to indicate viable policy paths than are the broad-brush patterns that emerge from doing cross-national statistical analysis with global samples. The latter tend to be very much driven by differences between OECD countries and "the rest."

• Other research has drawn our attention to particular cases and categories of successful human development strategies in poor countries. These include (1) variants of mobilizing socialism (China, Cuba, Tanzania), (2) labor-intensive growth leading to fast-rising real wages (Taiwan and South Korea), and (3) the exceptional cases of deeply rooted and successful public "welfare" policies (Sri Lanka, Kerala State in India, Costa Rica) (see, e.g., Sen 1981). By taking into account the full range of cases among poor countries, our analysis provides a different type of knowledge. This knowledge is useful to people who need to think about general patterns. It also helps draw attention to problem categories of countries—notably the mineral exporters. Our findings do not compete with explanations (e.g., Sen 1981) that focus on individual national cases. Our statistical analysis has at best explained 55 percent of the variance in human development performance in relation to income, leaving 45 percent unexplained.

• We have only been able to try to explain cross-sectional variations between countries in the 1980s and 1990s. Lack of reliable data prevents us from examining changes over time within countries. There is always the possibility that our explanation is wrong because we had no (adequate) data series on other potential determinants of intercountry variations in RICE. Two such potential determinants are of particular concern: the degree of income inequality and the amount of money that governments spend on health and education services. Income inequality is clearly a potential additional or alternative explanation to those we have advanced for intercountry variations in RICE. It is also likely that RICE will be high in countries with low levels of income inequality because, all else being equal, the poorer sections of the population have more income per head than the poor in similar countries with high income inequality. The amount of public spending on health and education is, potentially at least, an intermediary variable influencing RICE, and it could be an independent variable. There are data series on both of these variables. We did not include them in our main analysis because there are many observations missing from these data series. Our country sample would be even smaller and less representative of the poorest countries. We did, however, run some rough checks that strongly suggested that neither of these variables was a significant influence on intercountry variations in RICE.[31]

The results reported in regressions 8 and 9 (table A3) are our best estimate of the determinants of RICE. Let us repeat that, bearing in mind that our measures of the explanatory variables are indirect and imperfect, the statistical relationships are relatively robust and strong. We can be confident that we have four important sets of conclusions.

RICE IS A USEFUL CONCEPT

The first conclusion is, from the political science perspective, essentially methodological and technical. The idea behind our RICE variable—measuring the relative efficiency of national political-economic systems in converting national material resources into human development—appears to provide a useful new way of thinking about and researching governance-poverty connections. However, such measures need to be explored and refined to take account of the extent to which variations in the human and natural environments affect the conversion process. It is clear that high population density is a favorable factor. It reduces the unit cost of providing health and education services and may increase the effective political demand for them. It is likely also that the conversion process is inherently more difficult in environments, such as those of West Africa, where tropical diseases are endemic.

THERE IS NO EVIDENCE THAT DEMOCRACY
LEADS TO PRO-POOR POLICIES

It is part of current conventional wisdom, at least in aid donor circles, that democracy and a policy emphasis on tackling poverty are among the good things of life that go together. We found no evidence of this in our results. The issue merits an essay in its own right and cannot be fully treated here. Let us simply note two reasons why there might be no detectable statistical association between democracy and RICE:

- First, there are institutional prerequisites for the effective representation of the interests of the poor in public policy. In particular, either (1) the poor should themselves be organized politically along interest lines or (2) governments should be influenced by groups or organizations that for some reason—notably ideology or legitimation pressures—are impelled to take a pro-poor stance. Votes are not enough. In personalistic or patrimonial political systems, the potential numerical power of the votes of the poor is neutralized by their fragmentation among numerous, competing, particularistic networks and interests.[32]

- The second reason is at first sight more concrete and contingent. Our statistical data relate mainly to the 1980s and early 1990s. Our conclusions are shaped by the experience of the cold war, which (1) narrowed the scope for radical or socialist policies within the often democratic states allied with the West; and (2) permitted and encouraged the emergence of a group of states (roughly the "people's democracies") that were often very pro-poor, in the sense in which we have used the term here, without being democratic in any substantive electoral sense. Given the virtual disappearance of this latter category of pro-poor but nondemocratic countries, the present and the future may look different. There might be a statistical connection between democracy and RICE or other measures of pro-poorness.

Whatever the truth of these suggestions or of alternative explanations of our statistical findings, the basic conclusion seems sound: the degree of electoral democracy alone is not a strong determinant of the pro-poorness of states.

DEPENDENCE OF GOVERNMENTS ON MINERAL RESOURCES IS BAD NEWS FOR THE POOR

Polities that are dependent on mineral resources are particularly bad at translating material resources into mass welfare. There is some evidence that the same is true in the case of high dependence on foreign development aid. These findings chime in well with a growing body of theory and evidence, summarized earlier, that connects poor governance in developing countries to the existence of states that are relatively dependent on extrinsic resources and support—and are therefore relatively autonomous of, and disconnected from, their own citizens.

STANDARD ICRG MEASURES OF THE QUALITY OF GOVERNANCE ARE MISLEADING, INSUFFICIENTLY POLITICAL, AND IDEOLOGICALLY BIASED

This conclusion is in some respects technical, but it has important political implications in a world in which international aid and development agencies are producing indicators of the quality of governance in poor countries in order to influence aid policies and allocations. We found that the higher government institutions are scored by the ICRG, for the information of international investors and lenders, the worse those governments perform in converting national income into human development. Since those ICRG scores have been used as proxies for the general quality of governance,[33] we need to explore a little further this surprising and apparently perverse finding.[34]

The ICRG score (QUALPOL) is a composite of five separate indicators: government corruption, the quality of the public service, risk of expropriation of investments, observance of the rule of law, and risk of repudiation of contracts by government. It is clear that there is an emphasis on the factors most likely to concern ICRG's clients: international investors and lenders. The point at issue is whether a measure that focuses on these dimensions of government is a plausible indicator of the quality of governance either (1) in some more general sense or (2) in relation to the poor and poverty. To date, the ICRG scores have enjoyed almost a clear field, at least as a measure of the general quality of governance. One reason may be the ideological appeal, especially to Washington-based international institutions, of assessing governance from a business perspective. Other reasons are more contingent: the lack of alternative data series for measuring governance and the absence of any strong challenge to the credibility of these ICRG scores. Our findings provide a basis for such a challenge.

Suppose that the ICRG scores that we have aggregated into the QUALPOL variable really do capture differences between countries in the quality of governance—according to conceptions of good governance that would command wide assent. The implications would be quite profound. We could no longer be confident that better governance would tend to lead to poverty reduction and would seriously have to confront the possibility of a perverse relationship. Surely the ICRG measures must be seriously awry? They are—through the interaction of a series of related deficiencies rather than because of any one glaring error. There are at least four problems that beset both of these particular ICRG measures of the quality of governance and, to varying degrees, the alternative available measures. We can group them loosely into pairs of technical and conceptual problems.

The first technical problem is that alternative measures of the quality of governance do not correlate very closely with one another.[35] There may be several reasons for this, including, as we discuss later, ambiguity about exactly what is being measured. An immediate concern with the ICRG measures in particular is the absence of public information on the criteria and procedures employed. It is known that they depend essentially on the subjective judgment of a small number of experts. They are vulnerable to a "halo effect," that is, a tendency to attribute good or bad national economic performance (and investment opportunities) to the behavior and qualities of whatever governments happen to be in power. That is connected to the second technical problem: the fact that there is actually little variation in the ICRG scores of quality of governance among poor countries. Among our sample of sixty-one (poor) countries, actual scores range only from 2.0 to 7.3 on a ten-point scale, and 79 percent (forty-eight out of sixty-one) scores are in the range 3.0 to 5.9 (table A1). Such narrow differences result in blunt analytic tools and must give rise to a concern that the ICRG measures reflect general stereotypes of poor countries.[36]

Our first concern about the conceptual basis of conventional governance measures might at first sound "academic" in the pejorative sense of the term: these are essentially measures of "correct" governmental procedure and behavior in a rather narrow sense. How much corruption is there? How competent are public officials? Does government honor the agreements it makes with big investors? These types of concerns are very important. But there is a widely accepted view that the big differences in state capacity, especially among poorer countries, are influenced not only by such "intrastate" factors but by the ways in which and the effectiveness with which sections of the state apparatus relate and interact with societal groups, especially their clients. The role of these interactions in shaping the effectiveness of popular mobilization against poverty is the core element of the polity-centered framework explored by Peter Houtzager in his chapters in this volume. In Peter Evans's words: "variations in internal state and state-society relations create differential degrees of developmental capacity" (1995, 73).

Governments are more effective when they can obtain information of various kinds from social or interest groups; use these linkages to get support for their policy choices; and secure the cooperation of society in policy implementation and monitoring.[37] This kind of state-society "synergy" is especially likely to be helpful in the effective provision of the public services with which we are dealing here: mass health and educational services to poor, often rural, populations. We have in table A1 two outstanding scorers in the RICE stakes: Vietnam and Sri Lanka. It is likely that this reflects synergistic relationships developed between parts of their state apparatuses and the mass of their rural poor because of particular historical experiences. In the Vietnamese case, this was a long sequence of mobilizing armed conflicts with French, Saigon-based Vietnamese, American, and Chinese armies from the 1940s to the 1980s. In the Sri Lankan case, a long period of highly competitive democratic politics, beginning in 1931, appears to have generated a similar outcome. The

ICRG procedures for assessing governance are likely to undervalue such relationships, and focus too narrowly on the "intrastate" dimensions of governance.

Our second concern about the conceptual basis of the standard governance measures follows directly. These relations between state apparatuses and societal groups are rarely constructed and conducted at the level of the state or nation but at lower levels, within the domains of specific government organizations: individual ministries, directorates, agencies, or provinces. If these relations are significant influences on state capacity, there is likely to be considerable variation within individual states in the quality of governance. Standard governance measures are country averages and may therefore be seriously misleading. There are other reasons to suspect that this may be the case.

The standard governance measures relate principally to the effectiveness of those central government institutions concerned mainly with economic and investment policy—what Rauch and Evans term "the core economic agencies" (2000, 54).[38] Neither Rauch and Evans nor any other scholars have consistently tried to measure, for a number of countries, intranational differences in the quality of government agencies. However, more than one school of thought in comparative politics warns us to expect considerable variation within countries. There is, for example, a literature on "islands of efficiency" in public service in countries where the overall quality of governance is low (Evans 1995, 60–73) and a broader literature emphasizing how far different agencies within the same state can vary in quality and competence (Skocpol 1985, 17–18; Weiss 1998, chap. 1). Further, there is a more structuralist argument about the intrastate variations in the quality of bureaucratic "performance" that emanate from the differential roles of various parts of the governmental apparatus in seeking to fulfill the different (and conflicting) functions or imperatives of the state. For example, it is argued that, even during its heyday as a model "developmental state" from the 1950s to the 1970s, the Japanese polity simultaneously encompassed another set of relations more reminiscent of a "clientelist state." Different state organizations played leading roles within these "developmental" and "clientelist" spheres. Efficient, admired, and relatively unpoliticized ministries (Trade and Industry, Finance) promoted Japanese primacy in internationally competitive industries. Meanwhile, the electoral and financial basis of the ruling party, located especially in protected and inefficient sectors like construction, agriculture, and retailing, was served by a much less effective, patronage-ridden, and corrupt set of government organizations (Woodall 1996, 1–23). It would be misleading to assess the general quality of the public bureaucracy in Japan solely on the basis of the core economic ministries and agencies.[39]

In sum, comparative politics provides a plausible set of hypotheses to explain our surprising statistical finding: that quality of governance, as measured by the ICRG, not only fails to contribute to higher RICE scores but appears to consistently depress those scores. All ICRG scores are narrow in two senses: they embody a statecentric concept of the determinants of state capacity; and they focus on only one part of the spectrum of state activities and functions. Even if it is technically adequate, a low conventional governance score might indicate the coexistence within one country of (1) a rather ineffective set of core economic agencies unable to help mobilize much private investment with (2) a set of agencies that are effective in providing mass health and education from limited resources—in part because of the political and organizational relations they have with client groups. It is not that "good governance is bad for poverty reduction." Rather, our standard measures of good governance are conceptually (as well as technically) inadequate and possibly perverse. Contrary to the implications they convey, conflict of interest has not entirely faded away in the politics of poor countries. What is good for international lenders and investors may not always be good for the poor.

Appendix:
Data Set and Main Regression Results

TABLE A.1. THE SAMPLE COUNTRIES AND VALUES OF THE
DEPENDENT AND MAIN INDEPENDENT VARIABLES

	RICE (dependent variable)	AID (aid as % of GDP)	MINERAL (mining sector as % of GDP)	QUALPOL (quality of government institutions, scale 0–10)	POP-DENSE (population density)
Vietnam	0.23	2.0	0	4.5	545
Sri Lanka	0.21	8.2	2	4.5	733
Philippines	0.14	1.5	2	2.7	550
Jamaica	0.14	7.4	7	4.5	630
Honduras	0.12	6.5	2	3.5	116
Kenya	0.12	8.7	0	6.1	104
Paraguay	0.11	1.5	0	3.6	28
Jordan	0.10	13.6	0	4.5	89
Costa Rica	0.09	4.8	0	6.2	154
India	0.08	0.9	2	5.8	769
Trinidad and Tobago	0.08	0.1	23	5.2	680
Peru	0.08	1.3	12	3.2	45
Dominican Republic	0.08	2.7	4	4.4	393
Malawi	0.08	16.8	0	4.9	229
El Salvador	0.07	8.3	0	2.7	683
Congo Brazzaville	0.07	4.2	18	3.9	17
Ecuador	0.07	1.1	13	4.9	98
Zambia	0.07	11.0	9	4.0	27
Tanzania	0.07	20.1	0	4.7	74
Nigeria	0.06	0.6	15	3.1	272
Indonesia	0.06	1.2	19	3.1	269
Bolivia	0.06	7.6	14	2.0	16
Uruguay	0.06	0.2	0	5.1	51
Syrian Arab Republic	0.06	4.9	11	3.6	167
Panama	0.05	1.0	0	3.7	87
Malagasy	0.04	9.1	16	5.1	52
Colombia	0.02	0.2	3	5.3	88
Ethiopia	0.02	8.3	0	3.9	125
Argentina	0.02	0.1	2	4.7	33
Zimbabwe	0.02	4.3	7	4.8	64

Mexico	0.01	0.1	3	4.7	117
Thailand	0.01	1.1	3	5.7	298
Ghana	0.00	6.2	0	3.7	166
Chile	0.00	0.2	8	5.5	48
Cameroon	0.00	3.1	11	5.4	64
Venezuela	–0.01	0.1	16	5.5	58
Egypt	–0.01	5.2	14	4.7	139
Tunisia	–0.01	20.1	10	4.5	139
Brazil	–0.01	0.1	2	6.6	48
Turkey	–0.01	0.5	2	5.2	194
Pakistan	–0.03	2.7	0	4.3	373
Haiti	–0.03	7.6	1	3.0	637
Guatemala	–0.03	1.7	0	2.9	220
Uganda	–0.05	8.9	0	3.1	214
Papua New Guinea	–0.07	11.7	13	6.7	23
Guinea-Bissau	–0.07	45.9	0	3.1	94
Malaysia	–0.07	0.6	10	7.3	143
Morocco	–0.08	5.2	4	4.7	145
Mali	–0.08	23.4	2	2.7	18
Angola	–0.09	2.7	28	4.3	19
Sierra Leone	–0.09	6.6	8	5.4	150
Côte d'Ivoire	–0.11	2.8	1	6.5	93
Gambia	–0.13	36.9	0	5.6	226
Oman	–0.15	1.4	41	5.4	19
Senegal	–0.16	14.4	0	4.9	99
Saudi Arabia	–0.16	0.0	47	5.5	17
Burkina Faso	–0.17	13.1	0	5.1	86
Niger	–0.18	14.9	9	6.0	15
Gabon	–0.21	2.1	41	5.3	9
Guinea	–0.21	12.1	0	4.7	61
Botswana	–0.23	7.6	48	6.9	6

TABLE A.2. COUNTRY CLASSIFICATION FOR LOCATION/AFRICA
DUMMY VARIABLES

	AFRICA (Africa)	DEPEND (dependent)	FRAFRICA (francophone Africa)	WAFRICA (West Africa)
Angola	✓			
Botswana	✓			
Burkina Faso	✓	✓	✓	✓
Cameroon	✓	✓	✓	✓
Congo Brazzaville	✓	✓	✓	✓
Côte d'Ivoire	✓	✓	✓	✓
Egypt	✓			
Ethiopia	✓			
Gabon	✓	✓	✓	✓
Gambia	✓			✓
Ghana	✓			✓
Guinea	✓		✓	✓
Guinea-Bissau	✓			✓
Kenya	✓			
Madagascar	✓	✓	✓	
Malawi	✓			
Mali	✓	✓	✓	✓
Morocco	✓		✓	
Niger	✓	✓	✓	✓
Nigeria	✓			✓
Senegal	✓	✓	✓	✓
Sierra Leone	✓			✓
Tanzania	✓			
Tunisia	✓		✓	
Uganda	✓			
Zambia	✓			
Zimbabwe	✓			

TABLE A.3.   REGRESSION RESULTS (DEPENDENT VARIABLE = RICE; SIGNIFICANCE LEVELS IN PARENTHESES)

Regression	α	β_1 (AID)	β_2 (MINERAL)	β_3 (QUAL-POL)	β_4 (POP-DENSE)	β_5 (SEE ALTERNATIVE DEFINITIONS IN TABLE)	R^2	F
		β_5: Africa/location dummy variable = DEPEND						
1 PM	0.124	−3.4E03	−2.9E03	−2.0E02	1.3E04	−5.7E02	0.47	9.72
$n = 61$	(1%)	(0.8%)	(0.3%)	(3%)	(2%)	(6%)		
2 PM-A	0.114	−2.8E03	−2.8E03	−1.9E02	1.3E04	−6.1E02	0.45	8.83
$n = 59$	(3%)	(17%)	(5%)	(5%)	(2%)	(6%)		
3 PM-M	9.0E02	−2.8E03	1.3E03	−1.7E02	1.3E04	−6.8E02	0.38	6.15
$n = 56$	(7%)	(3%)	(45%)	(7%)	(2%)	(3%)		
		β_5: Africa/location dummy variable = AFRICA						
4 PM	0.134	−2.383E03	−2.763E03	−2.071E02	1.206E04	−4.617E02	0.47	9.60
$n = 61$	(1%)	(10%)	(0.5%)	(3%)	(3%)	(7%)		
5 PM-A	0.126	−1.618E03	−2.722E03	−1.967E02	1.23E04	−4.936E02	0.45	8.68
$n = 59$	(2%)	(48%)	(1%)	(4%)	(3%)	(7%)		
		β_5: Africa/location dummy variable = FRAFRICA						
6 PM	0.128	−3.044E03	−2.914E03	−1.927E02	1.161E04	−7.548E02	0.47	11.45
$n = 61$	(0.7%)	(1%)	(0.2%)	(3%)	(3%)	(0.5%)		
7 PM-A	0.112	−1.379E03	−2.8E03	−1.742E02	1.195E04	−8.7E02	0.51	10.85
$n = 59$	(2%)	(49%)	(0.3%)	(6%)	(3%)	(0.3%)		
		β_5: Africa/location dummy variable = WAFRICA						
8 PM	0.132	−1.893E03	−2.918E03	−2.049E02	1.177E04	−9.282E02	0.55	13.46
$n = 61$	(0.4%)	(13%)	(0.1%)	(2%)	(2%)	(0.000%)		
9 PM-A	0.132	−2.349E03	−2.958E03	−2.001E02	1.173E04	−9.285E02	0.54	12.25
$n = 59$	(0.6%)	(20%)	(0.1%)	(2%)	(2%)	(0.000%)		

Note: PM = preferred (regression) model; PM-A = preferred model minus AID influential points; PM-M = preferred model minus MINERAL influential points.

NOTES

This is a revised version of an essay written for the Governance Department of the U.K. Department for International Development (DFID) as a contribution to a research project on the responsiveness of political systems to poverty reduction. The original essay was discussed at a meeting held at Castle Donnington, United Kingdom, August 16–17, 1999. We are grateful to the participants for their comments. Graham Davis, Peter Houtzager, Steven Knack, Martin Ravallion, Steven Poe, and Fernando Limongi have been especially helpful in providing detailed comments and suggestions.

1. Readers familiar with cross-national statistical analysis will be aware that one can generate endless, apparently significant statistical relationships simply by including rich and poor countries in the same global sample.

2. For a summary presentation of these two perspectives, see Poggi 1978 (chap. 1). The best-known statement of the statist case in relation to developing countries is Huntington 1968.

3. The criteria they used were: specificity with which the indicators implicate particular institutions, specificity with which the indicators define the outcomes of good government in operation, the replicability and transparency of the indicators, the quality and accuracy of the indicators, and data coverage of the indicators (Knack and Manning 2000).

4. It is for these reasons that the Freedom House measures of political and civil liberties are so widely employed in cross-national statistical analysis, despite concerns about their relevance and accuracy. They constitute consistent long-term data series.

5. For a recent warning, see Srinivasan 2000. Note that data on income distribution that are insufficiently reliable to indicate changes over time within individual countries may still give us a reasonably accurate picture of differences between countries.

6. For an excellent recent review of the state of knowledge, see Kenny and Williams 2001.

7. For precise details on the calculation procedures, see UNDP 1990.

8. Sixty-seven percent of the intercountry variation in HDI* was explained by differences in GNP per head. Conceptually, we are trying to account for the one-third (33 percent) of variation in HDI* left unexplained.

9. They are discussed in appendix 1 of an earlier version of this chapter (Moore et al. 1999). There is also an issue about statistical procedure that merits some comment. The purpose of our analysis is to explain variations in RICE. RICE is, however, derived, through regression analysis and estimation of residuals, from the variable HDI*. From a statistical perspective, we have used a two-step procedure that can be described as a half partial regression—a mixture of simple and partial regression. An alternative way of conducting the analysis is to undertake single-step multiple regression analysis, in which we try to explain variations in HDI* using our measure of income as one of the explanatory variables. Fernando Limongi suggested to us that the method we chose might bias the results in certain ways and that the single-step procedure would be preferable. At

the conceptual and theoretical level, we prefer the two-step procedure. This involves a clear specification of what it is we are trying to explain, that is, variations between countries in RICE. However, we also reestimated our model as a single-step multiple regression to test Limongi's suggestion. The results were virtually identical to those obtained from our preferred model.

10. We have been more successful at providing a statistical explanation of a measure of RICE that combines both human development components (i.e., longevity and education) than in explaining separate RICE measures for longevity (RICE-LONG) and education (RICE-ED), respectively. When we attempted the latter exercises—that is, explaining separately (1) deviations between actual life expectancy and the levels predicted on the basis of GNP per capita and (2) a similar measure for the education of HDI—we did not come up with consistent statistically significant relationships, although the general direction of the statistical relationships was as expected (Moore et al. 1999, 23–26). This implies that there is not a high degree of correlation between the longevity and the education components of HDI. The factors that explain relative levels (and changes in levels) in longevity are not (completely) the same as those that explain relative levels and changes in education/literacy. That accords with the results of other research in this area, for example, Dasgupta 1990; and Sen 1981.

11. To the extent that our model incorporates time lags, it takes some account of history. Note, however, that, like other statistical analyses of this type, it cannot accommodate the possibility of historical path dependence in the strong sense of that term, that is, the notion that because of increasing returns processes two or more countries that initially differ only in relatively small ways might become set on relatively diverging paths (Pierson 2000).

12. We did not test alternative time lags; data constraints would make this difficult. There was a particular reason for measuring our independent variables over the 1980s. Income from mineral exports was hypothesized to be an important explanatory factor and indeed proved to be. But world mineral prices are not very stable. The decade of the 1980s was a period of relative stability.

13. These are autocracy (AUTOC), democracy (DEMOC), executive recruitment regulation (XRREG), executive recruitment competition (XRCOMP), executive recruitment openness (XROPEN), executive constraints (XCONST), regulation of participation (PARREG), competitiveness of participation (PARCOMP), and centralization of state authority (CENT).

14. These are risk of repudiation of contracts by government, risk of expropriation, corruption, rule of law, and bureaucratic quality.

15. We used a chi-square test for association between the variables, rather than correlation analysis, for two reasons. First, the correlation coefficient is a measure of the extent of a linear relationship between the two variables. It will identify nonlinear relationships only imperfectly. Second, the scores used in measuring some of the variables are categorical, that is, the increment between 1 and 2 need not be the same as that between 2 and 3. They are therefore inappropriate for the correlation model. There are ninety-one possible combinations of the fourteen variables. About half the pairings (forty-four of the ninety-one) were

significantly associated at the 5 percent level and about a third at the 1 percent level. We grouped together those variables that were significantly associated at the 5 percent level. This left eight out of the nine Polity III variables in one cluster, with CENT standing alone, and all five ICRG variables in a second cluster.

16. The processes that encourage effective popular political mobilization in densely populated rural areas appear to be similar to those that explain why left-wing popular movements are typically centered in cities.

17. We took an average for the years 1980, 1985, and 1989. Note that average population density is not the perfect measure of our underlying concept: average population densities would be the same for one country with its population equally dispersed over space and another, identical in area and total population, where 90 percent of the population lives in 10 percent of the area. Yet the latter would yield more economies in service provision. Visual inspection of our data indicated that Bangladesh is an anomaly: its population density is three times the level of the next country on the scale. This outlying observation was going to distort the regression results. We therefore omitted Bangladesh from the sample.

18. For some discussion of these issues, see, for example, Inkeles 1990 (3–6); and Alvarez et al. 1996. For evidence on the inconsistency of different data series, see McHenry 2000.

19. For explorations of the political consequences of oil dependence, see Karl 1997; Luciani 1994; Vandewalle 1998; and Yates 1996. Aid has not yet been examined in the same detail. Brautigam (1999) provides a very useful discussion of the issues, and Knack (2001) presents statistical evidence that high aid levels do undermine the quality of government and public institutions. Other key references to this body of work are Bates and Lien 1985; Chaudhry 1989, 1997; Guyer 1992; Levi 1999; Moore 2001, Ross 1999; Shambayati 1994; and Tilly 1992.

20. For the apparent reasons, see Moore 2001.

21. This is simply demonstrated by looking at the proportion of countries in different income groups for which the World Bank feels it can confidently cite recent figures on a statistic as basic as total central government revenue: 92 percent of high-income countries; 72 percent of middle-income countries; and 33 percent of low-income countries (World Bank 1997, table 14, relating to 1995). See also Moore 1998.

22. One can do the exercise for some individual countries through Herculean efforts. Ross (2001) uses a similar measure to ours.

23. To reduce the labor input, we took the average of three years: 1980, 1985, and 1989.

24. Details on the scoring procedures and criteria are not publicly available.

25. This required us to rescale three of the indicators from a zero to six to a zero to ten range and then to average the five indicators on a zero to ten scale.

26. The classification was made by consulting three experts on contemporary Africa without telling them the purposes behind the consultation. The countries classified as dependent are Burkina Faso, Cameroon, Côte d'Ivoire, Gabon, Madagascar, Mali, Niger, Congo Brazzaville, and Senegal. All are former French colonies. The following former French African colonies in the sample were not classified as dependent: Guinea because the country broke away (and was

expelled from) from the francophone club under the leadership of Sekou Toure and has never returned; and Morocco and Tunisia because, while in some respects they remain close to the French government, they have also maintained close relations with other Western governments, notably the United States, and have generally kept domestic politics relatively separate from relationships with Paris.

27. For details of these outliers, see Moore et al. 1999 (app. 5).

28. We are dealing here with a small window into a complex pattern of relationships. Unlike incomes from minerals, aid revenue sometimes has strong policy voice(s) attached. Some aid donors might succeed in efforts to ensure that aid is used to promote human development.

29. For a useful discussion of location and disease incidence, see Gallup and Sachs 1999. The authors provide maps of disease incidence only for malaria. Other parts of the tropics face similar problems of intensive disease concentration. The reason this does not come through in our analysis is probably that we have a large number of observation points (countries) located in West Africa. The tropical areas of Asia and Latin America cover fewer countries. And some of these countries (e.g., Brazil) have large populations living in nontropical areas.

30. However, these disease- and health-mediated processes do not appear to comprise the full story. When we attempted to explain separately the longevity (RICE-LONG) and the literacy/education components (RICE-ED) of RICE, the West Africa dummy (WAFRICA) is very significant in both cases (Moore et al. 1999). West African location appears to reduce the efficiency with which material resources are converted into *both* longevity and literacy/education. Since we do not have the data to explore this issue adequately, we do not comment on it further.

31. In this smaller sample of forty-seven countries for which we obtained data on income inequality and the proportion of government expenditure devoted to health and education (from World Bank sources), our measure of mineral dependence (MINERAL), taken alone, was significantly associated with variations in RICE. By contrast, there was no statistical association at all between RICE and either (1) any measure of income inequality or (2) the proportion of government expenditure devoted to health and education.

32. To give one recent example, Niles (1999) shows that in democratic poor countries governments were more likely to try to protect poor people against the economic consequences of structural adjustment policies when political parties were relatively stable and institutionalized.

33. For a partial list of their use in cross-national statistical analysis, see Aron 2000, 107.

34. Martin Ravallion has suggested to us that our statistical results could reflect a situation in which the quality of governance affected the level of average incomes but left health and education outcomes untouched. Countries with good governance would then have low health and education attainments in relation to income levels, that is, low RICE scores. This is logically possible, but it is unlikely that it will explain the facts we have observed. We know that income levels are generally quite good predictors of health and education levels. To the extent that

there exist styles of governance that manage to "insulate" general levels of health and education from the normally benign effects of rising incomes, then, this simply illustrates our argument that the quality of governance might be good on one set of criteria (e.g., promoting economic growth) but bad from the perspective of those concerned about the priority given to poverty reduction.

35. For an examination of this issue, see Rauch and Evans 2000.

36. In these standard sets of national governance scores, high individual scores are assigned mainly to high- or upper-middle-income countries (Evans and Rauch 1999, 763). It is mainly the inclusion of richer countries that (1) gives the data sets an appearance of being usefully discriminatory and (2) generates substantial correlation among some of the different sets. Given a global sample of countries, including rich and poor, it is especially easy to generate all kinds of statistically significant correlations among social, economic, and political variables. It is questionable how far such "cheap" correlations are meaningful for analytic or policy purposes.

37. For two classic variants of this general argument, from very different perspectives, see Evans 1995 and Migdal 1988.

38. It is clear why this should be the focus of the measures of governance that derive from country risk analysis for international investors and lenders, including the ICRG. The main alternative measure is that recently produced for thirty-five poor and middle-income countries by Evans and Rauch (1999). But they, too, produced "national" scores by measuring attributes of the core economic agencies. The fact that their measures correlate substantially similar ICRG measures may reflect the fact that they set out to measure similar attributes and functions of states (Rauch and Evans 2000).

39. For more general arguments about how the capacity of individual state agencies stems from their patterns of interaction with societal groups and interests, see Skocpol 1985 (19); and Weiss 1998 (chaps. 1–3).

REFERENCES

Ades, A., and R. Di Tella. 1999. "Rents, Competition, and Corruption." *American Economic Review* 89, no. 4: 982–93.

Alvarez, Michael, José Cheibub, Fernando Limongi, and Adam Przeworski. 1996. "Classifying Political Regimes." *Studies in Comparative International Development* 31, no. 2: 3–36.

Aron, J. 2000. "Growth and Institutions: A Review of the Evidence." *World Bank Research Observer* 15, no. 1: 99–135.

Ascher, W. 1999. *Why Governments Waste Natural Resources: Policy Failures in Developing Countries.* Baltimore: Johns Hopkins University Press.

Bates, R. H., and D.-H. Lien. 1985. "A Note on Taxation, Development, and Representative Government." *Politics and Society* 14, no. 1: 53–70.

Brautigam, D. 1999. *Aid Dependence and Governance.* Stockholm: Almqvist and Wicksell International.

Chaudhry, K. A. 1989. "The Price of Wealth: Business and State in Labor Remittance and Oil Economies." *International Organization* 43, no. 1: 101–45.

————. 1997. *The Price of Wealth: Economies and Institutions in the Middle East.* Ithaca and London: Cornell University Press.

Dasgupta, P. 1990. "Well-Being and the Extent of Its Realisation in Poor Countries." *Economic Journal* 100 (400 [Supplement]): 1–32.

Dollar, D., and A. Kraay. 2000. "Growth Is Good for the Poor." World Bank, <worldbank.org/research>.

Evans, P. 1995. *Embedded Autonomy. States and Industrial Transformation.* Princeton: Princeton University Press.

Evans, P., and J. Rauch. 1999. "Bureaucracy and Growth: A Cross-National Analysis of the Effects of 'Weberian' State Structures on Economic Growth." *American Sociological Review* 64, no. 3: 748–65.

Gallup J. L., and J. D. Sachs. 1999. "Geography and Economic Development." *International Regional Science Review* 22, no. 2: 179–232. Reprinted from the Annual World Bank Conference on Development Economics, 1998, Proceedings.

Guyer, J. I. 1992. "Representation without Taxation: An Essay on Democracy in Rural Nigeria, 1952–1990." *African Studies Review* 35, no. 1: 41–80.

Huntington, S. P., ed., 1968. *Political Order in Changing Societies.* New Haven: Yale University Press.

Inkeles, A. 1990. "On Measuring Democracy." *Studies in Comparative International Development* 25, no. 1: 3–6.

Karl, T. L. 1997. *The Paradox of Plenty. Oil Booms and Petro-States.* Berkeley, Los Angeles, and London: University of California Press.

Kenny, C., and D. Williams. 2001. "What Do We Know about Economic Growth or Why Don't We Know Very Much?" *World Development* 29, no. 1: 1–22.

Knack, S. 2001. "Aid Dependence and the Quality of Governance: Cross-Country Empirical Tests." *Southern Economic Journal* 68, no. 2: 310–29.

Knack, S., and P. Keefer. 1995. "Institutions and Economic Performance: Cross-Country Tests Using Alternative Institutional Measures." *Economics and Politics* 7, no. 3: 207–27.

Knack, S., and N. Manning. 2000. "Why Is It So Difficult to Agree on Governance Indicators?" Washington, DC, World Bank. Manuscript.

Levi, M. 1999. "Death and Taxes: Extractive Equality and the Development of Democratic Institutions." In I. Shapiro and C. Hacker-Cordon, eds., *Democracy's Value,* 112–31. Cambridge and New York: Cambridge University Press:

Luciani, G. 1994. "The Oil Rent, the Fiscal Crisis of the State, and Democratization." In G. Salame, ed., *Democracy without Democrats? The Renewal of Politics in the Arab World,* 130–55. London and New York: I. B. Tauris.

McHenry, D. E. 2000. "Quantitative Measures of Democracy in Africa: An Assessment." *Democratization* 7, no. 2: 168–85.

Migdal, J. S. 1988. *Strong Societies and Weak States: State-Society Relations and State Capabilities in the Third World.* Princeton: Princeton University Press.

Moore, M. 1998. "Death without Taxes: Democracy, State Capacity, and Aid Dependence in the Fourth World." In M. Robinson and G. White, eds., *The Democratic Developmental State: Politics and Institutional Design.* Oxford: Oxford University Press.

————. 2001. "Political Underdevelopment: What Causes 'Bad Governance'?" *Public Management Review* 3, no. 3: 385–418.

Moore, Mick, Jennifer Leavy, Peter Houtzager, and Howard White. 1999. "Polity Qualities: How Governance Affects Poverty." Working Paper 99. Institute of Development Studies, Sussex.

Narayan, Deepa, Robert Chambers, Meera Kaul Shah, and Patti Petesch. 2000. *Voices of the Poor: Crying Out for Change.* Oxford and New York: Oxford University Press for the World Bank.

Niles, K. 1999. "Economic Adjustment and Targeted Social Spending: The Role of Political Institutions (Indonesia, Mexico, and Ghana)." Paper presented at the IDS-DFID conference Responsiveness of Political Systems to Poverty Reduction, Castle Donnington, United Kingdom, August 16–17.

Pierson, P. 2000. "Increasing Returns, Path Dependence, and the Study of Politics." *American Political Science Review* 94, no. 2: 251–68.

Poggi, G. 1978. *The Development of the Modern State: A Sociological Introduction.* London: Hutchison.

Rauch, J., and P. Evans. 2000. "Bureaucratic Structure and Bureaucratic Performance in Less Developed Countries." *Journal of Public Economics* 72, no. 1: 49–71.

Ross, M. L. 1999. "The Political Economy of the Resource Curse." *World Politics* 51, no. 1: 297–322.

———. 2001. "Does Oil Hinder Democracy?" *World Politics* 53, no. 3: 325–61.

Sala-I-Martin, X. X. 1997. "I Just Ran Two Million Regressions." *American Economic Review* 87, no. 2: 178–83.

Sen, A. 1981. "Public Action and the Quality of Life in Developing Countries." *Oxford Bulletin of Economics and Statistics* 43, no. 4: 287–319.

Shambayati, H. 1994. "The Rentier State, Interest Groups, and the Paradox of Autonomy: State and Business in Turkey and Iran." *Comparative Politics* 26, no. 3: 307–32.

Skocpol, T. 1985. "Bringing the State Back In: Strategies of Analysis in Current Research." In Peter Evans, Dietrich Rueschemeyer, and Theda Skocpol, eds., *Bringing the State Back In,* 3–43. Cambridge and London: Cambridge University Press.

Srinivasan, T. N. 2000. "Growth, Poverty Reduction, and Inequality." Paper presented at the World Bank conference Development Economics, Europe, Paris, 26–28 June 2000.

Tilly, C. 1992. *Coercion, Capital, and European States, A.D. 990–1992.* Cambridge, MA, and Oxford: Blackwell.

UNDP. 1990. *Human Development Report, 1990,* New York: Oxford University Press.

United Nations. 1992. *United Nations National Account Statistics: Main Aggregates and Detailed Tables, 1990.* Pts. 1–2. New York: United Nations.

Vandewalle, D. 1998. *Libya since Independence. Oil and State-Building.* Ithaca and London: Cornell University Press.

Wantchekon, L. 2000. "Why Do Resource Abundant Countries Have Authoritarian Governments?" Paper presented at the annual meetings of the American Political Science Association, Washington, DC, 31 August–3 September 2000.

Weiss, L. 1998. *The Myth of the Powerless State. Governing the Economy in a Global Era.* Cambridge: Polity.

Woodall, B. 1996. *Japan under Construction: Corruption, Politics, and Public Works.* Berkeley and Los Angeles: University of California Press.

World Bank. 1997. *World Development Report, 1997: The State in a Changing World.* Washington, DC: World Bank.

———.1998. *World Development Indicators, 1998,* Washington, DC: World Bank.

Yates, D. A. 1996. *The Rentier State in Africa. Oil Rent Dependency and Neocolonialism in the Republic of Gabon.* Trenton, NJ, and Asmara, Eritrea: Africa World Press.

8 Do Political Regimes Matter?

POVERTY REDUCTION AND
REGIME DIFFERENCES ACROSS INDIA

John Harriss

India constitutes something of a laboratory for the study of political factors that influence the development and implementation of pro-poor policies. Its major states have different political histories and contemporary patterns of politics, yet, contained as they are within the framework of a federal democracy, they also have important features in common. This combination of difference and commonality makes possible a comparative analysis to identify the political factors that have significantly influenced poverty reduction in India. This chapter focuses on how different subnational political regimes of the major Indian states affect (1) factors that are instrumental in reducing rural poverty (notably how they may influence the rate and nature of agricultural growth) and (2) the adoption and financing of pro-poor public policies.

I first identify what there is to explain: variation in the performance of the different states in poverty reduction. In accounting for different levels of, and trends in, poverty, I take into account a strong historical path dependence. I then define the different regime types found in the states in terms of the balance of caste/class power and the nature of party organization. The third section reviews evidence on the possible influence of regimes on policies, expenditure patterns, and poverty outcomes. The focus throughout is on "poverty" conceived in the limited sense of income/consumption poverty levels, measured conventionally by the head count ratio (the proportion of the population below a defined "poverty line").

A starting point for this study is Kohli's work *The State and Poverty in India,* which is one of two substantial attempts to date to explore the Indian "laboratory," as Kohli himself refers to it (1987, 3–4). Kohli's strong conclusion, based on a comparison of the performances of West

Bengal, Uttar Pradesh (UP), and Karnataka in poverty reduction policies (land reform, small farmer support, and wages and employment supports for the landless), was that "a tightly organized ideological party can penetrate the rural society without being coopted by the propertied groups." Conversely, he found that "multi-class regimes with loose organization and diffuse ideology are not successful at reformist intervention" (8).[1] In other words, it is most likely that pro-poor redistribution will be accomplished by regimes dominated by well-organized left of center parties exactly like the one that has held power in West Bengal since 1977.

According to Kohli, such a party regime has the following critical characteristics: (1) coherent leadership, (2) ideological and organizational commitment to exclude propertied interests from direct participation in the process of governance, (3) a pragmatic attitude toward facilitating a nonthreatening as well as a predictable political atmosphere for the propertied entrepreneurial classes, and (4) an organizational arrangement that is simultaneously centralized and decentralized so that the regime is both "in touch" with local society and not being subjected to local power holders. These regime attributes, Kohli argues, "make the institutional penetration of society possible, while facilitating a degree of regime autonomy from the propertied classes" (1987, 11).[2] By contrast there is, he says, "little evidence in India's experience—including that of Punjab— to suggest that, over time, growth 'trickles down'" (225). These findings, he suggests, show that there is "room for manoeuvre," even in the context of a democratic capitalist polity with a regime at the center that is "incapable of imposing authority (and) typically provides economic incentives to propertied groups to buttress its own political support and at the same time to stimulate productive activities" (8).

Kohli argues emphatically, therefore, that politics does make a difference. Others perhaps disagree. In summing up the findings of comparative studies of public intervention and rural poverty alleviation in nine states, Vyas and Bhargava, for example, argue emphatically that "success in poverty alleviation efforts was not significantly affected . . . [at least] by the professed political ideology of the ruling parties in the different states" (1995, 2572).[3] Against this, I find a good deal of evidence to support Kohli's conclusions. Extending Kohli's work, I argue in this chapter that there are other types of regimes, beyond the left of center ones of West Bengal and Kerala, that have been relatively successful in poverty reduction. In particular, those states where populist politics have been institutionalized—Andhra Pradesh and Tamil Nadu—appear to have performed more strongly in reducing poverty than might have been predicted.

The exercise that I have undertaken also builds upon the work of Frankel and Rao, the other substantial exploration of the Indian laboratory and the most ambitious comparative project so far. Frankel and Rao develop a comparative framework that focuses on the problematic of "the decline of dominance," which they define as "the exercise of authority in society by groups who achieved socio-economic superiority and claimed legitimacy for their commands in terms of superior ritual status" (1989, 2). My analytical framework draws on the idea of the decline of dominance as one key to the understanding of variations in state political regimes and so develops further the case studies that Frankel and Rao bring together in their two volumes.

VARIATIONS IN POVERTY REDUCTION ACROSS STATES

There are of course many different studies of poverty across Indian states and much variation in the results according to the methods employed, the data sources used, the periods of time covered, and so on. Minhas, Jain, and Tendulkar (1991) and Datt and Ravallion (1998) provide two authoritative studies. The former examined trends in rural poverty alleviation performance in two periods, 1970–71 to 1983; and 1983 to 1987–88. They finally ranked the major states, in terms of changes in the poverty head count ratio and in absolute numbers of poor rural people across both periods (see table 1).

Datt and Ravallion have analyzed a comprehensive data set for the period 1960 to 1990. Examining rates of progress in reducing rural poverty, growth in average consumption, and the relationship between these two trends, they came up with a somewhat different ranking. They find that "by and large, the same variables determining rates of progress in reducing poverty mattered to the growth of average consumption [so that] there is no sign here of trade-offs between growth and pro-poor distributional outcomes" (1998, 34). They also find, contrary to Kohli, that the economic growth process in the adjacent and formerly unified states of Punjab and Haryana "was unusually pro-poor" (23).[4] Table 1 shows their ranking of states in terms of reduction in the incidence of poverty from around 1960 to around 1990, by the poverty head count index (the best comparator with the findings by Minhas, Jain, and Tendulkar).

On all measures of states' records in poverty reduction (according to Datt and Ravallion), and according to both teams of authors, both Kerala and Andhra Pradesh are high-performing states and Karnataka, Jammu and Kashmir, and Assam are clearly among the low-performing states. Tamil Nadu, West Bengal, and Orissa are states that have done fairly well, and consistently (according to different measures and different authors) better than Maharashtra; and the first two of these three states consistently better than what are commonly considered to be the "poverty heartland" states of northern India: Bihar, Uttar Pradesh, Madhya Pradesh, and Rajasthan. The findings are most ambiguous for Gujarat.

From the two studies, it is apparent that, contrary to Kohli's suggestions, there are states that have not had in place a regime like that of the
Left Front in West Bengal and that seem to have done as well, or even
better, in terms of rural poverty reduction.
Datt and Ravallion argue that the main causes of variation among
states in poverty reduction are differences in (1) the trend rates of growth
of average farm yields; and (2) initial conditions, especially better irrigation infrastructure, higher levels of literacy, and lower infant mortality
rates. Variations in levels of state development spending (as officially
defined in the budgeting procedures employed in India) were not found
to be significant, but this, the authors argue,

does not necessarily mean that such spending is irrelevant to
progress in reducing rural poverty, since other (significant) variables in the model may themselves be affected strongly by development spending. The impact of initial conditions presumably reflects
in part past spending on physical and human infrastructure [e.g.,

TABLE 1. TWO RANKINGS OF MAJOR
INDIAN STATES BY EXTENT OF RURAL
POVERTY REDUCTION

	Minhas, Jain, and Tendulkar 1991[a]	Datt and Ravallion 1998[b]
1	Andhra Pradesh	Kerala
2	Kerala	Andhra Pradesh
3	West Bengal	Punjab-Haryana
4	Tamil Nadu	Gujarat
5	Madhya Pradesh	Orissa
6	Uttar Pradesh	West Bengal
7	Haryana	Tamil Nadu
8	Rajasthan	Maharashtra
9	Bihar	Uttar Pradesh
10	Orissa	Rajasthan
11	Maharashtra	Karnataka
12	Karnataka	Jammu and Kashmir
13	Himachal Pradesh	Madhya Pradesh
14	Assam	Bihar
15	Punjab	Assam
16	Gujarat	
17	Jammu and Kashmir	

[a]Major states are ranked according to the extent of changes in the poverty
head count ratio and in the absolute numbers of poor rural people from
1970 to 1971 and from 1987 to 1988.
[b]States are ranked according to the extent of reduction in the incidence of
poverty, measured by the head count index, from around 1960 to around
1990.

investment by the colonial state in irrigation in Punjab and investments in education in the princely states of Travancore and
Cochin]. It can also be argued that agricultural and non-agricul-
tural output are determined in part by public spending on (for
example) physical infrastructure and public services." (1998, 31)

Abhijit Sen, commenting on an earlier publication by Datt and Ravallion, which he says shows that "state development expenditure is the
most significant variable . . . decreasing poverty both by increasing average income and improving income distribution," and, reporting the
results of his own comparable exercise, argues that "the importance of
state expenditure and of the relative food price appears to be fairly robust
as factors explaining poverty both across time and space" (1996, 2473). It
seems reasonable, then, if we follow these authors, to argue that state
development expenditure does matter and the broad structural determinants of variations in this expenditure must therefore be taken into
account. These are considered in the next section.

INITIAL CONDITIONS AND HISTORICAL "PATH DEPENDENCE"

There is a marked pattern of regional differentiation within India that is
rooted in the colonial period and resulted from the mutually reinforcing
effects of the different ways in which land revenue was raised. How this
was done influenced modes of surplus appropriation in agriculture and
patterns of public investment. Srivastava (1993, 149) argued that "investment in irrigation was concentrated chiefly in areas where gains in productivity could be skimmed off in additional revenue . . . [and] the mutually reinforcing elements resulted in widely differing growth dynamics in
the different regions." The result was that, at independence, the states of
the Northwest and "the southern region around Madras and Bombay,
and especially what later became the state of Gujarat, was better placed
and had a better start in terms of both agriculture and industry" (150).
Bharadwaj, too, in her analysis of regional differentiation, remarked
upon the kind of virtuous spiral that was established in these regions of
the country, connecting public investment, agricultural growth, industrial development, and the general level of well-being (1982). The initial
conditions that Datt and Ravallion emphasize were to a large extent the
outcome of interventions by the colonial state in India.

Subsequently, for all the "overwhelming economic power wielded by
the Centre" in India's (limited) form of federalism (Chelliah 1998, 346),
and the interventions of both the Planning Commission and the quin-
quennially appointed Finance Commissions, which advise on the allocation of public sector resources between the central government and the
states, it "appears evident that there are inherent political-economic con-

straints on the Centre's ability to impart significant progressiveness to its investment or transfers to backward states" (Srivastava 1993, 185). Despite the efforts of the central government to reduce economic equalities between the states, strong connections are still observed, at state level, between average per capita income (measured in terms of domestic product), rates of economic growth, and levels and rates of growth of public development expenditure. The recent findings of Rao, Shand, and Kalirajan are eloquent.

> Contrary to the predictions of neoclassical growth theory . . . [there are] widening interstate disparities [in levels of income] . . . mainly caused by the allocation of private investments which, in turn, has been influenced by the inequitable spread of infrastructure. The inequitable nature of public expenditure spread across states is attributed to the inability of the intergovernmental transfer mechanism to adequately offset the fiscal disabilities of the poorer states as well as [the] regressive nature of the invisible interstate transfers." (1999, 769)

Table 2 shows development expenditure per capita, on the Revenue Account,[5] for four selected years in eight major states. It bears out the findings of the general literature on interstate disparities.

Datt and Ravallion argue that, in addition to the set of initial conditions, interstate variations in performance in reducing rural poverty have been strongly influenced by the trend rate of growth of agricultural yields. The rate of growth of farm yields, according to the results of much research, are influenced in turn by levels of investment in agricultural infrastructure (e.g., Mohan Rao 1993). Levels of public and private investment in agricultural infrastructure, which often seem to complement each other, correspond rather closely with long-running historical

TABLE 2. DEVELOPMENT EXPENDITURE PER CAPITA AT THE STATE LEVEL (RUPEES, CURRENT PRICES)

	1980–81	1985–86	1990–91	1995–96
Andhra Pradesh	159	355	589	969
Karnataka	162	344	597	1,185
Kerala	197	379	614	1,104
Madhya Pradesh	143	271	499	835
Maharashtra	202	436	771	1,342
Orissa	151	250	468	899
Tamil Nadu	170	342	728	1,251
West Bengal	143	262	516	759

Source: Calculated from *Reserve Bank of India Bulletin,* various issues.

differences in income levels and levels of developmental expenditure. One recent study generates the following ranking of states on an index of levels of agricultural infrastructure: Punjab, Kerala, Tamil Nadu, and Haryana are better endowed than Karnataka, Gujarat, Maharashtra, and Andhra Pradesh, which in turn stand above West Bengal, Uttar Pradesh, Orissa, Madhya Pradesh, Bihar, and Rajasthan (Bhatia 1999, A–47).

There is quite a close correspondence between this index and rates of growth of farm yields. Table 3 reports recent estimates by Bhalla and Singh (1997) of rates of growth of crop yields from 1962 to 1995. They reckon that, despite what is reported to be a rather high level of agricultural infrastructure, the rate of growth of yields in Kerala has been low; Maharashtra has performed rather less well than the comparably endowed Andhra Pradesh, Karnataka, and Gujarat (though its irrigation endowment is less good); and Rajasthan and Uttar Pradesh performed much better than Orissa, Madhya Pradesh and Bihar.

There are strong indications, therefore, of long-running historical path dependence in the connections of levels of income in the different states, levels of public expenditure on a per capita basis, levels of investment in agricultural infrastructure, rates of growth of farm yields, and the progress of poverty reduction. There are also interesting divergences.

- *Andhra Pradesh* is a middle-income state with middling levels of development expenditure and middling agricultural infrastruc-

TABLE 3.   RATE OF GROWTH OF CROP YIELDS (PERCENTAGE OF ANNUAL COMPOUND GROWTH RATES)

	1962–65 to 1970–73 (%)	1970–73 to 1980–83 (%)	1980–83 to 1992–95 (%)	1962–65 to 1992–95	
				(%)	Rank Order
Andhra Pradesh	0.9	3.7	3.4	2.8	3
Bihar	1.1	0.1	2.9	1.5	12
Gujarat	2.1	2.8	2.3	2.4	8
Haryana	3.3	2.0	4.1	3.2	1
Karnataka	3.6	1.6	2.8	2.6	5
Kerala	1.6	–0.5	2.0	1.1	14
Madhya Pradesh	1.1	0.8	3.8	2.0	10
Maharashtra	–2.6	4.9	2.6	2.0	11
Orissa	–0.1	0.7	2.6	1.3	13
Punjab	4.2	2.7	2.9	3.1	2
Rajasthan	3.1	0.5	4.0	2.6	6
Tamil Nadu	2.1	1.0	4.0	2.5	7
Uttar Pradesh	1.8	2.4	3.4	2.6	4
West Bengal	1.3	0.6	4.4	2.3	9

Source: Bhalla and Singh 1997, A–4, table 3.

ture (although it had a relatively high level of irrigation among its initial conditions), but it has had a comparatively high rate of growth of farm yields and has been successful in reducing poverty.

- *Karnataka is* also a middle-income state, generally with slightly higher levels of development expenditure and middling agricultural infrastructure (though a smaller irrigated area than Andhra Pradesh), and it too has had a comparatively high rate of growth of farm yields. Yet by all accounts it appears to have been one of the states that has been least successful in reducing poverty.
- *Kerala,* another middle-income state with fairly good infrastructure and a higher level of development expenditure, has done very well in reducing poverty despite a poor agricultural performance.
- *West Bengal,* also middle income, has relatively low levels of development expenditure and relatively poor agricultural infrastructure on Bhatia's index, but it has done well in raising farm yields in the recent past and has a relatively good record on poverty reduction (though better according to Minhas, Jain, and Tendulkar than on the reckoning of Datt and Ravallion).
- *Maharashtra* is a high-income state with high levels of development expenditure but rather a poor performance both in increasing farm yields and in reducing poverty.
- *Orissa* is a poor state, and according to Bhalla and Singh it has a poor record in increasing yields, yet according to Datt and Ravallion it has done rather well in reducing poverty.
- *Uttar Pradesh* is a poor state, well endowed in terms of irrigation and enjoying one of the higher rates of growth of crop yields, yet its record in poverty reduction is only middling.

Is it possible to explain apparent divergences of these kinds from the trends set by long-run dynamics of economic development in terms of differences in political regimes?

DEFINING REGIME DIFFERENCES IN INDIA

The principal focus of this chapter is on variation in the democratic functioning of different Indian states, which I will describe in terms of regime types. Democracy may be defined as: "government by the people; the form of government in which sovereign power resides in the people and is exercised either directly by them [participatory democracy] or by officers elected by them [representative democracy]." Clearly, this is a statement of an ideal, for it evades the real problems of collective action,

which arise from the fact that the goals held by individuals ("the people")
rarely coincide absolutely. Approaching the ideal of democracy, therefore, depends (in large part) upon the differentiation of the realm of politics from overall systems of inequality in a society—so that collective
decisions are not made by particular individuals or groups of people
because of the power derived from their economic or social status
(Rueschemeyer, Stephens, and Stephens 1992, 41ff).

In practice, democratic forms of government, involving the accountability of the executive to an assembly of representatives elected through
free, open elections in the context of freedom of expression and association, can never eliminate altogether the significance of differences of
wealth, power, and status in society. Marxists have generally rejected
such representative democracy as a sham that conceals the exercise of
power by the dominant class. The view that is expressed by
Rueschemeyer and his coauthors is that the ideal of democracy is
approached more or less closely according to the balance of class power
in a society and the nature of the state system. The development of capitalism is, in some ways, actually conducive to approaching the democratic ideal. It weakens the power of landlords and strengthens subordinate
classes, shifting them from the relatively unfavorable environment of
peasant agriculture in which, as Marx argued in *The Eighteenth Brumaire,* they are "like potatoes in a sack"—divided from each other, lacking a sense of a collective interest, and given their identity by the more
self-conscious classes that make up the rest of society.

The democratic ideal is approached more closely, too, if the state system (the organization of the state) is relatively autonomous in relation to
society. But there is a narrow gap between the Scylla of a state system
dominated by particular interests within society, such as those of landlords, industrial or finance capital, and the Charybdis of a state system,
which is absolutely autonomous and able to exercise dictatorship over
society, overriding the interests and aspirations of "the people." This is
where "civil society" enters the equation. The more developed is the
sphere of private, voluntary association, of civil society, the wider is the
gap between the Scylla and the Charybdis and the greater the space for
democracy, for it implies that different interests are organized within
society and able to hold the organizations in the state system to account
(derived from Rueschemeyer, Stephens, and Stephens 1992).

In the light of this short discussion of democratic political systems, we
may expect there to be a greater likelihood that the needs and strategic
interests of poor people will be met in circumstances in which they are
more effectively organized. Critical questions in distinguishing between
the regimes of various Indian states, then, are these: are there appreciable
differences between them in terms of the balance of class power and the

extent of political participation of historically subordinated, lower classes? What is the nature of this "participation," ideologically and organizationally, and what are the relationships among the lower classes and other classes?[6]

Tackling these questions in the Indian case requires study of the evidence on class structures and their relationships with caste/ethnicity and historical structures of dominance (as defined by Frankel and Rao [1989–90]). "Class formation" is always and everywhere a problematic concept. The relationships between "objective" differences between groups of people, in terms of their roles and relations within productive systems, and the subjective categories in terms of which people experience and understand these roles and relations—between "class in itself" and "class for itself"—have always to be treated contextually and historically. In the Indian case, this means studying the relationships between class and caste. We know that there is no neat mapping between class and caste, but there are strong, broad correspondences, for example, between landownership and caste position. We also know that in many instances class relationships are experienced as relations between castes (see Harriss 1994). Sometimes potential or actual class political mobilization is crosscut by caste relations and vice-versa—and sometimes not. But in practice we have to study the class/caste bases of different regimes in order to address the critical question of the balance of class power.

The further steps in the analysis mean examining political organization, including the formation of different types of association and the ideology, organization, and class alliances underlying different regimes. What are their stated objectives? How do their leaders seek to win support ideologically and organizationally? What are the alliances on which they depend? What are the relationships between local power and state-level politics? Questions concerning leadership and organizational and ideological coherence—which Kohli also highlighted—enter here.

Measuring regime differences is obviously difficult, both conceptually and practically. My approach has been to develop a framework for the comparison of Indian state politics worked out by Roderick Church (1984). At that time, Church argued, there was a "crisis of participation" among lower castes/classes. This was in the context of a fourfold distinction between caste categories. If Brahmans, Kshatriyas, and Banias, who include most of the more important property owners and professionals in Indian society, are described as "upper castes," then the principal farming castes across India—*jats, yadavs,* and *kurmis* in large parts of the north or *marathas* and *patidars* in the west—may be called "middle castes." This leaves a diverse group of middle castes—marginal farmers, sharecroppers, and agricultural laborers as well as members of traditional service and artisanal castes—sandwiched between the middle castes and the fourth category: Scheduled Castes and (Scheduled) Tribes. The latter are mostly laborers and, though subject to particular disabilities because of their caste status, also the objects of positive discrimination by the Indian state. By the 1960s, it was very often the "lower castes" that were most excluded, and thereafter political trends in the states were influenced significantly by the ways in which these groups became mobilized politically.

The Congress Party, until recently the hegemonic national political party, succeeded in establishing strongholds in Maharashtra and Karnataka in 1977 in part because of the support it won from the lower castes (see Lele 1984; and Manor 1984). In the 1980 State Assembly elections in Gujarat, the Congress[7] built a winning coalition with the so-called KHAM strategy. This was a deliberate attempt to bring together rather numerous but low-ranking Kshatriyas—an important fraction of the lower castes there—with Harijans, Adivasis (i.e., Scheduled Tribes, or "tribals") and Muslims (see Wood 1984). In Uttar Pradesh, Paul Brass has suggested, "In the struggle among the landed castes [the middle castes and some from the upper castes in our terms], the Congress and the Bharatiya Kranti Dal/Lok Dal [middle castes, richer farmer-based parties] have been fairly evenly divided, which means that the low castes hold the balance electorally" (1984, 47). In Bihar, the lower castes continued to be excluded. In West Bengal and Kerala, the Congress Party had lost the support of the lower castes to the Communist Party of India (Marxist).

Around the early to middle 1980s, therefore, Church argued, the pattern of politics in different states could be understood in terms of the extent and mode of political participation of the lower castes:

> First, there are those states in which lower castes have achieved positions of power in the legislature and government and *where government policy to some extent addresses the concerns of the poor*. These include West Bengal, Gujarat, Karnataka, Kerala and (perhaps to a lesser extent) Maharashtra. Uttar Pradesh and Bihar remain states where the lower castes have made little progress. Second, among states in which the lower castes have made the most progress, there are those in which the Congress has taken the initiative in recruiting the lower castes and bringing change [and those in which lower-caste power has been associated, rather, with the ousting of Congress]. (Church 1984, 236–37; my emphasis)

Taking account of subsequent political developments, this analysis for the early 1980s may be extended to the late 1990s. The regime categories employed are shown in table 4 and discussed in sequence in the following pages. A key variable is the extent to which the electoral dominance of the formerly hegemonic and inclusive Congress Party has been eroded.

STATES WHERE UPPER CASTE/CLASS DOMINANCE HAS PERSISTED

Madhya Pradesh and Rajasthan were both created largely by merging former princely states.[8] Some of the former ruling families have remained politically powerful in both cases. Historically, right-wing parties—Swatantra in the 1960s, then the Jan Sangh, which became the Bharatiya Janata Party, the current ruling Hindu nationalist party—have been strong here. Neither state has offered much opportunity for left-wing political parties or ideologies. Stable patterns of two-party competition developed at an early stage. Power is now contested in each state between the BJP and the Congress. While political leadership in Rajasthan was

TABLE 4. A TYPOLOGY OF INDIAN STATE REGIMES

Ai: States in which upper-caste/class dominance has persisted and the Congress Party has remained strong in the context of a stable two-party system ("traditional dominance" rather than politics of accommodation vis-à-vis lower classes)

Madhya Pradesh	(low income)
Orissa	(low income)
Rajasthan	(low income)

Aii: States in which upper-caste/class dominance has been effectively challenged by middle castes/classes and Congress support has collapsed in the context of fractured and unstable party competition (both "dominance" and the politics of accommodation have broken down)

Bihar	(low income)
Uttar Pradesh	(low income)

B: States with middle-caste/class-dominated regimes, where Congress has been effectively challenged but has not collapsed and there is fairly stable and mainly two-party competition (the politics of accommodation vis-à-vis lower-class interests have continued to work effectively, especially in Maharashtra and Karnataka, and least so in Gujarat)

Andhra Pradesh	(middle income)
Gujarat	(high income)
Karnataka	(middle income)
Maharashtra	(high income)
[Punjab?]	(high income)

C: States in which lower castes/classes are more strongly represented in political regimes and where the Congress lost its dominance at an early stage

Kerala	(middle income)
Tamil Nadu	(middle income)
West Bengal	(middle income)

divided between (upper caste) Brahmans and Rajputs and (middle caste) Jats, and the State Assemblies were dominated by these three groups (along with the Scheduled Castes), Jenkins has shown how the BJP has been a vehicle for extending Rajput dominance (1998). Narain and Mathur remarked that "The day when the placidity and civility of Rajasthan politics will be rocked by the 'power-drive' of the agricultural castes, while bound to arrive, is difficult to predict" (1990, 53). It has still not come. Jaffrelot's work on politics in Madhya Pradesh (1998) similarly, shows the continuing preeminence of (upper caste) Brahmans, Rajputs, and Banias in both the BJP and the Congress.

Orissa has features in common with Madhya Pradesh and Rajasthan. It too was partially constituted by former princely states, and like Madhya Pradesh it has a high proportion of Scheduled Tribes within its population. The princes of Orissa seem to have been less successful in retaining political power, but the right-wing parties, initially Swatantra—to which some of the princes gravitated and which took part in a coalition government after 1967—and later the Jan Sangh/BJP, have long been influential. Mohanty argues that "a *brahman-karan* ["upper caste" in our terms] middle class dominates society and politics in contemporary Orissa" (1990, 321). Left-wing parties have never won much support outside small pockets. The most outstanding political leader from Orissa has been the late Biju Patnaik, who maintained a political following in opposition to Congress for over two decades. This widened the social base of electoral politics and mobilized the rising "agrarian middle class," as Mohanty described it, including notably Khandayats, numerically the largest single caste group, who should probably be considered to be middle caste—although they do not have the political clout that these middle castes enjoy elsewhere. The politics of Orissa has had an unusually strong personal element, and party contests have been governed by intraelite competition. Latterly the main competition has been between the Congress and Patnaik's following, which has passed substantially to his son Navin, now leader of the Biju Janata Dal, which is in alliance with the BJP. The two operate from the same social base, and "Monopolising the competitive arena they [have] pre-empted alternative popular forces from acquiring political significance" (Mohanty 1990, 356).

STATES WHERE UPPER CASTE/CLASS DOMINANCE HAS BEEN EFFECTIVELY CHALLENGED

Bihar and Uttar Pradesh are the core states of the "Hindi Heartland," where the upper castes are relatively much more numerous than in most parts of India. The Congress Party in both states has been dominated by members of these upper castes: "Upper caste domination provided the framework of political bonding in a fragmented society" (Hasan 1998,

19). But groups officially categorized as Other Backward Classes (OBCs)—middle castes in our terms—have become politically powerful in both states. The Congress Party has very substantially destroyed itself after ruling each state for most of the time from independence until 1989–90. Politics in each is fragmented and bitterly contested between formations that derive either from the Lok Dal, in which OBCs are strong; the BJP, to which the upper castes have gravitated but which seeks, as elsewhere, to win support from lower castes as well; and parties based on Dalits—the former Untouchables.[9] The rule of law has broken down to a greater extent in Bihar than elsewhere in India. The home minister of India went on record in the Lok Sabha (the Indian parliament) in March 1997 to state that UP is moving toward "anarchy, chaos and destruction."

STATES WITH REGIMES DOMINATED BY THE MIDDLE CASTES/CLASSES

There are of course many differences between these states. But they are alike in having powerful middle castes/classes—numerically significant groups whose dominance extends over wide areas—that have generally exercised pervasive political influence. Prime examples are the Reddys and Kammas of Andhra Pradesh (who make up, together, about 20 percent of the population); the Patidars of Gujarat (about 12 percent); the Lingayats and Vokkaligas of Karnataka (around 30 percent); and the Marathas in Maharashtra (around 30 percent).[10] Upper castes (Brahmans, Banias, and Kshatriyas) have been significant in the politics of all these states, but especially so in Gujarat, where Brahmans and Banias generally dominated the ruling Congress Party up to and through the 1960s (Wood 1984).

In all of these states, the dominant middle castes (and the upper castes) have been challenged by lower castes or they have accommodated lower-caste aspirations, but the political grip of the middle castes has remained strong, though with subtle variations. They are also states in which the BJP now has a substantial presence.[11] This is significant in relation to current concerns, especially because of the way in which the BJP has mobilized support from both middle classes and some groups of poor people, though not in a way that promises to deliver very much to the latter.

In Andhra Pradesh, politics has continued to be dominated by Reddys and Kammas, locally termed Forward Castes. They are major landholders and, in the case of the Kammas especially, successful industrialists who historically have pursued effective strategies of political accommodation of the interests of the lower castes/classes. They have been assisted in this by the fact that, although those officially described as Backward Castes make up about 50 percent of the population of Andhra Pradesh, they are unevenly distributed and divided into a large number of small groups. A very significant shift took place, however, in the forms of political mobilization in the state because of the success of Mrs. Gandhi's populist strategy in the early 1970s. This resulted in the breaking down of client-patron relations at local level, which is attested in detail by Robinson (1988) and also by Kohli's observations on Guntur District (1990). The same kind of breakdown seems not to have occurred in Karnataka (according to Kohli's observations [1990]) or in Maharashtra.

Then, in the early 1980s, Mrs. Indira Gandhi's frequent interventions in Andhra Pradesh politics, and a rapid succession of ineffectual chief ministers, built up resentments that were successfully exploited by the film star N. T. Rama Rao, who established a new political party, the Telugu Desam. Stepping into the political vacuum created by the decline of the Congress, Telugu Desam won office in the state in 1983 (see Kohli 1988; and Ram Reddy 1989). Thus, one charismatic leader (Rao) effectively replaced another (Gandhi), but one was a national leader and the other regional: "It was [Rao's] charisma that dominated the electoral scene, rendering most of the organized political parties irrelevant" (Ram Reddy 1989, 286). The Telugu Desam offered "to restore the dignity of the Telugu people." The policies it proposed were frankly populist (notably promising rice at two rupees per kilo) and attempted to accommodate youth, women, and the lower castes/classes—indicating "the continuity in political style" (Ram Reddy 1989) with Mrs. Gandhi's Congress in the 1970s. Subsequently, the Telugu Desam and the Congress have continued to compete for power in the state. In the process, the Telugu Desam (in spite of internal conflicts) appears to have become relatively well institutionalized. Recently, under a new but also charismatic leader, Chandrababu Naidu, the Telugu Desam succeeded both in retreating significantly from its earlier populist policies—this partly under the tutelage introduced by its independent negotiation of loans with the World Bank—and in retaining power in the state in the 1999 elections.

Gujarat has a more complex caste-class structure, which has made for a politics that is even more byzantine than is usual in India. I noted earlier that the pursuit of the so-called KHAM strategy brought lower castes/classes into power in a Congress regime in the early 1980s. This meant that there was a discrepancy between political power and social dominance in the state. The economy was dominated by (upper-caste) Brahmans and Banias and by (middle-caste) Patidars, but political power was held mainly by Rajput and (lower-caste) Koli "Kshatriyas." Wood remarked, insightfully, that "the haves, possessing social and economic power but excluded from access to political power in the Congress-I, appear to have nowhere to turn except to hopelessly weak and divided opposition parties, or to lawless behaviour" (1984, 221). He anticipated the violence and turbulent conflict that characterized Gujarat's politics over the following decade. By the end of the 1980s, the "haves" did find in the BJP a party to turn to, although, after the party took power in the state in 1995 it was rapidly split by a conflict that reflected the traditional rivalry between Patidar and Rajput-cum-Koli leaders. Overall, significant regime shifts occurred in the later 1970s and 1980s in the period of the KHAM strategy and again in the mid-1990s with the assumption of power by the BJP and the realignment of economic and political power.

Karnataka is described by Manor as a state with a conservative social order in which "the disparities in wealth, status and power have not been so severe as to undermine the comparative cohesiveness of society" (1989, 323). He later argues that this cohesion is "rooted in small peasant proprietorship" (331). State politics has been dominated by the Lingayat and Vokkaliga castes. As I noted previously, there is no evidence here of the challenging of local power—typically embodied in client-patron relations—in the way that has evidently occurred in Andhra Pradesh. Crook and Manor argue that democratic decentralization in Karnataka—through local assemblies, the *panchayats*—has improved political participation and government performance, but, they say, "even [this] the most successful of [the cases they studied] showed little evidence of having been particularly responsive to 'vulnerable groups,' the poor or the marginalised" (1998, 301).

In Karnataka, there was no mechanism or political process for checking the exercise of local power, such as might be supplied, they imply—à la Kohli—by prominence in the political system of a leftist party. We should not then "expect democratic decentralization in India to assist in poverty alleviation over the short to medium term, unless the centralized system is dominated by a leftist party" (Crook and Manor 1998, 77). In Karnataka, however, not only has the Left been particularly weak (Manor 1989), but party competition, too, has been notably fragmented and factionalized, on the part of both the Congress and the Janata (later Janata Dal) opposition, which took power for the first time in 1983. It is striking that Karnataka, unlike its neighbors, has not given rise to a truly regional party. None of the parties in the state persisted in the pursuit of populist policies for the mobilization of political support—as has happened in both Andhra Pradesh and Tamil Nadu—perhaps because of the continuation here, unlike in those two states or (perhaps) Gujarat, of clientelism.

Jayant Lele, who has written extensively on the politics of Maharashtra, says of the Marathas that "In no other state do we find an ideologically guided and economically differentiated caste cluster of this size" (1990, 180). Rob Jenkins sums up Lele's views on the politics of the state as follows: "the *maratha* caste cluster has constructed a system of elite-pluralist hegemony, which subsumes many unprivileged members of that caste cluster as well as other disadvantaged castes, and has cut short a 'coalition of the disadvantaged' . . . this system is flexible enough to respond to most challenges of change" (1996, 210, n. 12).

One outcome of the system was that Congress rule proved most durable in Maharashtra, among all the major states. The State Legislative Assembly elections of 1995 brought the BJP-Shiv Sena alliance to power, and for the first time in the history of the state it had a real non-Congress government and one not dominated by Marathas from rural areas. The caste composition of the Assembly did not change very much in 1995, but its social character was changed in other ways. Maratha strength was maintained—but the kinds of Marathas who won were different from those who had held seats in previous Assemblies. The Maratha Maha Sangh, a caste association, was allied with the Shiv Sena, but successful Maratha candidates who won on the Shiv Sena ticket were young and had little or no support from Maharashtra's cooperatives or other established institutions: "They are those disgruntled elements who are not absorbed in the local power structure by the clannish marathas of the Congress" (Vora 1996, 173). One commentator argues that in India's most urbanized and industrialized state "the rural-based Congress is becoming irrelevant" (172). The BJP-Shiv Sena seems to accommodate different class interests very effectively, though in a different way from the old Maharashtrian Congress system. The implications in the longer run of the challenge to Maratha dominance locally, and to the elite-pluralist hegemony described by Lele, may be profound. However, the Congress returned to power in the state in 2000. Overall, lower-caste/class interests have probably been more effectively accommodated, by selective inclusion/exclusion, in Maharashtra than in any other state.

STATES IN WHICH LOWER CASTES/CLASSES HAVE BEEN MORE STRONGLY REPRESENTED

Kerala, Tamil Nadu, and West Bengal contrast with the other states discussed here because their caste/class structures have historically been quite fragmented. In none of them was upper-caste dominance as strongly entrenched as in the North (although Brahmans had positions of importance in all of them). None of them has middle castes extending local dominance over wide areas, as is the case with the Marathas, the Reddys, or the Lingayats and Vokkaligas. In all three, there are strong indications of higher levels of political mobilization and participation by lower castes/classes than is true elsewhere. Essays in Wood 1984 substantiate this case for Kerala and West Bengal. Although the mobilization of lower castes/classes is in both cases associated with the organizational and electoral strength of the CPIM, there clearly are significant differences between them. Accounts show much more extensive organization in civil society in Kerala (Nag 1989), and there is a great deal of political competition there, whereas the CPIM has become rather monolithic in West Bengal. But the idea of "stronger representation of lower castes/classes" can certainly be supported.

The case of Tamil Nadu is more problematic. Narendra Subramanian, however, in his recent, authoritative study of Tamil politics, argues emphatically that the populist approach to mobilization practiced by the Dravidian[12] parties "attracted groups with limited access to the state [as long as] Congress dominated Tamil Nadu politics (until the mid-1960s). . . . Dravidian populism successfully addressed the intermediate and lower strata" (1999, 47). In office, he suggests, the Dravidian parties have governed through "populist clientelism," which "channels patronage through the extensive social networks of party subcultures, both to supporters and to others from the intermediate and lower strata" (69).

REGIME DIFFERENCES, FACTORS THAT INFLUENCE POVERTY REDUCTION, AND PRO-POOR POLICIES

It would be nice now to go on to show that, corresponding with these political regime differences, there are systematic variations in the resourcing of agricultural infrastructure (including irrigation) and the social services (basic education and primary health care)—both of which we know exercise a great deal of influence on poverty reduction, directly and indirectly—as well as in the adoption of specifically pro-poor policies and programs. But public accounts rarely tell such straightforward stories, and an examination of trends in state public expenditure, on the Revenue and Capital Accounts, provides no exception to this general rule.[13] The story is complicated, anyway, because of the considerable power of the central government over the policies of state governments and the influence of bureaucratic conventions on the management of the state budgets and the way in which public accounts are presented. The following observations are based on an examination of the state-level accounts for eight states: Andhra Pradesh, Karnataka, Kerala, Madhya Pradesh, Maharashtra, Orissa, Tamil Nadu, and West Bengal.

Variations over time in spending per capita on the Revenue Account and hence on development functions (which account for 65 to 75 percent of all expenditure on this account; see table 1) between the eight states have been rather constant. Expenditure has been highest in the high-income state of Maharashtra, which has been consistently ahead of the middle-income states of Tamil Nadu, Kerala, and Karnataka. These three have usually spent rather more than the other middle-income state of Andhra Pradesh. The latter has been ahead, in turn, of the low-income states of Orissa and Madhya Pradesh as well as middle-income West Bengal, whose level of expenditure is strikingly low given that its state domestic product per capita, between 1973 and 1986, was close to that of Maharashtra and Gujarat and was distinctly higher than those of Karnataka, Kerala, Tamil Nadu, and Andhra Pradesh.

In all the states, the most important single item of what is officially defined as "developmental spending" is education. The quinquennial average percentages of the developmental budget allocated to this heading are shown in table 5.

Kerala, followed by West Bengal, has consistently spent a greater share of public funds on education than other states do. Madhya Pradesh and latterly especially Andhra Pradesh have spent less than others. Taking account of the differences in levels of development expenditure per capita, these proportional allocations mean that Kerala has been spending about twice as much on education, per person, as Madhya Pradesh. Figures for two selected years, for illustrative purposes, are shown in table 6.

The well-known bias toward social expenditure in Kerala appears very clearly in these data, and it is followed by West Bengal, although, because of lower levels of development expenditure per capita in West Bengal, this state is outstripped in absolute terms by both Maharashtra and Tamil Nadu. The level of expenditure on education in Andhra Pradesh, relatively and absolutely, seems rather low, given both the level and the rate of growth of the state domestic product—which corresponds with the state's comparatively poor record in terms of human development objectives.

Allocations of developmental expenditure on medical and health ser-

TABLE 5. PROPORTION OF DEVELOPMENTAL EXPENDITURE ON EDUCATION IN EIGHT STATES, 1980–81 TO 1997–98

	1980–81 to 1984–85	1985–86 to 1989–90	1990–91 to 1994–95	1995–96 to 1997–98[a]
Andhra Pradesh	28	26	26	24
Karnataka	29	29	30	28
Kerala	44	43	43	40
Madhya Pradesh	24	25	26	25
Maharashtra	28	28	30	32
Orissa	27	31	31	33
Tamil Nadu	28	30	27	32
West Bengal	33	36	39	38

Source: Calculated from data given in *Reserve Bank of India Bulletin,* various issues.

[a]Note that the figures for 1996–97 and 1997–98 are the budget estimates; others are from the accounts.

vices vary rather little between these eight states, usually being around 12 percent, and are somewhat higher (14 to 15 percent) in West Bengal, Kerala, and (less predictably, perhaps) Madhya Pradesh. Allocations of expenditure to agriculture, irrigation, and community development (and these three headings, with education and medical and health expenditures, together make up around two-thirds of all developmental expenditures on the Revenue Budget) vary more between states, though in none of them in at all a distinctive way. In general, it appears that "economic" expenditure on irrigation and agriculture has formed a higher percentage of the total in Maharashtra, followed by Karnataka and Madhya Pradesh, and Kerala and West Bengal have usually spent rather less than the other states under these headings.

The story of spending on nutrition alone stands out. Tamil Nadu has spent more than 4 percent of its developmental outlays on nutrition since the early 1980s, when the then chief minister, M. G. Ramachandran, introduced his Nutritious Noon Meals Scheme, which became one of the most significant nutrition interventions anywhere in the world. Andhra Pradesh seems to have followed suit after the return of the Telugu Desam to office in the mid-1990s. Karnataka increased its nutrition spending at the time of the Janata government in the 1980s. In no other state is nutrition spending at all significant.

The main conclusion that it seems to be possible to draw from this examination is that Kerala, West Bengal, and Tamil Nadu—as we would predict—do indeed give greater emphasis in their spending to social expenditure. They have spent more relatively, and in the case of Kerala and Tamil Nadu (probably) absolutely as well, than high-income states such as Maharashtra.

TABLE 6. EXPENDITURE PER CAPITA ON EDUCATION IN EIGHT STATES, 1980–81 AND 1990–91 (RUPEES, CURRENT PRICES)

	1980–81	1990–91
Andhra Pradesh	43	151
Karnataka	46	177
Kerala	88	264
Madhya Pradesh	33	137
Maharashtra	60	218
Orissa	40	142
Tamil Nadu	49	229
West Bengal	45	200

Source: Calculated from accounts given in *Reserve Bank of India Bulletin,* various issues.

What may be described as India's Poverty Alleviation Program has three major components—the Integrated Rural Development Programme (IRDP), which aims to put productive assets into the hands of the poor; the rural public works program, Jawahar Rozgar Yohana (JRY); and the Public Distribution System (PDS), which is intended to allow the poor— the great majority of whom must purchase their food—to secure basic staples at low prices. It is a program of the central government, which also pays for 80 percent of JRY and IRDP. So with regard to these important pro-poor programs the role of the states is principally in implementation. Are there differences in performance that are politically determined?[14]

Variation in performance seems to be most marked with regard to the Public Distribution System. Offtake under the scheme has been particularly low in the states with the greatest concentrations of poverty. In research conducted in the 1980s, D S Tyagi calculated the level of "desired distribution," taking account of the incidence of poverty, agricultural production, and income levels in the different states, and compared it to the actual distribution of food grains through the Public Distribution System. His results are shown in table 7.

Tyagi's firm conclusion was that "the distribution of foodgrains through the PDS has not gravitated in favour of areas with a higher proportion of the poor" (1990, 91). Subsequent research by Thamarajakshi

TABLE 7.   "DESIRED DISTRIBUTION" AND
"ACTUAL DISTRIBUTION" OF FOOD IN MAJOR
STATES UNDER THE PUBLIC DISTRIBUTION SYSTEM,
LATE 1980S (KILOGRAMS PER CAPITA)

	Desired Distribution	Actual Distribution
Andhra Pradesh	8.1	8.3
Bihar	11.6	4.7
Gujarat	6.3	5.0
Karnataka	5.8	5.8
Kerala	6.4	10.4
Madhya Pradesh	7.6	3.2
Maharashtra	11.4	9.6
Orissa	3.7	2.3
Punjab	1.3	1.1
Rajasthan	4.9	4.4
Tamil Nadu	8.4	9.9
Uttar Pradesh	15.2	5.3
West Bengal	8.2	11.9

Source: Tyagi 1990, 93. The "actual" figures relate to 1988–89. Data reproduced by Tyagi for the quinquennium ending in 1988 show a similar "actual" distribution across states.

(1997) confirms this conclusion. By 1995–96, Andhra Pradesh, Tamil Nadu, Kerala, Karnataka, and West Bengal—but barely Gujarat and not Maharashtra—had benefited from a higher share of total PDS distribution of wheat and rice than one would expect on the basis of their share of the poor population of the country. This has been achieved through subsidies, which keep the PDS price below the open market price and ensure that PDS grain accounts for relatively high shares of total grain consumption—around a quarter in Andhra Pradesh and Tamil Nadu. But the cost is high, not least in terms of foregone public investment in agriculture. Latterly, as the government of Andhra Pradesh has dealt independently with the World Bank, it has made commitments to cut back on its subsidized rice scheme in response to conditionality. Whatever the arguments for and against food subsidies, it is striking that they have played a much more prominent role in some states than in others, notably in Andhra Pradesh, Tamil Nadu, and Kerala, followed by Karnataka and Gujarat.

The analysis shows quite strikingly that those states that have most clearly pursued what might be described as a direct approach to poverty reduction, through investments in the key social sectors of education and health and by means of food subsidies, are those in which there is evidence that the lower castes/classes are most strongly represented in the political regime. These were Kerala, Tamil Nadu, and West Bengal, followed by Andhra Pradesh (food subsidies rather than social sector spending) and then by Karnataka and Gujarat—well ahead, among the states that are still dominated by middle castes/classes, of Maharashtra.

This middle-caste/class dominance has been challenged most strongly in Andhra Pradesh, which has also come to have a stable two-party system in which both the Congress and the regional party, the Telugu Desam, compete for popular votes. When the Congress returned to office in the early 1990s, it was unable to get rid of the subsidized rice scheme introduced earlier by the Telugu Desam, despite pressures to do so in the context of economic reforms. It then lost office again in 1995, significantly because the Telugu Desam was widely considered to run the scheme better.

Maharashtra, on the other hand, is the state in which the Congress rural party machine, dominated by Marathas, has endured longer than anywhere else. Here political accommodationism has been most effective, and the Congress (at least until its defeat, for the first time, in 1995) has not been subject to the same kinds of competitive pressures as in Andhra Pradesh or Gujarat and Karnataka. In Karnataka, although there has been party competition, it has been rather fragmented, and the dominance of the middle castes/classes has not been challenged in the way that it has in both Andhra Pradesh and Gujarat.

CONCLUSION: THE BALANCE OF CLASS POWER
MATTERS AND SO DO PARTY SYSTEMS

The divergences of different states from long-run historical path dependency can be explained, then, in terms of the balance of class power and
the character of party systems in different states, which are reflected in
patterns of public action.

Kerala, West Bengal, and Tamil Nadu, where levels of pro-poor social
expenditure have been relatively high, stand out as states in which there
has been much greater political participation than elsewhere by lower
castes/classes. This has been the case in Kerala and West Bengal because
of the activities of a left of center party (the CPIM) that has combined
coherent leadership, pragmatism toward the propertied classes, and ideological and organizational commitment and has successfully challenged
local landed power holders. In both states, there have been more
significant efforts made at asset redistribution through agrarian reform
than elsewhere. Kerala, however, has a more developed civil society and
more political competition, whereas the CPIM in West Bengal has
become rather a monolithic machine. Nonetheless, the work of Crook
and Sverrisson (this volume) shows that among all the instances of decentralization that they have been able to identify and study from across the
world, West Bengal's has been most successful. They argue that most successful cases of decentralization, like that of West Bengal, have occurred
where a higher level of government not only had an ideological commitment to pro-poor policies but was prepared to engage actively with local
politics to challenge local elite resistance if necessary and to ensure implementation of policies. Where central governments had not confronted
local elites, the results of decentralization in relation to the poor were
universally dismal.

In Tamil Nadu, the participation of lower castes/classes has been artic-
ulated by a regional party that at one time propagated cultural nationalism and has had charismatic leaders who have successfully appealed to
lower castes/classes through populist programs. Cross-class political
alliances have been established by fairly well institutionalized political
parties, and there have been consistent pressures to maintain social
expenditure in the context of vigorous electoral competition.

In the group of states where middle castes/classes have been dominant,
Andhra Pradesh has done better in poverty reduction than the other middle-income state of Karnataka; between the high-income states, Gujarat
probably has done better than Maharashtra. In each pairing, the relatively successful state has hosted a greater electoral challenge to the
power of the locally dominant castes/classes. Agricultural growth in Karnataka has been slower than in Andhra Pradesh, and probably less pro-

poor as well, through lower levels of increase in labor absorption and lower rates of increase of real wages in agriculture. In Maharashtra, it has been slower and less pro-poor than in Gujarat. This reflects the continuing power of locally dominant castes/classes, which can lead to what has been described as "responsive wage deceleration" or the bidding down of wages by the locally powerful.

Andhra Pradesh has a more institutionalized party system than does Karnataka, where the party system is increasingly fragmented—although it is still dominated by the locally powerful middle castes/classes. Unsurprisingly, Crook and Sverrison (this volume) found that decentralization was less effective in relation to poverty alleviation in Karnataka than in West Bengal because the central (state) government made no attempt to challenge local power. There has been more party competition in Gujarat than in Maharashtra, which may have made for rather greater responsiveness to the poor, for example, through use of the Public Distribution System.

There appears to be a relationship between a history of upper-caste/class social and political dominance and economic backwardness. Uttar Pradesh started off with a relatively favorable endowment of public investment in irrigation and has had a relatively high rate of growth in agriculture. But this has not translated into benefits for lower castes/classes, nor has it been supplemented by a direct attack on poverty. This is unsurprising given the long persistence of the local power of upper castes/classes and, more recently, competition between these elites and an elite from middle-caste/class groups, which has resulted in the fragmentation of party competition. If it is true, as seems to be the case according to Datt and Ravallion, that Orissa has done relatively well in poverty reduction among this group of poor, upper-class-dominated states, it may be because of a history of political competition in which one particular leader (the late Biju Patnaik) mobilized support across the middle and lower castes/classes.

Madhya Pradesh has been poorly placed in terms of initial conditions of agricultural infrastructure and subsequent agricultural growth, and it has also had a very conservative party regime. This may be changing now in the context of rather stable two-party competition in which the Congress Party in particular now has a leader of long standing who has the prestige of having retained office for a second term and who has been building a party organization that reaches down to the lower castes/classes in a way that has not been true before. Correspondingly, the Congress government of the state has latterly implemented a number of progressive innovations. It may be doubted, however, whether the current program of decentralization in Madhya Pradesh will be successful in the absence of a significant challenge to local power holders.

Three broad conclusions emerge from this study. First, the structure and functioning of local (agrarian) power and the relations of local- and state-level power holders exercise a significant influence on policy processes and development outcomes. They show that politics does "make a difference," though within the constraints of long-running historical path dependence in patterns of economic and social development.

Second, they show that populist regimes relying on charismatic leadership—those of the regional parties All India Anna Dravida Munnetra Kazhagam (AIADMK) and Dravida Munnetra Kazhagam (DMK) in Tamil Nadu or the Telugu Desam in Andhra Pradesh—can become relatively well institutionalized and that they can deliver pro-poor policies and programs. It is important that both cases involve competitive populism carried on by institutionalized parties. How sustainable the resulting pro-poor policies are is another question. However, in both these states relatively productive agricultural systems and relatively high rates of growth in crop yields[15] help sustain poverty reduction. The political regimes of Andhra Pradesh and Tamil Nadu have certainly generated more poverty reduction than clientelist patterns of politics in Maharashtra and Karnataka, where the lower castes/classes have been accommodated through selective inclusion.

Finally, these findings seem to confirm the view that well-organized left of center parties, which successfully confront local landed power through even modest agrarian reforms, are probably best able to deliver poverty reduction. But of course such social democratic regimes—any more than competitive populist as opposed to clientelist regimes—are not a policy choice.

1. This last statement referred particularly to the Janata government of Uttar Pradesh. In Karnataka, "Coherent leadership and populist ideology [in the time of Devaraj Urs' chief ministership in the 1970s] facilitated a modicum of reform. The organisational base, however, was weak and the propertied classes penetrated the ruling groups" (Kohli 1987, 8).

2. This conclusion anticipates the "embedded autonomy" thesis developed more recently by Peter Evans (1996) and, after him, by Michael Woolcock (1998).

3. Vyas and Bhargava (1995) base their argument on the findings of comparative studies of public intervention and rural poverty alleviation in nine states. This was a program of work undertaken by a group of Indian scholars between 1989 and 1993 in Andhra Pradesh, Karnataka, Maharashtra, Haryana, Bihar, Gujarat, Rajasthan, West Bengal and Kerala. The results were published in *Economic and Political Weekly,* October 14, 1995.

4. Datt and Ravallion treat the two states as one unit because their earlier data refer to the undivided Punjab.

5. Under the Indian budgeting system, the government fund is made up of the Revenue (or Current) Account and the Capital Account. There are receipts and expenditures under each of these two accounts; and outlays may be divided between "nondevelopment" and "development" expenditures. Receipts on the Revenue Account of a state government (within India's federal system of government) include tax and nontax revenues, grants received from the central government, and taxes devolved from the center. Disbursements on the Revenue Account include mostly recurring expenditures (such as wages and salaries). If disbursements on the Revenue Account are less than receipts, the surplus may be devoted to capital expenditures.

6. It has often been argued that Indian politics is characterized by "political accommodationism," referring to the way in which dominant elites build coalitions of political support among sections of dependent groups by means of a strategy of selective inclusion.

7. This was actually the Congress-(I), as the dominant group was labeled after Indira Gandhi split the party.

8. Under the British, princely states were subject to indirect colonial rule.

9. *Dalit* is the term used by activists to describe the former "Untouchables," those labeled with rather paternalistic good intentions by Mohandas Karimchard Gandhi as Harijans (children of God).

10. The Jat Sikhs similarly constitute more than 20 percent of the population of Punjab—a state whose politics I shall not consider here in view of its rather specific history of poverty reduction.

11. The BJP held power in Gujarat at the time of writing and, in an alliance with the Shiv Sena, did so in Maharashtra in 1995–99.

12. In this context, *Dravidian* connotes Tamilian nationalism.

13. I am extremely grateful to David Hall-Mathews, of the University of Leeds, for his valiant and conscientious efforts to record and make some sense of these data—though David is exonerated from any responsibility for what follows.

14. It is not part of my purpose here to assess the effectiveness of these programs. There is an abundant literature on this topic. See, for example, essays in Harriss, Guhan, and Cassen 1992.

15. Relatively high rates of growth of crop yields have been sustained over a long period in Andhra Pradesh. Growth rates have picked up recently in Tamil Nadu after a long period of stagnation.

REFERENCES

Bhalla, G. S., and G. Singh. 1997. "Recent Developments in Indian Agriculture: A State Level Analysis." *Economic and Political Weekly,* 32, no. 13, Review of Agriculture, March 29.

Bharadwaj, K. 1982. "Regional Differentiation in India: A Note." *Economic and Political Weekly,* 17, no. 14–16, Annual Number, April.

Bhatia, M. S. 1999. "Rural Infrastructure and Growth in Agriculture." *Economic and Political Weekly,* 34, no. 13, Review of Agriculture, March 27.

Brass, P. 1984. "Division in the Congress and the Rise of Agrarian Interests and Issues in Uttar Pradesh Politics, 1952 to 1977." In J. R. Wood, ed., *State Politics in India: Crisis or Continuity?* Boulder and London: Westview.

Chelliah, R. 1998. "Liberalization, Economic Reforms, and Center-State Relations." In I. J. Ahluiwalia and I. M. D. Little, eds., *India's Economic Reforms and Development: Essays for Manmohan Singh*. Delhi: Oxford University Press.

Church, R. 1984. "The Pattern of State Politics in Indira Gandhi's India." In J. R. Wood, ed., *State Politics in Contemporary India: Crisis or Continuity?* Boulder and London: Westview.

Crook, R., and J. Manor. 1998. *Democratisation and Decentralization in South Asia and West Africa: Participation, Accountability, and Performance in Comparative Perspective*. Cambridge: Cambridge University Press.

Datt, G., and M. Ravallion. 1998. "Why Have Some Indian States Done Better Than Others at Reducing Rural Poverty?" *Economica* 65, no. 257: 17–38.

Evans, P. 1996. "Government Action, Social Capital, and Development: Reviewing the Evidence on Synergy." *World Development* 24, no. 6: 1119–32.

Frankel F., and M. S. A. Rao. 1989. *Dominance and State Power in Modern India: Decline of a Social Order*, Vol. 1. Delhi: Oxford University Press.

Frankel, F., and M. S. A. Rao. 1990. *Dominance and State Power in Modern India: Decline of a Social Order*. Vol. 2. Delhi: Oxford University Press.

Harriss, B., S. Guhan, and R. Cassen, eds. 1992. *Poverty in India*. Delhi: Oxford University Press.

Harriss, J. 1994. "Between Economism and Post-modernism: Reflections on the Study of Agrarian Change in India." In D. Booth, ed., *Rethinking Social Development*. London: Longman.

Hasan, Z. 1998. *Quest for Power: Oppositional Movements and Post-Congress Politics in UP*. Delhi: Oxford University Press.

Jaffrelot, C. 1998. "The Sangh Parivar between Sanskritization and Social Engineering." In T. Hansen and C. Jaffrelot, eds., *The BJP and the Compulsions of Politics in India*. Delhi: Oxford University Press.

Jenkins, R. 1996. "The Politics of Protecting the Poor during Adjustment." In U. Thakkar and M. Kulkarni, eds., *Politics in Maharashtra*. Bombay: Himalaya Publishing House.

———. 1998. "Rajput Hindutva, Caste Politics, Regional Identity, and Hindu Nationalism in Contemporary Rajasthan." In T. Hansen and C. Jaffrelot, eds., *The BJP and the Compulsions of Politics in India*. Delhi: Oxford University Press.

Kohli, A. 1987. *The State and Poverty in India*. Cambridge: Cambridge University Press.

———. 1988. "The NTR Phenomenon in Andhra Pradesh: Political Change in a South Indian State." *Asian Survey* 28, no. 10: 991–1002.

———. 1990. *Democracy and Discontent: India's Growing Crisis of Governability*. Cambridge: Cambridge University Press.

Lele, J. 1984. "One Party Dominance in Maharashtra: Resilience and Change." In J. R. Wood, ed., *State Politics in Contemporary India: Crisis or Continuity?* Boulder and London: Westview.

———. "Caste, Class, and Dominance: Political Mobilization in Maharashtra." In F. Frankel and M. S. A. Rao, eds., *Dominance and State Power in Modern India: Decline of a Social Order,* vol. 2. Delhi: Oxford University Press.
Manor, J. 1984. "Blurring the Lines between Parties and Social Bases: Gundu Rao and the Emergence of a Janata Government in Karnataka." In J. R. Wood, ed., *State Politics in Contemporary India: Crisis or Continuity?* Boulder and London: Westview.
———. 1989. "Karnataka: Caste, Class, Dominance, and Politics." In F. Frankel and M. S. A. Rao, eds., *Dominance and State Power in Modern India: Decline of a Social Order,* vol. 1. Delhi: Oxford University Press.
Minhas, B. S., L. R. Jain, and S. D. Tendulkar. 1991. "Declining of Poverty in the 1980: Evidence versus Artifacts." *Economic and Political Weekly* 26, nos. 27–28 (July 6).
Mohan Rao, J. M. 1993. "Agricultural Development under State Planning." In T. Byres, ed., *The State and Development Planning in India.* Delhi: Oxford University Press.
Mohanty, M. 1990. "Class, Caste, and Dominance in a Backward State: Orissa." In F. Frankel and M. S. A. Rao, eds., *Dominance and State Power in Modern India: Decline of a Social Order,* vol. 2. Delhi: Oxford University Press.
Nag, M. 1989. "Political Awareness as a Factor in the Accessibility of Health Services: A Case Study of Kerala and West Bengal." *Economic and Political Weekly* 24, no. 8 (February 25).
Narain, I., and P. Mathur. 1990. "The Thousand Year Raj: Regional Isolation and Rajput Hinduism in Rajasthan before and after 1947." In F. Frankel and M. S. A. Rao, eds., *Dominance and State Power in Modern India: Decline of a Social Order,* vol. 2. Delhi: Oxford University Press.
Ram Reddy, G. 1989. "The Politics of Accommodation: Caste, Class, and Dominance in Andhra Pradesh." In F. Frankel and M. S. A. Rao, eds., *Dominance and State Power in Modern India: Decline of a Social Order,* vol. 1. Delhi: Oxford University Press.
Rao, M. G., R. Shand, and K. Kalirajan. 1999. "Convergence of Incomes across Indian States: A Divergent View." *Economic and Political Weekly,* 34, no. 13 (March 27).
Robinson, M. 1988. *Local Politics: The Law of the Fishes.* Delhi: Oxford University Press.
Rueschemeyer, D., E. H. Stephens, and J. D. Stephens. 1992. *Capitalist Development and Democracy.* Cambridge: Polity.
Sen, A. 1996. "Economic Reforms, Employment, and Poverty Trends and Options." *Economic and Political Weekly,* 31, no. 35–37, special number (September).
Srivastava, R. 1993. "Planning and Regional Disparities." In T. Byres, ed., *The State and Development Planning in India.* Delhi: Oxford University Press.
Subramanian, N. 1999. *Ethnicity and Populist Mobilization: Political Parties, Citizens, and Democracy in South India.* Delhi: Oxford University Press.
Thamarajakshi, R. 1997. "Economic Reforms and State Intervention in Foodgrains Market." *Economic and Political Weekly* 32, no. 30 (July 26).

Tyagi, D. S. 1990. *Managing India's Food Economy: Problems and Alternatives.*
New Delhi: Sage.

Vora, R. 1996. "Shift of Power from Rural to Urban Sector." *Economic and
Political Weekly*, 30, no. 41–42 (January 13).

Vyas, V. S., and P. Bhargava. 1995. "Public Intervention for Poverty Alleviation:
An Overview." *Economic and Political Weekly*, 30, no. 41–42 (October 14).

Wood, J. R. 1984. "Congress Restored? The 'KHAM' Strategy and Congress (I)
Recruitment in Gujarat." In J. R. Wood, ed., *State Politics in Contemporary
India: Crisis or Continuity?* Boulder and London: Westview.

Wood, J. R., ed. 1984. *State Politics in Contemporary India: Crisis or Continuity?*
Boulder and London: Westview.

Woolcock, M. 1998. "Social Capital and Economic Development: A Theoretical
Synthesis and Policy Framework." *Theory and Society* 27:151–208.

9 Does Decentralization Contribute to Poverty Reduction?

SURVEYING THE EVIDENCE

Richard C. Crook and Alan S. Sverrisson

T he governments of developing countries have been decentralizing. Since the mid-1980s, decentralization reforms have been introduced in states ruled by virtually all varieties of national political regimes, from military dictatorships, authoritarian presidencies, and monarchies through single-party or dominant-party regimes to multiparty competitive democracies. There is no close connection between form of decentralization and regime type: elected, democratic local governments have been introduced by military regimes—mostly nonpartisan but even in one case (Bangladesh in the 1980s) with party competition—while technocratic, administrative deconcentration is to be found in a formally multiparty system such as that of Kenya, and, under Ghana's multiparty regime, which produced a peaceful transfer of power nationally in 2000, parties are banned from District Assembly elections.

Much of the literature tends to assume that decentralization of government has generic benefits that are independent of regime context. The most common argument is that, because decentralization by definition involves bringing government closer to the governed in both the spatial and institutional senses, government will be more knowledgeable about and hence more responsive to the needs of the people.[1] It is the more recent tendency to conflate decentralization with democratization and enhancement of participation at the "community" level, which underlies the belief that decentralization will lead to greater responsiveness to the needs of the "poor." Insofar as the majority of the population in developing countries is both poor and excluded from national elite or "high" politics, then any scheme that appears to offer greater political participation to ordinary citizens seems likely to increase their "voice" and hence (it is hoped) the relevance and effectiveness of government policy.

In this chapter, we address two linked questions: whether decentralized forms of government in general are more responsive to poor people, and whether there is any systematic relationship between variations in responsiveness and the political and regime context of decentralized systems. It will be argued that regimes, particularly the kinds of policy coalitions constructed within democratic ruling parties at both the central and local levels, do have an important impact on the pro-poor outcomes of decentralization.

We shall focus primarily on political and administrative decentralization, that is, the allocation of power among territorially defined and nested hierarchies.[2] The majority of cases examined will be either devolved local governments with or without federal systems or mixed forms of devolution with deconcentrated administrations. Pure deconcentrated administrations, whether general or sectoral, are of less interest unless (as is increasingly routine) they incorporate at least some participatory elements (or aspirations).

A review of the literature led to the selection of the following cases for which there was sufficient evidence to make a comparison of their responsiveness and social and economic performance outcomes: West Bengal and Karnataka States (India), Colombia, the Philippines, Ceara State (Brazil), Chile, Côte d'Ivoire, Bangladesh, Ghana, Kenya, Nigeria, and Mexico. The Indian states of West Bengal and Karnataka stand out as probably the most systematically studied and richly documented of any in the world, while the Philippines is beginning to generate a mass of research evidence that has yet to come to fruition. There are other interesting cases from the rest of Asia, Africa, and Latin America, but the evidence is frequently partial and contradictory. Bangladesh, Ghana, Côte d'Ivoire, Brazil, and Colombia count as among the best-documented cases from those continents, while Chile, Kenya, Nigeria, and Mexico provide useful contrasts on particular dimensions.

THE POLITICS OF DECENTRALIZATION

Different governments have different political purposes and motives for introducing decentralization reforms. These intentions are embodied in the details of the structure and form of the decentralization scheme or, more subtly, are revealed only in the way in which the system functions after it is introduced (the most revealing outcome often being a mode of implementation that virtually guarantees the "failure" of the reform!). We suggest that political variables determine the outcomes of decentralization (in terms of increased responsiveness and poverty reduction), not because of variations in formal structure or broad regime context, or technical failures of implementation, but because decentralization is essentially about the distribution of power and resources, both among different levels and territorial areas of the state and among different interests in their relationship with ruling elites. Understanding decentralization, like the other policy areas considered in this volume, has therefore to be rooted in a "polity-centered" approach. The politics of central-local relations explains what interests might gain or lose from a particular set of institutional opportunities, policy initiatives, and resource allocations and relates these factors to the political purposes of the decentralization reform. As Boone has noted in her recent analysis of state building in West Africa, decentralization schemes cannot be treated as technically neutral devices that can be "implemented" without constraint, as if there were no preexisting social context: "Governments may have important stakes in established powerbrokers and in established, local-level social and political hierarchies that can extend beyond the reach of the state" (1998, 25). Apparently similar decentralization reforms could have diametrically opposed purposes according to whether they aim to reinforce vested interests in existing patterns of patronage and central-local linkage or involve challenges to local elites from groups using decentralized institutions to "draw down" central resources to bolster local power struggles.

Our comparative analysis of the performance of decentralization focuses on five variables that seem most likely to explain differences in outcome, both among countries and among regions or localities within countries. They are as follows.

The first variable is relations between central and local governments, which reflect key regime characteristics such as the power bases of the ruling elite and their relationships with local elites. What kinds of alliances does the ruling elite have, or seek to build, with local or subnational elites? Does the ruling elite face potential challenges with which it must deal either through attack, circumvention, or co-optation? Is decentralization a help or a hindrance if elites have an ideological or transformational program to implement? Such relationships will determine the extent to which a central government attempts to support and use decentralization to further its own policies and whether those policies will be pro-poor or not. Four broad scenarios are likely.

1. The ruling elite or central authority seeks to build its power bases through alliances with established local or regional elites that are both congenial to its interests and have some degree of autonomy. In such a situation, decentralization is likely to involve bargaining and co-optation, and devolution of power and allocation of resources, through either fiscal decentralization or direct central government funding. Such bargains are likely to reinforce conservative forces and—in line with Smith's pessimistic view that decentralization is an inherently conservative strategy (1985, 193)—are unlikely to result in pro-poor outcomes.

2. The central ruling elite challenges or tries to circumvent locally powerful groups. The motives can range from party and ideological rivalry and class and ethnic conflict to the deep distrust often found in federal systems between institutional elites at different levels of government. The desire to challenge entrenched regional and provincial power holders can follow a popular revolution (as in the post-Marcos Philippines) or the victory of reforming social democratic or communist parties, as in a few exceptional Brazilian states[3] or the Indian states of West Bengal and Kerala. Decentralization strategy often involves centrally funded development and antipoverty or agrarian reform programs that have to be implemented by "decentralized" bodies. However, these strategies involve tightly controlled, deconcentrated central agencies and/or party structures that ensure implementation of reforms and prevent local elite capture of decentralized bodies.

3. If national elites are nervous about providing an institutional base for subnational, regional, or ethnic political rivals, or even potential separatists (e.g., if the regime depends upon maintaining a fragile coalition of ethnic interests or is based upon a single dominant, but not demographically majoritarian, group), then they will often adopt a decentralization scheme that deliberately fragments existing or potential local power bases into smaller, weaker units. This is often combined with central funding and control mechanisms, which permit spatial redistribution and/or centrally focused patronage linkages. Classic examples are the actions of the Nigerian military regime in using local governments to undermine state-based, ethnic challenges and transfer resources from the oil-producing to the non-oil-producing areas; the extreme weakness and fragmentation of the commune-based system in Côte d'Ivoire; and the delimitation of local government areas in Uganda in order to divide the main ethnic groups.[4]

4. The fourth scenario is associated with the consolidation or renewal of an already powerful ruling elite in a society where local elites do not have significant autonomous power. Here decentralization is usually predominantly of the deconcentration type. It is used to articulate the power and effectiveness of the regime down to the local level. If done rationally, this can produce more effective development administration and spatial redistribution (e.g., according to many observers, Indonesia). At its worst, it consolidates a system of corrupt patronage-based linkages (e.g., Bangladesh in the late 1980s and early 1990s).

This simple typology of local-central relations suggests that in situations in which there is greater local autonomy there is greater likelihood of conservative "elite capture" of the decentralized institutions. It may be hypothesized that pro-poor outcomes are more likely in situations in which continuing central intervention and external alliances for supporting the mobilization of the disadvantaged are linked to conflict between central and local forces.

Second, the degree of social and economic inequality and the extent to which it is translated into the structure of local politics will have an impact on the likelihood of elite capture of the decentralized system in each local society or area. The configuration of local societies is a variable that can influence the outcomes of decentralization within one country. The economic and social power of locally dominant groups (landlords, agribusiness elites, landed aristocrats) may be such that they can use the elections offered by democratic decentralization to reinforce their dominance. The danger of elite capture of decentralization was recognized in the literature many years ago, and if taken seriously it suggests that central intervention is nearly always needed to ensure progressive or pro-poor outcomes (Smith 1985, 193; Leonard and Marshall 1982).[5]

Third, there is variation in the extent to which the increased participation promised by decentralization (particularly democratic decentralization) actually leads to outcomes that are more responsive to the felt needs of ordinary citizens and the poor. This is most likely to be determined by a combination of the local political factors already outlined and the effectiveness of institutional and public accountability mechanisms (e.g., well-institutionalized and legally regulated bureaucracies or fair elections). Enhanced participation alone is not sufficient without institutional mediation.

Fourth, the system of allocating resources, both administrative and financial, will inevitably have a crucial impact on outcomes. This is not simply a question of "adequacy" of funding, which is little more than a tautology if used to explain the success or failure of a decentralization reform. While in most less developed countries (LDCs) locally raised revenues are almost by definition inadequate, this does not mean that success is guaranteed by generous allocations of central grants. More important is likely to be the stability, security, and degree of targeting of funding, from whatever source, together with effective mechanisms for its management, monitoring, and control.

The fifth variable is a simple factor that is often overlooked: the length of time a system has been in operation. Most decentralization reforms take some time to become established, and many are changed or abandoned after only a few years or one electoral cycle. In reality, it may take at least ten to fifteen years in a context of financial and political stability for a system to show any results that can be fairly judged.

ANALYZING THE OUTCOMES OF DECENTRALIZATION: CONCEPTS AND METHOD

Given the framework of political and structural variables outlined previously, we may now turn to our principal questions: how responsive have different forms of decentralization been to the needs of the poor (as measured by their impact on levels of poverty, either economic or social), and can variations in this responsiveness be explained by the combination of political and institutional factors suggested at the outset? We are interested in five categories of outcomes: four labeled "poverty outcomes," which are at least in principle measurable (economic growth that benefits the poor; increases in socioeconomic equality; human development; and spatial equity); and less tangible concepts of empowerment and responsiveness. We deal first with the latter.

EMPOWERMENT OF THE POOR AND RESPONSIVENESS

The assertion that decentralized governments are more responsive to the needs of ordinary citizens—and by extension to those of "the poor"—is derived from the notion that local, more participatory forms of government and development activity will offer more than just greater effectiveness in promoting economic development. *Institutional responsiveness* has been defined as the achievement of "congruence between community preferences and public policies" such that the public values the activities of the institution (Fried 1980). Others characterize it as the "learning capacity" of an organization or its ability to listen to both its own staff and the public and then alter its behavior accordingly (Moris 1991; Korten 1984).

Insofar as *poverty* is now defined as more than just material deprivation, pro-poor responsiveness is about more than just material outputs; it is a matter of the processes through which policies are devised, the degree of empowerment and "ownership" that is felt by those affected by them (to which parties the institution is responsive), and therefore the general legitimacy of the institution and the procedures by means of which it allocates resources. For these reasons, responsiveness is frequently seen as a product of increased participation, both in its social scope and in the numbers of people participating.

Some caution is necessary, however, when analyzing data on participation. It is often treated as an "input" factor when explaining the development of responsiveness. But empowerment and policy responsiveness do not automatically follow from increasing the level of participation, nor from increasing the representation of the poor and disadvantaged. For the former to happen, the impact of participation must be felt in the operation of accountability mechanisms, both internally within decentralized institutions (e.g., the accountability of bureaucrats to elected representatives) and externally in relations between local institutions and the public (e.g., the fairness and competitiveness of elections or the representativeness of elected councilors). In other words, as an input factor it is the effectiveness of participation that is being measured rather than its quantity or scope.

POVERTY OUTCOMES

The impact of decentralization on levels of social and economic poverty can be broken down for analytical purposes into four main areas.

1. Pro-poor growth or changes in the levels of economic activity, wages, or prices that increase the incomes of small farmers, sharecroppers, agricultural laborers, small traders, or urban workers, particularly in the informal sector.
2. Social equity or the extent to which there is redistribution of income or reduction in levels of inequality.
3. Human development or improvements in the quality of life and hence the life chances of poor people, as reflected in their access to health, education, sanitation, or justice.
4. Spatial or interregional inequality: the extent to which there is redistribution of resources or growth between deprived and economically more wealthy areas of a country.

Measuring whether the actions of decentralized institutions have had an effect on any or all of these areas is fraught with enormous difficulties. Comparison of national economic and human development statistics would be useful if it were possible to isolate the decentralization variable by comparing countries with and without decentralization schemes and over time. Some attempts have been made to compare using the degree of decentralization as the independent variable, but the measure normally used—subnational expenditures as a proportion of total government expenditures—is so flawed as an indicator of the character and functioning of any particular decentralization structure that the results obtained can be suggestive at most (see Huther and Shah 1998).[6]

A major difficulty facing any comparative analysis of the impact of decentralization on poverty is therefore that most of the data are based on case studies that are partial and not systematically comparable. Few case studies even satisfy the minimum requirements for a valid internal measure of performance: baseline and longitudinal data to enable comparisons to be made of the situation before and after a decentralization program was introduced; some sense of the overall significance and scope of local expenditures, both in relation to local needs and to the national development program; and some representative assessments of impact. In the absence of this kind of information, much of the evidence is anecdotal. This suggests that the most feasible research method is to evaluate and rate each case internally and only then undertake comparison of the configurations or patterns of explanatory factors in each case (see Ragin 1996).

A COMPARATIVE EXPLANATION OF OUTCOMES

Our cases are West Bengal (India), Karnataka (India), Colombia, the Philippines, Ceara (Brazil), Chile, Côte d'Ivoire, Bangladesh, Ghana, Kenya, Nigeria, and Mexico. Table 1 summarizes conclusions on the outcomes of decentralization that are derived from a study of the published research evidence. For each case, the outcomes for participation/responsiveness and the four dimensions of social and economic poverty reduction were rated on a five-point scale: "good," "fairly good," "mixed/ambiguous or neutral," "poor," and "very poor." Where the evidence was simply inadequate or unavailable, this is noted.[7]

It is immediately obvious that West Bengal stands out as the only case to rate an unambiguously positive outcome on both major dimensions, while Karnataka, Colombia, and Brazil show good results in some areas or for particular local cases. Both the Philippines and Chile have to be regarded as cases whose record is highly contested or awaits further evidence and must therefore be sidelined. The other cases—Ghana, Côte d'Ivoire, Bangladesh, Kenya, Nigeria, and Mexico—are all examples of the failure of decentralization to help the poor, with Ghana being the "least bad" in that its participation record was relatively good and recent increases in its funding mean that it may now have more potential, at least, to provide more development. But its Achilles' heel is its lack of accountability. Bangladesh, Nigeria, Mexico, and Kenya can be rated as unambiguous failures.

Because of its exceptional nature, it is worth describing the West Bengal case in some detail in order to demonstrate the analysis that led to such a judgment.

THE WEST BENGAL CASE

In 1978, a leftist coalition, known as the Left Front, led by the CPI(M) (Communist Party of India, Marxist), was elected to government in the state of West Bengal. In order to challenge the power of the Congress Party and the landlord classes in the countryside, and to provide a strong popular power base, the Left Front government aimed to increase the decision-making power of the poor by devolving implementation of government programs to the *gram panchayats* (village councils) and mobilizing poor peasants to participate using the CPI(M) machinery. It was a reform that anticipated by some thirteen years the 1993 Seventy-third

Amendment to the Indian Constitution, which mandated that the states should introduce a three-tiered, democratically elected local government system with the village assembly (*gram sabha*) as its foundation and reservation of seats for women and the Scheduled Castes and Scheduled Tribes (Meenakshisundaram 1994).[8]

One of the most significant political aspects of the reform was the opening up of local elections to party competition for the first time. The districts, or *zilla parishads,* the main level of authority in the three-tiered system, were devolved local government bodies that were legally obliged to liaise closely with the district-level offices of the West Bengal state administration without having direct authority over them. The power of the state government was exercised through the district magistrate, who was ex officio the chief executive of the *zilla parishads* (Meenakshisundaram 1994). All of the reforms carried out by the Left Front clearly had an ideological motivation. The political and economic empowerment of poor and landless peasants was intended to give impetus and mass support to the CPI(M)'s radical agrarian reform programs. The latter aimed to restructure the semifeudal basis of Bengali rural society through sharecropper protection and land redistribution.

Participation and Responsiveness

In terms of the scope of participation, West Bengal's record of representation of the poor is good, whether defined by caste, occupation, or landownership. In Birbhum District, for example, by 1988, 44 percent of all *gram panchayat* members were either small peasants, sharecroppers, or agricultural laborers or a combination of these (Lieten 1988, 2070–72). Webster's study showed that small peasants and the landless increased their share of representation between 1978 and 1988 (1990, 71), while the influence of the formerly dominant groups was reduced (Webster 1989, 206). Because seats were reserved for women in the 1993 elections, women now account for just over the statutory one-third minimum (Lieten 1996, 127).

Although representation of the poor and previously excluded in West Bengal has increased significantly as a result of the *panchayat* reforms, it has nonetheless to be recognized that mobilization through the party machine has meant that the electoral necessity to build broad cross-class coalitions has also played its part. The electoral success of the CPI(M) had by the early 1990s attracted a substantial group of "middle-class" or white-collar employees (schoolteachers, clerks) and middle peasants, the so-called rural middle strata, who formed a new "party elite" in the *panchayats* (Echeverri-Gent 1992a).

Although representation of the poor has improved and compares favorably with the situation in other Indian states, this does not appear to have translated into meaningful participation in the affairs of the *pan-chayats*. One study showed that *panchayat* members from scheduled castes or tribes rarely spoke in meetings, and if they did they tended to be ignored (Westergaard 1986, 88). This finding is supported by another study, which demonstrated that just 2 percent of Scheduled Caste and Tribe members spoke in meetings (Webster 1990, 113). Nevertheless, the Left Front has set in motion important changes that will encourage greater popular participation (Westergaard 1986, 89).

Measuring responsiveness in terms of perceived change under the *pan-chayat* system, Webster's survey of 150 households showed that the majority of landless or land-poor (under two acres) respondents felt there had been substantial positive changes under the *panchayat* system, as did the vast majority of interviewees of Scheduled Caste and Tribe back-grounds (Webster 1992, 158). However, the impact of participation has been restrained by the kinds of functions and resources that have been devolved to the local government level. The ability of local government institutions to provide a "voice" to the poor is limited by the fact that their main designated role is to implement government programs (partic-ularly those relating to poverty alleviation) rather than influencing policy (Webster 1989, 206). Their main function is to select beneficiaries for poverty program benefits such as work or loans.

Poverty Reduction

When combined with land redistribution, sharecropper programs, and the popular mobilization programs of the Left Front, democratic decen-tralization has resulted in significant benefits to the poor of West Bengal. The state remains one of the poorest in India, ranking second only to Bihar in the incidence of rural poverty (Echeverri-Gent 1992a, 1403). Nev-ertheless, the material changes in the state since the election of the Left Front government have been considerable, particularly in agricultural production and the provision of infrastructure (Webster 1992, 161). The continuing high levels of support for the Left Front government can also be used as a yardstick for its success (Webster 1989, 205).

Any assessment of the effect of decentralized institutions in West Ben-gal must acknowledge the general political context of the CPI(M)'s devel-opment strategies. Many of the ascribed benefits are only indirect results of decentralization, as the Panchayati Raj reforms went alongside the restructuring of the agrarian political economy, in particular, the share-cropper programs (Operation Barga) and the redistribution of land. Sev-eral authors agree that this combination of reforms has resulted in an improvement in West Bengal's agricultural performance (Sanyal, Biswas, and Bardhan 1998; Bagchi 1998),[9] with West Bengal's agricultural econ-omy growing faster than those in other eastern Indian states between

1981 and 1991 (Rawal and Swaminathan 1998). Furthermore, this growth has reduced poverty (Ghosh 1998). As Chatterjee (1998) notes, after a careful analysis of planning commission and expert group data on poverty levels between 1972 and 1993–94, "both the percentage of poor and the number of poor in rural West Bengal has declined sharply during the 1980s . . . this decline is largely due to a combination of technology-induced productivity upsurge in agricultural production, and institutional reforms like Operation *Barga,* land redistribution and decentralized planning through elected panchayats" (3006).

The reforms have meant that elected institutions are now responsible for government development programs and that the benefits of such programs have gone to the poorest. In one case study, 85 percent of beneficiaries of one national works program were from the Scheduled Castes and Tribes (Webster 1990, 112). There are allegations that the benefits of works programs tended to go to CPI(M) members (Westergaard 1986, 91–92), although this does not square easily with the reputation of the Left Front and CPI(M) for avoiding corruption (Webster 1990, 59–60).[10]

There is some, albeit limited, evidence of improved human development indicators in West Bengal. Bhattacharya notes that the state's Human Development Index improved slightly between 1981 and 1991, and the extent of deprivation relative to other states also decreased (1998). Other studies have shown that the poor themselves perceive that they now have greater human dignity, insofar as they have greater access to administrative and justice systems, sometimes to the exclusion of the wealthy (Lieten 1988, 2069–70). Webster shows that villagers themselves saw improvements in the provision of water (1992, 159). Since 1977, when tubewells were shallow and the upper castes had privileged access; the tubewells have been dug three times deeper; general access has improved, with most wells being within walking distance; and there is a decreased likelihood of water-borne disease (Webster 1990).

Evidence of the spatial impact of decentralization in West Bengal is difficult to come by, but it appears that it has not been uniform across the state. The state government's joint director of the Panchayati Raj argued that, while decentralization had been successful in five districts, there had been problems in other districts (Webster 1992, 160). However, most of the evidence is based on small samples, mainly in the more central districts. There are no conclusive data on the spatial impact of decentralization.

IS WEST BENGAL UNIQUE? COMPARISON WITH THE OTHER CASES

How can the exceptional performance of the West Bengal case be explained? We suggested that there are five main variables likely to explain the poverty impacts of decentralization. Comparison with the other cases according to these five variables does throw into sharp relief the critical differences between West Bengal and the less successful decentralized systems, particularly the extreme cases of poor performance.

(1) RELATIONS BETWEEN LOCAL AND
NATIONAL POLITICAL ELITES

West Bengal clearly falls into scenario 2 in our typology of local-central relations, in which an elite ruling at the central level challenges locally dominant groups. The CPI(M) government not only had an ideological commitment to pro-poor policies but was prepared to engage actively in local politics (even if for its own electoral reasons), to challenge local elite resistance if necessary, and to ensure implementation of policies.

The same was true of Ceara State in northeastern Brazil. Here a federally funded antipoverty program, the Northeast Rural Development Program, which was administered by local governments in response to community demands, recorded positive results partly because it was able to bypass obstructive local patronage networks (van Zyle et al. 1995). In Ceara, the election of a reforming governor from the Brazilian Social Democratic Party (PSDB) in 1987 led to the launching of state programs in preventive health and employment-generating public works for drought relief that have been outstanding and innovative. One of the key conclusions drawn by Tendler and others is that improvements in the performance of these local pro-poor programs were the result of a three-way dynamic between local government, civil society, and an active central (state) government rather than decentralization per se (Tendler 1997, 145). The 1988 reforms meant that the state government was forced to share power with local governments. By using the political, financial, and capacity-building incentives offered by the new schemes in a conditional way, the state government was able to bring "onboard" an initially reluctant local government establishment. The actions of the state also helped to develop a more active public interest in demanding accountability and decent standards of service from local employees (Tendler 1993, xxii; Tendler and Freedheim 1994; Tendler 1997). It is also clear, however, that the case of Ceara and another success story, Rio Grande do Sul in the southeast, are not typical of the Brazilian decentralization system as a whole but resulted from the particular political circumstances and regimes present in those states at a particular time. In Rio Grande do Sul, it was the election of candidates of the radical Workers Party in a number of important cities that led to the introduction of participatory democratic reforms in those municipalities in the 1990s—reforms that have undoubtedly benefited the residents of the poorer districts

In West Bengal and Brazil, therefore, pro-poor outcomes were in fact a product of the synergy between local and central factors—centrally funded, poverty-relevant programs implemented in cooperation with local governments—and were given a strong ideological and organizational impetus at the local level by the commitment of local employees and political activists. To achieve this, it was necessary to have either a strong political party that mobilized an electoral coalition in favor of such policies or elites that, in the process of competition, saw the policies as a way of constructing a new political base. It is this factor that distinguishes these cases from that of Karnataka, the other Indian state reviewed, where conditions were otherwise quite favorable.

The decentralization reform of 1987 in Karnataka was a type 1 decentralization scenario in that the newly elected Janata Party intended to build up its rural electoral base but in this case by giving power and resources to the dominant middle-peasant, landowning castes and associated elites. Even though the poor, women, and the Scheduled Castes increased their participation, this was not effective in that the new councils were judged not to have been very responsive to the needs of those groups (Meenakshisundaram 1994, 83; Subha 1997; Crook and Manor 1998, 40; Sivanna 1990, 198; Kurian 1999). Sivanna highlights a telling detail: selection for benefits under the national antipoverty Integrated Rural Development Program (IRDP) in Karnataka was based on information provided by *panchayat* chairmen and other influential leaders, and this meant that many quite well off families were included (1990, 200).

The Colombian case, by contrast, illustrates a mixture of type 1 and type 2 scenarios. The limited success that it achieved can be explained by elements of a type 2 strategy, in which directed central funding was accompanied by the emergence in particular municipalities of an elected leadership that made a virtue out of its commitment to popular participatory policies. These mayors provided strong leadership in a participatory style, particularly where they had emerged as challengers to Colombia's two traditionally dominant parties, which were embedded in local patronage networks. According to Fiszbein, these popular and electoral pressures led in turn to measurable improvements in the effectiveness of service delivery in key areas of education, roads, and water supply (1997; see also World Bank 1995). On the other hand, the Colombian successes remained limited in that they were not supported more generally through the program of a strong national party. It should also be noted that none of these developments would have been possible in the successful cases without regular, competitive elections.

In Nigeria, Bangladesh, and Mexico, decentralized governments were also supported by large allocations of central funding and development programs that were centrally directed and locally administered. In Bangladesh, the decentralized system introduced by the military government of President H. M. Ershad in 1985 was intended to help build his new Jatiyo Party by co-opting rural landed elites and power brokers, offering them access to patronage resources that they otherwise lacked—a type 4 scenario (Ingham and Kalam 1991, 4). The subdistrict councils had very limited revenue-raising powers and in practice were dependent upon the (generous) funding given by the central government. In fact, considerable resources were allocated to job-creation projects and relief schemes in the rural districts—the majority of them in the form of "grain for work." These programs were, however, used primarily for patronage purposes by the elite politicians who were elected as subdistrict chairmen (Crook and Manor 1998, 104; Khan 1987, 411).

The Mexican national poverty alleviation program, the National Solidarity Fund (PRONASOL), was ostensibly similar to that of Brazil in that it transferred considerable funds down to local governments for them to administer and allocate to local community projects. But such was the pressure on state-level officials to produce rapid and tangible results from the program that the main consequence seemed to have been a vast increase in the building of infrastructure, much of which has only marginal relevance to poverty alleviation, for example, basketball courts (Fox 1995, 12). The dominant political logic of the scheme was in fact the desire of the then ruling Party of Revolutionary Institutions (PRI) to bolster its position in states where it was facing real electoral challenges from opposition parties, another type 4 scenario in that the government was using dependent, politically loyal, local elites to implement its "decentralization" scheme. The allocation of funding was skewed toward middle-income rather than poorer states, where the PRI had no need to bolster its supporters against any local opposition challenges (Fox 1995; Fox and Aranda 1996).

Party building or renewal by a national ruling elite was not the political motive behind the continuing support and increasingly generous allocation of powers and funds to local governments by federal military governments in Nigeria from 1983 to 1999. In the early 1990s, federal funds accounted for 90 percent of local government revenues (Awotokun 1995). The aim in increasing the numbers of local authorities and in giving local governments responsibility for major federal programs was to bypass and weaken possible challenges from state-based political and ethnic elites and to create dependent local support bases for the military, a type 3 scenario (Olowu 1989, 1997). The "presidential"-style local council chairmen, armed with substantial federal patronage, became feared and entirely unaccountable figures unrestrained even by viable audit and control mechanisms (Gboyega 1998; Wunsch and Olowu 1996–97). Military clientelism created a system characterized by rampant corruption, inefficiency, and an utter lack of accountability.

The essential difference, therefore, between West Bengal and the

Brazilian states, on the one hand, and Bangladesh, Nigeria, and Mexico, on the other, is not that the latter governments did not allocate sufficient funds to the decentralized authorities or that they lacked centrally funded development and antipoverty programs. The real difference was that they failed to ensure that central funds were used in a responsible and accountable manner and failed to ensure implementation of pro-poor policies where these formally existed. The explanation for this is to be found in the politics of central-local relations: in none of these three countries was it likely that decentralization would empower any kind of challenge to local elites resistant to, or uninterested in, the development of pro-poor policies. On the contrary, the logic of their decentralization systems was that of scenarios 3 or 4 set out at the beginning of this chapter. The central governments, acting on behalf of particular elite interests, were using local government or decentralized service funding either to create ab initio, or to consolidate, an alliance with local elites based on the availability of patronage opportunities.

Neither Ghana nor Côte d'Ivoire can be placed in the same extreme category as the previous three cases, but the same factors are relevant to explaining aspects of their decentralization outcomes. In Côte d'Ivoire, a "Mexican" logic was initially at work: in 1985, the long-established, dominant ruling party (the Parti Démocratique de la Côte d'Ivoire or PDCI) established elected commune authorities for the ninety-eight small towns of the "interior." Its motive was to renew itself by offering openings to new cadres and allocating resources to the small towns of the rural areas but in a way that would prevent the emergence of any broader political challenge to the regime—a type 3 scenario. It was only in 1990 that multiparty competition was permitted. However, the PDCI maintained control of 93 percent of all communes in the 1990 elections and 80 percent in the 1996 elections. The indirectly elected mayors, who were mostly of elite status and lived or worked in the capital city, were simply an extension of the ruling party network. In the absence of any national program or commitment to pro-poor policies and very weak accountability to local electorates, the reform was virtually guaranteed to remain a fairly conservative, elite-based exercise (Crook and Manor 1998, 171).

In Ghana, it is possible that, had the initial "revolutionary" trajectory of the Jerry Rawlings's 1982 military regime persisted, a West Bengal scenario might have developed. The elected District Assemblies created in 1989 were based on radical populist ideas of direct participation and no-party "people's democracy." In practice, they were linked to Rawlings's attempt to pursue a type 1 scenario: to create a rural power base, embodying in the District Assemblies a privileged position for the pro-Rawlings revolutionary organizations and mechanisms for co-opting rural business, professional, and agrarian elites. By the late 1980s, the rev-

olutionary organizations were little more than "Rawlings loyalists."
Once they were converted into a conventional political party—the
National Democratic Congress (NDC)—which won power for Rawlings
in the 1992 multiparty elections, they became part of a centrally controlled power and patronage system, working with co-opted local elites
where possible and excluding the opposition elites where necessary.
More important, perhaps, even after 1992 party activity in the assemblies
was banned; the government retained executive control of the assemblies
through centrally appointed district chief executives and assured the continuation of a privileged role for the former revolutionary organizations.
In Ghana, therefore, the structure of local-central relations undermined
the ability of the assemblies to respond to popularly defined local priorities (Crook and Manor 1998; Crook 1999).

(II) THE CONFIGURATION OF LOCAL
SOCIETY AND ELITE CAPTURE

The impact of local social and political structures on the likelihood of
"elite capture" of decentralization is clearly illustrated in the cases of
Côte d'Ivoire, Bangladesh, Colombia, Brazil, and the Philippines. In Côte
d'Ivoire, a combination of business and professional elites and large commercial farmers was actually encouraged by the government to become
involved in the local communes. In Ivorian society (as in other parts of
West Africa), there is a strong social expectation that the more successful
sons and daughters of a town or village will use their influence and
patronage to help the development of their "hometown"; the communes
provoked a political discourse on how to persuade these elites to become
involved rather than on how to increase the representation of the poor or
disadvantaged (Crook and Manor 1998, 162).[11] In Bangladesh, the impact
of Ershad's decentralization scheme was to "intensify already extreme
inequalities" (Crook and Manor 1998, 99), as the elected councils were
captured by the wealthy landed classes; the landless were excluded, and
even middle peasants achieved only minority representation.

The structure of local society also influences variations in outcomes
within a particular country. In the Philippines, there is enormous variation in the extent to which the legally prescribed system for associating
NGOs and peoples organizations with the new, post-Marcos, local governments has been successful. These variations are clearly associated with
local political dynamics, particularly in areas where local government
reform has reempowered semifeudal landed elites and even, according to
some analysts, regional "warlords." These local power structures in turn
influence the behavior of officials of both the local governments and the
field agencies of central departments (Cariño 1992, 34; Brilliantes 1998;
Rood 1998). In Brazil, too, the 1988 constitutional reforms of local gov-

ernment had the effect of restoring the power of the states and of state-based patronage machines and increasing spatial inequalities between rich and poor areas. In the absence of the special factors and centrally funded programs present in the states of Ceara and Minas Gerais, it was these factors that probably continued to shape the performance of local governments.

Doubts about the overall success of the Colombian experiment also arise from the conflicting assessments that emerge from different localities. Fiszbein's work on a selected group of sixteen municipalities emphasizes the importance of local political leadership and the degree of real political competition (World Bank 1995). But other studies of particular towns and cities are much less optimistic, reporting the continued dominance of traditional elites and patronage politics (Forero and Salazar 1991; Velasquez 1991).

The contrast with West Bengal is again very clear. As Echeverri-Gent argues, elite capture by an "antipoor" class was prevented by a combination of competitive electoral politics and the ability of a "counterelite" (the Communist Party) to mobilize a broad alliance of the poor, middle peasants, and *salariat* (salary earners) against the old landlord class (Echeverri-Gent 1992a, 1992b).

(III) PARTICIPATION AND ACCOUNTABILITY

The presence of effective mechanisms of public and institutional accountability also helps to explain why greater popular participation was translated into improved outcomes in some countries but not others. In particular, the ability to sustain a system of fair and competitive elections emerges as a key factor in the most successful cases, such as West Bengal and particular localities in Brazil and Colombia. Even in cases like those of Bangladesh and Ghana, elections have had important effects at certain points when they operated to throw out local elected officials even though the general regime context prevented the results from changing the real character of the local governments.

At the level of institutional accountability, the difference between the better- and worse-performing cases is absolutely clear. In the Indian states, an existing tradition of democratic government, a well-established civil service, and the scale of the authorities themselves at district level meant that there was a good balance between the political clout that elected politicians could exercise and the ability of civil servants and council committees to invoke legal and accounting norms if politicians tried to exceed or abuse their powers. In other states of India, of course, this balance has been severely challenged, but relative to cases such as those of Bangladesh or Nigeria the situation in West Bengal or Karnataka is clearly of a different order. In Bangladesh, local accountability mechanisms were so weak that there were few restraints on the behavior of elected chairmen, whose main concern was to maintain their political relationships with the national patronage machine controlled by President General Ershad. In Nigeria, the behavior of local council chairmen led eventually to a wave of ineffective "impeachment" proceedings that were themselves an abuse of procedure. The contrast with the Brazilian cases is again instructive: although in Brazil the local political elites were not instinctively sympathetic to the policies they were being asked to implement or support, the strongest possible accountability was ensured through organizational and public controls.

The importance of accountability for pro-poor outcomes lies simply in the fact that if a pro-poor political force is represented at the institutional level (through either participation or sympathetic elites) then its interests can be manifested in the development and implementation of policy. Thus, the Karnataka outcome can be explained by the lack of actual representation of the poor within the *panchayati* institutions. One of the factors explaining the Ghana outcome is the failure of elected politicians, whoever they represented, to establish control over the administrative and financial machinery of district government.

Another variation in this set of factors underlies the low responsiveness of the Ivorian communes to local popular needs. Although elected officials (the mayors) are able, because of their political status and the effectiveness of the Ivorian state administrative and financial system, to establish good control over their administrations, their connections to the electorate are so weak that their public accountability is virtually nonexistent. This is partly due to the nature of the electoral system: the commune council elects the mayors, but the council itself is the product of a single, closed list system without ward representation. The winning list, which takes all the seats (thereby excluding all opposition) is in effect the list put together by the powerful political entrepreneur who is hoping to become the mayor. The lists therefore represent—or exclude—main factions or interests in the community. Even when they do incorporate poorer or more marginal groups, the councils themselves have very limited functions and powers. The responsiveness of the communes studied by Crook and Manor to popular preferences was therefore very low, and their record of consultation with local citizens was dismal (1998, 190). This may be directly compared to the Colombian cases, in which the most successful mayors clearly had established a public constituency for their approach.

(IV) SYSTEMS OF RESOURCE ALLOCATION

As was indicated in the analysis of local-central relations, simply allocating generous amounts of financial or administrative resources to decentralized authorities is not sufficient to ensure successful performance, even though it is obviously necessary. The funding systems of the most successful cases in our review were characterized by the following.

1. Secure and adequate earmarked funding to accompany the allocation of specific sectoral functions, particularly that associated with deconcentration, together with "ring-fenced" allocations from general taxation (India, Northeast Brazil, Colombia).

2. Targeted central poverty-relevant programs or "social funds" for development (with the appropriate accountability) (West Bengal, Northeast Brazil, Colombia). In Chile, there is considerable debate over the success of the targeted funding approach, which began under the Pinochet regime in 1981. Some studies argue that poverty, as measured by such factors as infant mortality, nutrition levels, and access to education, was reduced (Castaneda 1992; Graham 1994), while others argue that privatization and a reduction in real levels of government support widened the gap between rich and poor (Stewart and Ranis 1994; Parry 1997; Raczynski, Serrano, and Bousquet 1990). Success in ameliorating spatial inequality only came (as in Colombia) with the allocation of such funds using an adequate equalization formula.

3. A hierarchy of authorities that at the larger end (regions, districts in India, states in some federal systems) have sufficient scale to handle the resources, raise some of their own revenues, and provide effective support to the lower-level, grassroots bodies.

With respect to administrative resources, the successful cases were able to overcome the standard problems of lack of both high- and middle-level staff and lack of administrative "infrastructure" by using existing, well-established administrations at a level where there was sufficient strength for careers, recruitment, and management not to suffer. Apart from their other problems, the decentralized experiments in Ghana, Bangladesh, and Nigeria all suffered from attempting to set up new authorities with inadequate staffing and poor management and failing to address the legal and personnel problems that inevitably arose. They also underestimated the costs both of the extra staffing required and of the interagency/parallel hierarchy conflicts that arose.

A further aspect of administrative capacity lies in the organizational commitment and "morale" of the local administrations. In the unsuccessful cases, this was clearly low; indeed, it had probably been made worse by the kind of decentralization they had experienced (the fear of Nigerian public servants faced with decentralized control is instructive).

252 Changing Paths

In West Bengal, Karnataka, Brazil, and Colombia, in contrast, the evidence shows that commitment and willingness to serve the public improved. In Brazil, this was connected to the specific organizational form of the programs, which, it must be recognized, had little to do with decentralization and more to do with trying to evade the implications of purely local control. In the other cases, political leadership was clearly a crucial factor.[12]

(V) THE TIME FACTOR

The relative success of West Bengal may also be an effect of the time factor. The West Bengal decentralized system has enjoyed the longest and most stable existence of any of the schemes examined (twenty-two years). Unlike other decentralization schemes, structures were not changed or abandoned after a few years or left to languish by regimes that had found new priorities. Financial and administrative structures have had time to establish themselves and rectify faults. Although many detailed studies have thus been able reveal the system's faults over the long term, it has a record of relative achievement that few other systems can yet emulate.

CONCLUSION

Our comparative analysis shows that, on the evidence of the cases examined, accountability and responsiveness to the poor are still most likely to emerge locally where representation of their interests can be supported externally in the context of a conflict between local and central forces with different power bases.

The key variables accounting for the emergence of such pro-poor outcomes are the politics of local-central relations and the extent to which it affected the likelihood of elite capture of decentralized governments. It is these factors that serve to distinguish the successful from the unsuccessful cases. West Bengal, Karnataka, Brazil, Bangladesh, Nigeria, and Kenya all set up decentralized bodies that were extensively funded and supported by the central governments. But in West Bengal and Brazil, the only two with positive social and economic outcomes, conservative elites were challenged locally by groups supported externally by an ideologically committed government and/or party. In Karnataka, as in other states of Brazil, elite capture probably undermined the otherwise positive effects of the reform, while in the Colombian cases cited electoral competition seems to have produced a more reform-minded local elite. In Bangladesh, Nigeria, and Kenya, in contrast, conservative elite capture of decentralization was actually facilitated by the government's desire to create and sustain a power base in the countryside and to prevent opposition forces from coalescing. In Ghana, a similar motivation took over after an initial commitment to radical reform faded. Côte d'Ivoire and

TABLE 1. THE OUTCOMES OF DECENTRALIZATION, BY COUNTRY

| | Outcomes | |
	Participation by/Responsiveness to the Poor	Impact on Social and Economic Poverty (human development [HD])
West Bengal	Good: improved participation and representation, improved responsiveness	Good: positive on growth, equity, HD; evidence lacking on spatial equity
Karnataka	Fairly good: improved representation, but participation of poor less effective and responsiveness low	Neutral: did little directly to help pro-poor growth or equity; HD and spatial equity indirectly benefited from funding allocations and development programs
Colombia	Fairly good: evidence on participation/representation ambiguous, but responsiveness improved	Fairly good: little evidence on growth or equity, but good results on HD and spatial equity
Philippines	Mixed: representation and participation improved through people's organization (POs) and nongovernmental organizations (NGOs), but evidence on responsiveness contested and local elites still powerful	No evidence presented
Brazil	Little evidence, but thought to be poor, as spoils/patronage system run by powerful mayors and governors still dominant	Good on equity and HD in exceptional areas where state or federal programs are combined with decentralization; poor generally on spatial equity
Chile	No evidence presented	Mixed: growth and equity good as result of targeting, but evidence on HD and spatial equity contested; tends to show negative effects
Côte d'Ivoire	Poor: participation and representation low, responsiveness very low	No evidence presented, but spatial equity probably improved through government allocations to rural areas
Bangladesh	Poor: some improvement in participation, but very negative on representation of poor; responsiveness low	Very poor on all criteria, undermined by corruption and political patronage
Ghana	Mixed: participation by poor and community groups improves; limited improvement in representation, but responsiveness low	Limited evidence shows that resources involved were too insignificant to have made much impact; spatial equity may have improved through government allocations
Kenya	Very poor: politically run deconcentration scheme	Some impact on spatial equity through politically motivated redistribution
Nigeria	Very poor: low participation and representation, very bad record of responsiveness and lack of accountability	Poor: very bad record on equity and HD; spatial equity subject to political manipulation and urban bias
Mexico	No evidence presented, but assumed that party-dominated patronage system remains little changed	Poor in spite of significant central funding allocations; equity, spatial equity, and HD undermined by political patronage considerations and "basketball court" syndrome

Mexico exemplify the fourth scenario, in which decentralization was used by a ruling party to renew and extend the party's support without any real commitment to pro-poor policies that might disturb entrenched networks of influence and patronage.

In effect, the comparative evidence suggests that elite capture of even democratic decentralization remains the main obstacle to the possibility that decentralization might result in pro-poor outcomes. This possibility becomes less likely only where central ruling elites and/or democratic parties have a political motivation to challenge or circumvent locally powerful conservative groups and can give broader external support to antielite forces at the local level.

There is no convincing evidence for the notion that there is a predictable or general link between decentralization of government and the development of more pro-poor policies or poverty-alleviating outcomes. People who advocate decentralization on these grounds should be more cautious. However, it is possible that there are other important benefits, particularly in the field of participation and empowerment.

Our comparative analysis highlights the importance of "regime" in understanding the circumstances under which decentralization of government might benefit the poor. Parties, and the ideological character of parties, do matter. Decentralization in the cases we reviewed only produced more pro-poor outcomes when a national (or state-level) party and government were elected with a commitment and a program for social and economic redistribution and the capacity to prevent locally hostile elites from sabotaging such a program (see Harriss, this volume). This requires both adequate central state capacity (in order to monitor local government performance), the willingness to provide positive financial and administrative support to decentralized governments, and the emergence of a pro-poor coalition within the ruling party. These are essentially political factors that can be comprehended primarily through a "polity-centered" approach.

NOTES

1. This is an assumption questioned by few—except, for example, Peterson (1994) and Tendler (1997).

2. *Decentralization* can also be defined in functional terms, as when authority to carry out or manage a particular function is delegated within an institution or transferred to a parastatal or nonstate agency. In the more recent literature, even privatization and marketization of government functions have been described as decentralization insofar as they remove functions from the central "bureaucratic" state (Bennett 1994; Turner and Hulme 1997, 155; Litvack, Ahmad, and Bird 1998, 6).

3. In Ceara State, for instance, it was a newly elected reforming social democratic party (PSDB) governor who launched successful state programs in preventive health and in emergency public works. In fact, these bypassed the municipal mayors, who might have regarded them as a threat to their local patronage systems (Tendler 1997, 145). In Minas Gerais State, a reformist state governor was similarly responsible for devolving funding and authority in the education sector, using state government funds rather than the local governments (World Bank 1997, 123); note, too, the role of the Brazilian Workers' Party (PT) in the major cities that it took over after 1988 (Fox 1994, 111).

4. See Barkan and Chege's analysis of the Kenyan situation, in which they propose an hypothesis that "the probability that decentralization will serve the political interests of the regime varies inversely with the power and resources of the ethno-regional base on which the regime rests" (1989, 21).

5. Echeverri-Gent, however, argues that, while elite capture is not inevitable if a pro-poor radical party can mobilize the poor at the grass roots, the logic of electoral politics will still inevitably tend to blur the interests of the poor within a broader alliance serving the needs of the successful party, however radical (1992a).

6. The figure is misleading in the most basic sense in that it aggregates locally determined spending and spending on sectors or programs for which the finances are simply transferred to local governments for them to implement (Litvack and Seddon 1999, 19).

7. See Crook and Sverrisson 2001 for a full account of the case material.

8. The Scheduled Castes are the groups formerly referred to as Untouchables in preindependence India.

9. Annual agricultural growth for the period 1949–80 was 1.74 percent; whereas between 1981–82 and 1990–91 it is estimated to have been 6.4 percent (Sanyal, Biswas, and Bardhan 1998). Harriss (1992) plays down the role of institutional factors in this improvement, stating that the main cause was improvements in irrigation technology. However, Sanyal, Biswas, and Bardhan conclude that, although difficult to measure exactly, institutional reforms must have had an effect on breaking West Bengal's "agrarian impasse."

10. There are also criticisms that the West Bengal reform program did not go far enough in alleviating poverty. Although the landless and land poor were the main beneficiaries of government policies—indeed, no large or middle farmers received benefits from government credit programs—the resources provided were insufficient, and the poor, particularly sharecroppers, are still mainly dependent on landowners. As Westergaard argues, in a situation of such extreme land scarcity and pauperization, any improvement requires a fundamental transformation of agricultural production and the development of an industrial sector (1986, 84). Other critics point out that the government credit programs in West Bengal failed to reach women and the landless (Webster 1990, 103). Similarly, although the *panchayats* have been much better at coordinating relief work following natural disasters such as floods or droughts, this is criticized from within the CPI(M) as a move away from addressing the structural issues that cause vulnerability (41). This is part of a debate concerning the CPI(M)'s overall political strategy, as the approach has had to be softened to maintain electoral support (Webster 1989, 205–6).

11. In her comparative analysis of Ghana, Côte d'Ivoire, and Senegal, Boone argues that differences in the strength and autonomy of local elites actually determined the degree of devolution and central control in the decentralization scheme set up by central government (1998).

12. In Uganda, two districts studied by Sverrisson showed increases in morale that were a combination of the greater control provided by decentralization and the encouraging effects of generous donor sponsorship (Sverrisson 1999).

REFERENCES

Awotokun, A. M., ed. 1995. *New Trends in Nigerian Local Government*. Ile-Ife: Department of Local Government Studies, Ofafemi Awolowo University.

Bagchi, A. K. 1998. "Studies on the Economy of West Bengal since Independence." *Economic and Political Weekly* 33, nos. 47–48: 2973–78.

Barkan, J. D., and M. Chege. 1989. "Decentralizing the State: District Focus and the Politics of Reallocation in Kenya." *Journal of Modern African Studies* 27, no. 3: 431–53.

Bennett, R. J., ed. 1994. *Local Government and Market Decentralization: Experiences in Industrialised, Developing, and Former East Bloc Countries*. Tokyo: United Nations Press.

Bhattacharya, B. 1998. "Urbanisation and Human Development in West Bengal: A District Level Study and Comparison with Inter-state Variation." *Economic and Political Weekly* 33, nos. 47–48: 3027–32.

Boone, C. 1998. "State Building in the African Countryside: Structure and Politics at the Grassroots." *Journal of Development Studies* 34, no. 4: 1–31.

Brilliantes, A. B. 1998. "Decentralised Democratic Governance under the Local Government Code: A Governmental Perspective." *Philippine Journal of Public Administration* 42, nos. 1–2: 38–57.

Cariño, J. K. 1992. "The Local Government Code of 1991 and People's Organisations and Non-governmental Organisations in Northern Luzon." CSC Working Paper 20. Cordillera Studies Centre, University of the Philippines College, Baguio City, Philippines.

Castaneda, T. 1992. *Combating Poverty: Social Policy and Decentralization in Chile in the 1980s*. San Francisco: ICS Press.

Chatterjee, B. 1998. "Poverty in West Bengal: What Have We Learnt?" *Economic and Political Weekly* 33, nos. 47–48: 3003–14.

Crook, R. C. 1999. "No-Party Politics and Local Democracy in Africa: Rawlings' Ghana and the Ugandan Model in the 1990s." *Democratization* 6, no. 4: 114–38

Crook, R. C., and J. Manor. 1998. *Democracy and Decentralization in South Asia and West Africa: Participation, Accountability, and Performance*. Cambridge: Cambridge University Press.

Crook, R., and A. Sverrisson. 2001. "To What Extent Can Decentralised Forms of Government Enhance the Development of Pro-poor Policies and Improve Poverty Alleviation Outcomes?" IDS Working Paper 130. Institute of Development Studies, University of Sussex, Brighton.

Echeverri-Gent, J. 1992a. "Public Participation and Poverty Alleviation: The Experience of Reform Communists in West Bengal." *World Development* 20, no. 10: 1401–22.

———. 1992b. "Politics of Development and the Development of Politics." *Contemporary South Asia* 1, no. 3: 325–50.

Fiszbein, A. 1997. "The Emergence of Local Capacity: Lessons from Colombia." *World Development* 25, no. 7: 1029–43.

Forero, H., and M. Salazar. 1991. "Local Government and Decentralization in Colombia." *Environment and Urbanisation* 3, no. 2: 121–26.

Fox, J. 1994. "Latin America's Emerging Local Politics." *Journal of Democracy* 5, no. 2: 105–16.

———. 1995. "Governance and Rural Development in Mexico: State Intervention and Public Accountability." *Journal of Development Studies* 32, no. 1: 1–30.

Fox, J., and J. Aranda. 1996. *Decentralization and Rural Development in Mexico: Community Participation in Oaxaca's Municipal Funds Programme*. La Jolla: Centre for U.S.-Mexican Studies, University of California, San Diego.

Fried, R. C., and F. F. Rabinovitz. 1980. *Comparative Urban Politics: A Performance Approach*. Englewood Cliffs, NJ: Prentice-Hall.

Gboyega, A. 1998. "Decentralization and Local Autonomy in Nigeria's Federal System: Crossing the Stream while Searching for the Pebbles." In J. Barkan, ed., *Five Monographs on Decentralization and Democratisation in Sub-Saharan Africa*: Occasional Papers 45–49. International Programs, Iowa City: University of Iowa.

Ghosh, M. 1998. "Agricultural Development, Agrarian Structure, and Rural Poverty in West Bengal." *Economic and Political Weekly* 33, nos. 47–48: 2987–95.

Graham, C. 1994. *Safety Nets, Politics, and the Poor: Transitions to Market Economies*. Washington, DC: Brookings Institution.

Harriss, J. 1992. "Does the Depressor Still Work? Agrarian Structure and Development in India: A Review of Evidence and Argument." *Journal of Peasant Studies* 19, no. 2, 189–227.

Huther, J., and A. Shah. 1998. "Applying a Simple Measure of Good Governance to the Debate on Fiscal Decentralization." Policy Research Working Paper 1894. Washington, DC, World Bank Operations Evaluations Department, Country Evaluation and Regional Relations Division.

Ingham, B., and A. K. M. Kalam. 1992. "Decentralization and Development: Theory and Evidence from Bangladesh." *Public Administration and Development* 12, no. 4: 373–85.

Khan, M. M. 1987. "Paradoxes of Decentralization in Bangladesh." *Development Policy Review* 5, no. 4: 407–12.

Korten, D. C. 1984. *People Centered Development*. West Hartford, Conn.: Kumarian Press.

Kurian, G. 1999. "Empowering Conditions in the Decentralization Process: An Analysis of Dynamics, Factors, and Actors in Panchayati Raj Institutions from West Bengal and Karnataka, India." Working Paper 288. Institute of Social Studies, the Hague.

Leonard, D. K., and D. R. Marshall. 1982. *Institutions of Rural Development for the Poor: Decentralization and Organisational Linkages.* Berkeley: Institute of International Studies, University of California, Berkeley.

Lieten, G. K. 1988. "Panchayat Leaders in a West Bengal District." *Economic and Political Weekly* 23, no. 40: 2069–73.

———. 1996. *Development, Devolution, and Democracy: Village Discourse in West Bengal.* New Delhi, Thousand Oaks, and London: Sage.

Litvack, J., J. Ahmad, and R. Bird. 1998. *Rethinking Decentralization in Developing Countries.* Washington, DC: World Bank.

Litvack, J., and J. Seddon, eds. 1999. *Decentralization Briefing Notes.* Washington, DC: World Bank Institute.

Meenakshisundaram, S. S. 1994. *Decentralization in Developing Countries.* New Delhi: Concept Publishing.

Moris, J. R. 1991. "Institutional Choice and Local Development: What Kind of Social Science Do We Need?" In R. Crook and A. M. Jerve, eds., *Government and Participation: Institutional Development, Decentralization, and Democracy in the Third World.* Bergen: Chr. Michelsen Institute.

Olowu, D. 1989. *Achievements and Problems of Federal and State Transfers to Local Governments in Nigeria since Independence.* Washington, DC: World Bank.

———. 1997. "Decentralization in Africa: Appraising the Local Government Revitalisation Strategy in Nigeria." In G. Nzongola-Ntalaja and M. C. Lee, eds., *The State and Democracy in Africa.* Harare: AAPS Books.

Parry, T. R. 1997. "Decentralization and Privatisation: Education Policy in Chile." *Journal of Public Policy* 17, no. 1: 107–33.

Peterson, G. E. 1994. *Decentralization Experience in Latin America: An Overview of Lessons and Issues.* Washington, DC: Urban Institute.

Raczynski, D., C. Serrano, and E. Bousquet. 1990. "Escuelos y Educación Basica: La Mirada de Padres y Apoderados en Penalolen Alto." *Apuntes Cieplan* 95. Santiago: CIEPLAN.

Ragin, C. 1996. "Political Methodology: Qualitative Methods." In R. Goodin and H. Klingemann, eds., *A New Handbook of Political Science.* Oxford: Oxford University Press.

Rawal, V., and M. Swaminathan. 1998. "Changing Trajectories: Agricultural Growth in West Bengal, 1950 to 1996." *Economic and Political Weekly* 33, no. 40: 2595–2602.

Rood, S. 1998. "An Assessment of the State of Knowledge Concerning Decentralised Governance under the Philippine 1991 Local Government Code." *Philippine Journal of Public Administration* 42, nos. 1–2: 58–82.

Sanyal, M. K., P. K. Biswas, and S. Bardhan. 1998. "Institutional Change and Output Growth in West Bengal Agriculture: End of Impasse." *Economic and Political Weekly* 33, nos. 47–48: 2979–86.

Sivanna, N. 1990. *Panchayati Raj Reforms and Rural Development.* Allahabad: Chugh Publications.

Smith, B. C. 1985. *Decentralization: The Territorial Dimension of the State.* London: Allen and Unwin.

Stewart, F., and G. Ranis. 1994. "Decentralization in Chile." Human Development Report Occasional Papers 14. New York, UNDP.

Subha, K. 1997. *Karnataka Panchayat Elections, 1995: Process, Issues, and Membership Profile.* New Delhi: Concept.

Sverrisson, A. S. 1999. "The Politics of Poverty Alleviation in Sub-Saharan Africa under Structural Adjustment." Manuscript. Glasgow Caledonian University, Glasgow.

Tendler, J. 1993. "New Lessons from Old Projects: The Workings of Rural Development in Northeast Brazil." Washington, DC, Operations Evaluation Department, World Bank.

———. 1997. *Good Government in the Tropics.* Baltimore: Johns Hopkins University Press.

Tendler, J., and S. Freedheim. 1994. "Trust in a Rent-Seeking World: Health and Government Transformed in Northeast Brazil." *World Development* 22, no. 12: 1771–91.

Turner, M., and D. Hulme. 1997. *Governance, Administration, and Development: Making the State Work.* Basingstoke: Macmillan.

van Zyle, J., T. Barbosa, A. N. Parker, and L. Sonn. 1995. "Decentralised Rural Development and Enhanced Community Participation: A Case Study from Northeast Brazil." Policy Research Working Paper 1498. Washington, DC, Agriculture and Natural Resources Department, Sector Policy and Water Resources Division, World Bank.

Velásquez C., F. E. 1991. "Local Governments in Intermediate Cities in Colombia: Municipal Administration for Whom?" *Environment and Urbanisation* 3, no. 1: 109–20.

Webster, N. 1989. "Agrarian Relations in Burdwan District, West Bengal: From the Economics of the Green Revolution to the Politics of Panchayati Raj." *Journal of Contemporary Asia* 20, no. 2: 177–211.

———. 1990. "Panchayati Raj and the Decentralization of Development Planning in West Bengal: A Case Study." CDR Project Paper 90.7. Copenhagen, Centre for Development Research.

———. 1992. "Panchayati Raj in West Bengal: Participation for the People or the Party?" *Development and Change* 23, no. 4: 129–63.

Westergaard, K. 1986. "People's Participation, Local Government, and Rural Development: The Case of West Bengal, India." CDR Research Report 8. Copenhagen, Centre for Development Research.

World Bank. 1995. "Colombia Local Government Capacity: Beyond Technical Assistance." World Bank Report 14085–C. Washington, DC, World Bank.

———. 1997. *World Development Report: The State in a Changing World.* New York: Oxford University Press.

Wunsch, J. S., and D. Olowu. 1996–97. "Regime Transformation from Below: Decentralization, Local Governance, and Democratic Reform in Nigeria." *Studies in Comparative International Development* 31, no. 4: 66–82.

10 *Arguing the Politics of Inclusion*

Mick Moore

W hat are the prospects for inclusionary development, in the sense that Peter Houtzager uses the term in chapter 1? By 2015, in how many countries will poor people be receiving an enhanced share of the material fruits of economic growth? And how many of these improvements in income distribution will be sustainable because they reflect some embedding into policy-making processes of political parties, movements, and institutions that give greater voice and influence to the poor? I have no idea of the answers and will make no serious attempt at prophecy. My objective here is more instrumental: to try to prevent the unwarranted use of academic social science in the service of pessimism—or reaction. Several years of research into the politics of poverty reduction in poor countries leave a strong impression that the future is not determined. Some countries could move toward inclusiveness; others could go in the opposite direction. Given the enormous diversity of the polities, societies, and economies of poor countries, one can safely predict diverse outcomes. But that is not the central message of the vast range of recent literature on this rather nebulous subject. The weight of this material tends toward pessimism, toward the conclusion that, within countries, the poor are in future likely to command an even smaller share of material resources and even less political influence than they do today. This pessimism is fed from two particularly abundant contemporary sources. One is a set of arguments about how *globalization*—a term that is often used to mean nothing more than international economic liberalization—allegedly is undermining the political incentives and capacities of states to address poverty. The other source, which is more narrowly confined to academic social scientists, is in the first instance more methodological than substantive: modeling politics on the assumption that the main driver of political action is rational self-interest. As is explained later, this method has an "elective affinity" with pessimism about the prospects for more inclusive politics.

There is a disjuncture between the pessimism about inclusiveness that is embedded in much contemporary literature on poverty and some more optimistic or open-minded scenarios that emerge from the scholarly material and ideas represented in this volume. This chapter is an attempt to reconcile these two perspectives. It is, however, reconciliation with a purpose. Ideas are not innocent. Marcus J. Kurtz observes, in chapter 6, that "the system of ideas that comes with particular economic strategies constrain the range of antipoverty policies that local decision makers consider." He is referring particularly to Chile and Mexico. Scaled up, his argument encapsulates the motivation behind this chapter. "Academic" ideas about the politics of poverty can make a big difference. Intellectual backing for the notion that positive change is possible can stimulate and embolden reformers and dishearten opponents. Conversely, according recognition to arguments that deep historical forces lie behind growing inequality and the further disempowerment of the poor may have a self-fulfilling element (Ascher 1984, chap. 1).[1] And research findings do not always emerge independently of the context in which they are used. We know that, in applied development studies, the cumulative conclusions of even apparently "hard" quantitative research have a way of changing over time to reflect changes in the ideas and concerns of dominant institutions.[2] There are good reasons to suspect that the pessimism embodied in much of the recent research and theory on politics and poverty reduction reflects a similar adjustment on the part of researchers to the neoconservative principles that have enjoyed such a free rein in recent decades. Until very recently, the dominant international development institutions have been signaling opposition to the redistribution of resources or power to the poor and have helped create an environment that rewards researchers who demonstrate why any such redistribution is impossible, difficult, or dangerous.[3]

The purpose of this chapter is not to try to rally progressive or radical spirits by claiming that some serious opportunities to change to a better path lie just around the corner. The objectives are more modest: to explore and critique how social science arguments recently have been deployed in making general statements about the politics of poverty reduction in poor countries; to thereby demonstrate that—contrary to much extant literature—there are no strong grounds for generalized pessimism about the prospects for more inclusive political and economic strategies; and to indicate how some of the key ideas in this volume can help us make the best of the current intellectual battle around the term *empowerment.* I pursue these objectives by examining three social science debates:

- Arguments about the political consequences of globalization.
- The use of formal political economy models to examine the politics of poverty.

- A more recent debate, likely to intensify in the near future, over the substantive interpretation of the increasingly popular concept of empowering the poor.

My conclusions on each point areas follows.

- There is no reason to believe that globalization consistently undermines the political willingness or capacity of states to tackle poverty.
- Formal political economy models of the politics of poverty have contributed very little to our understanding of the field to date and are unlikely to do so for the foreseeable future. In particular, their exponents have failed to validate the assumption that political responses to poverty are dominantly driven by "rational egoism": the ways in which political actors conceive their own (narrow, material) self-interests.
- The fact that so many international development organizations are now declaring priority for empowerment of the poor represents an advance and an opportunity. The term *empowerment* is rarely defined, however, and the various implicit meanings are sometimes weak and watery. There is a major struggle to be fought over operational definitions. To win that struggle, we would do well to follow Laurence Whitehead and George Gray-Molina (chap. 2) and redefine the objective as enhancing the political capabilities of the poor. To open up paths to the achievement of that objective, the polity approach to political analysis explored by Peter P. Houtzager in chapters 1 and 4 is an invaluable intellectual tool.

THE POLITICAL CONSEQUENCES OF GLOBALIZATION

Globalization is used here as a narrow shorthand for international economic liberalization—the reductions in trade barriers and increases in the international mobility of capital that were so marked over the final quarter of the last century.[4] There is a widespread perception that during this period the distribution of income has become increasingly unequal, both within and between nations.[5] This is a major cause of the growing interest in the politics of inclusion (see chap. 1). The purpose of this section is to refute the most deterministic interpretation of the political implications of the apparent growth of inequality: the notion that globalization is bringing about changes in the character of national political processes that fatally undermine the prospects for more inclusionary politics in poor countries.

If income distribution has indeed become more unequal over recent decades, what is the reason? There is no consensus on the answer, and there are many candidates. It is, however, overwhelmingly likely that the answers lie mainly in the economic sphere: in the changing structure of economies and in market forces. For it is in the economic sphere that the world recently has become more interconnected and homogeneous. Given the continuing diversity of states and national politics and policies, it is unlikely that a general global trend toward inequality would be immediately driven by changes in politics at the national level.[6] Further, there are plausible accounts of how international economic liberalization might be expected to exacerbate inequality through market processes (e.g., Wood 1994). However, intellectuals have a generic tendency to overexplain. This is especially the case when they are trying to account for "big picture" changes. Currently there is a widespread view that globalization has led to a fundamental weakening of the political capacity of governments to tax or redistribute income or capital and to preserve or increase social protection. I summarize in the following pages the three main causal sequences through which globalization is often claimed to undermine prospects for practicing the politics of inclusion. There is limited evidence on whether these claims are valid. To the extent the evidence exists, it does not appear to support the most widespread argument about the politically erosive effects of globalization—that these work through the direct political consequences of increased international capital mobility.

Before looking at the arguments in detail, it is useful to provide a little context. For two to three decades after the end of World War II, the world economy boomed. The 1970s saw the beginning of an equally long period of relative economic recession. For several decades, social scientists have been trying to explain the onset of that recession. Interpretations are of course diverse. There has, however, been a strong preference for explanations that abstract from or sideline the instability and crises that are inherent in capitalism and instead locate the cause in the political power of particular social groups. Within the advanced capitalist countries, the favored explanation, from all parts of the political spectrum, has been the alleged increased political power of organized labor and its capacity to extract a higher share of economic surplus at the expense of capital, profits, and reinvestment rates.[7] The fact that this interpretation is not consistent with the evidence (Brenner 1998, 13–22) is relevant to current concerns in two ways. First, it is a warning against attempts to explain patterns of economic change that are relatively uniform across many countries through arguments that imply simultaneous changes in domestic politics within those countries. Second, there is a direct connection between these questionable explanations of economic stagnation in the 1970s and 1980s and current suggestions about the political impact of globalization. It is but one short, logical step from these (questionable) arguments to the proposition that higher rates of economic growth returned in the 1990s when and where the power of organized labor was broken. It is from there just another logical step to the conclusions that (1) there has been a fundamental and long-term shift of power away from labor and what the Latin Americans term "popular sectors," and (2) the future prospects for the politics of inclusion are correspondingly bleak. With that context in mind, we can examine the three main arguments about the politically erosive effects of globalization.

The most significant and plausible argument is that increased international capital mobility is undermining the capacity of governments to redistribute assets or income to the poor or to expand social provision. The greater the efforts that governments make to tax or redistribute income or capital, preserve or increase social protection, or influence where and how the private sector invests, the more they will be "punished" by capital. To protect their assets, profits, and prerogatives, controllers of capital (capitalists) do not need to get together to bribe governments or conspire against them. Adequate warnings will be conveyed and punishments inflicted by capitalists individually pursuing their own interests. They will individually reduce investments and liquid capital deposits in countries (and cities or regions) ruled by regimes lacking in "realism"—or they may simply threaten to do so, pointing out how easy it is for them to move money and production facilities to more favorable business environments. The specter or the actuality of declining tax revenues, rising unemployment, and falling political support will be enough to persuade most governments to accept reality: to reduce business taxes, cancel promises to redistribute land, dilute proposals to extend employee rights, and postpone plans to provide a basic income to all destitute households.[8] Rational voters will respond in the same way and withdraw support from progressive parties or movements.

This proposition is to be taken seriously. There are valid concerns, often expressed in terms of the metaphor "the race to the bottom," that pressures from mobile capital are leading governments to cooperate in undermining the employment conditions, social protection, and political influence of the poor. But the pessimistic case is clearly far too simplistic. There is much else going on in the world. There are two general reasons to be skeptical.

First, it is far from clear that it is in the interests of capitalists that states lose authority. In most circumstances, capitalists need effective states (e.g., to enforce property rights) and may therefore be unwilling to undermine the political legitimacy and stability of the regimes with which they wish to deal by encouraging the political exclusion of the poor (e.g., Evans 1997; Weiss 1998). Capitalists might even wish poor states to pursue active, inclusionary, social policies for reasons of political and labor force stability or to reduce political obstacles to economic adjustment (Rieger and Liebfried 1998).

Second, there is no historical justification or evidence for the expectation that higher degrees of economic openness of national economies will be associated with smaller or less economically interventionist states. On the contrary, there is a strong and positive historical connection between the degree of national economic openness and the extent to which states become involved in welfare provision. It has been known for two decades that, among the Organization for Economic Cooperation and Development (OECD) countries, the rate of growth of the public share of the economy—measured as the ratio of tax revenue to gross domestic product (GDP)—was significantly shaped by the degree of economic openness. This was believed to be related to the livelihood risks associated with economic openness (Cameron 1978). Recent work by Rodrik (1998) not only extends that general finding to a much larger sample of countries at all income levels but provides us with a more convincing analysis of the causal sequences at work. Rodrik takes measures of government consumption, rather than income, as his dependent variables. He shows that more precise measures of the risk associated with economic openness—the volatility of the terms of trade of individual countries and the extent to which their exports are concentrated on a few products—are better predictors of the growth of the state's share of the economy than are measures of economic openness per se. And he provides evidence that, whereas governments of richer countries tend to respond to the political pressures to cope with economic uncertainty by expanding social spending as we conceive it, governments of poorer countries, lacking the administrative apparatus to undertake compensatory social spending, tend to respond by expanding government consumption and employment.[9]

Neither history nor theory gives clear support to any version of the "race to the bottom" hypothesis of globalization. There are competing hypotheses. What about the evidence for developing countries? It is clearest in relation to state revenue: after two decades of international economic liberalization, states are not reducing their tax take (as a percentage of gross national product [GDP]).[10] The evidence on patterns of spending is more ambiguous. We appear to have a good causal statistical analysis only for Latin America. Kaufman and Segura-Ubiergo (2001) find that economic openness has indeed tended to lead to reductions in social spending but that virtually all the cuts fall on transfers (mainly pensions), with health and education spending apparently not clearly affected either way.

The OECD polities have considerable capacity to mediate the domestic consequences of globalization (Crepaz 2002). Governments in poorer countries may lack that capacity. We cannot reject the possibility that increased international capital mobility will in some respects erode the scope for more inclusive political institutions and for a greater political voice for the poor. There is sufficient smoke to indicate some kind of fire. But there is clearly much else going on, and it seems highly unlikely that the proposition is generally valid. There is a similar lack of confirming evidence on the two other main propositions about the politically erosive effects of international economic liberalization.

One proposition is based on the evident decline of trade union power in many parts of the world, consequent upon the ways in which globalization is changing the character and location of production. Production is increasingly disaggregated and dispersed, nationally and internationally. The roles of production workers are increasingly differentiated and specialized. The controllers of capital have gained in power relative to workers and their organizations because of their increasing scope—as a result of technical change and international economic liberalization—to (threaten to) relocate production to alternative sites on relatively short notice. The consequent weakening of the trade union movement represents a diminution of the power and political capabilities of the poor generally.

The second proposition concerns the effects of globalization on national political and economic elites—and indeed is based on the fear that they are becoming less "national." Both globalization (in the extended sense of the term) and international economic liberalization provide poor country elites with greater opportunities and incentives to move "offshore"—and into first world enclaves—their assets, their expectations and investments for their children's' futures, and much of their own time. Insofar as they retain a national presence and interest, elites may seek their own salvation in private, market provision of the health, education, pensions, security, and other social goods that might otherwise have been publicly provided. The overall effect is fewer pressures on governments to provide effective public services of any kind because the more wealthy and influential are abandoning the state.

These two propositions are clearly based on some valid observations. They are intriguing and present weighty challenges to social science researchers. But it would be unwise at this point to assume a general validity. The decline of "traditional" trade unionism is a clear fact in some parts of the poorer world, notably in much of Latin America, where it was relatively strong during the twentieth century (Keck 1989; Seidman 1994). But the decline is certainly less evident for some other parts of the world. Correspondingly, one might expect that, even if there has been some dilution of their own national identities and concerns, the elites that dominate many poor countries would become alarmed if the legitimacy of the state and public order were to decline to such a degree that their own interests were threatened. They, too, are potential supporters of the politics of inclusion. And the fear that international linkages have undermined the "national" character of third world elites goes back at least to 1960s dependency theory (e.g., Sunkel 1969).

In sum, we need clearly to separate out our concerns about growing income inequality from the assertions that (1) this is largely to be explained by changes in national-level political forces and therefore (2) the prospects for political action to combat inequality are particularly remote. There are at present no general grounds to be pessimistic that the globalization monster has undermined the prospects for more inclusionary politics in poor countries.

POVERTY IN FORMAL POLITICAL ECONOMY

The second main potential source of pessimism about the prospects for inclusionary politics is rooted in social science method. Recent decades have witnessed a great expansion within—and into—political science of rational choice analysis. In attempting even a summary characterization of this paradigm, one has to tread carefully. For the debates around rational choice still excite strong emotions within the (American) political science academy—the kinds of emotions that Jonathan Swift parodied so effectively almost three centuries ago in his characterization in *Gulliver's Travels* of the conflict between the "Big-endians" and the "Small-endians." Fortunately, it is not necessary here to engage deeply with the details of rational choice methods and research findings. The key points can be summarized relatively briefly, first by describing some major features of the rational choice approach.

- It is based on the application to political science of the positivistic, formal, and quantitative analytic methods that we normally associate with economics, notably: models of political processes that are clearly specified, often in algebraic form, in terms of the identification of the actors; their objectives, resources, and constraints; and the institutional context in which they operate. Frequently, quantitative data and statistical and econometric techniques are used to explore and test propositions.
- Although the rational choice method is in principle compatible with a very wide range of assumptions, perspectives, or ideological preferences, it is in practice possible to specify and test only models of political processes that are extremely simplified—with few variables and highly stylized assumptions (about the political actors; their objectives, resources, constraints; and the institutional context in which they operate).

- In particular, the actual practice of rational choice analysis
  almost always involves the assumption that, when they engage
  in politics, the political actors—voters, governments, politicians,
  organizations, and so on—are motivated (only) by "rational
  egoism," that is, some variant of perceived individual self-interest. Further, it is normally the case that this self-interest is (and
  can only be) specified in material terms.[11]
- The practitioners of rational choice analysis, who are just as
  likely to be economists as political scientists, frequently adopt
  the economists' style of writing, in which statements that are
  based on no more than logic—the assumptions they make when
  setting up their models, the deductive implications of the inter-
  active processes that they set out algebraically—are presented as
  if they were facts about the world. The statement "I have shown
  X" is used as a shorthand for "If all my assumptions, my algebraic modeling, and my statistical analysis are correct, then, in
  the specified circumstances, X would be true."

When it is used to analyze the politics of poverty, the rational choice
paradigm is liable to lead to systematically biased inferences. Its practitioners are forced by the inherent limitations of the method to make sim-
plifying assumptions that are contrary in spirit and substance to an inclusionary attitude toward the poor. To adopt the normal assumption of
rational egoism—the presumption that individual actors are pursuing
individual (material) self-interest—is to begin the analysis by coming
close to rejecting the possibility that rich or powerful people could
"rationally" support any redistribution of resources to the poor unless
that redistribution were also in the self-interest of the rich.[12]

To illustrate that the intellectual hazards of the rational choice paradigm are real and not simply conjectural, we need look no further than
an essay, published by the World Bank in 1997, that has the following
policy conclusion emblazoned on its front cover: "Will means-tested targeting help the poor? Economics might say yes, but politics say no" (Gelbach and Pritchett 1997). There are no qualifications to this conclusion.
No particular countries or contexts are specified. How did the two economists who authored this essay reach such a dramatic and gloomy conclusion about politics? Not by any reference to facts or experience. The
only poverty-related fact in twenty-seven pages is found in the first paragraph and concerns a verbal exchange in the American House of Representatives about the means testing of Medicare benefits. The argument in
the essay is purely deductive and abstract. It is derived from adding some
algebra to the following main assumptions.[13]

- Policy decisions derive solely from the relative numbers of citizens (voters) supporting alternative options. Politicians and governments are not actors in their own right but simply registers and instruments of the will of voters. Politicians do not set agendas, exercise leadership, organize bargains and trade-offs, or reflect international pressures.[14]
- Voters are all rational egoists, seeking to minimize their personal contributions to government revenue and maximize the subsidies they receive from government.
- In order for the algebra in the model to remain tractable, it is assumed that all voters behave according to their membership in one of a small number of interest groups defined purely in terms of income categories—rich, middle-income, or poor. Almost all the reality of politics is excluded. Voters do not have ambiguous concerns or identities. The politics of policy decisions relating to poverty is totally separate from the politics of other issues. Considerations of ethnicity, region, language, ideology, belief, religion, and established party loyalty play no role.
- There is a high level of public awareness of and information on complex policy options: people understand the net implications for them personally of attempts not only to, for example, increase public pension benefits but also to change the basis on which the prices of subsidized foodstuffs are adjusted for inflation or alter budgetary allocations for public works projects. Every piece of the public budget is the subject of highly informed political competition between those asked to fund it through taxes and those who might hope to benefit from it.

Given these assumptions, the "conclusions" of the essay follow in a couple of easy steps:

- Attempts to limit ("target") any income transfers only to poorer people will mean that the bulk of the population will not provide political support because they clearly perceive that they will obtain no direct personal benefit.
- Therefore, income transfer programs will survive the competitive business of electoral politics only if they are not targeted, that is, if large proportions of the population are in principle eligible.

That targeted antipoverty programs are politically vulnerable in this way is not in doubt. Joan M. Nelson explores the implications in her contribution to this volume. But the stark fact is that they exist in large numbers all over the world. We can have little respect for a theory that explains why they are impossible. The Gelbach and Pritchett essay adds nothing to our understanding of the issue and lays claim to radical and pessimistic policy conclusions that are without foundation. Their publication illustrates the extent to which the "conclusions" of rational choice analysis may be conditioned by the initial assumptions.[15] It follows that the rational choice method could be used for different purposes. With altered—or more realistic—assumptions, it might be a tool on the side of proponents of a more inclusionary approach to antipoverty policy. It has been used in this way in the *World Development Report, 2000–2001: Attacking Poverty* (World Bank 2000), which represents a symbolic and intellectual step down the inclusionary path by the World Bank. This step was possible, after some internal conflict within the World Bank, in part because some economists had employed rational choice analysis to provide suitable intellectual ammunition. Using cross-national samples, it had been shown that in recent decades countries with lower levels of (initial) intranational income inequality have enjoyed higher rates of economic growth. It is not clear that we really know the reason for this statistical relationship.[16] However, a number of respected economists had employed the rational choice framework and deductive reasoning to suggest a causal connection between inequality and low growth that was plausible and acceptable in a World Bank context: variants of the argument that, the higher the degree of income inequality, the greater the degree of citizen support for high rates of tax on capital and thus the greater the disincentives to capital investment and the lower the rate of economic growth. This evidence was good enough to persuade the authors of the *World Development Report* to at least acknowledge that inequality might hinder economic growth.[17]

If the rational choice method can be deployed on all sides of the debate about poverty reduction and inclusive politics, the important question is not about whether any particular piece of rational choice analysis is right or wrong but what significant, robust, and valid conclusions emerge from the application of the paradigm to the study of the politics of poverty reduction in poor countries. Fortunately, we do not have to review the literature afresh to reach a considered view on that question. Two accomplished practitioners of the art have recently published a careful review of the state of knowledge on the linkages among inequality, economic growth, and democracy in developing countries (Landa and Kapstein 2001). Their mission is not to critique the rational choice approach in any fundamental way. They are rather open-minded adherents asking scholarly questions and seeking convincing answers. They demonstrate the high degree to which the principal apparent "conclusions" in the field are contested and based more on deductive reasoning than empirical verification.[18]

To the degree that the rational choice research program has constituted a trawl for evidence to support the assumption that the politics of poverty reduction are fundamentally driven by rational egoism, it appears to have failed. That failure throws seriously into question the assumption of rational egoism. Self-interest is of course a significant driver of political action, but it comes in broad and enlightened long-term, as well as narrow and short-term, sizes. It is sometimes seriously diluted by morally—and ideologically—driven behaviors that verge on altruism.[19] Equally, the institutional context in which political leaders attempt to pursue antipoverty policies may have a major impact on outcomes. Leaders have some scope to manipulate this context.[20] Rational choice analysis might one day tell us more about the conditions under which we find one or another kind of political behavior in relation to poverty reduction. It has not done so yet. Its assumptions cannot be used as evidence that politically inclusive approaches to poverty are doomed to failure.

THE STRUGGLE OVER EMPOWERMENT

Almost two decades ago, A. F. Robertson wrote *People and the State: An Anthropology of Planned Development* (1984). Engaged in what would currently be termed a critique of applied development discourse, Robertson deconstructed (also not his term) many of the pieces of development jargon still widely used today. *Community* receives especially close scrutiny (142–50), while terms like *participation* and *grass roots* are examined with a cold eye (see especially 139). The word *empowerment* does not appear in the book. The story would be very different today. Any equivalent contemporary work would have to give *empowerment* pride of place. It has been creeping into the development lexicon for many years, impelled mainly by the increasing political and intellectual prominence of development nongovernmental organizations (NGOs), which frequently claim empowerment as their area of special expertise. The creep has accelerated to a canter over the past two or three years: many of the big international aid and development agencies have adopted the term with fervor, especially in relation to poverty reduction. The notion of empowering the poor is either the dominant or the most prominent concept framing discussions of the political dimensions of poverty reduction in three recent major reports on poverty: the United Nations Development Program's (UNDP's) *Poverty Report, 2000: Overcoming Human Poverty* (UNDP 2000); the World Bank's *World Development Report, 2000–2001: Attacking Poverty* (World Bank 2000); and the International Fund for Agricultural Development's (IFAD's) *Rural Poverty Report, 2001: The Challenge of Ending Rural Poverty* (IFAD 2001).[21] Empowerment is perhaps *the* signifier of the new politics of inclusion.

Should those of us concerned about political inclusion of the poor not rejoice? Is it not a matter for celebration that "our" language is becoming hegemonic? To a degree, yes. The new popularity of empowerment is a step in the right direction. But it is neither as big nor as firm a step as one would like. The term is now so widely and loosely used that it could become as much an obstacle as a stimulus to clear thinking and positive action. A little deconstruction is in order.[22] Reconstruction will follow.

It is likely that the international development agencies are embracing *empowerment* in part because it suits their own narrow organizational agendas.[23] Equally, there is every reason to believe that they have not thought seriously about empowerment: in none of the three high profile publications listed here is the term actually defined. The implicit meanings are diverse or primarily symbolic. If the opportunity provided by the current popularity of *empowerment* is to be seized, we need to inject into the debate a little rigor and some insights from political science. Let us begin with the question of why the term is employed so diversely.

Part of the answer is that *empowerment* is simply a fashionable term in many contexts, especially in the rich world. A more fundamental point is that the ambiguities about the term to some degree reflect the diverse meanings of the word *power* both in everyday English and in the political science academy.[24] Most important for present purposes, a close look at contemporary development discourse suggests that serious users of *empowerment* genuinely, albeit implicitly, differ among themselves about what they mean. Without engaging deeply in literature surveys and discourse analysis, one can detect at least three different axes or continua along which one can locate meanings of the term:

1. The word is used routinely to refer both to (1) the means to the goal and (2) the goal itself. Seeing the word *empowerment* on the page does not tell us whether the author had in mind the processes through which the poor and disadvantaged might become empowered or the end state of their being able to exercise power. Development and NGO activists tend to prefer the process interpretation (e.g., Rowlands 1995), while official agencies are more likely to emphasize the outcome dimension (e.g., IFAD 2001).[25]

2. There are political and economic/material interpretations of *empowerment* that are, at least at the poles, distinct from one another. It is particularly striking in contemporary development discourse that large official organizations like the World Bank take an economistic perspective. People are empowered

when they get access to jobs, credit, assets, and market opportunities: for example, "A range of measures in productive activities, notably microfinance and farming inputs, have produced
documented benefits in terms of increased yields (in Kenya for
example) and increased autonomy for women and better nutritional status of children" (World Bank 2000, 10). This highly
materialist conception of empowerment—and implicitly of politics in general—stands in contrast to the emphasis of NGO,
community, and political activists on the organizational and
ideational dimensions of politics and the empowerment
process.[26]

3. The third axis is the most significant: the tension between those
who interpret empowerment as taking place at the level of the
individual and those who view it fundamentally as a collective
phenomenon. One should be able to assert, with confidence,
that there is a clear right answer here. It is one of the "givens"
of political science that poor people in poor countries have few
political resources and become politically effective only through
collective action. It would follow that we should feel comfortable in making a clear distinction between (1) the genuine advocates of empowerment of the poor, who would give great priority to the collective and organizational dimensions; and (2) the
"false prophets" who, in using or promoting the individual
interpretation, are attempting to divert us from the true path.
We might classify organizations like the World Bank among
the false prophets, noting that the individualistic conception of
empowerment is in practice virtually identical to the materialist
or market-oriented concept mentioned earlier.

Unfortunately, the world is not so clear-cut. We cannot honestly or
usefully live with this simple dichotomy between good and bad. The picture is complicated on both sides of the divide.

Much of the recent discourse on empowerment emanating from the
large international development organizations, including the World
Bank, is collectivist in language, identifying the "community" as *the* site
of empowerment. This apparent radicalism is, however, less substantial
than it sounds. The community in question is implicitly the small, local,
spatially defined "village community"—not generally the prime arena for
the political mobilization of the poor and often the site of their worst
oppression. Insofar as there is any instrumental logic or purpose behind
the promotion of this set of ideas by organizations like the World Bank,
it probably lies in attempts (1) to obtain more political support from
international development NGOs by adopting NGO rhetoric; and (2) to

provide ideological bolstering to very large new lending programs, called social funds, that involve large direct allocations of money to local governments in many developing countries.[27]

It is more significant to our concerns here that there are strong threads of the individualist approach to empowerment even within the discourse of those whose commitment appears to be genuine. Why so? There are two likely reasons. One is largely incidental: there is in practice interaction and affinity among (1) community-level political activists, who tend toward the collective approach; and (2) therapists and personal counselors, who also use the language of empowerment but necessarily do so at the individual level.[28] The second reason is more weighty: the individualist and the collective interpretations of *empowerment* are inevitably intermingled within the sphere where so much of the thinking and action has taken place recently in rich and poor countries alike—in the domain of gender relations. The subordination of women is experienced, and contested, not only at the level of a generic or categorical phenomenon, involving relationships between women in general and men in general, but also at the very individual level, within the context of close personal relations between particular women and particular men. The empowerment of women is simultaneously an individual and a collective process. The two reinforce one another. It is quite appropriate that there should be an individualist dimension to conceptions of empowerment that reflect gender concerns (e.g., Mayoux 2001). The British official aid agency has this to say in its recent flagship statement "Poverty Elimination and the Empowerment of Women."

> Empowerment means individuals acquiring the power to think and act freely, exercise choice, and to fulfil their potential as full and equal members of society. The United Nations Development Fund for Women (UNIFEM) includes the following factors in its definition of women's empowerment:
>
> - acquiring knowledge and understanding of gender relations and the ways in which these relations may be changed;
> - developing a sense of self-worth, a belief in one's ability to secure desired changes and the right to control one's life;
> - gaining the ability to generate choices and exercise bargaining power;
> - developing the ability to organize and influence the direction of social change to create a more just social and economic order, nationally and internationally. (DfID 2000, 11)

The interpretation of *empowerment of the poor* will continue to be much debated and contested. There will be continuing disagreements over at least three issues. One is the extent to which empowerment is viewed as a process or an outcome. Another is how far empowering the poor (and disadvantaged people generally) should be understood and pursued at collective or individual levels. The third is how far empowerment should be interpreted strictly, in terms of the (also contested) concept of power, and how far one should accommodate the range of notions that are causally related to power in a contingent way but not intrinsically or necessarily a component of power: choice, knowledge, operational autonomy, self-worth, self-confidence, participation, and even enrichment.[29] These phenomena clearly contribute directly to empowerment. At the same time, allowing them into the definition of the concept potentially legitimizes programs that, while justified in terms of empowerment, at best offer only knowledge, only choice, or only enrichment and may in practice offer much less.

MOVING BEYOND EMPOWERMENT

As it is employed in contemporary development discourse, *empowerment* is essentially a mobilizing term. It helps to muster and motivate troops willing to fight for greater political and economic inclusion. It does not, however, provide them with much sense of direction. We need other, better tools to help us decide where and how to deploy the troops. This volume provides several: an informed skepticism about the intrinsic value of decentralization (Richard C. Crook and Alan Sverrisson) and the interpretation of measures of good governance (Mick Moore, Jennifer Leavy, and Howard White), a grasp of the constraints that economic ideology can impose on the public policy menu (Marcus J. Kurtz), an appreciation of the progressive potential of institutionalized democratic competition between "populist" political parties (John Harriss), an understanding of the scope for cross-class alliances among the poor and not so poor (Joan M. Nelson), and an awareness that the political possibility theorem of agrarian reform is becoming outdated (Ronald J. Herring). It is, however, in the first two chapters of this volume that we find the analytic tools that are of the broadest use in building on, and advancing beyond, the empowerment mantra: the concepts of political capabilities of the poor and the polity approach to political analysis.

Lawrence Whitehead and George Gray-Molina define *political capabilities of the poor* as "the institutional and organizational resources as well as collective ideas available for effective political action" (chap. 2). Like *empowerment*, this is a very abstract term. Those wishing to employ it for analytic purposes need to find more operational definitions. It is, however, superior to *empowerment* as a way of thinking about strategies for promoting political inclusiveness. The notion of political capabilities draws attention to the longer term; the process of political learning; the ways in which the ideas, identities, and collective self-awareness that constitute valuable political resources in one context can be reframed to suit other contexts; and the importance of the intersection between the three arenas driving pro-poor policy-making—the institutional characteristics of the state, the organizational resources of the poor, and the content of policy itself. When talking about the political capabilities of the poor, we are sure we are referring to ways of enhancing their power and policy leverage. By contrast, the promiscuous employment of the term *empowerment* to allude to or embrace associated concepts like choice, knowledge, operational autonomy, self-worth, self-confidence, participation, or enrichment has stripped the term of any clear, agreed upon, analytic content.

The goal is to enhance the political capabilities of the poor. The polity approach to political analysis, explained and explored by Peter Houtzager in chapters 1 and 4, respectively, is a powerful analytic tool to help the kind of people who read books like this to think through how they might, directly or indirectly, help achieve that goal. The core insight of the polity approach is that the state and public policy on the one side, and civil and political society on the other, are mutually constitutive. They shape one another. In chapter 1, Houtzager summarizes the four components of the framework as follows.

> [It] focuses on how societal and state actors are constituted, how they develop a differential capacity to act and form alliances, and how they cooperate and compete across the public-private divide to produce purposeful change. The capacity and nature of both state and societal actors are understood as the outcome of a two-way exchange that is shaped in substantial ways by the institutional terrain in which it takes place. The ability of political actors to produce a politics of inclusion is in large measure contingent on their ability to engineer *fit* with political institutions that grant some actors greater leverage in the policy process than others. The capacity to engineer fit, however, is severely constrained by a variety of factors, including institutional ones.

The strategic implications of the polity approach for those struggling for the political inclusion of the poor are only partly explored in chapters 1 and 4. Some appear relatively straightforward. For example, if organizations representing poor people are better organized at local rather than national levels, it will be helpful to decentralize to local levels much of the management of public programs intended to benefit the poor. Conversely, if the poor are locally weak but nationally more influential, centralization of program management is likely to be in their interests. Other implications of the polity approach are less direct. I will end this chapter by discussing two that are of broad relevance to many poor countries. Both concern the potential value of indirect strategies that help create a context conducive to the popular political action needed to increase the political capabilities of the poor. It is in supporting the creation of "enabling environments," rather than in engaging directly popular politics, that many of the kinds of people likely to read this book are best placed to make their contribution.

My first point is essentially a reframing of arguments already made by Houtzager: the implications for political activism of the fact that many states in Africa, Asia, and Latin America are weak. Unlike "modern states," they have not eliminated rival internal centers of power and lack authority over portions of the populations and territories they nominally control. Further, the activities of different parts of the state apparatus are often uncoordinated and incoherent. The authority and coherence of modern states provide the basis for social groups to organize on a national scale and to create collective identities that cut across geographic regions. Whether social groups organize to influence the state depends on whether they believe the state has the authority and capacity to meet their demands. If the national state has little authority, why bother to organize at the national level? Better to concentrate limited political resources—and political resources are always limited—on exercising influence in different ways: negotiating an acceptable level of informal taxes with the guerrilla movement in this region, using ethnic linkages with a minister to remove oppressive policemen from this town, or building up connections with the aid donors who might provide money for local NGOs in that district. Creating large membership movements of the poor is unlikely to be the most efficient means of exercising influence through these kinds of channels. Global maps of effective states and social movements would look very similar. Where the state is fragmented and ineffective, social movements are likely to be rare, weak, particularistic, localized, often closely connected with armed secessionists and smugglers, or the creation of external actors like international aid donors. As aid donors are learning, it is difficult under such circumstances to effectively promote "civil society" or social mobilization of any kind.[30] The NGO and other intermediary organizations that donors fund themselves use particularistic political linkages and pursue particularistic strategies and are therefore unable to overcome the problem of organizational fragmentation. Under these kinds of circumstances, measures intended to enhance the influence and coherence of public authority—which involve forging links with some societal actors—may be as good a way to stimulate effective organizations of the poor as direct attempts at political mobilization.

The second implication of the polity approach is that there may be scope for relatively small groups of politicians and bureaucrats to engage in purposive institutional redesign to create a political and institutional environment that encourages and helps poor people to develop political capabilities. This is especially likely in public programs providing services to the poor. One very substantial and relatively complex example is the Employment Guarantee Scheme, a very large public works program in Maharashtra State, India, which has been in operation for almost thirty years. This program was designed by a group of astute politicians in such a way that it would both satisfy a range of potentially competing social groups—notably rural employers and the laborers whom it is principally intended to benefit—and embody permanent incentives and encouragement for laborers to organize to pressure for the opening of local works programs when employment is scarce. Important components of the institutional design include a formal right to employment, which, while not actually legally enforceable, provides a strong moral basis for making political claims; a financing mechanism that gives sections of the public bureaucracy incentives to implement a program that is so problematic from their administrative perspective that its natural fate would be official neglect followed by decay; and a procedural emphasis on assessing demands for work and providing employment within small, local, administrative units, such that potential beneficiaries can organize to demand work within the social networks that they employ in daily life (Joshi and Moore 2000). The introduction in Britain of a legal minimum wage in 1998 is a more straightforward example of the same kind of process. Promoted in terms of social justice and economic efficiency, it had the consequence—no doubt intended by some supporters but not anticipated by other participants in the debate—of providing a new motivation for low-paid workers to join trade unions and a new field of union activism. Having been in decline for many years, union membership increased after the legislation was enacted.

There appear to be many interesting and positive ramifications of the insight that political-institutional environments can be redesigned, from "above," to support processes that enhance the political capabilities of the poor. For example, corporatist arrangements originally designed to enable the state to structure and control the political expression of the interests of subordinate social groups can, in some circumstances, provide the organizational basis for quasi-autonomous movements of those same groups.[31] There may be much more to explore. The polity approach provides a stimulus for thinking about these issues and a much broader framework for considering alternative means of enhancing the political capabilities of the poor than do theories and attitudes that locate the mainsprings of popular political action solely within ("civil") society itself.

NOTES

I am much indebted to Peter Houtzager for inspiration and to Peter, Joan Nelson, and two anonymous referees for very useful comments on an earlier draft.

1. On the general political roles and uses of ideas, see Berman 2001; and Reich 1988.

2. For example, Przeworski and Limongi (1993, 60) note that most studies published up to 1987 either find that nondemocratic regimes performed better economically or find no clear pattern, while studies published in 1988 or later nearly all find that democracy leads to faster economic growth. The same pattern is found when one looks at the more recent studies that they did not review (Moore 1996, 66). This reversal is far too sudden and too complete to be a reflection of actual changes over time in the relationships between types of political regime and economic growth rates. Since there was in the 1980s, even more in the realm of "development" than in the world more generally, a marked shift of opinion in favor of democracy, one has to share the suspicions of Przeworski and Limongi (1993, 61) about "the relation between statistics and ideology."

3. See, for example, the work of Gelbach and Pritchett (1997), which is discussed in more detail in the text. Hirschman (1991) provides a useful classification and overview of the types of arguments that historically have been used against progressive public policies.

4. There is no complete consensus over the interpretation of the term *globalization*, but there is agreement that, if the term is to have any identifiably distinct meaning, it refers to some notion of the increasing intensity and speed of interactions between agents across the globe (Held et al. 1999; Scholte 2000). By contrast, I use it here as it is conventionally deployed in policy debates.

5. There is continuing debate on this. One reason is that the concept of income inequality can be measured in a number of ways. Wade (2001) demonstrates that, if one employs a range of measures, the balance of probabilities point strongly to increased inequality. The editorial staff of the *Economist* now accepts this as a fact: see the issue of June 16–22, 2001.

6. The analytical separation of political from economic spheres is defensible for this purpose.

7. There is a close analogy in developing countries in the theory of "urban bias": the argument that a fundamental obstacle to economic growth lay in the power of political coalitions that transferred resources from small farmers to more wealthy groups and undermined agricultural investment (Bates 1977; Lipton 1977). These arguments played an important role in legitimizing policies of structural adjustment in the 1980s and 1990s.

8. An excellent account of the political consequences of the mobility of capital is to be found in Winters 1994, 1996 (chap. 1). Winters is not himself a proponent of globalization arguments.

9. Studying fifteen OECD countries at various intervals over the 1980s and 1990s, Crepaz (2002) finds higher levels of openness of national economies to be associated with increases in the extent to which national governments actually redistribute income through taxes and transfers. This general line of argument is congruent with the view that the political drive behind the creation of welfare states in the industrial countries was as much a matter of collective risk sharing—which benefited wide swathes of the population—as income redistribution to the poor (e.g., Baldwin 1990).

10. Tanzi and Zee (2000, 8) show that average tax revenues as a proportion of GDP increased for every major region of the world between 1985–87 and 1995–97. For non-OECD countries as a group, the figure increased from 17.5 to 18.2 percent. The facts and the reasons why the expectation of a shrinking state have not been realized are explored in detail for OECD countries by Swank and Steinmo (2002). They show that, between 1981 and 1995, the mean tax take for eighteen countries increased from 38 to 40 percent of GDP, with, on average, some shift of the tax burden from capital to labor.

11. The assumption of the pursuit of individual material self-interest is the equivalent in economic and political economy analysis to the assumption in biological analysis that individual actors can be assumed to be motivated by the drive to pass on genes. Both sets of assumptions have been very fruitful but also have clear limits, especially when dealing with the behavior of highly socialized species like humans.

12. It is logically possible to square the circle by hypothesizing indirect benefits to the rich from inclusionary policies, for example, reductions in crime, disease, or political unrest and higher rates of national economic growth through the increased consumer demand of a higher-quality labor force. But the algebra in such models is very intricate and the data required to test them are not available.

13. For a more detailed presentation of the ideological context and implications of this kind of analysis, see Moore 1999.

14. In Dunleavy's terms, politicians are assumed to be preference takers not preference makers (1991, chap. 5).

15. For references to similar material, see Moore 1999.

16. It is possible that income inequality is not part of the causal story and that this "finding" reflects a complex of contingent processes that happened to generate high rates of economic growth in a region of the world with low inequality (East Asia) and low rates of growth in high-inequality regions (Africa, the Middle East, and Latin America).

17. This acknowledgment is guarded. If the argument were valid, the policy implications would be radical. See chapter 3 of the report in general (World Bank 2000) and particularly the sentence on page 56 referenced with footnote 31. The articles on the inequality-growth connection most widely cited are Alesina and Rodrik 1994 and Persson and Tabellini 1994.

18. A prominent American political scientist sympathetic to rational choice and quantitative analysis recently referred to "the stubborn fact that few applications of formal theory have yielded new insights sufficiently powerful to have a

significant impact on the study of the questions that concern most non-mathematical comparativists" (Wallerstein 2001, 23). See also Green and Shapiro 1994, which is sympathetic to the rational choice method but critical of the tendency of practitioners to rely too much on deductive argument and not enough on empirical testing.

19. For explorations of how privileged sections of society develop active empathy for the poor, see, for example, Himmelfarb 1992 on late Victorian England and Toye 1997 on contemporary developing countries.

20. For a detailed exploration of this idea, see Ascher 1984.

21. See especially IFAD 2001 (chap. 6); UNDP 2000 (chap. 7); and World Bank 2000 (chaps. 6 and 7).

22. Aficionados of the sport of deconstructing international development discourse will see close parallels between what I have to say about *empowerment* and what others have said about *popular participation*.

23. One reason is that international development organizations are increasingly dependent for political support on development NGOs in OECD countries and the language of *empowerment* is especially appealing to this constituency. Another is that *community empowerment* in particular can help validate a great deal of lending by these organizations on social funds programs that may not meet normal lending criteria. See Moore 2001; and, on social funds, Tendler 2000.

24. Keeping things simple, one can point to two major causes of disagreement about the use of the term. First, there is a clear difference between (1) the "zero-sum" or despotic concept of "power over," the capacity of one agent to command the obedience of another; and (2) the more generative concept of "power to," the ability of leaders to mobilize other agents to undertake some collective activity. Second, there is an implicit continuum, from the very direct and overt exercise of power (e.g., the landlord commands all peasants to bow as he passes by) to a form of power that is highly indirect and covert (e.g., peasant children bow to landlords because they have internalized this as correct and respectful behavior in school, where the schoolteacher simply assumed that he or she had no choice other than to teach this). In the latter case, there may be genuine disagreement between rational and informed individuals over whether the landlord—as an individual or a member of a class—can be said to exercise power in relation to the bobbing heads of the peasants. For some insight into this concept of layered depths of power, see Lukes 1974. The indirectness of the exercise of class or institutional power through mental conditioning has been a major concern of radical social commentators such as Antonio Gramsci and Michel Foucault.

25. To insist on the usefulness of distinguishing process from outcome for analytical purposes is fully consistent with the view that processes and outcomes are closely linked in a causal sense, that is, the view that genuine (outcome) empowerment of the poor results (only or mainly) from their active participation in the process.

26. See, for example, Friedman 1992; Menike 1993; Oakley 2001a; Rowlands 1995; and Thomas 1992.

27. For a more detailed exploration of the points made in this paragraph, see Moore 2001.

28. For an example, see Oakley 2001b; and Rowlands 1995 (103).

29. For evidence of the conflation of these various terms with *empowerment* see, in addition to the sources cited earlier, Craig and Mayo 1995.

30. Ottoway and Carothers (2000) provide a neat summary of aid donors' disappointments in this sphere.

31. See, for example, Houtzager 2001 in relation to rural labor in Brazil; and Cross 1998 in relation to street vendors in Mexico.

REFERENCES

Alesina, A., and D. Rodrik. 1994. "Distributive Politics and Economic Growth." *Quarterly Journal of Economics* 109, no. 2: 465–90.

Ascher, W. 1984. *Scheming for the Poor. The Politics of Redistribution in Latin America*. Cambridge and London: Harvard University Press.

Baldwin, P. 1990. *The Politics of Social Solidarity. Class Bases of the European Welfare State, 1875–1975*. Cambridge: Cambridge University Press.

Bates, R. 1977. *Markets and States in Tropical Africa. The Political Basis of Agricultural Policies*. Berkeley: University of California Press.

Berman, S. 2001. "Ideas, Norms, and Culture in Political Analysis." *Comparative Politics* 33, no. 2: 231–50.

Brenner, R. 1998. "The Economics of Global Turbulence. A Special Report on the World Economy, 1950–98." *New Left Review* 229:1–265.

Cameron, D. R. 1978. "The Expansion of the Public Economy: A Comparative Analysis." *American Journal of Political Science* 72, no. 4: 1243–61.

Craig, G., and M. Mayo, eds. 1995. *Community Empowerment. A Reader in Participation and Development*. London and Atlantic Highlands, New Jersey: Zed.

Crepaz, M. M. L. 2002. "Global, Constitutional, and Partisan Determinants of Redistribution in Fifteen OECD Countries." *Comparative Politics* 34, no. 2: 169–88.

Cross, J. C. 1998. *Informal Politics: Street Vendors and the State in Mexico City*. Stanford: Stanford University Press.

DfID. 2000. *Poverty Elimination and the Empowerment of Women*. London: Department for International Development.

Dunleavy, P. 1991. *Democracy, Bureaucracy, and Public Choice. Economic Explanations in Political Science*. New York and London: Harvester/Wheatsheaf.

Evans, P. 1997. "The Eclipse of the State? Reflections on Stateness in an Era of Globalization." *World Politics* 50, no. 1: 62–87.

Friedman, J. 1992. *Empowerment. The Politics of Alternative Development*. Cambridge, MA, and Oxford: Blackwell.

Gelbach, J. B., and L. H. Pritchett. 1997. "More for the Poor is Less for the Poor." Policy Research Working Paper 1,799. Washington, DC, World Bank.

Green, D., and I. Shapiro. 1994. *The Pathologies of Rational Choice*. New Haven: Yale University Press.

Held, D., A. McGrew, D. Goldblatt, and J. Perraton. 1999. *Global Transformations: Politics, Economics, and Culture*. Stanford: Stanford University Press.

Himmelfarb, G. 1992. *Poverty and Compassion. The Moral Imagination of the Late Victorians.* New York: Vintage.

Hirschman, A. O. 1991. *The Rhetoric of Reaction. Perversity, Futility, Jeopardy.* Cambridge and London: Belknap Press of Harvard University Press.

Houtzager, P. P. 2001. "Collective Action and Political Authority: Rural Workers, Church, and State in Brazil." *Theory and Society* 30:1–45.

IFAD. 2001. *Rural Poverty Report, 2001: The Challenge of Ending Rural Poverty.* Oxford and New York: Oxford University Press for the International Fund for Agricultural Development.

Joshi, A., and M. Moore. 2000. "Enabling Environments: Do Anti-poverty Programmes Mobilise the Poor?" *Journal of Development Studies* 37, no. 1: 25–56.

Kaufman, R. R., and A. Segura-Ubiergo. 2001. "Globalization, Domestic Politics, and Social Spending in Latin America: A Time-Series Cross-Section Analysis, 1973–1997." *World Politics* 53, no. 4: 553–87.

Keck, M. 1989. "The New Unionism in the Brazilian Transition." In A. Stepan, ed., *Democratizing Brazil.* Oxford: Oxford University Press.

Landa, D., and E. B. Kapstein. 2001. "Inequality, Growth, and Democracy." *World Politics* 53, no. 1: 264–96.

Lipton, M. 1977. *Why Poor People Stay Poor. Urban Bias in World Development.* London: Temple Smith.

Lukes, S. 1974. *Power. A Radical View.* London and Basingstoke: Macmillan.

Mayoux, L. 2001. "Participatory Programme Learning for Women's Empowerment in Micro-finance Programmes: Negotiating Complexity, Conflict, and Change." In P. Oakley, ed., *Evaluating Empowerment,*152–67. Oxford: INTRAC.

Menike, K. 1993. "People's Empowerment from the People's Perspective." *Development in Practice* 3, no. 3: 176–83.

Moore, M. 1996. "Is Democracy Rooted in Material Prosperity?" In R. Luckham and G. White, eds., *Democratization in the South. The Jagged Wave,* 37–68. Manchester: Manchester University Press.

———. 1999. "Politics against Poverty? Global Pessimism and National Optimism." *IDS Bulletin* 30, no. 2: 33–46.

———. 2001. "Empowerment at Last?" *Journal of International Development* 13, no. 3: 321–29.

Oakley, P., ed. 2001a. *Evaluating Empowerment.* Oxford: INTRAC.

Oakley, P. 2001b. "Understanding Empowerment." In P. Oakley, ed., *Evaluating Empowerment,* 11–23. Oxford: INTRAC.

Ottoway, M., and T. Carothers, eds. 2000. *Funding Virtue. Civil Society Aid and Democracy Promotion.* Washington, DC: Carnegie Endowment for International Peace.

Persson, T., and G. Tabellini. 1994. "Representative Democracy and Capital Taxation." *Journal of Public Economics* 55, no. 1: 53–70.

Przeworski, A., and F. Limongi. 1993. "Political Regimes and Economic Growth." *Journal of Economic Perspectives* 7, no. 3: 51–69.

Reich, R., ed. 1988. *The Power of Public Ideas.* Cambridge and London: Harvard University Press.

Rieger, E., and S. Liebfried. 1998. "Welfare State Limits to Globalization." *Politics and Society* 26, no. 3: 363–90.

Robertson, A. F. 1984. *People and the State: An Anthropology of Planned Development*. Cambridge: Cambridge University Press.

Rodrik, D. 1998. "Why Do Open Economies Have Bigger Governments?" *Journal of Political Economy* 106, no. 5: 997–1032.

Rowlands, J. 1995. "Empowerment Examined." *Development in Practice* 5, no. 2: 101–7.

Scholte, J. A. 2000. *Globalization: A Critical Introduction*. London: Macmillan.

Seidman, G. W. 1994. *Manufacturing Militance: Workers' Movements in Brazil and South Africa*. Berkeley: University of California Press.

Sunkel, O. 1969. "National Development Policy and External Dependence in Latin America." *Journal of Development Studies* 6, no. 3: 23–48.

Swank, D., and S. Steinmo. 2002. "The New Political Economy of Taxation in Advanced Capitalist Democracies." *American Journal of Political Science* 46, no. 3.

Tanzi, V., and H. H. Zee. 2000. "Tax Policy for Emerging Markets: Developing Countries." Working Paper WP/00/35. Washington, DC, International Monetary Fund.

Tendler, J. 2000. "Why Are Social Funds So Popular?" In S. Yusuf, S. J. Everett, and W. Wu, eds., *Local Dynamics in the Era of Globalization*, 114–29. Oxford: Oxford University Press for the World Bank.

Thomas, A. 1992. "Non-governmental Organizations and the Limits to Empowerment." In M. Wuyts, M. Mackintosh, and T. Hewitt, eds., *Development Policy and Public Action*, 117–46. Oxford: Oxford University Press.

Toye, J. 1997. "Nationalizing the Antipoverty Agenda." In L. Emmerij, ed., *Economic and Social Development into the Twenty-first Century*, 521–30. Washington, DC: Inter-American Development Bank.

UNDP. 2000. *Poverty Report, 2000: Overcoming Human Poverty*. New York: United Nations Development Program.

Wade, R. 2001. "Winners and Losers." *Economist*, April 28, 79–82.

Wallerstein, M. 2001. "Bridging the Quantitative/Non-quantitative Divide." *APSA-CP. Newsletter of the Organized Section in Comparative Politics of the American Political Science Association* 12, no. 2: 1–23.

Weiss, L. 1998. *The Myth of the Powerless State. Governing the Economy in a Global Era*. Cambridge: Polity.

Winters, J. A. 1994. "Power and the Control of Capital." *World Politics* 46, no. 3: 419–52.

———. 1996. *Power in Motion. Capital and the Indonesian State*. Ithaca and London: Cornell University Press.

Wood, A. 1994. *North-South Trade, Employment, and Inequality: Changing Fortunes in a Skill-Driven World*. New York: Oxford University Press.

World Bank. 2000. *World Development Report, 2000–2001: Attacking Poverty*. New York: Oxford University Press.

Contributors

RICHARD C. CROOK is a Fellow at the Institute of Development Studies, University of Sussex. He has published extensively on comparative political systems and administration in West Africa and South Asia and particularly on decentralization and democratization. His most recent book is *Democracy and Decentralisation in South Asia and West Africa: Participation, Accountability, and Performance* (Cambridge University Press, 1998), with James Manor.

GEORGE GRAY-MOLINA is Professor of Public Policy and Director of the Bolivian Catholic University's Public Policy Graduate Program. He is currently doing research on pro-poor politics, popular participation, and social exclusion. He holds a D.Phil. in Politics from Nuffield College, Oxford University, and a Masters Degree in Public Policy from the John F. Kennedy School of Government, Harvard University.

JOHN HARRISS is Professor of Development Studies at the London School of Economics and former Dean of the School of Development Studies at the University of East Anglia. Much of his research has been in and on India. He is the author of *Capitalism and Peasant Farming: Agrarian Structure and Ideology in Northern Tamil Nadu* (Oxford University Press, 1982) and the joint author of *Reinventing India: Economic Liberalization, Hindu Nationalism, and Popular Democracy* (Polity, 2000). He was the coeditor of *Sociology of "Developing Societies": South Asia* (Macmillan, 1989) and *The New Institutional Economics and Third World Development* (Routledge, 1995). He is currently a managing editor of the *Journal of Development Studies*.

RONALD J. HERRING is Director of the Mario Einaudi Center for International Studies at Cornell University, where he is the John S. Knight Professor of International Relations and Professor of Government. His earliest academic interests were in agrarian relations, and he is the author of *Land to the Tiller: The Political Economy of Agrarian Reform in South Asia* (Yale University Press, 1983). Recent work has included issues of state property rights in nature and the politics of genetic engineering. His edited volume *Carrots, Sticks, and Ethnic Conflict: Rethinking Develop-*

ment Assistance (with Milton Esman) was published by the University of Michigan Press in 2001.

PETER P. HOUTZAGER is a Fellow at the Institute of Development Studies, University of Sussex, and co-coordinator of the IDS Program in Law, Democracy, and Development. He has taught at Stanford University and St. Mary's College in the United States. His work on the relationship between collective action and institutional change has appeared in *Theory and Society, Comparative Studies in Society and History,* and the *Journal of Development Studies.* His book *Remaking Authority and Collective Action in Brazil* is currently under review.

MARCUS J. KURTZ is Assistant Professor of Political Science at Ohio State University. His research interests center on the role of rural politics in national regime outcomes. His work in this area has appeared in *Politics and Society, Comparative Studies in Society and History,* the *Journal of Latin American Studies,* and *Theory and Society.* His book manuscript *Free Market Democracy? The Sectoral Foundations of National Politics in Chile and Mexico* examines the relationship between market-based economic strategies and national democratic regime formation.

MICK MOORE is a Professorial Fellow at the Institute of Development Studies, University of Sussex. He was Visiting Professor at MIT from September 1994 to December 1995. During 1996–2000, he was the convenor of two large research programs on poverty located at the IDS and was extensively involved in preparing background material on the politics of poverty for the World Bank's *World Development Report, 2001–2002: Attacking Poverty.* He is now Director of the Centre for the Future State at IDS. He has extensive field research experience in Asia and is the author of two books and numerous book chapters and articles on the political and institutional dimensions of economic policy and performance in developing countries, antipoverty policy, and governance in "the South."

JOAN M. NELSON is a Senior Scholar at the Woodrow Wilson Center of the Smithsonian Institution and Scholar in Residence at the School of International Service, American University. Her primary research interests are the politics of economic reforms and the interactions between market-oriented reforms and democratization in middle- and low-income countries. Her current work focuses on the politics of social sector reforms in rapidly evolving national and international contexts. She has taught at MIT, the Johns Hopkins School of International Studies, and the Woodrow Wilson School at Princeton University. Among her publications are *Transforming Post-communist Political Economies* (coeditor with Charles Tilly, National Academy Press, 1998); *Intricate*

Links: Democratization and Market Reforms in Latin America and Eastern Europe (editor, Transaction Press, 1994); *Global Goals, Contentious Means: Issues of Multiple Aid Conditionality* (Overseas Development Council, 1993); *Encouraging Democracy: What Role for Conditioned Aid?* (Overseas Development Council, 1992); *Economic Crisis and Policy Choice* (editor, Princeton University Press, 1990); *Fragile Coalitions: The Politics of Economic Adjustment* (editor, Overseas Development Council, 1989); *Access to Power: Politics and the Urban Poor* (Princeton University Press, 1979); *No Easy Choice: Political Participation in Developing Countries* (with Samuel Huntington, Harvard University Press, 1976); and *Aid, Influence, and Foreign Policy* (Macmillan, 1968).

ALAN S. SVERRISSON was pursuing his Ph.D. at Glasgow Caledonian University until his tragic passing last year.

LAURENCE WHITEHEAD is an Official Fellow in politics at Nuffield College, Oxford University, and a Senior Fellow of the college. He currently serves on the General Board of Faculties. He also does graduate teaching in contemporary Latin American politics and economic policy at Oxford's Latin American Centre and has held various appointments as a visiting scholar at universities in the United States and Latin America. His recent work has been on international aspects of democratization and the relationship between democratization and economic liberalization. His publications include the five-volume series *Transitions from Authoritarian Rule*, with Guillermo O'Donnell and Philippe C. Schmitter, editors (Johns Hopkins University Press, 1986). Since 1989, he has been coeditor of the *Journal of Latin American Studies*. He is also editor of the Oxford University Press series Studies in Democratization. The first book in the series (Laurence Whitehead, ed., *International Dimensions of Democratization: Europe and the Americas*) was published in 1996.

Subject Index

Author Index